AF229683

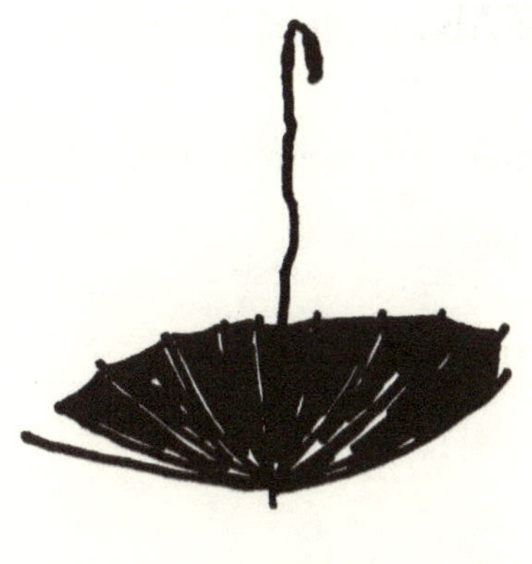

good deed rain

**Books by Allen Frost**

Ohio Trio
Bowl of Water
Another Life
Home Recordings
The Mermaid Translation
The Selected Correspondence of Kenneth Patchen
The Wonderful Stupid Man
Saint Lemonade
Playground
Roosevelt
5 Novels
The Sylvan Moore Show
Town in a Cloud
A Flutter of Birds Passing Through Heaven:
A Tribute to Robert Sund
At the Edge of America
Lake Erie Submarine
The Book of Ticks
I Can Only Imagine
The Orphanage of Abandoned Teenagers
Different Planet
Go with the Flow: A Tribute to Clyde Sanborn
Homeless Sutra
The Lake Walker
A Hundred Dreams Ago
Almost Animals
The Robotic Age
Kennedy
Fable
Elbows & Knees: Essays & Plays

# Elbows & Knees

Allen Frost

*Elbows & Knees: Essays & Plays* © 2018
Allen Frost, Good Deed Rain
Bellingham, Washington
ISBN 978-1-64467-465-9

Writing: Allen Frost
Cover: Madison Dowling
Cover Production: Aaron Gunderson
Map: Michael Paulus
2 Drawings: Allen Frost
Apple: TFK!

> "We learned that the films we loved the most were badly made."
>
> —Raul Ruiz, *Poetics of Cinema*

*The W. Lee Wilder from Space, Trees in the Asylum Garden, Entering the Water and Escaping, Visions of Raven, Haunting Birds* were first published online by *Habits of Waste* from 2003-2006.

*The W. Lee Wilder from Space* published in England by *Zoo Nation 6*, 2005.

*Open the Windows, Open the Doors*, first published in *d.a. levy and the mimeograph revolution*, Bottom Dog Press, Edited by Larry Smith & Ingrid Swanberg, 2007.

*Robert Huff in Bellingham*, first published online by *Poetry Northwest*, 2013.

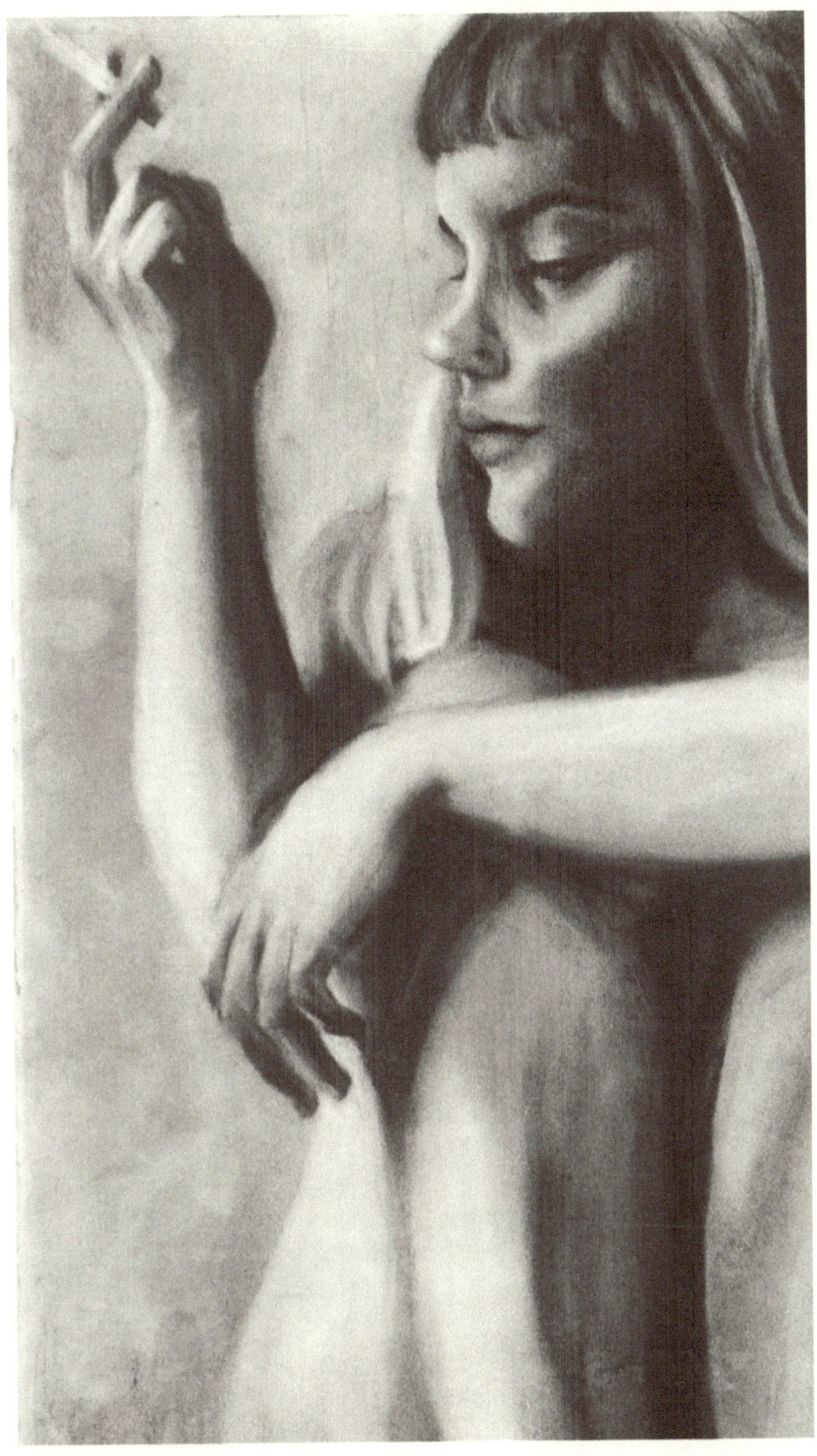

## *INTRODUCTION*

My interest in writing essays began against all the odds in college, with an essay on Chaucer. Page 1 was a standard sort of thing, until you turned it and saw the first page repeated—the same, except that words were crumbling. Page by page, this repeated, words splintering, paragraphs falling away, until the last page revealed Willie Mays with his bat, standing amid an essay rubble. There were other essays like that too (all met with utter mystification by the department instructors) but my favorite experiment was one entitled "Essay is a Saddle Sore." It starred a student trying to write an essay, when he is jumped by cowboys and country singers! They carouse and disrupt and fill his dorm room with song. Furthermore, instead of turning it in, I had the nerve to post each page on the trees in the quad!

The following essays are about subjects that have interested me long before and long after college: writers, artists and movies.

There are also a couple other entertainments tossed in the mix: a play and a Super-8 screenplay. My friend Mike and I previously made a Super-8 movie called *Caruso* (an operatic pig tragedy) and *The Jimbaroo* was meant to be our next masterpiece. Mike even prepared a big black and white map of Papua New Guinea that the camera would slowly climb over. *Little Italy* is another unfilmed script—a couple oddities, but they fit in with this book's themes of monsters and B-movies. Also I just couldn't resist the rhyme of 'essays & plays.'

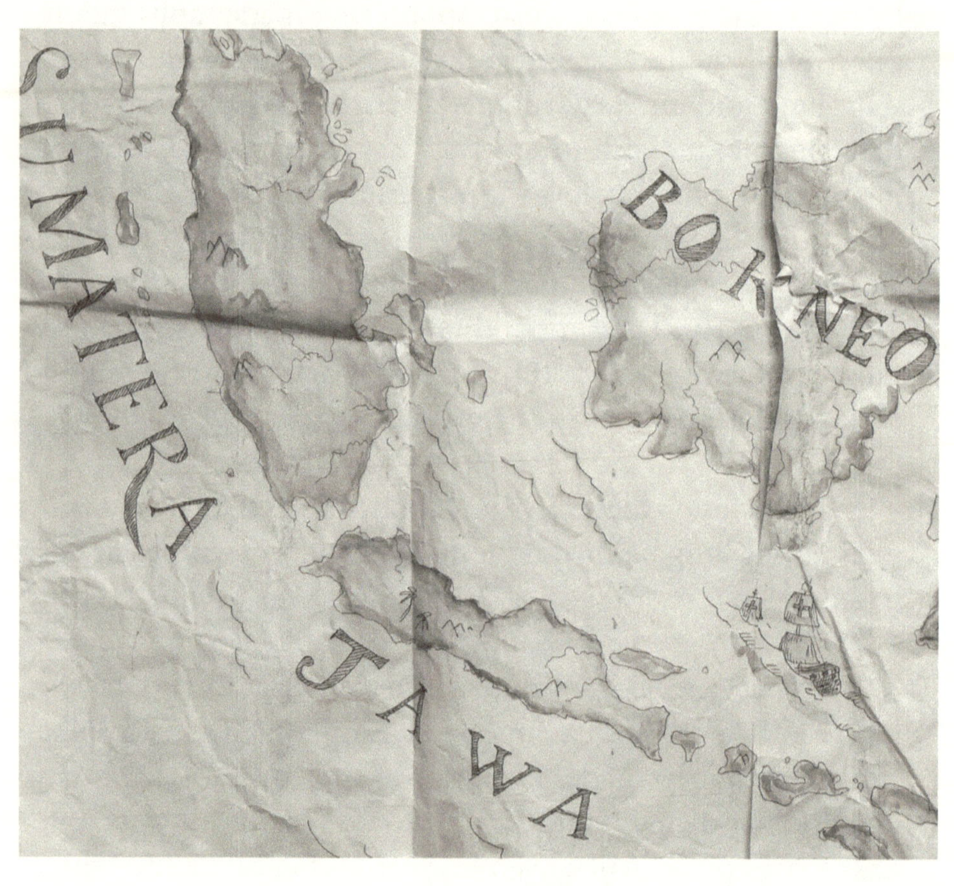


*Michael Paulus, detail of map for* The Jimbaroo

This is a different sort of writing from my usual books, but you're sure to see the similarities. *Elbows and Knees* is a book of things that rubbed and pointed and bent to be looked at. I've kept this collection for a long time without really knowing if you would enjoy them. I hope so. They ought to carry you to some unexpected places.

Allen Frost
Bellingham, WA
Fall 2018

## CONTENTS:

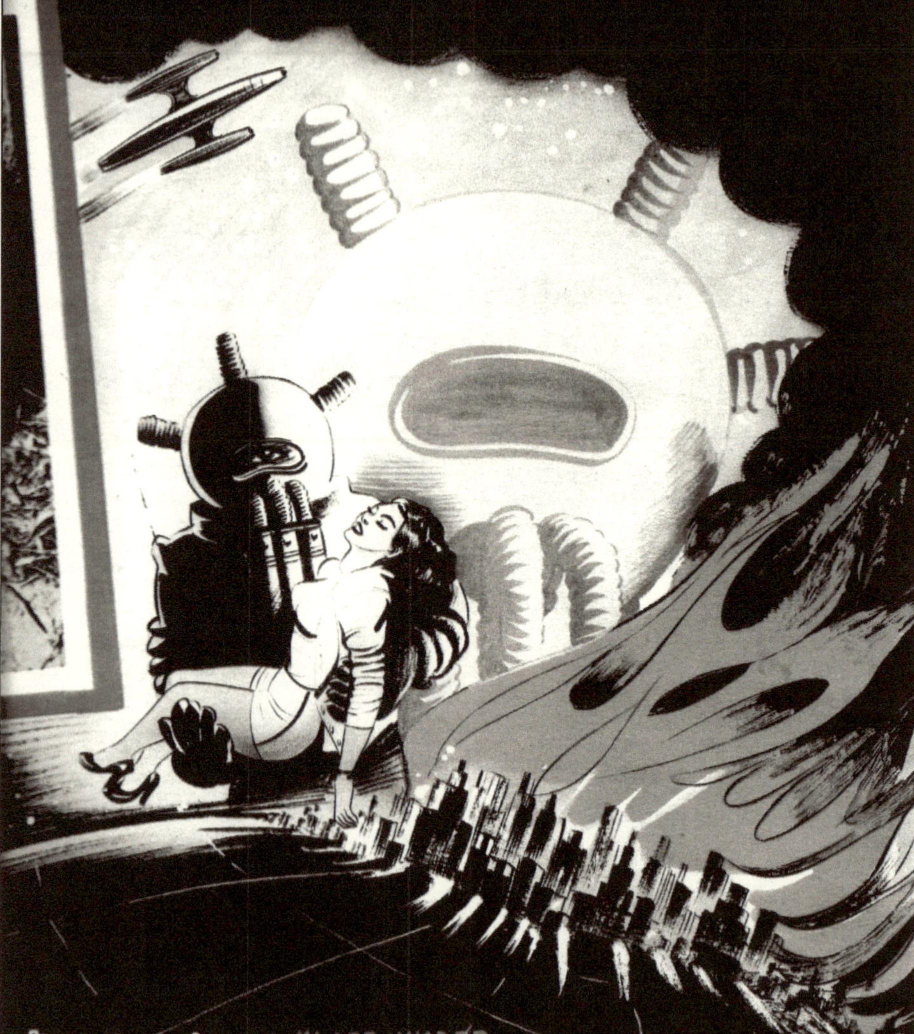
MA DEL ESPACIO
(PHANTOM FROM SPACE)
PRODUCTOR Y DIRECTOR W. LEE WILDER

## *THE W. LEE WILDER FROM SPACE*

An Old Testament opening of black and white clouds with lightning breaking. *Phantom from Space.* "It began after sundown…" The warning, then the leap into stock footage. An unidentified object is traced by time above Alaska, flying across British Columbia on to California, disappearing in Los Angeles. Mobile units set out, a couple of thick cars with antler antennas, in and out of shadows. Flushed from the night, a woman runs up from the water's edge, "This man, he just kept coming at us, it was awful." "Who?" "I don't know! He was wearing a suit like a diver."

W. Lee Wilder directed this opening in 1953, eight years after arriving in Hollywood. Soon, he would make two more films, *Killers from Space* and *The Snow Creature* in 1954. In an endless night sky, this trilogy will survive the trials of planet Earth as his everlasting memory.

Before he landed at Republic Studios, among the fabled Poverty Row horrors, Willie Wilder had emigrated from across the Atlantic Ocean to grow in New York City. The years passed there as he directed the Manhattan everyday workings of Wm. Wilder Co, Inc., Original Handbags. From the broken poverty of a Europe after war, he seemed to have found his way in to the American dream. In such spirits, in 1935 he sent for his younger brother, Samuel "Billy" Wilder, to join him in the new world.

Billy Wilder recalls the day, "My memories of my brother are like old faded photographs from a long time ago when we were children in the Astro-Hungarian Empire, which was in the Dark Ages…I remember him in his place on Long Island when he met me at the ship—when America was new for me and when the snow was white and fresh." (1)

A man with a bandaged head is grilled at the police station, snapping, "How would you feel if somebody with a crazy helmet with pipes sticking out of it came at you in the dark? Look, I know this sounds crazy but there wasn't any head in that helmet." Searching for a lost signal, a "mysterious interference," the sedans, mounted with gigantic kitchen whisks, continue to scour the muddy night sky. There are so many day for night shots jarring with such sincere narrated effort to pin down shifting time and place that by now the film has dropped into the surreal. More weird witnesses testify. Burning oil fields, trailing a disturbance, Theremin, cigarettes, coffee. A crazy reporter with a pipe and a photo of the Moon: "If you want to know how things turned out, read the *Chronicle* in the morning." Chased around pallets, catwalks, hunted by Geiger counter, The Phantom finally removes its helmet and suit, escaping invisibly. It may be free, but it is trapped in the Griffith Institute labyrinth without its radioactive, magnetic, indestructible suit and its breathing apparatus helmet. The Phantom's one chance for survival in a strange land comes when it tries vainly to communicate with a human named Barbara.

Likewise, Billy Wilder admits, "My brother and I never talked much. We were never close in anything except age…We never had much to say to each other." (2)

"A code…" Barbara observes as the invisible being taps scissors on the table. "1…1,2…1…1,2,3…" but when she happens to reveal the Phantom's hand with an ultra-violet lamp, she lets out a shriek, and the chase is on again. "Too bad he got wise to us and took off his uniform, or we'd have been able to catch up with him by now." "But if he was trying to tell us something, why did he run away?" The minds of scientists and police devise a simple plan. Yet it is a barking house pet named Venus who finally hunts the Phantom down.

*Phantom from Space* introduces itself as "the story of a handful of people who in the course of one desperate night held back a wave of panic and pandemonium." Hardly. Most of the time it drifts like a slow pale kite. The Phantom, who can't even be seen, poses no danger, except accidentally. This is simply the tragic tale of an astronaut doomed to wander a hostile planet as long as his one air tank holds out.

Movies like this live in another realm altogether, especially when viewed in context of the big budget films of the day. It's no wonder that one such Hollywood director Billy Wilder would observe: "My brother went to America. He had a good business in New York. He was in leather, but he sold his company to make movies. They weren't anything that interested me, so I didn't see them. I saw one. I didn't expect much of it, and it didn't let me down. It wasn't even bad, which is worse. He should have stuck with leather purses." (3)

But W. Lee Wilder, in his rather tedious and heavy crafted fashion, created a work of recognition—matched by the gray light and gloomy shadows of dawn—it is filmed insomnia. Who would want to go to this world? Unless you already know it for what it is: the place in between dreams.

January 23, 1954, were there spotlights above neon Hollywood? Were there long lines of black limousines pulled to curbs, mobs of thrilled crowds and flashbulbs? The RKO Theater boomed with: "Soledad Flats, Nevada. The time 6:15 AM...Climax arduous planning, Operation A-Bomb Test underway." The narrator's strict observation of time and place, the military stock footage, the feel of a cracked newsreel...This is the opening of *Killers from Space.*

As with the previous year's *Phantom from Space*, W. Lee Wilder is once again intent on stressing the reality of the unfolding picture. Yet it is a sort of cardboard and tin approach to how his brother Billy Wilder explained filming *Double Indemnity*:

"We had to be realistic. You had to believe the situation and the characters, or all was lost. I insisted on black-and-white, of course, and in making operettas I'd learned that sometimes one technical shot destroyed a picture...I tried for a very realistic picture—a few little tricks, but not very tricky...It was a picture that looked like a newsreel. You never realized it was staged. But like a newsreel, you look to grab a moment of truth, and exploit it." (4)

The Wilder brothers may have discussed such commonality, but Billy's advice was received by string-can telephone.

Another observation worth noting is W. Lee Wilder's disregard for the dangers of radiation (a reflection, of course, of American culture that continues to this day). In *Phantom from Space*, the scientists and police casually handle The Phantom's radioactive suit with bare hands. And now, as an atomic bomber nears Detonation Minus Two Minutes, "Military personnel from buck private to top raking grad... men from research and news services move into position" setting up folding chairs or standing in trenches before the blast. They wear sunglasses, one man in a cowboy hat, "ready to record the radioactivity from the closest possible vantage point." That's when Doctor Martin enters the picture, in a ghostly silver model jet, spiraling on a wire in the clouds.

With the explosion, only four minutes into the film, the jet goes into a nosedive in a sequence that is the height of radio suspense-theater. If there is one glaring thing that distinguishes this from Wilder's last film, it is Action!

"Mayday, Mayday...Search for Tar Baby Two..." A distraught wife, a framed photo of Ike. "It's Dr. Martin! Call the base hospital!" "I remember the controls froze, the next thing I saw was the main gate of the base." A scar over the heart. The FBI enters, accepts a cigarette, "Did you ever stop to think that perhaps this Dr. Martin isn't really *the* Dr. Martin?" Fingerprints check. Home. Eyes glare through the window slats. Insomnia, after 3. "I wondered if there were any last minute orders on another atomic test?" "You go put the coffee on while I get dressed." Another Atom Bomb Exploded. "Me? A security risk? My current state?" The hand of time again. There is an echo of Billy Wilder's memorable scene in *Double Indemnity* where Barbara Stanwyck hid behind a door from Edward G. Robinson.

Presenting the Wilder/Robinson aside: W. Lee Wilder's son Myles remembered when his uncle Billy Wilder "brought me together with Edward G. Robinson's son, Eddie Robinson Jr., who was already a full-fledged sneak thief and before he was sixteen he was living with an older woman, and drinking a bottle of whiskey a day. That was the kind of playmate Uncle Billy got me." (5)

"Another woman?" Bronson Canyon. "Code 4." Phone booth, pneumatic tubes. Eyes! "They're here...They're going to destroy us..." "What did you give him?" "Truth serum. It will deprive his mind of any imagination." "It was my own heart." Memory. Underground. "Here, in our machines magnetically propelled across the electron bridge we have created...We are accumulating the energy released with each of your atomic explosions...Our eyes developed to this state to combat the ever growing darkness."

A word needs to come through from Harry Thomas, who created The Killers, "I knew that these types of pictures would be remembered for the makeup. It wouldn't be for the hackneyed stories or the poor acting; it would be for the makeup." Thomas revealed:

"The director wanted the space aliens to have large, protruding eyes. An optical shop said that it would cost at least $900 to make eight pairs of glass eyes for the movie. The producer rejected the cost right away, and then someone suggested using ping pong balls. I decided that I would not use ping pong balls for this. They're much too thin and they don't have the depth that I need for the sclera of the eye. I spent that night and most of the next morning wondering how I'd make realistic eyes for these aliens. I was almost completely discouraged when I went to get something to drink from the refrigerator and there was my answer—a white plastic egg tray. The plastic tray had the perfect shiny, almost translucent appearance that I was looking for. I yelled, I've got it, I've got it.....laughing and dancing around like a fool. I sliced the bottoms of the tray off with a heated screwdriver, leaving me with half-spheres of plastic. I pierced the center of each one with the heated screwdriver, so the actors could see. Then, I painted Irises on them, and drew in some red blood vessels. The producers wouldn't give me enough time to make the eyes and the aliens effective...The director did allow me the time to create one effect. The director kept telling me to "hurry up, hurry up," I told him that this would only take a minute and he would love the effect. If you watch the head alien while he's giving his long speech to Peter Graves in the cave, you'll see his eyes move....just a little. I did this by placing a second set of eyes, thinner than the first set, over his original alien eyes. Then, I attached fine wires to the edges of each eye and very carefully moved the eyes for the camera." (6)

Escape in the caverns. Giant roaring tarantulas and reverb creatures. "We are breeding our—shall I say—armies." Dr. Martin, a dead man, stuck underground, trapped by electricity. "You will listen and obey. What have you seen and heard here?" "Nothing." Filling notepad pages. Escape in a car to cut off the power supply. Catwalks, shadows, dials in the control room. Lunging in his bathrobe. "What's the matter with you? You sleep walking?" "Cut the power!" Power turned off for a hundred miles. Eight seconds pass. A blinding scene in the slatted window curtain. "Just as he said."

It's almost as if W. Lee Wilder himself exploded; the restraint of *Phantom from Space*, all that slow flowing below erupts in *Killers from Space*. Where did it come from? Had Wilder been influenced by his peers? 1953 had seen: *The Atomic Man, Invaders from Mars, War of the Worlds, The Beast from 20,000 Fathoms, Donovan's Brain, Robot Monster, It Came from Outer Space, Glen or Glenda?, Magnetic Monster*. Inspiration! Did Wilder want to be remembered with them? Did he research? Leaning on the blue and chrome steering wheel, taking notes at the Drive-In? Tuning in to dreams? Reading the pulps? Listening at diners and the chatter between double features? Clearly this time he was pushing to deliver a popular product for the masses. Complying with their wishes, *Killers from Space* answers the existence of UFOs in the Atomic Age and provides a universal mythic hero. Dr. Martin dies in pursuit of the knowledge of fire. In a hell within the upper crust of the Earth, he is revived, mesmerized and robotized to betray the world, then, overcoming his spell, he battles out of darkness, disbelief and insomniac night terrors to finally save the planet. Doctor Martin is a hero Director Wilder drew from inside, identifying with what was readily becoming a sci-fi trait: the hero seen as crackpot—the hero nobody believes—the hero who must prove the unbelievable believable.

"If there's one yeti, there must be a whole civilization."
—*The Snow Creature*

The question of where W. Lee Wilder would go next, after an invisible phantom and underground killers, was answered in November, 1954.

A map fills the screen, the camera climbs between the Ganges and "the mysterious plateau of Tibet," onto the Himalayas. Among the snow and lightning peaks, an expedition has come "to find and study plant-life which had heretofore been unknown or inaccessible. This is the story of that mission, of how a small group of people bound themselves in pursuit of a crude and primitive civilization which once only existed as a figment of the imagination." *The Snow Creature.*

1935's *The Werewolf of London* began with a similar zoom in on a map of Tibet, where sherpas abandon a botany expedition, looking for "a strange flower which grows only in Tibet and which it is said takes its life from the moon." Continuing without guides, to a valley filled with demons and invisible phantoms, Dr. Wilfred Glendon discovers the flower but gets attacked by a creature. The next scene transplants the suffering man and flower to England, mansion and artificial moonlight machinery.

Wilder's Japanese-speaking Tibetan sherpas also mutiny when a creature disrupts their botany expedition, tracking off with the lead guide's wife. Although Dr. Frank Parrish must tear his attention from flora to fauna, following the snow creature's footprints, he realizes, "Finding one would more than compensate for my failure as a botanist." And his wish comes true.

Discovered in a tunnel, the snow creature desperately claws at the stones, causing a cave-in upon itself. Dr. Parrish takes a living pulse from its huge mitten paw and the expedition sets off down the mountain with the yeti on a stretcher. Soon the resourceful doctor acquires a fabulous "refrigerator unit" from Bombay so he can transport the creature to America. Stock footage glides them over ocean, New York's Statue of Liberty, the Grand Canyon, then leads to the most fantastic image in the film. There, in the glaring Los Angeles sun, standing on the tarmac next to the parked Lockheed Constellation, is an astonishing sight. In what looks like a converted white phone booth, the yeti mimes behind the frosted window glass, fuming, so far away from home.

Meanwhile, the intellectuals in the U.S Dept. of Immigration office ponder the eternal question: "Is it a beast or a man?" "The Department's main interest is to classify this specimen, as you call it, as being not human." "I have to determine whether his brain is a calculating brain." While the debate rages, the yeti escapes into the shadowy parking garages and dark repeating alleyways of the city. The creature is even spotted at a meat packing plant. Wilder reuses the same stock footage from *Phantom from Space* and *Killers from Space* of a watch on a hairy arm. The police lieutenant is baffled, "This is a white elephant, any three year old child could spot him. The question is, how does he cover seven miles without being seen?"

In June of 1954, five months before *The Snow Creature* opened, another movie filmed in Los Angeles was released. Giant ants trooped through the sewer system tunnels and had to be hunted down by army jeeps, bazookas and flame throwers. *Them!* was a monster hit. Surely W. Lee Wilder saw it. Maybe he caught an afternoon matinee during a break in making his own low-budget film.

"Lieutenant, there are 4,800 miles of storm drains under the city," the city engineer drones. By now, Wilder can present an establishment that is well organized and capable of accepting whatever surreal invasion presents itself. Carrying lantern and rolled-up map, a net, a pistol, cigarettes and radio, they go underground in search. It's too bad that dog Venus of *Phantom From Space* couldn't trek down Mt. Palomar to help them track this creature too. Still, it's only a matter of time before the police can radio, "We just finished the job." The lieutenant receives a cryptic reply from the station, "There's a creature waiting for you. Eight pounds, three ounces, a boy, lieutenant." While driving botanist/yeti hunter Dr. Frank Parrish back home, the lieutenant jokes, "Maybe I'll name my kid Frank. Frank Dunbar, sounds great." Then, he quickly grins, "I don't know. I'm not too sure I like it." That's it.

This strange scrawl of humor at the end can only be the signature of the story and screenplay writer, W. Lee Wilder's son, Myles Wilder. He was trying something new after writing *Phantom from Space* and *Killers from Space*, where humor never seems to appear. Even a contemporary film review book grades *Killers from Space* a BOMB, noting, "Poor in all departments—and too dull to be funny." (7) Yet humor would become the chosen field for Myles Wilder, who later went into television, writing scripts for *Get Smart, Gomer Pyle, My Three Sons, The Paul Lynde Show*, and *Welcome Back, Kotter*, among many others. W. Lee Wilder continued to influence his son's writing though, as can be seen in an episode of *The Dukes of Hazzard* where: "Boss Hogg's plan to plow up a cemetery rattles a con man who is supposed to be dead and buried there." (8) And Myles Wilder's paperback *Freeze*, a cryogenic shocker, features a laboratory where "the whole scene was beginning to look like something out of an old B picture." (9)

On another street in Hollywood, Billy Wilder was asked if he wanted to say anything about his brother:

"No, he was a fool. [Wilder swivels slowly in his chair, turns and looks toward the dictionary as he discusses his brother. Somehow he manages to be both wistful and dispassionate.] He lived in America many years before I even came here. I came here, really kind of pushed by Hitler. He was in the leather-goods business—he manufactured handbags. And then one day he said, 'Well, if my brother can do it, I can do it too.' He sold his business, he bought a house here, and started making pictures, one worse than the other, and then he died." (10) Or, seen another way, through a telescope seeking the grand picture, W. Lee Wilder fades in black and white, from fabric, to film, to television, into a dawn colored dream.

**Footnotes**:

(1) *Nobody's Perfect: Billy Wilder, A Personal Biography*. Charlotte Chandler. Simon & Schuster. New York. 2002. Page 29.

(2) *Ibid*. Page 28.

(3) *Ibid*. Page 28-29.

(4) *Conversations with Wilder*. Cameron Crowe. Alfred A. Knopf. New York, 2001. Page 53.

(5) *Billy Wilder in Hollywood*. Maurice Zolotow. Limelight Editions, New York. 1977. Page 146.

(6) *Filmfax*. Evanston, IL. Number 21, July 1990.
(7) *Leonard Maltin's Movie and Video Guide*. Leonard Maltin, editor. Signet Books, New York. 2000 Edition. Page 732.
(8) *Duke Lover's The Dukes of Hazzard Episode List*. Online address: www.geocities.com/Hollywood/4497/episodes/season. Season 2, Episode #36, "R.I.P Henry Flatt" originally aired 3/14/80.
(9) *Freeze*. William Raynor & Myles Wilder. Critics Choice Paperback from Lorevan Publishing Inc. New York, 1988. Page 100.
(10) *Conversations with Wilder.* Cameron Crowe. Alfred A. Knopf. New York, 2001. Page 324.

**Featuring quotes from:**
*Phantom from Space* (1953)
*Killers from Space* (1954)
*The Snow Creature* (1954)

"It is like the pollard willows of our Dutch meadows or the oak bushes of our dunes; the rustle of an olive grove has something very secret in it, and immensely old. It is too beautiful for us to dare to paint it or to be able to imagine it."

—Letter from Vincent Van Gogh, May 1, 1882 (1)

"There was something that lurked in the dark. It could not be imagined. It could not be described."

—*The Monster from Earth's End* (2)

Amid the cabbage plants, mosses and lichens, tussock grass, stunted forest tangled with daisies and buttercups, something else spread across the tundra of Gow Island in 1959. The violence, insanity and horror that steadily took over there appealed to director Michael Hoey who confessed, "Around 1959, I read a book called *The Monster from Earth's End* by Murray Leinster. I was very taken with it and thought, 'Gee, this could be an exciting film.'" (3)

The administrating officer, Drake, tries to remain rational throughout his experience on the small island, "In a real world, everything follows natural laws. Impossible things do not happen. There is an explanation for everything that does happen." (4) Despite such assurance, Drake begins to slip and admits to himself, "On the other hand, if something sufficiently unlikely occurred, he might disbelieve the evidence of his senses. He might become convinced of his own insanity. He could act on the assumption that he himself had gone mad." (5) As people, dogs and birds die and fear takes over, it becomes clear that existence is as much a battle for sanity as it is a battle against an unknown terror. Drake insists, "But I've been having all the experiences of a madman. I've got to be a little bit stern and make him tell his hallucinations. They may not be delusions. Maybe they're facts. On this island you can't use the standards of a sane world to decide what's crazy and what isn't!" (6) What caused such a collapse and unleashed the hysteria and bloodshed to follow? The sight of trees…

"Its actual appearance in that place was as if some insane artist had traveled thousands of miles to create."

—*The Monster from Earth's End* (7)

"As for me, I tell you as a friend, I feel impotent when confronted with such nature, for my Northern brains were oppressed by a nightmare in those peaceful spots, as I felt that one ought to do better things with the foliage."

—Letter from Vincent Van Gogh, 1889 (8)

If only Drake and the others trapped on Gow had been aware of a parallel place with an open door to their shadows. Thousands of miles away on the mirror other side of the world lies the North Pole, "that enchanted continent in the sky, land of everlasting mystery." (9) Long a land of free imagination, this arctic source of myth and legends includes the horror of Mary Shelley's *Frankenstein.* In 1818 she set the scene: "I feel a cold northern breeze play upon my cheeks...Inspirited by this wind of promise, my daydreams become more fervent and vivid. I try in vain to be persuaded that the pole is the seat of frost and desolation; it ever presents itself to my imagination as the region of beauty and delight...there snow and frost are banished; and, sailing over a calm sea, we may be wafted to a land surpassing in wonders and in beauty every region hitherto discovered on the habitable globe." (10) This vision became part of Admiral Byrd lore when the polar explorer hinted at greater mysteries in 1947, "I'd like to see the land beyond the Pole. That area beyond the Pole is the center of the great unknown." (11) There are rumors that Byrd found that 'center of the great unknown' and even flew inside to explore, landing and finding that both poles have holes leading into the Hollow Earth. Already revealed in Jules Verne's *Journey to the Center of the Earth*, Oz historian L. Frank Baum also used this location for *Dorothy and the Wizard in Oz*, published in 1908. Dorothy says, "We are somewhere in the middle of the earth, and the chances are we'll reach the other side of it before long. But it's a big hollow, isn't it?" (12) She and her traveling companions observe, "On some of the bushes might be seen a bud, a blossom, a baby, a half-grown person and a ripe one." (13) It doesn't take long before one of these plant creatures threatens them with a cruel death.

Then in 1951, a long flight from Alaska, "Botanists, physicists, including a pin-up girl" were at war with "Our superior in every way...a being from another world, as different from us as one pole from another." *The Thing from Another World* revealed, "an intellectual super-carrot" from the crashed ice remains of a flying saucer. The North Pole base came under attack, dogs were mauled. Presiding Captain

Patrick Hendry gathered the forces, arming his fellows with weapons, guns, gasoline and electricity.

In opposition to the vigilante mentality, scientist Dr. Carrington is committed to keeping a sane approach to the escalating violence. It is his goal to study the creature. He decides "science rather than the army" should lead. Even in the face of death, he is sure, "Knowledge is more important than life." So it is a pivotal moment when he introduces himself to the Frankenstein-like monster in a dark Quonset hallway with, "You're wiser than anything on Earth—" only to get clubbed to the slatted floor. Like the night crawling menace of Gow Island, the Thing is also a deadly plant creature that lives on blood.

Inspired by *The Thing from Another World*, director Michael Hoey bought the rights to *The Monster from Earth's End* in 1961 "for a horrendous sum, like around $4,000." (14) Yet it took until 1966 to be filmed and Hoey sadly confirms the result, "By the time the film was completed, I would have been ashamed to talk to [the author] because of what happened." (15) In any case…

"When I bought the book, I thought, '*Monster from Earth's End*…that's too exploitative a title. I'd like another title.' One day I'm driving down the street and I see a sign on some guy's lawn, NIGHTCRAWLERS FOR SALE. Obviously he was talking about worms, but I thought, 'Boy, that's a great title for this project!' So I called it *The Nightcrawlers*. But Jack Broder, who was the executive producer, retitled it *The Navy vs. the Night Monsters*, which is an abominable title. I remember the day when I was rehearsing and Broder walked in and announced what the new title was going to be. The entire cast was ready to walk out—they were furious that he would give it that title. Such an exploitative, dumb title."

—Michael A. Hoey (16)

"The picture is one of the ugliest I have done…I have tried to express the terrible passions of humanity by means of red and green."

—Letter from Vincent Van Gogh, 1888 (17)

A painted sunset or sunrise appears as an orange and blue canvas backdrop for the words, *The Navy vs. the Night Monsters*, and actor names. "I have observed that a very simple flat frame in vivid orange lead would produce the desired effect in conjunction with blues of the background and the dark green of trees." (18) The picture fades in favor of a narration intoned over a bleak collection of stock footage ice, "Antarctica, the frozen continent at the bottom of the world. A continent as mysterious and unknown as the other planets of our solar system. Or a world in deep space a million light years away." But the movie takes place on a tropical island. Gow Island resembles California or Vietnam.

Like the script of a paperback left out in the rain, the movie follows a warped version of the book. It seems clear that the film is directed more at a teenage Drive-In audience, especially with its mordant jokes about egg salad, balloons and girls. The sitcom atmosphere is quickly shattered though when death arrives whistling like a tea kettle in the night.

Antarctic trees crash land on Gow and begin to stalk. "It was a living fossil, with a basic structure remote from all experience. Its cellulose fibers were extraordinarily long. They were oriented like flax-fibers, from which linen is made." (19) The sight of it is so terrifying to the people in the movie that their reaction may seem strange. Their horrific tortured nightmare of the psyche comes across in today's light as a walking, sprouting sleeping bag. This didn't go unnoticed by the director though. In an interview with Tom Weaver, Michael Hoey describes the film as a battle between his vision and the budget, but more specifically a war with his ham-fisted producer Jack Broder.

Jack Broder had ultimate control over the final cut. After Hoey turned in his reels and went to San Francisco to begin shooting *Dr. Goldfoot and the Bikini Machine*, Broder added 12 minutes to the running time to market the film for television. 720 more seconds result in a lot of comic book scenes: Mamie Van Doren's blueprint dress, a beach full of tree stumps crawling, but the most surreal touch is saved for the closing moments, in the napalmed jungle finale: "The picture ends with a stock shot with the four Blue Angels, with multi-colored streamers going out the back. No combat plane in its *life* ever did anything like that! It was footage from an air show. The logic that went into it was almost non-existent!" (20)

Hoey had his own artistic logic, "The premise that I functioned under was 'less is more,' and if you don't show it, the audience's imagination would create a much more vivid monster than we could ever create visually." (21) The breaking point for him was the sight of the trees. "I wanted the trees to look like the *other* trees, so that there wouldn't be the feeling that they stood out like sore thumbs, which is what those stupid things did. Broder hired some guy who did them for $1.98. When they showed up on the set the first day, I refused to film them, I was so upset." (22) Broder vs. Hoey was a contrast as polar as night and day and it literally came down to that in the filming of the trees. "They brought in one tree where a guy could get inside and wiggle his arms, and two other 'dummy' trees which just stood there. Stanley Cortez and I looked at each other and said, 'How are we gonna shoot this?', and I said, 'How 'bout no lights?' And he said, 'Well, that's probably the only way we *can* do it.' So we literally tried to light it so that it was so dark that the only time you would see the trees was when the Molotov cocktails were exploding around them. Well, Broder didn't like that and he had that scene 'printed up' [brightened] so that the trees are vividly lit. But that was never our intention of how we would show 'em." (23)

"I can't imagine a thing which prefers darkness attacking things because they're light."

—*The Monster from Earth's End* (24)

The imagining of it is where the horror lies. The monster Michael Hoey wanted to see is something that could hide in Vincent Van Gogh's paintings of poplars, willows, or olive trees. In fact, it could *be* one of those trees! The way Van Gogh portrays them fits perfectly:

"*The Roots* shows some tree roots on sandy ground. Now I tried to put the same sentiment into the landscape as I put into the figure: the convulsive, passionate clinging to the earth, and yet being half torn up by the storm. I wanted to express something of the struggle for life... in the black, gnarled and knotty roots." (25)

Also, compare the pastels of the Nightcrawlers' jungle to the *Night Café*:

"The fact is that the sun has never penetrated us people of the North...a street stretching away under a blue sky spangled with stars...dark blue or violet and there is a green tree. Here you have a night picture without any black in it, done with nothing but beautiful blue and violet and green, and citron-yellow color." (26)

And the big screen repeats the view out his asylum window:

"These high trees stand out against an evening sky with violet stripes on a yellow ground, which higher up turns into pink, into green...Now the nearest tree is an enormous trunk, struck by lightning and sawed off. But one side branch shoots up very high and lets fall an avalanche of dark green pine needles. This somber giant—like a defeated proud man—contrasts, when considered in the nature of a living creature, with the pale smile of a last rose on the fading bush in front of him. Underneath the trees, empty stone benches, sullen box trees; the sky is mirrored—yellow—in a puddle left by the rain. A sunbeam, the last ray of daylight, raises the somber ocher almost to orange. Here and there small black figures wander around among the tree trunks." (27)

This is the sight of trees that haunted Gow Island, painted with the vision of one haunted by worse monsters as he went out in his last days:

"A man called Jullian, who in later life went on to be the municipal librarian, recalled with shame how as a youth he had taken part in the baiting: 'I remember—and I am bitterly ashamed of it now—how I threw cabbage-stalks at him! What do you expect? We were young, and he was odd, going out to paint in the country, his pipe between his teeth, his big body a bit hunched, a mad look in his eye.'" (28)

**Footnotes (Stock Footage)**

1) *Dear Theo, The Autobiography of Vincent Van Gogh*; Edited by Irving Stone; Houghton Mifflin Company, Boston; 1937; p. 504

2) *The Monster from Earth's End*, by Murray Leinster; Gold Medal Books; Fawcett Publications Inc. Greenwich Conn. 1959; p. 79

3) *I Was a Monster Movie Maker: Conversations with 22 SF and Horror Filmmakers*, by Tom Weaver; McFarland & Co. Inc. Jefferson, NC, 2001; p. 96

4) *The Monster from Earth's End*, by Murray Leinster; Gold Medal Books; Fawcett Publications Inc. Greenwich Conn. 1959; p. 92

5) *Ibid.*, p. 32

6) *Ibid.*, p. 135

7) *Ibid.*, p. 154

8) *The Complete Letters of Vincent Van Gogh*, Volume Three, New York Graphic Society, Greenwich, Connecticut, 1958; p.232

9) As quoting Admiral Byrd; *The Hollow Earth, The Greatest Geographical Discovery in History, Made by Admiral Richard E. Byrd in the Mysterious Land Beyond the Poles—The True Origin of the Flying Saucers*; by Dr. Raymond Bernard; Bell Publishing Company; NY; 1969; p.20

In 1947, "Before he left on his seven hour flight from his Arctic base over iceless land beyond the North Pole (leading to the interior of the Earth), Admiral Byrd said: 'I would like to see that land beyond the Pole. That area beyond the Pole is the center of the Great Unknown.' Admiral Byrd did not cross over the North Pole and travel 1,700 miles south on its other side. If he did, he would enter icebound territory. Instead he entered a land with a warmer climate, free from ice and snow, consisting of forests, mountains, lakes, green vegetation and animal life. This new unknown land over which he flew for 1, 700 miles, which was not on any map, existed inside the polar opening leading to the hollow interior of the

Earth, where it is warmer than on its outside, which is here a land of ice and snow." (29)

10) *Frankenstein*, by Mary Shelley; Viking, New York; 1998, p. 11

11) *The Hollow Earth, The Greatest Geographical Discovery in History, Made by Admiral Richard E. Byrd in the Mysterious Land Beyond the Poles—The True Origin of the Flying Saucers*; by Dr. Raymond Bernard; Bell Publishing Company; NY; 1969; p. 44

12) *Dorothy and the Wizard in Oz*, by L. Frank Baum; Books of Wonder, Harper Collins Publishing; 1990; p.28

13) *Ibid.*

14) *I Was a Monster Movie Maker: Conversations with 22 SF and Horror Filmmakers*, by Tom Weaver; McFarland & Co. Inc. Jefferson, NC, 2001; p. 98

15) *Ibid.*, p.97

16) *Ibid.*, p.98

17) *Stranger on the Earth; a Psychological Biography of Vincent Van Gogh*, by Albert J. Lubin; New York, Holt, Rineheart Winston; 1972; p.142

18) *The Complete Letters of Vincent Van Gogh*, Volume Three, New York Graphic Society, Greenwich, Connecticut, 1958; p.258.

19) *The Monster from Earth's End*, by Murray Leinster; Gold Medal Books; Fawcett Publications Inc. Greenwich Conn. 1959; p.62

20) *I Was a Monster Movie Maker: Conversations with 22 SF and Horror Filmmakers*, by Tom Weaver; p.106

21) *Ibid.*; p.102

22) *Ibid.*; p.104

23) *Ibid.*; p.104

24) *The Monster from Earth's End*; p. 49

25) *The Complete Letters of Vincent Van Gogh*, Volume One, New York Graphic Society, Greenwich, Connecticut, 1958; p.360

26) *The Complete Letters of Vincent Van Gogh*, Volume Three; p.444

27) *Ibid.*; p. 524

28) *Van Gogh, His Life and His Art*; David Sweetman; Crown Publishers, Inc. New York; 1990; p.299

29) *The Hollow Earth, The Greatest Geographical Discovery in History, Made by Admiral Richard E. Byrd in the Mysterious Land Beyond the Poles—The True Origin of the Flying Saucers*; p.24

**Featuring film quotes from:**
*The Thing from Another World* (1951)
*The Navy vs. the Night Monsters* (1966)

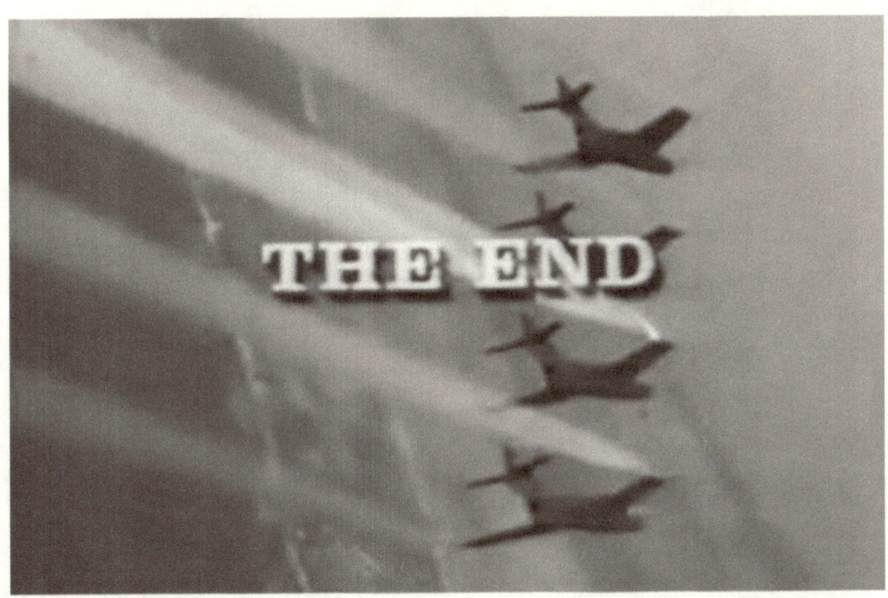


"Gow Island. In the past, virtually unknown to the rest of the world. Today, a famous landmark in man's struggle with the unknown. Another step forward in the march of science."

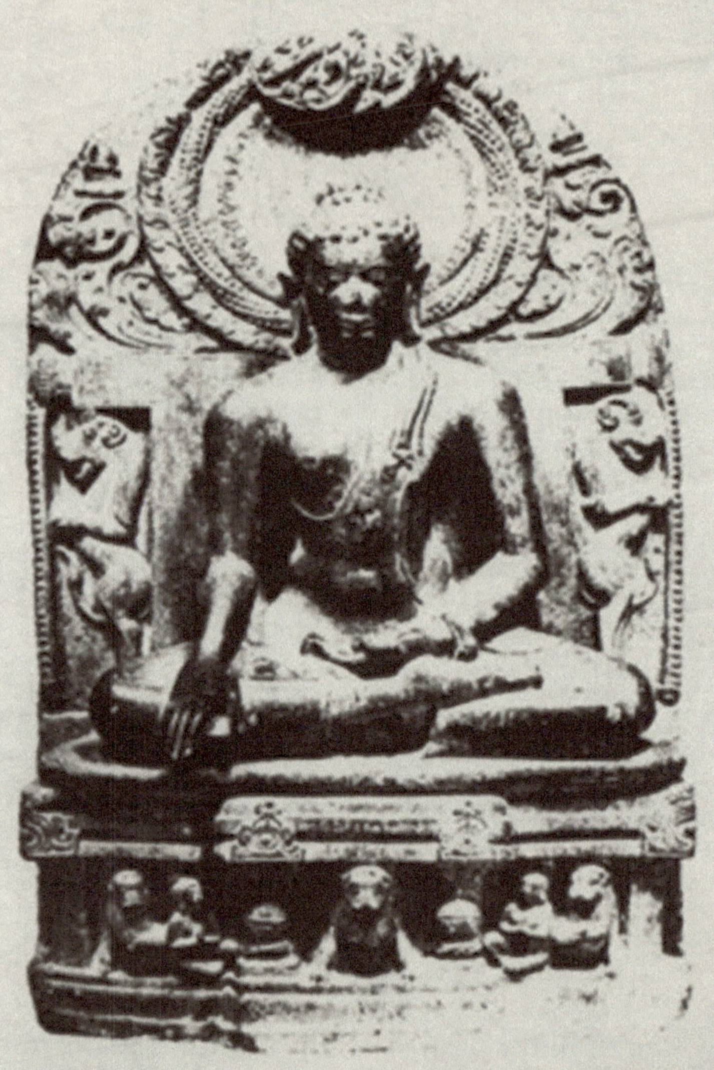

the GREATEST REVOLUTIONARY "GAME" is LEARNING TO LIVE with, SURVIVE FOR, & LOVE YOURSELF AND then to REALLY KNOW - YOU ARE otherpeople

For Tom Kryss

## *OPEN THE WINDOWS, OPEN THE DOORS*

Like the view from a bird or a big silver angel, Ohio tilts below, the Cleveland towers and bridges, the industrial flats, the great gray lake and all the rivers of cars. On the May Mother's Day weekend of 1967, airplane windows watch the ground. From a height, the sight wanders from the Asphodel Book Shop, past the Trinity Cathedral's Gate and the Well coffeehouse, along Euclid Avenue, over the Continental Theatre and the Case Auditorium. Every door opens to the poetry of d.a. levy.

"i have nothing to say
if you turn away
they made a machine
of / yr mind—once-
contained infinite doors

who let them be closed
one by one"

These words in levy's 1967 poem "Tombstone As A Lonely Charm," mention doors in Part 1 and Part Two: "the wind of the universe/ lies behind those doors/ who closed them/ one by one/...what can i tell you/ of re-opening those doors/...the mis-use of the mind/...everyone runs from/ words that carry light/ from the closed doors/ of the mind..."

From a letter to friend Tom Kryss, levy explained, "as for motivations behind a poem? motivations? hallucinations? the liberation seems to come thru misunderstanding

& struggling from one reality to another—one dimension to another—from one empty sphere to another." (1) While levy never shied from revealing the unchecked monstrosities in the necropolis of Cleveland, America, he also pointed the way out. d.a levy's poetry is a window in the wall and a Cleveland door thrown open. To let in light, to open eyes to a new vision is revolutionary.

All the doors in "Tombstone As a Lonely Charm" lead to the Part 3 conclusion, where levy determines:

"if you want a revolution
grow a new mind
& do it quietly
if you can

...if you really want
a revolution
learn how to change
your internal chemistry
then go beyond that"

d. a. levy's vision is there in his collages and art, in his poetry and editorials in the *Buddhist Oracle*, where ultimately: "the greatest revolutionary 'game' is learning to live with, survive for, & love yourself and then to really know—you are other people." (2)

Those words happened to have come at a time when America was in a state of war, overseas and at home, outside and in. Because of his message, levy was targeted with the determination accorded a radical revolutionary. d.a levy's secret indictment by the Cuyahoga County Grand Jury in

December 1966, police seizure of his mimeograph and writings, arrest, (along with Jim Lowell, owner of the Asphodel Bookshop), hearing, jail and release on bail, then March 1967 arrest again, made it clear the authority's response was simple: it was at war. Get the bookseller, get the poet, and then the light goes out.

The *Swamp Erie Pipe Dream* reported the first shot:

"On December 1, 1966 James Russell Lowell, owner of the Asphodel Bookshop in Cleveland was arrested and charged with possession and distribution of allegedly obscene literature. Over the years Mr. Lowell has acquired a reputation as one of the most singularly important bookdealers and collectors in all of the United States, if not the entire world. His dedication to new writing, particularly the Small Presses and little poetry magazines (manifested in his extreme willingness to market their product) has played a vital role in the incubatory states of the literature of the future. It was for dealing in this literature that Mr. Lowell was arrested by the Cleveland Police." (3)

And with Lowell went levy.

The underground *Swamp Erie* issue was mockingly dedicated to "psychotic prosecutor" George Mascarino, who "successfully managed to censor information and stop it from reaching the people of this city. He has accomplished this by declaring such information Obscene or Subversive. Obscenity is a christian neurosis. And Subversive is not necessarily Un-American, or Anti-American." (4)

If we compare the underground press coverage with the mainstream press, we see that it was a war with words, and a war on words—the overthrow of the 1st Amendment was easy when the establishment newspapers allowed it to happen. In the reporting of the *Cleveland Press* and the *Plain Dealer*, it's plain to see the press is simply a mirror for the fears and distorted views of their authorities:

"Beatnik Poet in Secret Indictment on Filth" (5), "D.A Levy is a little man of 24 with a scraggly beard who talks in a soft voice and uses dirty words when he writes." (6) It was made-to-order entertainment: "The Cleveland Civil Liberties Union will consider offering further assistance to beatnik poet D.A Levy, charged with acting in such a way as to tend to contribute to the delinquency of minors by reading poetry to them" , (7) later citing "...charges of dealing in obscene material and of acting in a way which tends to contribute to delinquency of minors." (8)

levy's poetry was finally reviewed in a Cleveland paper, but by a police officer and printed in the *Cleveland Press*: "Sgt. Burt Miller described some of the readings as 'obscene, weird and way out.' He compared them to foul language of the kind seen on lavatory walls." (9)

The media-engineered presentation of levy was a caricature, depicting an easy to draw enemy: "Darryl A. Levy, poet and leading figure of the beatnik community," (10) "the archetype of a beatnik", (11) "A widely known figure around the University Circle beatnik haunts." (12)

Read levy's description of these 'beatnik haunts' in the first *Buddhist 3rd Class Junkmail Oracle*: "There are many small coffeehouses hidden throughout Cleveland. <u>They are not</u> hangouts for beatniks, junkies & dopepeddlars...Please visit the coffeehouses, you may be surprised to learn that you have something to offer the spiritual development of this city." (13)

Finally, after all the propaganda, levy would call out: "Tell the teeny-boppers who admire me in droves that I am not a romantic figurehead," he said. He explained this term for the pseudo-beat teen-agers as those who "think they're hip but don't know who Kerouac is." (14) A year later, and fed up with the distortion, levy will recall, "3 years ago i was a beatnik leader, last year i was a hippie leader, a month ago i was a psychedelic assassin! Sorry to disappoint all you weaklings looking for a leader, & all you revolutionaries looking for an assassin, & all you politicians looking for a scapegoat. .but for the past 6-8 years i haven't been anything but a poet writing about what i see around me...I am a poet & i will read poems if anyone wants to put up some cash." (15)

If they had only listened to the man himself, they would see that he was aware and more than eloquent to the *Cleveland Press* speaking from the 6th floor of County Jail: "I am part of a movement to make the planet more civilized. I use those words you call shocking because I am trying to communicate. That's the way I hear people talk. That's the way they talk in here anyhow. I don't see any reason for people to be shocked...I'm not throwing bombs. I'm writing poems. When the bombs start to fall, we will need poems." (16)

Spelling it out clear: "This is supposedly a Free Country and we are all very sick of the christian moral laws that are only enforced when someone threatens temporal power structure. We are trying to grow, to be free to establish our own values, we are not trying to overthrow the Government of the United States." (17)

levy realized his poetry had incited a revolutionary reaction:

"THE POLICE KNOW what is most important to protect the security of the $warlords$ that control the minds of the people is To stop change/To suppress anything alien & different. Even if what is different is an expression of love. All forms of power must be kept in check Even if it is the Power of Friendship or knowledge." (18)

While grounded in a realization of revolutionary overthrow, levy's vision also opens to an exciting expression of what freedom, inspiration and friendship can accomplish. The experiences of those who were close to him are still carried. In my ongoing dialogue with poet Tom (T.L.) Kryss, he shares his memories:

"In the summer of 1966, after my graduation from high school, I read an article about levy in the Cleveland Press. The article, "Small Cause Champion Can't Fight Effects," is attached here at bottom. After reading the article, I began delivering mimeograph paper, canned food, and fresh produce to the Asphodel Book Store, asking Jim Lowell to pass this stuff. along to levy. This was when, not incidentally, I met Jim and began buying the 7 Flowers and Renegade Press booklets and magazines arrayed on a rack near the front door. The deliveries, two or three times a week, went on for maybe a couple of weeks before I ran into levy at the store. He asked me to STOP delivering these items to the Asphodel and gave me the address for his apartment on Savannah, which is where I took them in the future. The Asphodel's floor space was far less than the men's room today at Tower City, and since levy would come in for his mail about once a week the back room was fast piling up in the heat with unrefrigerated bananas, cans, and reams of paper. Years later Jim told me he often drove d.a. home to East Cleveland with the care packages. The indiscriminate purchase of 7 Flowers and Renegade Press publications stopped on that day, as he now just gave them to me, but in controlled numbers so as to save a few for somebody else." (19)

My wondering what it was like to visit levy's apartment in East Cleveland, brought this response from Kryss:

"Taped to the door of the apartment, first and last landing up from the tiny entrance foyer, was a home-made sign threatening peddlers, and anyone who would mindlessly disturb the resident's peace. It is remembered more for its humor—written in the style of an Egyptian curse with a drawing of the sacred eye for emphasis. One knocked on the door, just below the sign, and perhaps stood back a few inches as the crack between door and fame appeared and gradually widened to a look of surprise." (20)

And inside levy's room:

"The papers donated that summer were used, it seems, in the production of *Paideumic Dreams* (Sauls), *North American Book of the Dead, Coming forth by Day* (an Egyptian text). They were spread across the floors of the apartment, stacked and undergoing collation on sporadic trips to Savannah Avenue. The designs and colors in the Oriental rug did well by the unassembled booklets. On one occasion the 7 Flowers editor sat on the floor, legs impossibly crossed (but not full lotus), pulling pages and slapping them together from the piles arranged in a leading semi-circle like the curved windshield of a cockpit. It is thought that he had answered the door, let the visitor in, and returned to that position on the floor for a few minutes before reaching some stage of completion known only to himself. Then he stood up, wiped the hair back from his forehead, and whistled through his teeth." (21)

Tom Kryss elaborates in another letter:

"d.a.'s response to a gathering of John Scott, Grady Jones, and myself in his apartment on Christmas Eve 1966 is recorded in his poem "Jaywalking Blues." It is more than a response to a gathering. I remember the visits to his apartments more clearly than the walks, but what we spoke of is lost. That Christmas Eve, shortly after learning of his arrest, I returned to Cleveland on the Greyhound and walked up to his apartment. There was snow on the ground, but the stars could be seen in the sky. In my duffel bag were ten copies of Exupery's "Little Prince" I'd purchased a few hours before in a little bookstore on North Clark Street in Chicago. When I knocked on his door around midnight, he answered it the way I've described in excerpts above and showed me into the kitchen where we always sat. John and Grady were already seated there. John said they'd been waiting for me. I never told anyone I was returning to Cleveland, and didn't even know whether levy would be home." (22)

It was the strength and devotion of their friendship that allowed their circle to remain unbroken against persecution and to mount a defense against the city pressure and the police.

*A Tribute to Jim Lowell*, produced by T.L. Kryss, became the first response. Kryss had by then dropped out of Northwestern University and allied himself with small press operator Douglas Blazek of Chicago. As Tom Kryss explained: "I conceived of the idea, bought the equipment and materials, contacted the contributors, printed and assembled the book, and then pretty much turned it over to Jim (and

Jaspar Wood of the Defense Fund)." (23)

Kryss continues his description from inside the underground press movement:

"Indisputably the idea for this book (arising from Jim's arrest in late 1966 for selling 'obscene' literature) lit the fire for the purchase of a mimeograph—Sears Roebuck. Cleveland winter of '67...rj was about to disappear into the County Workhouse for the summer and wanted the ammunition ready for his return. And ammunition it was, as the machine's metallic thumping echoed through the bare and unappointed rooms, only a little masked by the clanking of dishes from the restaurant kitchen in front. Jim's Tribute was preceded by several test attempts that summer at smaller memeo'd books, all conceived in response to police and prosecutorial harassment. It was an easy machine to operate, almost self-explanatory, and did not require too much study...After 37 years the chemicals from the paint have, in spots, bled into the facing pages, imbuing them with ghost images and inhaling deeply, you detect strong scents of Royal Blue." (24)

Although Kryss received "No response from Ginsberg and Patchen when I solicited them by mail," (25) writers in the book included Denise Levertov, Jonathan Williams, Charles Olson, James Laughlin, Michael McClure, rjs, in all, 48 authors and editors:

"The 48 essays, poems, and statements of solidarity that were backbone to the *Tribute to Jim Lowell* came together in a few short weeks in the spring of 1967. The distances involved, the speed of mail, even the gamut of temperaments among contributors all underscore the uniqueness of the outpouring of sentiment on behalf of the Cleveland bookseller. The person putting the book together and soliciting the material would have been unknown to a large share of contributors, but mention along of the Asphodel and Lowell sparked rushes of response." (26)

From Douglas Blazek's contribution, entitled "Wisdom Shop" comes: "The door to his shop is the veritable 'door to perception;' the way to dispel fear, hatred and ignorance as best as is humanely possible. Beyond that door is the greatest amalgam of Thinkers our world has yet to produce."

Charles Bukowski wrote:

"Good art, Creation, is generally 2 decades to 2 centuries ahead of its time in relationship to the establishment and the police state, good Art is not only not understood but also feared because to make the future better it must state that the present is bad, very bad, and this is hardly an endearment to those in control...a hundred years from now those books that you are confiscating will be taught in your universities if your leaders are not silly enough to get us blown to hell. I think that when you raid that you raid own fear, you raid your own conscience (what little there is) and your raid, in anger, the lostness of your souls."

d.a. levy's poem for the collection ends with the walk away:

"& wander home
knowing

<u>the light still evades us</u>

the pigs wallow in their
euphoria/ i walk futilely
trying to hitch a ride

dreaming as jim lowell
restacks the mind-bending
poetry in freezers
& turns off

the neon-lites"

In the May issue of *Swamp Erie Pipe Dream, A Tribute To Jim Lowell* was announced for a June 15th release. Though Kryss wrote me, "The book was not linked in my mind, at the time, with the Benefit," (27) the issue also includes notice of the next maneuver in the defense of Lowell and levy.

On April 24th the *Cleveland Press* announced the Defense Benefit planned for May 14th at Masonic Hall "to raise money for the defense of bookseller James Lowell and hippy poet D.A. Levy." Less than a week later, the *Plain Dealer* reported the cancellation of the event after the Masonic Temple's commander-in-chief of the Lake Erie Consistory of the Masons discovered the nature of the benefit. It was not for a Vietnam veteran as assumed but for veterans of the censorship wars at home.

Working quickly, Jaspar Wood, founder and chairman of the Citizens for Freedom of the Mind, along with the University Circle Teach-In Committee found a new auditorium. The Committee's coordinator told the *Plain Dealer*: "We feel a particular responsibility to the poets of our city so that they can write and speak without police harassment and censorship. The action of the Masonic Association was a simple act of censorship and a denial of freedom of speech. We must keep the community open for the free flow of opinions." (28)

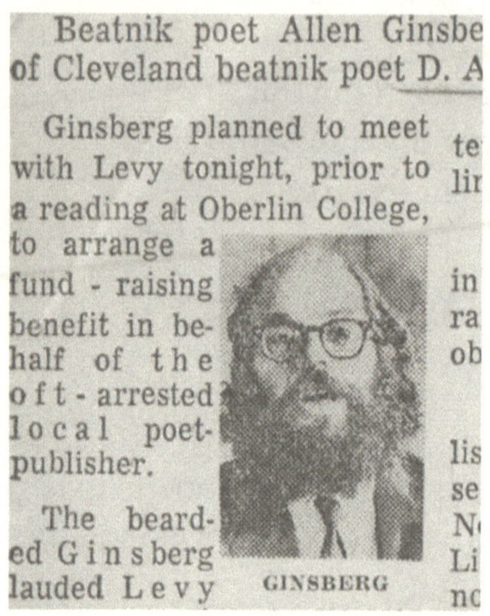

Beatnik poet Allen Ginsbe
of Cleveland beatnik poet D. A

Ginsberg planned to meet with Levy tonight, prior to a reading at Oberlin College, to arrange a fund - raising benefit in behalf of the oft - arrested local poet-publisher.

The bearded Ginsberg lauded Levy

GINSBERG

"I will haunt these States
with beard bald head
eyes staring out plane window"
—"A Vow," Allen Ginsberg; 1966

All through *The Fall of America*, Allen Ginsberg is looking out windows, from planes and buses and cars, observing the times; he is the window prophet: "Blue sunray on air heights, bubbled with thick steam roofing the planet…heard a sweet drone in the plane whine…language in the sky—And in the city, brick veils…it can drive yr eyes inward…anger at heart base all over the Nation…Fascism in America… kidnapped by phantoms conspiring to win elections…To sit at the window & moan…Elbow on windowsill, I lean and muse…dreams invented for your eyes… typewriter at window silver panorama…cloud-cities adrift

& dissolving...glimpsed from air-roads smogged thru heavens toward Illinois...Floating armchairs descend from sky in sunlight, rocking back & forth in polluted fields of air... the plane bounds down above gas tanks, gas stations, smokestacks flaring poison mist, Superhighways razored through hairy woods, Down to Earth Man City... ...how to end the poetry movie in the mind?" (29) Like Walt Whitman, Ginsberg was the watchman of the nation, but not the only one and he surely recognized an ally in d.a levy. After all, Ginsberg's *Howl* had been given similar treatment in 1957 with its branding as 'obscene literature,' followed by arrests and a much-publicized trial.

Landing in Cleveland, Ginsberg immediately defended levy for "attempting to lift the spiritual basis of Cleveland...Instead of persecuting him," Ginsberg told reporters, "he should be given a prize by the city for his poems about Cleveland. He stands alone in his effort to lift Cleveland... He is learned and sincere, but he is being made to suffer in the classic American way." (30)

It was Ginsberg's second trip to Cleveland in less than a year. The first time was less eventful, as felt in Ginsberg's June 1966 calm poem, "Cleveland Airport" and in the melancholy vision of "Cleveland, The Flats." This swirling sight of the city, finally settling in University Circle and Oms, was dedicated to d.a. levy.

As Tom Kryss remembers:

"Ginsberg was in Cleveland during the summer of 1966, too, with Ed Sanders and the Fugs (before I met or had heard of levy, I think). There was an article in the *Cleveland Press* Friday entertainment supplement concerning the man and his appearance in Cleveland shortly before the reading he gave at Amasa Stone Chapel. On information from Judy Prusnek, who was the youth writer for the *Press*, I went up on the bus to the Euclid Tavern with a tape recorder and a list of questions. Ginsberg and his group had a room all to themselves in the back, seated around a long table. I couldn't get the tape recorder to work, hadn't brought paper and pencil, the questions fizzled out (Ginsberg, I thought, was gracious and kind), and I left. Killed some time on the streets and walked up to the church where I stood in the back (the place was packed) and listened to a few minutes of the reading." (31)

*The Cleveland Press* reported: "Last night, the controversial poet read his works for two hours to 650 students jammed into the Amasa Stone Chapel at Western Reserve University. It was the poet's first visit here. His rough, stimulating verse resounded in striking contrast against the wooden walls of the chapel, where students come to pray...singing in Chinese, then English, a Zen Buddhist chant...he then read aloud seven free-verse poems peppered with obscenities, literary imagery and political comments against the Vietnam war." (32)

levy's friend rjs also recalled meeting Allen Ginsberg. Ginsberg was aware of him as a result of inclusion in the anthology, *Where is Vietnam? American Poets Respond*, published in 1967. rjs had a poem entitled, 'war-monger.' "i was 17, & had just been included in "Where is Vietnam" and thought I was hot. dont recall much of reading but at a party thereafter i was confronted by Ginsberg on the front porch & he had a taperecorder & wanted to interview me! pushing the mike in my face spooked me, so i just said 'rjs—poet—no comment & someday you will hear from me' levy must have instigated it." (33)

That summer Ginsberg had words with Ohio newspapers, knowing the role of writing and duty of word. From a letter printed in August 1966:

"Sirs,
A liberal policy where there is objective representation of private views attitudes and language characteristic of Persons who make up our nation is necessary if we are not to suffocate." (34)

And he warned:

"CENSORSHIP of language is direct censorship of consciousness; and if i don't fit in I can't change the shape of my mind." (35)

By the time he returned to Cleveland for the May Defense Benefit, Ginsberg was dropped into what was now a warzone. That summer of 1967 cities all over America were erupting in riots and Cleveland was no exception. Ginsberg paints the picture of those times in his depiction of the events the night before the big reading:

"In New York we had already had problems because the police wanted us to get entertainment permits, you know, as if it were a night club, and we were just reading poems in a coffeeshop. So in New York legally we were liberated. But out there [Ohio] the police were particularly violent and brutal. So we went into the Gate before the reading, and we were going to have some sort of poetry reading, but then we were told that according to the police, if we had a poetry reading in the coffeehouse, everyone would be busted. So we decided we'll go to the gig anyway, and we'll all sit around and have coffee and talk, and maybe…sing some music of something. I was sitting at a table with levy and Ed Sanders, and maybe

Kryss and a couple other people. After a while, big crowd, lots of people there, big excitement, and then there were police coming in. So we started singing, 'We Shall Overcome' or something, and so that wasn't poetry reading, just people singing 'We Shall Overcome.' And then you know we started singing Hare Krishna's… 'Hare Krishna…Hare Krishna. Krishna Krishna, Hare, Hare, Hare Llama, Hare Llama, Llama Llama, Hare, Hare…' And we were singing these devotional songs, when all of a sudden the doors burst in, and about 50 policemen with big shiny leather boots, and heavy crash helmets, and big black coats, and long truncheons, and guns rushed into the room and said, 'Everybody up against the wall. You're under arrest.' (chuckles) So I said to the guy standing next to me, a big policeman standing next to me who was one of the leaders, 'Who's in charge here, anyway? You got a warrant?' And he says, 'We don't need any warrant around here.' So I said, 'Well, who's in charge.' And he said, 'Nobody's in charge.' (laughs). I think I had a right asking who's in charge, and his 'Nobody's in charge.' And it's true nobody was in charge, maybe the devil or something… not that I believe in the devil…but aggression was in charge, police state was in charge, unconstitutional behavior was in charge, un-Americanism was in charge." (36)

d.a. levy recalled:

"allen was here with the fugs yesterday and we collected another grand for the defense of us/allen was greeted by 26 police cars & a gun in his gut & witness to the beating of several negros while the police seemed unable to break up the fight…all this at the coffee house on 115th Sat. night may 13 while i was watching a warhol movie at the continental & had to leave in a flash of light to run to the coffeehouse

& find out if allen got busted…he didn't…allen chanting mantras to chase away evil spirits…" (37)

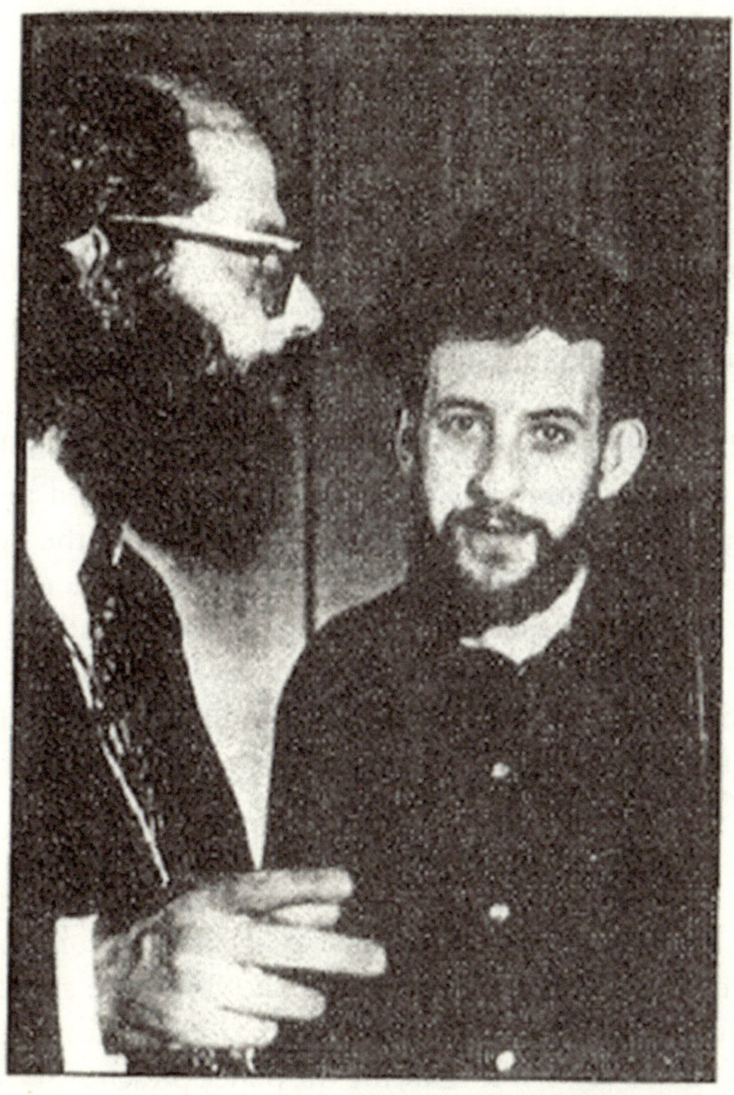

*Allen Ginsberg and d.a. levy*

New York poet and bookstore proprietor Ed Sanders, who performed on Sunday with the Fugs, recalled, "The day of the benefit we tried to do a preliminary poetry reading at the Gate in Trinity church but the fuzz broke it up. 1967 was a year in which you didn't give up and d.a. was no exception." (38)

rjs shared this:

"for the benefit reading, i was in the workhouse but letters & visitors told me of a Ginsburg read at E115 COFFEE-HOUSE that was busted by the COPS & Ginsberg was arrested. everyone thought it was great because "police riots" at that corner were common, & everyone thought A.G. could bring that to light. kids would tell me of police billyclubbing the male students & tearing clothes & groping (raping?) the girls…paddy wagons for the resistors. the one i stumble into, i was in parking lot across the street. cop pointed to me & angrily shouted "COME HERE" pointing to the curb. so i crossed the road to his spot, & he clubbed me & pushed my head into brickwall & busted me for jaywalking! i had bruised forehead & backhead. those times were bad & i really dont relish the memories. the cops in question were CLEVELAND 6th DISTRICT and University Circle under control of CWRU Board of Directors." (39)

According to Clevelander Jake Marx who attended the benefit, "When I walked in Strosacker Auditorium, I saw all the cops. I got a little afraid. The cops were shoulder to shoulder all around the theatre, all around with crash helmets on." (40) While ignoring the police presence at the benefit, the *Plain Dealer* article from Monday, May 15, 1967 derided Ginsberg's appearance there: "What had sounded like a Japanese kabuki actor was, Ginsberg assured his audience, a Buddhist prayer." Before an audience of 600, levy read two poems, Lowell "sat on the stage and didn't read anything," while Allen Ginsberg reread the poem that got levy arrested, though its potency didn't apply to his own arrest. The newspaper accounting of Ginsberg concluded, "the bearded one" promised to return in the summer, to "do some social work."

When Ginsberg did return years later, the *Plain Dealer* from April 12, 1971 would report:

"Ginsberg dedicated the program to D.A. Levy, Cleveland poet who committed suicide at 25 in 1968. Ginsberg had come to Cleveland several times to raise funds for the defense of Levy, who had been indicted for dealing in obscene literature because his poems contained four-letter words. The charges were eventually dropped. "The way the police harassed him was unique to Cleveland," Ginsberg said. "They even came into a coffee shop on Euclid Avenue while I was here and lined us all against the wall at gunpoint."

After the 1967 benefit though, when Ginsberg left, it only got worse. As levy related in the *Buddhist Oracle*:

"What i really want to say is, today is July 16 and I am afraid. I said, 'I AM AFRAID!' Its getting time for those pre-election busts and i wonder if im going to be one of them. I wonder how many of my friends are going to go to jail, no they're not all criminals, some of them are like me, they just talk too much. I am afraid that i wont have enough money to get this paper printed before i get assassinated, in one way or another, but then they may leave me alone, just to keep you deluded into believing that we still have freedom of the press." (41)

With Cleveland forces crashing down on them, levy dedicated *The Tibetan Stroboscope* to Allen Ginsberg and spoke to him in "poem for lama ginsberg":

"& now you are telling us about tomorrow & yesterday
& no one is listening…

& when you tell the people
how to stop america from dying
they will stop following you
Allen/America is dead
i didn't want to say it"

But the poem does say it, and he's talking to himself too, "in my psycho-drama/ there is a similarity in our blood/ perhaps in a past life/ we swept toilets together/ now the things i know/ are called paranoia/egocentricity/messianic complex/ hallucinations & other excuses not to listen to me…perhaps — ill see you next lifetime &/ you can take me on another journey/ toward the sun..."

And so the benefit reading ended, but that wasn't quite the end. Before Allen Ginsberg left town to float over a falling America again, d.a. levy took him down the street.

At 13931 Euclid Avenue, near his Wymore Street apartment, levy had a sanctuary, just the sort of temple he needed to get away from the outside Cleveland—a place to open a door and be in a dark room with one wall of light. This was the Continental Art Theatre, honored in many of his poems, "a great place to get it or just to dream about it because no one does get it except in european movies." (42)

The manager of the Continental, artist George Fitzpatrick, spoke with me on the telephone. "I liked him [levy].

He would hand out poems and his newspaper. Depending on what sort of film we had. He would be there. He also had a table in the theater..." And just like a movie, Fitzpatrick revealed this scene:
"On the day of that event, a Sunday, I was working at the theatre. Early that evening I was working in the box office and d.a. comes over with Allen Ginsberg to introduce me. I'm in the box office selling tickets and so I asked him if he would sign my picture postcard of him—that famous one of him in the top hat. Ginsberg was at the theatre and during an intermission went into the front of the Continental Theatre—the theatre didn't have a stage—and gave a Tibetan chant. That actually happened." (43)

After the prayers, the poets remained for the next movie to begin. With the end of the benefit day already fading, levy could open to light and go, as in his poem, "The Old Bohemian Hall 1967" which ends like his life with a revolving door:

"i am moving ahead in time
the american people have survived
the revolution
everyone is happy
no one is alive
everything is run very efficiently
someone old is reborn
haunted
& starts looking into his head

he is already programmed to not
look into his head
the sky explodes....etc."

**Footnotes:**

1) d.a. levy letter to Tom Kryss; September 1966; quoted with permission
2) *The Buddhist Third Class Junkmail Oracle*; Volume 2 #3; August-Sept 1968
3) *Swamp Erie Pipe Dream*; Vol. 1; No. 1; May 1967
4) *Ibid.*
5) *Cleveland Press*; January 6, 1967
6) *Cleveland Press*; March 30, 1967
7) *Cleveland Press*; March 31, 1967
8) *Cleveland Press*; April 12, 1967
9) *Cleveland Press*; January 6, 1967
10) *Cleveland Press*; January 6, 1967
11) *Plain Dealer*; January 19, 1966
12) *Plain Dealer*; January 16, 1967
13) *Buddhist Junkmail Third Class Oracle*; June 1967
14) *Cleveland Press*; July 15, 1966
15) *Buddhist Third Class Junkmail Oracle*; #7; October 1967
16) *Cleveland Press*; March 1967
17) *Swamp Erie Pipe Dream*, Vol. 1, No.1, May 1967
18) *The Marrhawanna Quarterly*
19) Tom Kryss letter to author; June 7, 2006
20) *The Search for the Reason Why: New and Selected Poems*; Tom Kryss; Bottom Dog Press; Huron, Ohio; 2006; p.70-71
21) *Ibid*; p.70
22) Tom Kryss letter to author; June 5, 2006
23) Tom Kryss letter to author; June 26, 2006
24) *Ibid.*
25) Tom Kryss letter to author, June 15, 2006
26) Tom Kryss letter to author, June 26, 2006
27) *Ibid.*

28) *Plain Dealer*; May 4, 1967
29) *The Fall of America: poems of these states 1965-1971*; Allen Ginsberg; City Lights Books; San Francisco, CA; 1972
30) *Cleveland Press*; April 12, 1967
31) Tom Kryss letter to Larry Smith; June 3, 2006; used with permission
32) *Cleveland Press*; June 9, 1966
33) rjs letter to Larry Smith; June 13, 2006; used with permission
34) Allen Ginsberg letter to Cleveland State University *Cauldron*; August 3, 1966
35) *Marrahwannah Quarterly*; Volume 3, Number 3; 1967
36) *If I Write I Scratch*; Kon Petrochuk; 1981
37) d.a. levy letter to d.r. Wagner
38) "A Biography of d.a. levy"; Ed Sanders; *Woodstock Journal*; 2004
39) rjs letter to Larry Smith; June 13, 2006; used with permission
40) Jake Marx, phone conversation with author, September 10, 2006
41) *Buddhist Third Class Junkmail Oracle*; #3; July 1967
42) d.a. levy; "I found It At the Movies"
43) George Fitzpatrick phone call with author; 4:35 PM, June 14, 2006

## *ENTERING THE WATER AND ESCAPING: From Houdini to the Hoodoo Sea*

"What was the Unspeakable Secret of the SEA OF LOST SHIPS?"

—Poster for *Creature from the Haunted Sea*

It's common knowledge that Harry Houdini planned to reach out after death and contact this world of the living again. But did Bogart plan the same escape? And did he succeed, channeled into the part of a way-below B-movie actor in a film entitled *Creature from the Haunted Sea*?

"If it's possible for anyone to get through after death, that person will be me." This was the vow of showman/magician/ultraman Harry Houdini. Time after time, across the country, around the world, he defeated death by out-smarting it. Whether locking himself underwater in a safe, enduring The Water Torture Cell, or throwing himself bound in chains into an icy river, he came out alive again. Water was his favorite element to challenge, though he was known to hang tied upside down in the air, or while staging another feat in California, he confessed, "I tried out 'Buried Alive' in Hollywood, and nearly did it. Very dangerous; the weight of the earth is killing." (1) Then in 1919, he ventured into the early life of motion pictures, which he saw as realizing "the American ideal of speed and activity." (2) His movie *The Man from Beyond* promised, "A man Entombed in a Massive Casket of Ice 100 Years Comes Back to Life. The Weirdest and Most Sensational Love Story Ever Screened" and featured his famous dethawing act from vaudeville. His experience conquering water even allowed him to share his Promethean knowledge, patenting a new and improved deep sea diving suit “arranged to permit the diver, in case of danger for any cause whatever, to quickly divest himself of the suit while being submerged and to safely escape and reach the surface of the water.” (3)

But when he died in Detroit on the Halloween of 1926, contact was lost. “The ordinary people of Europe and America mourned the death of Houdini, but they knew of his promise to come back. It was said that in the manner of his return he would demonstrate immortality so vividly that no one would ever be able to disbelieve again and all the world would be converted.” (4) For ten years, his wife Bess worked the air in séances (the very thing Houdini crusaded against, the spotlight of fraud mediums and phony spiritualists), reaching for the ten word code she would know him by, finding nothing before she finally let him go. Where are you? What more could she do? This mystery of human existence seemed to baffle her. Winds blew, curtains fell, magic stopped, things were laid to rest.

Is life after death possible, probable, more than the mystical, or the ravings of B-movies and pulp dreamers? Time. Reception reaches. Across the continent, over an ocean, up mountains to Tibet where life and death have been the hum of meditation for well over a thousand passing years. “In nature an embodiment of the ocean of buddhas/ With concentrated attention I call to you:/Send out waves of your compassionate energy.” (5) In 1933, after the 13th Dalai Lama wrote these verses, he passed away and the search was on to find him again.

Reincarnation is the path he follows. In the words of the Buddha of Compassion: “Both mind and body must have immediate sources…the immediate source of a body is that of its parents. But physical matter cannot produce mind, nor mind matter. The immediate source of a mind must, therefore, be a mind which existed before the conception took place; the mind must have a continuity from a previous mind. This we hold to prove the existence of a past life." (6)

So how could anyone discover, or rediscover this great man who returned to life? Lake Lhamo Lhatso held the answer. "The people of Tibet believe that visions of the future can be seen in the waters of this lake...Sometimes the visions are said to appear in the form of letters, and sometimes as pictures of places and future events." (7) Houdini's ten word code come to life. The blue sky on water revealed the clues and in 1937, after four years out of sight, the 14th Dalai Lama was found, a two year old boy under a turquoise roof, who knew who he was.

"Here lies one whose name was writ in water"
—John Keats' tombstone

In the meantime, America continued. Only 18, while Harry Houdini was making his first movies, Seaman Humphrey Bogart floated the ocean aboard The Leviathan. The U-Boats let him pass back and forth unsunk and after the war he drifted, closer to where he would become. Trying his hand at directing a film called *Life* was the opening door for him to act. Parts in plays and early pictures followed, then it happened: from the stage production of *The Petrified Forest* his gangster character was projected over theater screens in 1936. Going rough through the Depression into the next war years, reflecting the time-culture in the roles that made him bright, Bogart was created. "To his cynicism, his own code of ethics, his hatred of the phoniness in all human behavior, he now added the softening trait of tenderness and compassion and a feeling of heroic commitment to a cause." (8)

Like Houdini's water shows, Bogart seemed to truly glow when he was filmed on the ocean. T*o Have and Have Not* (1945), *Key Largo* (1948), *The African Queen* (1951) put Bogart on the waves and it's real, he's in control, steering the careening boat around danger. It's that vision of him that is timeless. At his funeral services in 1957, a glass display case holding the model of his yacht The Santana took the place of a coffin and the whistle from *To Have and Have Not* was interred with his ashes. Director John Huston decided, "He is quite unreplaceable. There will never be anybody like him." Sealing Bogart's memorial was Alfred Lord Tennyson's poem 'Crossing the Bar,' tolling Time and sea: "But such a tide as moving seems asleep,/Too full for sound and foam,/When that which drew from out the boundless deep/Turns again home."

"Everything is wrong...strange...We can't be sure of any direction. Even the ocean doesn't look as it should."

—Flight Leader, Flight 19, gone in 1945.

Roger Corman was born in 1926, the year Houdini died. After he served in the Navy, he made his first film *The Monster from the Ocean Floor* in 1954. Fiendishly, he returned again and again to explore the power from water. There was *The Phantom from 10,000 Leagues* (1956): "SHEER HORROR as a living nightmare stalks the ocean floor!" "See! The battle for life at the bottom of the sea!" and *Attack of the Crab Monsters* (1957): "From the depths of the sea...A TIDAL WAVE OF TERROR!" So it was only natural that he would be drawn to The Hoodoo Sea.

"The Bermuda Triangle is a stretch of the Atlantic Ocean bordered by a line from Florida to the islands of Bermuda, to Puerto Rico and then back to Florida." (9) However, disappearances of ships and aircraft have strayed well beyond this anomalous area, to include the Caribbean island Martinique, location of *To Have and Have Not.* One year after that film was shot, in the winter of 1945, the five Avengers of Flight 19, a Flight Leader and 13 other men, were lost off the Florida Keys. Bogart and Bacall would return to this very place in three years for the making of *Key Largo.*

What brought Roger Corman to The Bermuda Triangle were the tax incentives. Arriving in Puerto Rico in 1961, he quickly directed *The Last Woman on Earth* and produced *Battle of Blood Island.* Then, with a week before the crew had to return to America, he decided, why not direct one more film?

Whereas Bogart had script writers like Raymond Chandler, Ernest Hemingway, William Faulkner and Truman Capote, Roger Corman had Charles B. Griffith, a man who had set new standards in black-comedy with his screenplays *Bucket of Blood* (1954) and *Little Shop of Horrors* (1960). Corman remembered telephoning the States, "'Chuck, I need another comedy-horror film and you've got a week to write it…There's no time for rewrites. I've got a small cast so write for them'…He was very sleepy and I wasn't certain he understood completely the story line we discussed, but he agreed." (10)

The result, Corman confessed was "truly insane." Inspired by the nearby revolution of Fidel Castro, *Creature from the Haunted Sea* "was a story about a band of Batista's generals making off with a treasure chest of gold from Cuba. The man they hire to captain their boat is a mobster. He murders the generals and covers up the crimes by inventing a story about an undersea monster who devours people. But there *is* an undersea monster." (11)

Corman's monster is none other than the $150 creation of soundman/actor Beach Dickerson who shares: "I decide to get five helmets and make this *giant* head. Then we get a wetsuit, some moss, lots of Brillo pads. Then we get tennis balls for the eyes. Ping-Pong balls for the pupils, and pipecleaners for the claws. Then we cover him with black oilcloth to make him look slimy. I mean, we decked him out and he was absolutely *glorious*. And I must say, that son of a bitch, he ran on land and swam underwater for the whole shoot and when it was all over he went to heaven." (12)

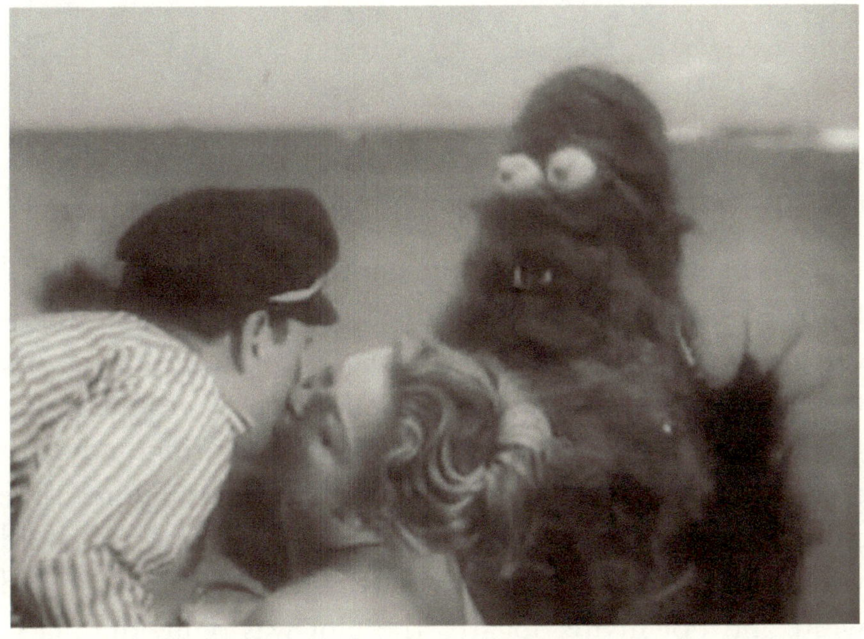

The monster is telling of the production itself, tossed together in a rush of crazed inspiration, allowing what's around to influence. It is seeing the movie inside someone's head...someone sleeping in the shade of the Bermuda Triangle. What a shock when into this dream assembly suddenly appears an Academy Award winning icon. Pulled through, after four years out of sight, Humphrey Bogart is back.

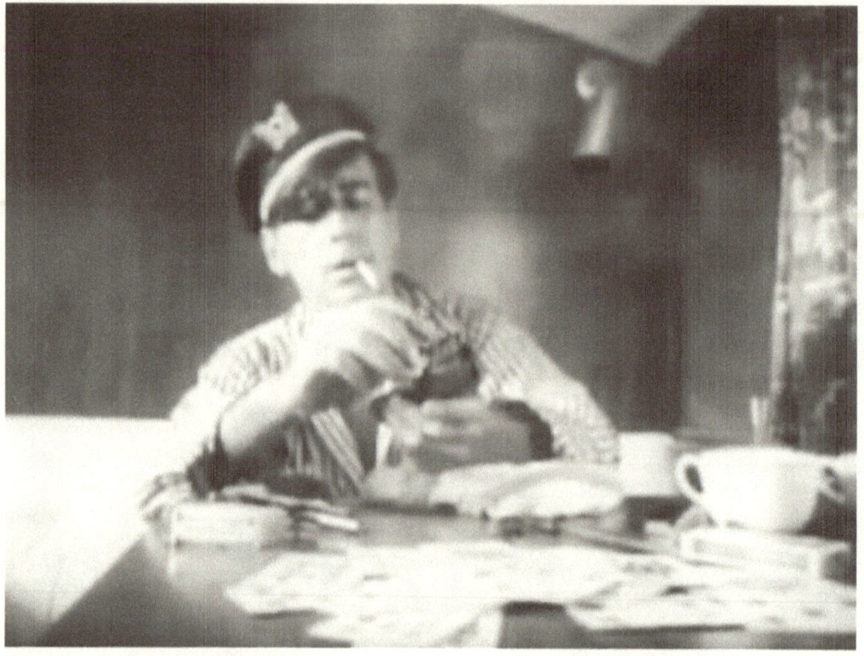

His first utterance in the dark under palms is, "I am," followed by, "Let's get on with it." Renzo Capeto, American gambler, gangster and yachtsman is Bogart's incarnation, though at times it seems his actor Anthony Carbone struggles to control the possession. The same posturing body language, the cigarette going, the sailor hat, the toughness, the smiles, his gaze, mannerisms and speech patterns. How could you possibly make a boat movie with gangsters in black and white and not invite Bogart? The plot was right, the place, the boat, everything agreed. It was an open door awaiting his reappearance.

So, coasting with the perfect ghost, the boat floats right into the plot of *To Have and Have Not*. As in that earlier film, while hoping to look like a fishing vessel, their mission has been discovered by a patrol boat and The Bogart of both films arms his deck hands for trouble. "Now let's appear casual," he orders in 1961 and, "Mary Belle, sing a song." Hoagy Carmichael backed Lauren Bacall, but Mary Belle has an out-of-the-blue piano track to make up a love song, as she bobs along. A shooting match erupts again and they escape again. Even the beyond-odd character Pete Peterson Jr., an animal mimic, is an impaired exaggeration of Walter Brennan's Eddy, with his dead bee routine. Boat full of thieves, the cramped onboard camera work resembles *Key Largo*, while Renzo plots for the chance to take over their course, and soon does.

But this is the Bermuda Triangle, a mysterious and dangerous place, unpredictable, as the theatrical trailer for *To Have and Have Not* already warned: "The danger zone of the Mid-Atlantic where strange ships slip through the fog with even stranger cargoes…where all barriers are down and the only law is the law of the Caribbean."

Prescient, in what amounts to his swansong, *Creature*'s Bogart echoes Tennyson in his conversation with an equally fated Cuban colonel, dreams of what to do, where to go next:

*"You can go anywhere you like. I'm going home."*

"To America?"

*"America? No, I can't go back there anymore."*

True, his encore appearance is over, he's bound for some unseen shore. The monster roars out of the water, there's no place to get away, and The Bogart runs out of life on the beach, unable to move, staring at the sky.

**Footnotes (Stock Footage):**

(1) *The Life and Many Deaths of Harry Houdini*, Ruth Brandon, Kodansha International, NY, 1993, page 151.
(2) *Ibid*, page 196.
(3) Houdini U.S Patent # 1,370,316 granted March 1, 1921. Quoted from www.magictricks.com/Houdini
(4) *Death and the Magician: The Mystery of Houdini*, Raymond Fitzsimons, Atheneum, NY, 1981, page 163.
(5) *The Fourteen Dalai Lamas: A Sacred Legacy of Reincarnation*, Glenn H. Mullin, Clear Light Publishers, Sante Fe, New Mexico, 2001, page 448.
(6) *My Land and My People, His Holiness the Dalai Lama of Tibet*, McGraw-Hill Book Co. Inc., NY, 1962, page 236.
(7) *Ibid*, page 21-22.
(8) *Humphrey Bogart*, Alan G. Barbour, Galahad Books, NY, 1973, page 96.
(9) www.unmuseum.org/triangle.htm
(10) *How I Made A Hundred Movies in Hollywood And Never Lost A Dime*, Roger Corman, Random House, NY, 1990, page 71.
(11) *Ibid*, page 237.
(12) *Ibid*, page 73.

**Film quotes from:**
*Creature from the Haunted Sea* (1961)

## *VISIONS OF RAVEN*
## *Jack Kerouac & Film Noir*

A man named Raven wakes up blearily to his alarm clock ringing 2:15 in the afternoon. Jazz piano and sunlight fill his rented room shambles. He picks up some typewritten words to read...Bridge Street...San Francisco...he dresses and feeds the black and white cat on the windowsill.

Watching the opening of *This Gun For Hire* aware of Jack Kerouac watching up there, "seated in the first row of the balcony in shirtsleeves" (1) reveals more and more about his own life visions. From the first frame, it is filled with the poetry Kerouac would surely pick up on. Stars surrounding the Hozomeen-like signature cold mountain logo of Paramount Pictures will recall his lookout window in *The Dharma Bums* and *Desolation Angels*: "Mist before the peak/—the dream/Goes on" (2)

This image is followed by a book with titles superimposed, names of actors and everyone involved, as though everything to be seen is part of a legend contained in pages. "The final scope of the Legend will be simply a completely written lifetime with all its hundreds of characters and events and levels interswirling and reappearing and becoming complete...a continuous tale." (3)

Then, when Raven drifts from the room, when the beat looking maid enters and attacks the cat, Raven explodes back at her. "Beat it, I said!" he sends her gone. She has committed the same crime described in Kerouac's "film of the angel child" (4) *Visions of Gerard*, mirrored in the holy rage of his saintly brother, "Bad girl! Don't you understand what you've done? When will you understand? We don't disturb little animals and little things! We leave them alone!...wake up, foolish girl!—realize what you've done!...There won't always be time!—Bad girl! Go on!" (5) From childhood on to his last days in Florida, Kerouac's remembering books took this commandment to heart, paging his works—cats walk all through the *Book of Haikus*—it was also the message Jack took down from the mountain in *Desolation Angels*.

In *Vanity of Duluoz*, Kerouac recalls his friendship with William S. Burroughs "Will Hubbard" ("Burroughs is Poe," (6) Kerouac revealed) and sets up his entanglement with "Franz Mueller," a role made for Laird Cregar, the heavy of *This Gun For Hire*. Kerouac nearly becomes the Poe-named Raven when, "Mueller took my little cat, wrapped Hubbard's tie around its neck, and tried to hang it from the lamp: a little kitty. Will Hubbard immediately took it down, undamaged and just slightly hurt I guess in the neck, I don't know, I wasn't there, I would have thrown that man out the window." (7)

Deep into that darkness peering, long I stood there wondering, fearing,
Doubting, dreaming dreams no mortal ever dared to dream before

—"The Raven" Edgar Allan Poe

Even though Kerouac admired Raven, "I wore great big felt hats all level to imitate Alan Ladd *This Gun For Hire,*" (8) he admits, "it wasn't so much the killing in those stories that we used to feed upon, it was rather the dark and mysterious labyrinthal movement of our heroes, the sibilant hiss of their secret sanctumed laugh, the fall of rain on Fifth Avenue mansion at night, the slow creeping menace of masked justice along Manhattan depths, and above all, our hero unmasked and posing before the dull eye of the world..." (9) In fact,

Kerouac rejected the violence, equating it with a nightmare, "it must be an educational movie from another Buddhaland showing Bodhisattvas why to reject violence and how horrible ignorance which not only projects an outside world but grasps at it, fights in it..." (10)

Nevertheless, Jack Kerouac's life became a film noir in 1944.

In the early morning a friend "like Alan Ladd" (11) came through his apartment window to confess Mueller's murder. "I've still got the knife and his glasses covered with blood." (12) Kerouac suggests their escape, "Let's take a subway downtown go see a movie" (13) which they do (as if they could walk into the screen, disappear into a dream). It all occurs in Book Eleven and Book Twelve, *Vanity of Duluoz*, shadows, murder, police, prison, all the elements. At the D.A.'s office, his wife visited him, "like in Jimmy Cagney movies when time's up they tell us it's time, she cries, hugs me, holds me, she waits to be dragged away like in the movies?" (14) and "Ma came to see me...in the jail, sat at the long table and talked to me in front of a guard just like in the John Garfield movies." (15)

"This was our dream, gleaned from going to the Rialto Theater and seeing movies"

—*Vanity of Duluoz* (16)

The next five minutes of film become a murder-dream framed by going up the stairs past the crippled girl then back down past her again and out to day. Each new place Raven goes becomes another dream sequence: the window framing the Golden Gate Bridge where Laird Cregar sets the doublecross in motion, the code for phony money, all these dreams building, forming the bigger sleep of the movie itself.

Life as a dream-movie is an awareness Kerouac fully explores in *Book of Dreams.* "Fact, I like to sleep so I can tune in see what's happening in that big show…My dreams (like yours) are fantastically real movies of what's actually going on." (17) His preface explains, "When I woke up from my sleep I just lay there looking at the pictures that were fading slowly like in a movie fadeout into the recesses of my subconscious mind." (18) In a dream right out of James Cagney's *White Heat* comes, "I'M LIVING WITH MA AGAIN—there are gangsters downstairs, I'm watching one all the time…" (19) It's easy to make a film noir from his dreambook, "There's a big murder case going on and cops, detectives keep coming to Ma's house to check on evidence, I'm in my room when the cop comes with my book…" (20) which winds to its thrilling ending escape: "DRIVING WITH MY DETECTIVE PUBLISHER FRIEND down a dry sand road…I HAD A WHITE BANDAGE on my head from a wound, the police are after me around the dark stairs of wood near the Victory Theater in Lowell, I sneak away—come to the boulevard where a parade of children chanting my name hide me from the searching police as I duck along their endless ranks, keeping low…" (21)

Dreams that become books become movies. Graham Greene wrote the inspiration, *This Gun For Hire.* Politicians and industrialists are ever eager to start another war, with some paid-off murder and marked bills. Raven, in a dark England setting resembling Richard Widmark in *Night and the City,* appears in a room, "His eyes, like little concealed cameras, photographed the room instantaneously…" (22) "Memories had never troubled him. He didn't mind death; it was foolish to be scared of death in this bare wintry world." (23) Raven finds the girl stuffed in a fireplace like Poe's "Murders in the Rue Morgue," but alive, rescues her from the doublecrossers and police, down night streets to the train tracks. "The lights went on in the city beyond the railway bridge, but where they were it was just a grey dusk and the sound of an engine shunting in the yard." (24) Hidden from the force in a tool shed he tells her his dreams, "I've been dreaming bad dreams lately" (25) and, "It seems your dreams mean things. I don't mean like tea-leaves or cards." (26) In the morning, a thick fog coming up from the river offers escape and the masked Raven vanishes to his doom. "It almost seemed as if Raven's act had had no consequences: as if to kill was just as much an illusion as to dream." (27) The book ends, war averted, looking out a train window as, "A mob of children went screaming down a street…" (28)

In 1941, just a year before *This Gun For Hire* hit screens, an equally influential Paramount movie begins with a book and opens turning pages. The star of *Sullivan's Travels*, Joel McCrea, vows, "I'm going out on the road," only to end up in a Hollywood diner with Veronica Lake. Free, talking, taking time, she becomes his traveling partner, hopping a train from a freight yard like *On the Road* later on. Kerouac was to invoke their meeting for 'The Mexican Girl' section of *On the Road* when he met Terry on a Hollywood morning, "In the gray, dirty dawn, like the dawn when Joel McCrea met Veronica Lake in a diner, in the picture *Sullivan's Travels*." (29) He needed to meet her, it had to happen, like Dean Moriarty.

"What do you think? You think all this is a dream?...How do we know we're not dreaming?"

—*Good Blonde* (30)

Another time Kerouac conjures Veronica Lake is for *The Dharma Bums*. Stuck in Santa Barbara, finding no luck hitchhiking, he was turning sinister, "blackly handsome in like Alan Ladd this gun for hire with murder anger" (31) when out of the blue "a brand new cinnamon colored Lincoln driven by a beautiful young blonde in a [white] bathingsuit flashed by and suddenly swerved to the right and put to a stop in the side of the road for me." (32) It was such a fantasy, he retold the story for *Playboy* as 'Good Blonde.' Kerouac questioned his temptations, her intentions and struggled with his response, "because since life is nothing but a short vague dream encompassed round by flesh and tears, and the ways of men are the ways of death…the ways of beautiful women such as those pictured in this magazine are eventually the ways of old age," (33) realizing, "Ah hell it's all a dream including beauty." (34)

But it's her wearied beauty attitude, her beatitude, her cool knowing like an angel who's watched Earth for a long, long time that attracts him to her. And Alan Ladd and Veronica Lake paired share the essence of beatitude that Kerouac was forever asked to define.

In another Paramount California film noir called *The Blue Dahlia* Veronica Lake foreshadows Kerouac's story. Like the unnamed blonde of *Sullivan's Travels*, she is the nameless good blonde traveler again, driving in white to pick up Alan Ladd on a rainy road night. Alan Ladd (like a wondering Kerouac) tells her, "You get around don't you? And your timing's good. It was good last night when you picked me up in the rain. Or was it? I don't know. I don't know anything. I don't even know your name." Even so, she's someone his unfolding story depends upon, telling her, "Every guy's seen you before—somewhere—the trick is to find you."

When Veronica Lake appears in *This Gun For Hire*, she is a dancing magician (her act includes little animals, canaries and gold fish) singing, "Now you see it, now you don't, because hocus pocus lo and behold, you get blinded by that moon of bright gold above," easily enchanting Laird Cregar "Will Gates" who hires her for his Neptune Club in Los Angeles. Like Ladd, Lake is for hire. Before her journey there, Miss Graham meets a senator in a black government car. "There's a handful of those heels in this country today. And they're powerful enough to sabotage our defense. We're trying to expose them." Monster Street Parade. Raven hides in a wooden phone booth while the police search his room. "They're after Mr. Raven because he passed a stolen bill in a dress shop."

It's on the night train to Los Angeles when they finally meet, while the rest of the car sleeps, she speaks, "Are you that broke? C'mon I know you're not asleep." "You talkin' to me? What d'you want?" But she can keep it calm, the five bucks is gone and back again, she sleeps beside him anyway.

In the morning, "They're looking for me for a job I didn't do and they're not gonna get me. You're gonna help." Off the train with a bundle like a baby they escape to a tire swing edge of the yard.

"Everything is prepared for the gas mask rehearsal, sir." "At eight o'clock tomorrow morning everyone will be wearing a gas mask." "This man Raven should be shot on sight." Meeting a knife sharpener to find Hollywood directions, "You can hitch a ride if you're broke." Gates' black mansion, tall lighted candles, thunder and rain; it's a set that resembles Count Condu's castle in *Doctor Sax*. "In a couple of hours the bridge over the reservoir will be deserted."

"Look I'm not gonna hurt you. You treated me okay." "There's a dragnet out for you, Raven." Pulled along on wet city cement, Veronica Lake leaves a trail of playing card clues. "It's the gasworks. We'll hide out inside until morning. Stay up on top until I get there. And don't try to run." "Raven.

I want to talk to you. You're bottled up, you can't get out. We're moving in when it's daylight. We don't want to shoot unless you make us…you hear me Raven?"

As Raven's pursuit closes in around him at the gasworks, as he ducks pipes, catwalks, tunnels and searchlights, it brings to mind other similar settings in film, like Lon Chaney's *Indestructible Man* and James Cagney's *White Heat.*

"The day after receiving Cassady's letter, Kerouac was so inspired that he sat down 'to write a full confession.' The result, written in white heat between December 28, 1950, and January 10, 1951, was nearly a hundred typed pages…" (35)

The source of this white heat which became Kerouac's *On the Road*, is Neal Cassady/Dean Moriarty, also known as Cody Pomeroy, star of *Visions of Cody*.

*White Heat* is a gangster vision of Cody, Cody Jarrett played by James Cagney, a role he plays with a fury. The film begins like *Sullivan's Travels*, with a train. First sight of Cody, he's looking at his watch, checking the time, the same as Raven with his clock beginning. This is fitting for time is the driving beat of *On the Road*—over and over again Dean Moriarty draws attention to it—"now is the time and *we all know time!*" (36), "Everything is fine, God exists, we know time" (37), "I want to be like him…he knows time, he has nothing to do but rock back and forth…You see, if you go like him all the time you'll finally get it." (38)

The train roars across the California state line. Cagney's Cody doesn't just jump the train to get on, he leaps to it from the overpass. The film exaggerates Kerouac, especially after the heist, at the gang's mountain hide-out, when his Ma is there to calm his terror, as he rocks back and forth. "It's these mountains, Cody. It's not good for you. Cold all the time," she comforts, bringing him back with a glass, "Top of the world, son."

Cagney's night confession in the garden makes their similarity clear, "All I ever had was Ma...My old lady never had anything, always on the run, always on the move... some life..." Cody and Ma, Kerouac and Memere, there is something there they share, but in film-noir it becomes a dark portrait, like the photograph Jack had taken in *On the Road*, "I took a straight picture that made me look like a thirty-year-old Italian who'd kill anybody who said anything against his mother." (39) *White Heat*'s Cody really does kill for his mother, becomes the fuel in a gas tank, wounded and burning up on the top of the world.

"I feel like Jimmy Cagney, I can feel the air with my fingers."
—*Visions of Cody* (40)

It did become harder and harder for Kerouac to function in the outside world, by 1963 it was "all a mad mixed up mess whenever I leave the house so I stay home." (41) Though he had proved perfectly capable on the road alone, in the woods, desert and mountain top, as time passed he seemed to do better with a companion and guide, as was Cassady, Ginsberg, Burroughs in Mexico, and Gary Snyder provided for *The Dharma Bums*. Alone could lead to the circling of *Satori in Paris* or awash on *Big Sur*. Memere provided that calm for him, offered him a place to go after journeys to reflect and build his legend. "I've always been 'settled with my mother' who supported me by working in shoe factories while I wrote most of my books years ago. She's my friend as well as my mother. When I go on the road I always have a quiet, clean home to come back to, and to work in, which probably accounts for the fact that I've published twelve books in the last six years." (42) Her influence can be felt throughout his books, he even took her on his travels, moving homes and hide-outs, Kerouac remained writing in her house until the end.

When Cody Jarrett uses the veil of teargas to escape from the chemical plant office, it mirrors Raven eluding the police into the shroud of the foggy rail yard morning. He leads his pursuers on a chase across a bridge that Kerouac recalled for *Visions of Cody*: "Last night at home I talked with Ma...woke up at four restlessly, hurried to Jersey City in a long foolish ride...got off at Erie Station, followed signs through the waiting room halls to the footbridge that's just like the one in *This Gun For Hire* with Alan Ladd (a pix incidentally that I saw the afternoon I signed on for Arctic Greenland in 1942, when I lay in the grass of Boston Common thinking of death..." (43)

Raven is lucky to escape the police bullets shot after him but—like the scene of doom in *Doctor Sax* Book Four, The Night the Man With the Watermelon Died: "I saw he was really dead and taken—his eyes had turned glassy on the milky waters of the night...that part which yet I see in dreams of Lowell and the bridge. I shuddered and saw white flowers and grew cold" (44)—Raven also knows death is only a matter of time. He has committed his own worst crime—only hours before, he killed a cat.

"One morning, in cold blood, I slipped a noose about its neck and hung it to the limb of a tree;—hung it with tears streaming from my eyes, and with the bitterest remorse at my heart;—hung it because I knew that it had loved me, and because I felt it had given me no reason of offence;—hung it because I knew that in so doing I was committing a sin."

—"The Black Cat," Edgar Allan Poe

Trains, rail yard sounds of engines pulling screeching wheels, spotlights over tracks, hiding out the night before in the ruined train car, a gray cat visited them, coming in through the open window. Raven smiles, "Cats bring you luck," he admits. But when the animal is heard by two men outside, Raven is forced to smother it. "I killed my luck," he tells her and the camera shows it in his eyes. "I'd like to crawl down there with you and sleep," he tells the cat, but, "It's no good, I'd only dream." Kerouac could sympathize, "It occurred to me, remembering last night's dream of me in a movie holding a kitty high over my head as a ravening hound leaped to eat it, that I was that hound, I wanted to eat and dissect the kitty of knowledge with my ravening mind." (45)

As the fog lifts morning, Raven promises her he's done with gun violence, he heads for the bridge Kerouac recalled in *Visions of Cody*. Up a dirt hill, he gets caught, gets out with a shot and runs again. Onto that wooden bridge, Raven passes a woman carrying a baby swaddled like a watermelon in her arms. He runs. Halfway across he stops and crawls through the slats and jumps down to the train passing below, just like Cody in *White Heat*.

James Cagney isn't done yet. His biography, *Cagney By Cagney*, reveals the story behind his only time directing, "when my old friend A.C. Lyles came to me in 1957 and asked me if I would direct his Paramount production of *Short Cut to Hell*, I was moved to do so out of friendship only. I said I would do it if he wanted me to, and he asked me how much I'd charge. 'How about nothing? Is that too much?' I asked him. We shot this updated version of Graham Greene's *This Gun for Hire* in just twenty days, and that was long enough for me." (46) A movie shot with the speed of Kerouac typing the holy roll of *On the Road*.

As Raven rushes off to the end, the air raid sirens sound

in the street. Raven, in a mask and uniform, gains entrance to Nitro Chemical. Caught, Gates blubbers to him, "I'm not to blame. You wouldn't—You wouldn't kill an innocent man, would you? It's all his fault. I was acting as his agent." Raven forces Gates to take him up the elevator, through four pairs of double doors to the president's office. In there he rounds up all the doublecrossers before his gun. There's a last doublecross as the old man's longtime nurse rips the alarm button from him, "For fifteen years dressing you, nursing you, cleaning you, listening to your dirty deals. Go ahead!" he shrieks at Raven, "Wipe him out!" Even Gates turns on the president, informing Raven, "I'll tell you. That new gas formula—he sold it to the highest bidder." The nurse agrees, "To the Japanese."

The doublecross is a film noir fixture. James Cagney's Cody was also betrayed by a close friend in *White Heat*, as Jack Kerouac suffered in *The Subterraneans* and *Big Sur*. Cagney and Kerouac were even doublecrossed by Florida doubles. Director Peter Bogdanovich wrote in *Pieces of Time*, "I finally met James Cagney the other day—the real one. There's a bearded fellow going around lately passing himself off as the actor. I was in Miami when this guy was there—they made him honorary mayor of Hollywood, Florida—and a paper printed pictures of him. Didn't look like Cagney to me. When Barbra Streisand was singing in Las Vegas around Christmas, they told her Cagney was in the audience so she introduced him from the stage and when this same bearded chap stood up, she thought, 'Doesn't look like Cagney to me.' Cagney himself seemed rather amused at this; he told several similar incidents that have occurred over the years..." (47) Likewise, when Kerouac lived in St. Petersburg, "He stoutly maintained that there were several imposters passing themselves off as Jack Kerouac and they were responsible for his receiving that kind of harassment." (48)

Police on the roof find a painter's scaffold, scale down on pulleyed boards. There's a birds-eye view of a 1940s parking lot in motion, a vision of Cody from *On the Road*: "He worked in a parking lot...rushed around in his ragged shoes and T-shirt and belly-hanging pants all by himself, straightening out immense noontime rushes of cars" (49) where there are hoods in sparkling rows, the little ticket shack, tall brick walls painted with the words of then, making canyons above the tar. Forced to sign a confession, the old man aims and shoots his pen at Raven but his heart gives out. "One final doublecross." Suddenly the windows and doors are blasted open. As if ready for sleep, laying down, covered by a black blanket, and full of bullets, Raven's last words ask her, "Did I do alright for you?" Veronica Lake, looking down on him maternally, nods silently with a smile. Now he can close his eyes, the same way he began the movie, on a different day.

That's the big epiphany for Raven. He has gone from believing "I'm my own police" and only showing heart to cats because, "They're on their own. They don't need anybody," to listening to Veronica Lake at night. By traveling through with him from the beginning, all along she sought to sway him into knowing, she impressed on him the meaning of the code he killed for, to see beyond the phony money and vengeance routine. That night of hiding in the train, she told him, "You know I've been figuring something. That chemical formula. I bet I know what it is. Gas—poison gas. They're selling it to our enemy...So tomorrow they'll ship it back in bombs...Do you hear what I said? It's important. This war is everybody's business. Yours too...Why don't you stop thinking about yourself for a minute."

If there's going to be a moment for redemption in film noir, this is it. It's a transformation repeated in so many scenes, seen in Humphrey Bogart films like *Casablanca* ("I'm not fighting for anything anymore, except myself. I'm the only cause I'm interested in") and *Key Largo* ("What do I care about Johnny Rocco, whether he lives or dies? I only care about me. Me and mine. Rocco wants to come back to America, let him. Let him be president. I fight nobody's battles but my own"). *Casablanca* and *Key Largo* endings come with the realization of involvement, dedicating one's life to a larger cause of freedom.

Veronica Lake took this lesson to her last movie, filmed in Florida, the year after Jack Kerouac died there. Filmed under the title *Time is Terror*, she allowed it three pages of her autobiography, hoping of it, "Some day soon, perhaps on your local television station during their daily horror film show, you'll be able to see" (50). At that time of writing though, "It sits in the can, some of the footage very good and imaginative, and will continue to sit there until the production company comes up with more money with which to go back and re-shoot master shots." (51)

The film was released with a new title, *Flesh Feast* and does include some relevance to time and dreams and America: "I've got a tremendous story and very little time", "I must have enough time for experimentation", "It is as if God turned back the clock," "These Americans…They're all dreamers. They want to rule the world." It's a Florida nightmare of, "That crazy feeling in America when the sun is hot on the streets and the music comes out of the jukebox or from a nearby funeral…sadness and strange secrecy of a shadow photographed scenes that have never been seen before on film." (52) But it moves with the pace of a sleepwalker, unrolling like flypaper, long slow stretches under palms and magnolias dazed by the steady twang of birds. But when Veronica Lake's mad doctor prepares to operate upon

Adolph Hitler in a suburban basement laboratory adorned with an overseeing framed, painted portrait of her mother, she delivers her alarming anti-fascist speech. Placing maggots on his face, "This one is for democracy!" she dishes them out, "It's you! Only you!" laughing maniacally, tossing handfuls of maggots like a karmic sentence on him, "Now you're going to get what you gave!"

One of Jack Kerouac's last written pieces "After Me the Deluge" shares her fury. In it, he denounces 'the politicians, the radicals, the cops and hoods, tax collectors and vandals,' warning them, "It's much like what do you think a parasite is thinking when he's sucking on the belly of a whale or the back of a shark?—'Where did this big, stupid brute get all that blood...How come he's so strong and free, not knowing how to live like I do?' So with human parasites feeding on their juicy national, personal, political, or racial host." (53) While his country self destructs in wars, Kerouac sizes up the times in *Vanity of Duluoz* at the end of his life, "in 1967 as I'm writing this what possible feeling can be left in me for an 'America' that has become such a potboiler of broken convictions, messes of rioting and fighting in streets, hoodlumism, cynical administration of cities and states, suits and neckties the only feasible subject, grandeur all gone into the mosaic mesh of Television where people screw their eyes at all those dots and pick out hallucinated images of their own contortion and are fed ACHTUNG!" (54)

"He identified himself with America," Allen Ginsberg told an interviewer, "He realized if he were put down that meant America was going to move through an immense amount of suffering and would inflict a lot of suffering on the world. He realized that his personal tragedy of being rejected by the official arbiters of culture meant that America was in for a bad, bad scene. The vision of America that he and Whitman had was going to be a flop and there was going to be great destruction." (55)

That vision was paved by a lifelong experience. Like the stars of film noirs, Kerouac knew the forces of destruction and suffering. "Society is organized cruelty and nothing else." (56) Washing dishes in World War 2, on a freighter full of TNT, made him question, "Who are these smiling Satans making all the money out of this? Whether they're Russian, American, Japanese, British, French or Chinese?" (57) knowing, "There oughta be a better way to die in this world than in the service of Ammunitioneers." (58) Taking that realization, after the war, the city, the murder and jail, he began to wander.

*This Gun For Hire* follows the circular trail from Raven's start, winding back up the tower to the source. Corruption began with the president of Nitro Chemical who employed a pushover, who paid off a killer to do the murder, steal and take the fall. Both Raven and Cody in *White Heat* were killed up there by police. Cody remained unrepentant, defiant to the end, Raven too, dying, asking Veronica Lake, "You didn't tell the cops, did you?" knowing full well her allegiance to them. He may have done the right thing taking out the president, but he didn't do it for the police society.

Jack Kerouac had enough experience with police and their mentality not to bow to them. The closest he came to their side was when he was a barracks guard, described in *On the Road*. "It was a horrible crew of men, men with cop-souls…I gulped at the prospect of making an arrest." (59) "They were always sitting around on their asses; they were proud of their jobs. They handled their guns and talked about them. They were itching to shoot somebody." (60) "I never had a gun in my life. It scared me even to load one. He desperately wanted to make arrests…This is the story of America. Everybody's doing what they think they're supposed to do." (61) As Allen Ginsberg reminds, "If you read his essays like *Lonesome Traveller*, they were really attacks on the police state. Always. The whole thrust of his work was toward individualism and freedom." (62) In *The Dharma Bums* when Kerouac traveled the roads and rails free as an enlightened wanderer, "The only alternative to sleeping out, hopping freights, and doing what I wanted, I saw in a vision would be to just sit in front of a nice television set in a madhouse...I saw so many cop cruising cars and they were looking at me suspiciously: sleek, well-paid cops in brand new cars with all that expensive radio equipment to see that no bhikku slept in his grove tonight." (63)All the more illuminating at the end of *On the Road* when they get to Mexico and Kerouac observes, "Such lovely policemen God hath never wrought in America. No suspicions, no fuss, no bother: he was the guardian of the sleeping town, period." (64) Beyond political corruption, betrayed by their laws and wars enforced by hired guns, Kerouac believes in the vision of a dream America, period.

*This Gun For Hire* is a dream Raven opening his eyes in the start and closing his eyes in the end. This was a reality that Jack Kerouac was well aware of by 1953 when his studies of Buddhism inspired him to write *Some of the Dharma*. "It was the bliss of knowing that our lives are but dreams, arbitrary conceptions, from which the big dreamer wakes—What could be more like a dream, with birth the falling-asleep, and death the awaking from sleep?—a dream, with beginning and ending..." (65)

"Life is a dream. My birth records, my family's birth records and recorded origins, my athletic records in the newspaper clippings I have, my own notebooks and published books are not real at all, my own dreams are not dreams at all but products of my waking imagination." (66) Since Lowell childhood, experiencing the death of his child brother, "Small wonder that the baby sees people in the world as giant put-together phantoms slashing in a violent projection INSIDE MIND," (67) the vision was instilled in him—it was all a dream movie—"I saw my father, my old girlfriends, my long Lowell night walks, clearly, without regret, on that Bliss Screen of Movies." (68)

*Some of the Dharma*, built over years, fed by scriptures of golden eternity, is filled with his thoughts on life as a movie. Beginning with the practice of meditation, which he envisioned: "You let it melt away, ignoring the dream of life for an examination of the mind itself the makes the dream appear…like watching a movie on a screen. But because it's like a movie on a screen, you realize the movie itself is unreal phantasms and the screen is the only reality. The 'screen' is your Mind Essence, the movie is forms that come and go." (69)

So when translating his visions to paper, he pictured "bookmovies", "movie novels", "mindmovies" with "prose concentration camera-eye visions of a definite movie of the mind with fade-ins, pans, close-ups, and fade-outs." (70)

He even hoped to turn writing into actual film. In *On the Road*, he describes coming to California expectantly, "I was to stay in a shack and write a shining original story for a Hollywood studio." (71) But it didn't work, "the first week I stayed in the shack in Mill City, writing furiously at some gloomy tale about New York that I thought would satisfy a Hollywood director, and the trouble with it was that it was too sad." (72) In fact it sounds like a description of *The Subterraneans*, a work that was made into a movie by Hollywood in 1960. A more successful dream into film was *Pull My Daisy*. Like the opening of *This Gun for Hire*, the camera pans around a black and white room, "early morning in the universe...the room's in a mess." Kerouac narrates his friends through the wonder, "Is it true that we're all in Heaven now and that we don't know it. And that if we knew it we would still know it but that because we don't know it we go around and act just the way that we do."

And Heaven being where all his ideas were anyway—"The Holy Ghost writes through me...I'm taking orders from Heaven" (73), "All these books are published in Heaven" (74)—that's also where the movie of *On the Road* glows: "I can see it now, Marlon Brando as Dean Moriarty and Montgomery Clift as Sal Paradise." (75) He could even translate the legendary plot for a Buddhist movie, "two brothers from the Himalayan Highlands floating down the Ganges on a home-made raft, to Benares, the sensual jealous lover and the goodhearted imbecile." (76)

The movie realization hit him deep, like a powerful spotlight projected beam. He was changed and haunted for life. From *On the Road*, "We decided to stay up in all-night movies on Skid Row...For thirty-five cents each we went into the beat-up old movie and sat down in the balcony till morning...We saw both of these things six times each during the night. We saw them waking, we heard them sleeping, we sensed them dreaming, we were permeated completely with the strange Gray Myth of the West and the weird dark Myth of the East when morning came. All my actions since then have been dictated automatically to my subconscious by this horrible osmotic experience." (77) So when he saw *This Gun For Hire* and lay on that Boston grass that day in the middle of America at war, his visions went out, he watched clouds going away, knowing he would go too. Life was a film and a legend and a dream and it starts every time the pages turn.

**NOTES:**

1) *Atop an Underwood*; Jack Kerouac; Viking; New York; 1999; p.236
2) *Desolation Angels*; Jack Kerouac; Bantam Books; New York; 1971; p.75
3) *Conversations with Jack Kerouac*; Edited by Kevin J. Hayes; University Press of Mississippi; Jackson; 2005; p.44
4) *Visions of Gerard*; Jack Kerouac; McGraw Hill; New York; 1963; p. 116
5) *Ibid*; p.18
6) *Selected Letters 1940-1956*; Jack Kerouac; Viking Press; 1995; p.472
7) *Vanity of Duluoz*; Jack Kerouac; Coward-McCann, Inc.; New York; 1967; p.219
8) *Doctor Sax*: Faust Part Three; Jack Kerouac; Grove Press; New York; 1959; p.47
9) *Atop an Underwood*; p.107
10) *Book of Dreams*; Jack Kerouac; City Lights Books; San Francisco; 2001; p.307
11) *Vanity of Duluoz*; p.209
12) *Ibid*; p.229
13) *Ibid*; p.232
14) *Ibid*; p.238
15) *Ibid*; p.256
16) *Ibid*; p.15
17) *Book of Dreams*; p.vii
18) *Ibid*; p.xvii
19) *Ibid*; p.94
20) *Ibid*; p.241
21) *Ibid*; p.303
22) *This Gun For Hire*; Graham Greene; The Viking Press;

New York; 1936; 1982; p.2
23) *Ibid*; p.56
24) *Ibid*; p.121
25) *Ibid*; p.144
26) *Ibid*; p.150
27) *Ibid*; p.215
28) *Ibid*; p.227
29) *On the Road*; Jack Keroauc; Viking; New York; 1955; 1997 edition; p.83
30) *Good Blonde & Others*; Jack Kerouac; Grey Fox Press; San Francisco; 1993; p.3
31) *Selected Letters 1940-1956*; p.522
32) *Good Blonde & Others*; p.5
33) *Ibid*; p.152
34) *Ibid*; p.11
35) *Selected Letters 1940-1956*; p.xxii
36) *On the Road*; p.114
37) *Ibid*; p.120
38) *Ibid*; p.127
39) *Ibid*; p.6
40) *Visions of Cody*; Jack Kerouac; McGraw-Hill Publishing Company; New York; 1972; p.377
41) *Selected Letters 1957-1969*; Jack Kerouac; Viking Press; New York; 1999; p.367
42) *Conversations with Jack Kerouac*; p.45
43) *Visions of Cody*; p. 102
44) *Doctor Sax*; p.129
45) *Some of the Dharma*; Jack Kerouac; Viking; New York; 1997; p.222
46) *Cagney By Cagney*; James Cagney; Doubleday & Co. Inc.; Garden City; New York; 1976; p.149
47) *Pieces of Time*; Peter Bogdanovich on the Movies; Peter Bogdanovich; Arbor House Publishing Company; New

York; 1973; p.106
48) *Empty Phantoms: Interviews and Encounters with Jack Kerouac*; Edited by Paul Maher Jr.; Thunder's Mouth Press; New York; 2005; p.392
49) *On the Road*; p.249
50) *Veronica: The Autobiography of Veronica Lake*; Veronica Lake; The Citadel Press; New York; 1971; p.260
51) *Ibid*; p.262
52) *The Americans*; Robert Frank; Jack Kerouac's Introduction; Grove Press; New York; 1959/1997; p.5
53) *Good Blonde & Others*; p.186
54) *Vanity of Duluoz*; p.105-106
55) *Spontaneous Mind: Selected Interviews 1958-1996*; Allen Ginsburg; Harper Collins; New York; 2001; p.448-9
56) *Some of the Dharma*; p.383
57) *Vanity of Duluoz*; p.134
58) *Ibid*; p.148
59) *On the Road*; p.65
60) *Ibid*; p.66
61) *Ibid*; p.68
62) *Empty Phantoms*; p.279
63) *The Dharma Bums*; Jack Kerouac; Signet Books; New York; 1959; p.96
64) *On the Road*; p.294
65) *Some of the Dharma*; p.250
66) *Safe in Heaven Dead: Interviews with Jack Kerouac*; Compiled and edited by Michael White; Hanuman Books; Madras & New York; 1990; p.124
67) *Some of the Dharma*; p.82
68) *Ibid*; p.93
69) *Ibid*; p.207
70) *Ibid*; p.342
71) *On the Road*; p.63

72) *Ibid*; p.64
73) *Empty Phantoms*; p.363
74) *Howl and Other Poems*; Allen Ginsberg; City Lights Books; San Francisco; 1959; Dedication to Jack Kerouac
75) *Selected Letters 1940-1956*; p.530
76) *Some of the Dharma*; p.304
77) *On the Road*; p.245-6
78) *Visions of Keroauc*; Charles E. Jarvis; Ithaca Press; Lowell, Massachusetts; 1996; p.201

**MOVIES QUOTED:**

*This Gun For Hire* (1942)
*Sullivan's Travels* (1941)
*The Blue Dahlia* (1946)
*White Heat* (1949)
*Casablanca* (1942)
*Key Largo* (1948)
*Time Is Terror/Flesh Feast* (1970)
*Pull My Daisy* (1959)

"...tell those Lowell politicians to take down that moldy Alan Ladd Monument in front of the city hall and put up a Zeusian statue of Ti Jean, Jack Kerouac, native son of Lowell." (78)

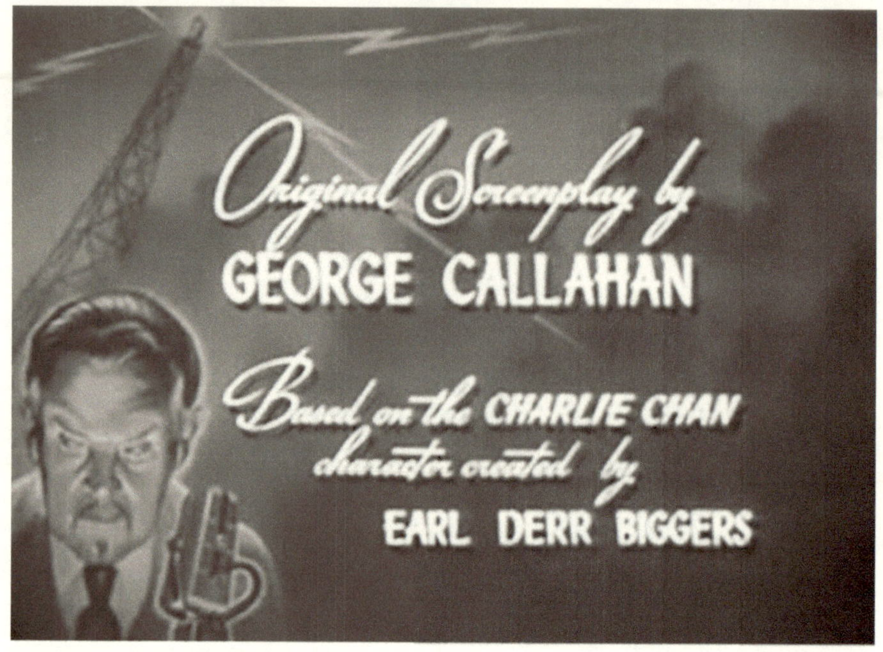
Original Screenplay by
GEORGE CALLAHAN
Based on the CHARLIE CHAN
character created by
EARL DERR BIGGERS

I've been watching Charlie Chan for over half this life but something new occurred while watching *The Shanghai Cobra* again. The film begins like a film noir with a café in the raining night. Inside, along the wall, there's a jukebox with a television camera connected to an operator who lives in a little dark room behind a bookshelf. Insert five cents for a song and a two-pronged needle shoots out and stings with cobra venom. Suddenly I wondered, who wrote this?? I restarted the movie and read the name, George Callahan.

Now I've been trying to find out about Callahan and it isn't easy. I went through the film books, detective encyclopedias and reference materials at the library but nothing turned up. The internet movie database gives the years of his life, born 1907 in Lawrence, Massachusetts (close to where Kerouac was born and *Doctor Sax* lurked), died in Los Angeles in 1989. He wrote 8 Charlie Chan movies from 1944-1946:

*Charlie Chan in the Secret Service* (1944)
*Charlie Chan in the Chinese Cat* (1944)
*Black Magic* (1944)
*The Jade Mask* (1945)
*The Scarlet Clue* (1945)
*The Shanghai Cobra* (1945)
*The Red Dragon* (1945)
*Dark Alibi* (1946)

There are no other details of his life, we can only observe his contributions to the famous detective and look for clues.

After Warner Oland died in 1938, Sidney Toler became the next Chan. Toler made eleven films playing Charlie

Chan ending with the excellent *Castle in the Desert*, as World War 2 began and 20th Century Fox dropped the series. Toler wanted Chan to go on. In 1942, he bought the film rights to the character from author Earl Derr Biggers' widow. Toler spent the next two years getting Chan back on the screen, landing at Monogram Pictures, the home of early 1940s films like *Phantom of Chinatown* and *King of the Zombies*.

What I wonder, as Toler searched Hollywood for a studio, surely he must have also been looking for a good writer. Toler's new series began with George Callahan's first screen writing credit, so it's possible Toler and Callahan met to thrash out the story idea for Monogram's initial product, *Charlie Chan in the Secret Service.*

Even knowing so little about George Callahan, there are things to be learned from these eight films—glimpses into the mind of Callahan, revealed by his writing for Charlie Chan:

*Charlie Chan in the Secret Service* takes place in a house full of curtains (a house that will be seen again and again in the unfolding films). A monster with photoelectric-cell eyes. A book titled *Magnetic Properties of Electricity*. Torpedo plans hidden in a Statue of Liberty.

*The Chinese Cat* has another book, *Murder By Madame* and its Raymond Chandler-like author. A foggy Fun House. Secret panels, more statues with secret compartments. Sea Tide Art Company. A skeleton in a closet. Gas through a keyhole.

*Black Magic* begins at a séance. A new book, *How To Disappear*. Mexican jumping beans. "Invisible bullet. That's dime novel stuff." A crystal ball transmitter connected to a basement room. A suspect maker of magician supplies. A newsboy points, a hypnotized woman walks off a building roof. Secret wall panels. The skeleton returns. A spring gun and a fake hand.

*The Jade Mask*. A television monitored gate in the fog. A steaming gas chamber laboratory with a voice-activated word combination secret wall panel. Experiments with puppets. Poison darts. "Dead men don't walk." A dictaphone. A disembodied ear. A deadly ventriloquist dummy.

*The Scarlet Clue*. The fog again. Radar secrets. "Cosmo Radio Center. They broadcast by television." An actor who parodies fellow Monogram star John Carradine, "Yes, once I was the foremost Shakespearean actor of my time...Now I am known only for the mask behind which I hide when I play the Mad Monster—on radio, screen, and television. But still, it is a living." A telltale shoe heel. A ghostly typewriter. A climatic tunnel. More Frankenstein electricity. Poison cigarettes. An elevator with a drop-away floor. A short-wave radio set used to explode a capsule.

Unfortunately, I couldn't find *The Red Dragon*, it seems to have gone underground. However, from reading the plot synopsis in a couple different books there are familiar signs we're in Callahan-land. A typewriter clue. Red Dragon ink. Mysterious bullets. The 95th element. A remote control thermostat.

*Dark Alibi*. A bank vault blast. Forged fingerprints. "It's not confusion, it's Confucius." Prison riot, cell block 4. A theatrical warehouse. The skeleton encores. The third missing man.

With a little more sleuthing (courtesy of interlibrary

loan) I was able to find a few mentions of Callahan in the books devoted to Charlie Chan on film. From *A Guide to Charlie Chan Films* (Charles P. Mitchell, Greenwood Press, 1999) : "George Callahan was the featured writer for the Monogram pictures, and the film's quality declined markedly after his departure." Sadly there is no mention of Callahan in the recently published *Charlie Chan* by Yunte Huang (W.W. Norton & Company, 2010). *Charlie Chan at the Movies* by Ken Hanke (McFarland & Co., 1989) offers the best insights:

"Callahan's difficulty lies in the area of story construction, which is limp and generally uninteresting" (*Charlie Chan in the Secret Service*).

"George Callahan's screenplay is most successful in fits and starts of clever devices and engaging exchanges..." (*The Jade Mask*).

"One of George Callahan's better screenplays...The basic mystery is better structured than a good deal of Callahan's work and is combined with the frequently sharp-toned dialogue of which he was capable, affording a very slick B picture indeed" (*The Scarlet Clue*).

*The Red Dragon* is "by far the silliest idea Callahan ever dreamed up and that is no mean fact."

*Dark Alibi* is "one of George Callahan's most witty and acid screenplays (his last for the series). The combination makes for a tight, beautifully made, often extremely funny sixty-one minutes of film, quite the last really good Toler Chan."

Finally, after Callahan left the Chan series, Hanke notes, "The replacement of George Callahan with the unlikely named Raymond Schrock as screenwriter is part of the problem...showing even less logic than his predecessor..." and "the plot, with its bizarre coincidences and secret identities makes George Callahan's occasional flights of fancy and lapses of logic in the Toler Monograms seem like models of sanity."

Obviously there was a big drop in the quality of picture-making as Charlie Chan jumped to a B-picture studio. At Monogram, he's mostly confined to rooms and hallways instead of his 1930s pre-war forays around the world on steamships and flying boats. But there is just as much enjoyment of a different sort to be had in these films. Callahan's storylines are filled with secret rooms, jewels and poison, fantastic machines, tricks and wobbling surprises. Also you can't overlook all the humor in his writing, mostly delivered by Mantan Moreland, who George Callahan featured in another non-Chan movie script he wrote, *Captain Tugboat Annie.*

But it isn't all 'dime novel stuff' that Callahan provided. It's interesting that Callahan foresaw the coming reign of television and worked this still fledgling invention into the plots of his stories. This was especially prophetic since that's where Charlie Chan would be reincarnated for the next generation of viewers. Likewise, this is where George Callahan would devote the last of his screenwriting, for TV programs like *The Man Called X*, and surprise, surprise, there's even an episode of *The Cisco Kid* he authored entitled "Chinese Gold" proving that Charlie Chan never really left his mind.

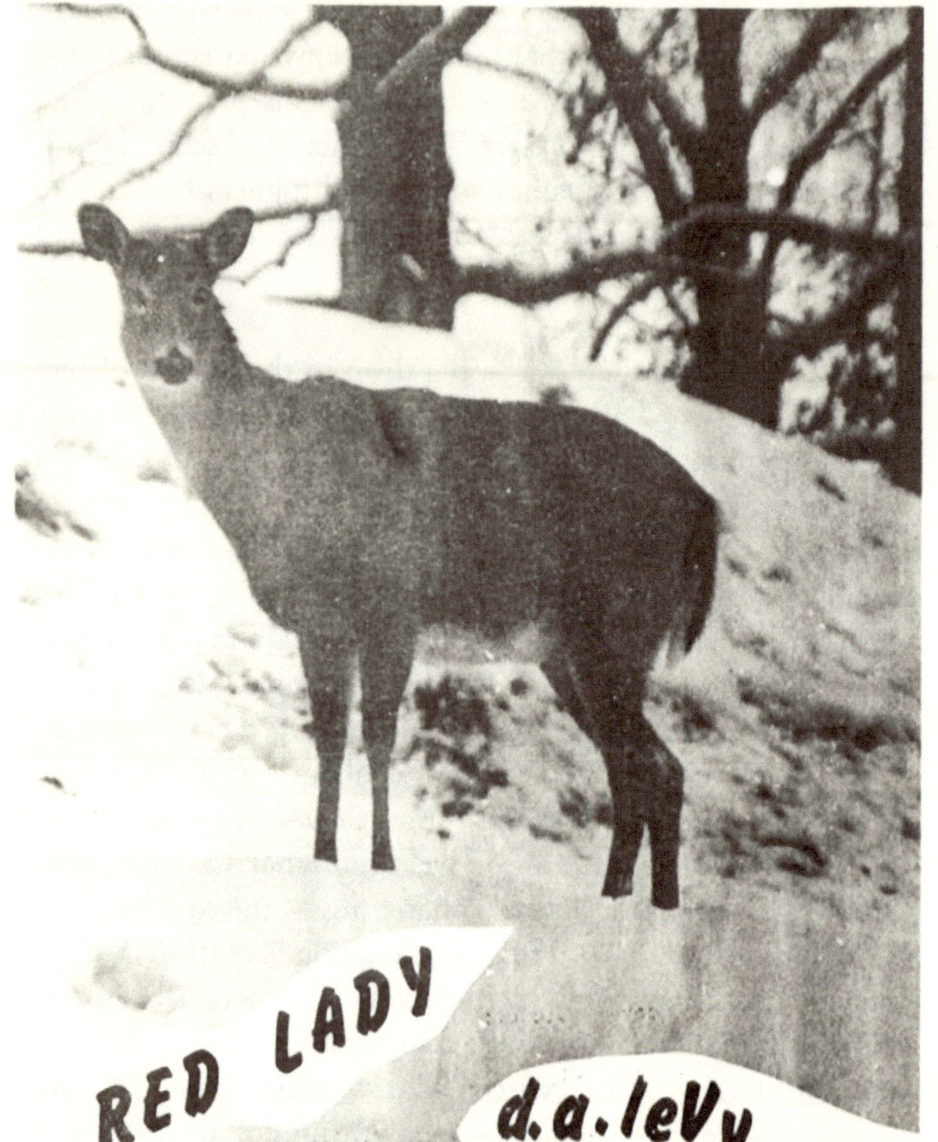
RED LADY
d.a. leVy

## *A CERTAIN STRANGE MEMORY*

Ten movie seconds of Jayne Mansfield in *Will Success Spoil Rock Hunter?*, leaning to look out a square window of the TWA Constellation hovered over city and then landing...

During the writing of an essay on Cleveland poet d.a. levy, a certain strange memory came my way. On the Mother's Day of 1967, a benefit was held in Cleveland to raise money for levy's defense fund. Allen Ginsberg was a featured attraction there, but could another star on the American scene, just as busy and planted in print as Ginsberg, have come into Cleveland without a word?

Larry Smith, Ohio poet and publisher related to me, "The story I heard about eight years ago involved the legal aid fund for levy...It was told to me by Dinsmore Wheeler, friend of James Lowell and the arts. According to Dinsmore, Jayne Mansfield came into town for the defense fund reading...She did it as a special thing for free speech." Further, "I once sat with Dinsmore Wheeler when he was in his 80s and living at his family home in Milan, Ohio. He was very cordial as we sat in his living room with loads of wonderful old books on the shelf. He told of starting the first foreign film series in Cleveland, together with bookseller James Lowell and others. They often were attacked by censors. Then he recalled a time when Jayne Mansfield came to town to speak for d.a.levy and James Lowell's Defense Fund...He said he drove out to the airport to pick up Jayne Mansfield as part of the May 14th program. He said he enjoyed the ride and that she was a very bright person, unlike her film persona. That's what I remember." (1)

Like Allen Ginsberg, Jayne Mansfield was in the midst of a busy spring tour that scheduled her in Britain and

Ireland. From her arrival in England her troubles with authorities began. Smuggling Chihuahuas was just the beginning. Lasting only weeks overseas, on May 14th, Mothers' Day, aghast Roman Catholics terminated her tour in Tralee.

So the question is, could she suddenly, clandestinely, have flown back to the States, to Cleveland, to witness the benefit for an underground poet?

And why would she?

"naturally I became interested in the intellectual type"

—Jayne Mansfield in *Will Success Spoil Rock Hunter?* (1957)

In 1963, the album *Shakespeare, Tchaikovsky and Me* was recorded. Jayne Mansfield purrs over her favorite poems and sonnets with lush accompaniment. Her material includes selections from Elizabeth Barrett Browning, Percy Shelley, Marlowe, Yeats, Wordsworth and Tennyson as well as Shakespeare and others. She had followed in the footsteps of Dylan Thomas and Caedmon Records.

It's not difficult to start wondering, and it soon becomes a myth of possibility.

With an interest in poetry, and always an eye on the papers, Mansfield would have read about Allen Ginsberg. She would have taken notice when Ginsberg praised harassed poet d.a. levy, commending his poetry, "It has obvious literary intent. I dig his poetry. He is learned and sincere, but he is being made to suffer in the classic American way." (2)

Since d.a levy's secret indictment by jury in December 1966, on charges of filth and obscenity, levy had been victimized for his poetic vision. There was police seizure of his mimeograph and writings, an arrest, trial, jail and release on bail, then a second arrest in March 1967 along with Jim

Lowell, owner of the Asphodel Bookshop. Allen Ginsberg had been through similar treatment with his *Howl* in 1957. He arrived in Cleveland to lend his support.

The story would have been familiar to Jayne Mansfield. But would she have stormed across the sea for poetry? Why would she call Dinsmore Wheeler anyway? Secrecy? Was he her connection to the underground? Was she afraid of attracting attention traveling by cab? Did she hide in some phone booth for him to arrive? And what if Dinsmore Wheeler was mistaken? (Nervous looks at a moviestar.) What if it wasn't Jayne Mansfield? Could she have been another Hollywood bombshell, incognito, *a substitute*, with enough resemblance to Jayne Mansfield to pass as her?

If she wasn't Jayne Mansfield, she could have been Mamie Van Doren. She was in America at the time, filming *Voyage to the Planet of Prehistoric Women.* And she knew about the Beat movement, even if cartoonishly; she had been featured in the 1959 exploitation film *The Beat Generation.* (3) She was also a friend of Jayne Mansfield who could double for her.

Mamie Van Doren's autobiography provides more.

"In the summer of 1967...I was again booked to do *Gentlemen Prefer Blondes*...Afterward I was scheduled for a ten-day engagement in Biloxi, Mississippi...I was due in Biloxi in July, but a complication arose...I was afraid I would have to return the money...Fortunately, Bill Loeb was able to schedule Jayne Mansfield to take my place, and reschedule me for later in the summer...now they were getting Jayne Mansfield *and* Mamie Van Doren the same summer." (4)

But it wouldn't happen that way, try as she might to imagine it. Both these women appearing on the stage in a play production of a film forever identified with Marilyn Monroe...It could only have been written that way.

Mamie Van Doren continued, "Jayne's death sharply brought home the many connections in the lives of Marilyn, Jayne Mansfield, and me, the three M's. We had become identified with an era because we made more movies and lived more flamboyant lives than many of the rest. They were connections that I'd tried to push out of my mind at the time of Marilyn's death. I continued to ignore them even more when I made *The Las Vegas Hillbillys* with Jayne Mansfield because I found it a constant reminder of how we seemed to be running out of time." (5)

Jayne Mansfield felt that too. Her last television appearance was to become apocryphal. On June 19, 1967, a month after levy's benefit and ten days before she would die, she was a guest on *The Joey Bishop Show* where she read poetry, Robert Herrick's "To The Virgins, To Make Much of Time" which begins famously:

> Gather ye rosebuds while ye may,
> Old Time is still a-flying:
> And this same flower that smiles to-day
> To-morrow will be dying.

"There is a history of calamitous and violent deaths among the glamour girls that boggles the mind and chills the blood," Mamie Van Doren writes, "If you make your living being beautiful, you've got to be willing to pay that price. You must realize that there is also something deep inside that is as beautiful as the outside; and that the beauty inside will *never* change for as long as you live." (6)

This was the same realization that levy points out in

his *Buddhist Oracle*, that ultimately: "the greatest revolutionary 'game' is learning to live with, survive for, & love yourself and then to really know—you are other people." (7)

Like the collage artwork levy had been creating for the Cleveland underground press, where he joined erotic imagery with Buddhist iconography to create a revolutionary picture, levy went beyond the surface level to draw on that power of the Hollywood Bombshell for his writing. This would become especially clear in his two short stories "The Beginning of Sunny Dawn" and "Red Lady." (8)

"I played games in the sun," Marilyn Monroe writes in *My Story*. "I daydreamed chiefly about beauty. I dreamed of myself becoming so beautiful that people would turn to look at me when I passed. And I dreamed of colors—scarlet, gold, green, white." (9)

From "The Beginning of Sunny Dawn" : "One young day the sun had teeth and softly whispered '<u>changes</u>' to an emerald place where the grass was withered and no one heard...That was the day Sunny Dawn fell out of bed...She decided to open the doors in her mind and let in the sun. Without a chance to grow old she naively went looking for a locksmith in the infinite plastic palaces of excitement." As an embodiment of beauty and light without seeing it, she's the most powerful revolutionary force: "She never met the underground who changed the game, but then, she never met herself." She doesn't know, "she was waiting for the dawn but she didn't understand she carried it within her mind."

Like Marilyn Monroe, "there was almost no one alive to teach her how to wait or what it meant if she saw the sunlight of herself." When Marilyn Monroe took acting lessons, her teacher realized, "You are a young woman who gives off sex vibrations—no matter what you are doing or thinking." So, "I realized that just as I had once fought to get into the movies and become an actress, I would now have to fight to become myself and to be able to use my talents." (10)

That's the story of levy's "Red Lady." The story is even seen as Three Movies (written with slide show images of William Burroughs, Charlie Chaplin, J. Edgar Hoover, flashcards, film clips and ads for bird seed, like one of those experimental films levy would watch every Saturday midnight at the Continental Theatre on Euclid Avenue). Time moves her from fairy tale to modern drive-in screen, "but she wanted something else, not to just get laid, she wanted something else,/hungry ghosts in the shadows of her brain…Red Lady said within her 'i am going'" like Sunny Dawn beyond, and in the morning when she is gone, "there were rumors of a woman who changed shapes in the darkness and whispered light in sleeping ears, a woman who left one thinking of the sun."

What comes to light will happen:

"She knew she was forever & the day would come when the others would understand her ways and leave her alone to fulfill her own destiny.

(crowds of people shouting before giant
posters of jean harlow, marilyn Monroe,
jane mansfield, jane fonda & faye dunaway
—they are firing guns in the air & scream-
ing FREEDOM NOW)"

Jayne Mansfield *was* included in his vision of revolution, but if she came to Cleveland to join him, it would have been done in the underground; the war was on, and bombshells and burning poets don't last long.

Anyway, on Mother's Day, the benefit really did happen. Allen Ginsberg was there, newspaper records were left behind. 600 people watched from the crowd. It's hard to imagine that Jayne Mansfield could have been there secretly (in sunglasses, hair under kerchief, made shadowy in long black coat) when everywhere she went she was falling out of pink, with photos flashing. All we have of her there is a memory in a car.

In a 2006 phone conversation with Continental Theatre manager George Fitzpatrick, I asked about Jayne Mansfield. He confirmed, "She was in Cleveland in Summer 1963 or 1964. She was pregnant at the time and she came to the theatre in full length pink mink coat." But he assured me the rumor of her appearing at the 1967 benefit never happened, and, "I don't know how these stories get started." (11)

**Footnotes:**

1) Letter from Larry Smith, May 18, 2006, used with permission
2) *Cleveland Press*, April 12, 1967
3) In a 1993 episode of *L.A Law* entitled "Rhyme & Punishment," Mamie Van Doren read from Allen Ginsberg's "Howl," while Jayne Mansfield's daughter Mariska Hargitay can currently be seen on television's *Law and Order.*
4) *Playing the Field: My Story*; Mamie Van Doren; G P Putnam's Sons; New York; 1987; p.226
5) *Ibid*; p.227
6) *Ibid*; p.231-32
7) *The Buddhist Third Class Junkmail Oracle*; Volume 2 #3; August-Sept 1968

8) I couldn't have written about d.a. levy without the help of his friend, Tom Kryss. He provided me with the 1969 Open Skull Press Edition of "The Beginning of Sunny Dawn" & "Red Lady" with the note:

"This was the first printing of 'Red Lady,' but the second appearance of 'Sunny Dawn,' which was first published by levy in Cleveland, March, 1968, under the Ghostflower Press imprint...I do believe the 'Sunny Dawn' story was written before 'Red Lady' but not by more than a few months, and in both cases the stories seemed to have gone into print shortly after they were written...Neither story, to the best of my knowledge, has appeared in print since 1970. Just a hunch—'Red Lady' always strikes me as something he brought back in his head from Madison, Wisconsin, and I suspect someone he met there lies at the core."

—Letter from Tom Kryss to author, May 25, 2006

9) *My Story*; Marilyn Monroe; Cooper Square Press; New York, New York; 1974/2000; p.19

10) *Ibid*; p.135

11) Author's phone call conversation with George Fitzpatrick conducted 4:35 PM, June 14, 2006.

**Film quotes from:**

*Will Success Spoil Rock Hunter?* (1957)

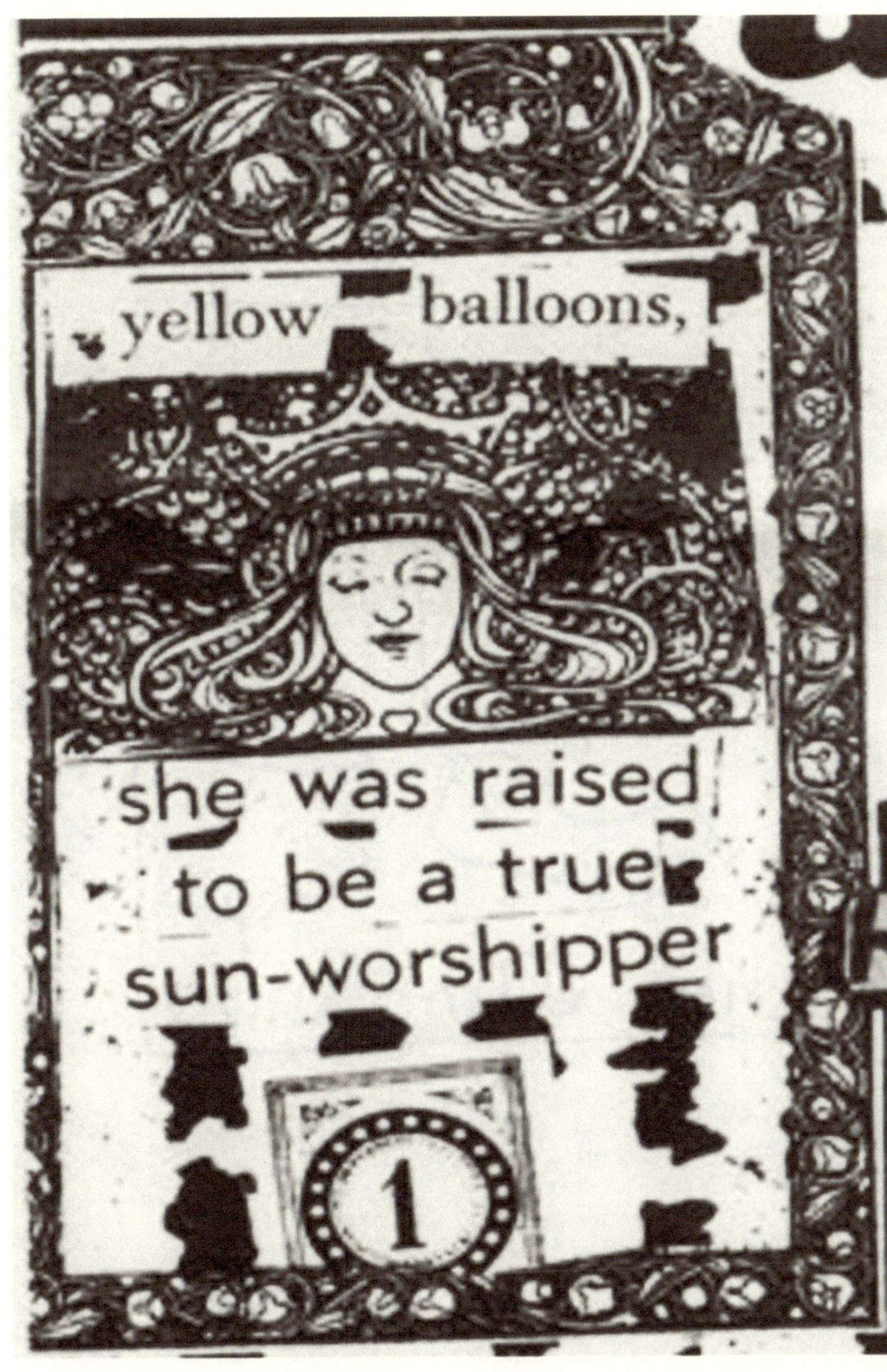
yellow balloons,
she was raised
to be a true
sun-worshipper
1

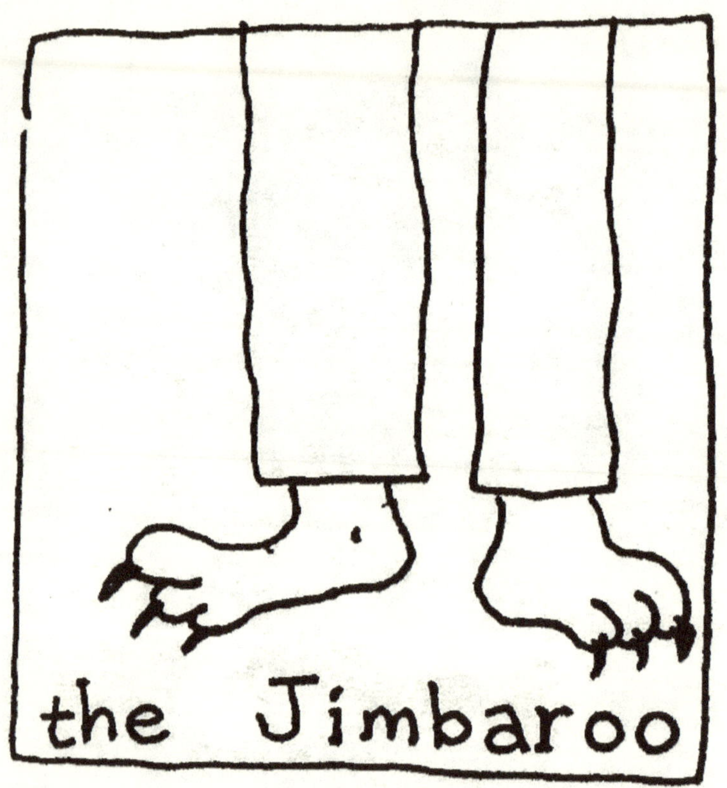
the Jimbaroo

## *THE JIMBAROO*

**Cast:**
Roz
Tyson
Lyle
The Jimbaroo

**Setting:**
A stark room with empty shelves, dresser, a lamp beside a bare mattress.
Into the room enters a young woman and man, Roz and Tyson.

Roz: "He'll like it, won't he?" (Looking around anxiously).

Tyson: "After being in Swaziland? Are you kidding? I bet this place is heaven compared to there. He was probably living in a mud hut. Besides, he was lucky to get out of there alive, with that epidemic or whatever it was. All those people dying mysteriously…He'll love it here, Roz."

Roz: "I hope so. You know we can really use the extra rent money."

Tyson: "You're telling me."

(Offstage a bell rings).

Roz: "That's him! He's here!"

Tyson: (Claps his hands) "Let's find out!"

(They leave the room and are heard greeting their new roommate, Lyle. Generic chatter about long-time-no-see, etc. as they reenter the room, all three).

Roz: "So, do you like it, Lyle?"

Lyle: (Sort of bewildered) "Yeah, it's good…Just…" (He drops his suitcase and sleeping bag on the floor).

Roz: "Plenty of room?"

Lyle: "Yeah, sure. Only…Well, I have a pet. I hope that's okay. I know I didn't say anything about it, but he's very well behaved."

(Roz and Tyson exchange looks).

Lyle: "I can't really live without him. He was given to me by a witch doctor in Swaziland."

Tyson: (Slowly) "I guess…It's okay with me, I guess."

Roz: "I have a cat. Will he get along with my cat?"

Lyle: "Oh yeah, sure! He loves animals. And people too! Makes no difference to him.

(Roz and Tyson look at each other).

Roz: "We can try it out, anyway."

Lyle: "Thanks guys! I'll get him!" (He whistles three times). "Oh yeah! I almost forgot, here's my rent, first and last deposit. I really appreciate this.

(Slowly, as if hypnotized, the Jimbaroo enters).

Tyson: "What the hell!"

(Roz claps her hands to her face).

Lyle: "It's a Jimbaroo."

Roz: "Jimbaroo…"

Tyson: "What's it do?"

Lyle: (Laughing) "Oh, don't worry. They're harmless. He just stands in the corner. See! There he goes. He won't move. He'll stay there."

Tyson: "It's kind of big…What's a Jimbaroo eat?"

Lyle: "That's the funny part! Practically nothing, I give him a glass of water a day and that's it."

Tyson: "He just stands there?"

Lyle: "Yep, like a hat rack."

Tyson: "Sure is strange." (Shakes his head). "They must have given you some weird looks on the plane."

Lyle: (Curtly) "There weren't other passengers for very long."

Roz: “I think he’s kind of cute.”

(They all stare at the Jimbaroo. It is motionless, as if in a trance).

Lyle: (Yawns) “Say, would you mind if I went to sleep now? I think we’re both pretty worn out…long flight.”

Roz and Tyson: (Both agreeing) “No, no, go right ahead. We’ll see you in the morning. Good night.” (They leave the room).

(Lyle unrolls his sleeping bag and tosses it onto the mattress. He takes off his coat).

Roz: (Reappearing) “Knock, knock! Hi again. I thought the Jimbaroo would like a glass of water.”

Lyle: “Oh, that’s kind of you.”

Roz: (Awkwardly holding glass) “Will he want it now?”

Lyle: “Oh no, the Jimbaroo only eats at midnight.”

Roz: “Ohh…Where should I put the glass?”

Lyle: “You can set it beside him. Thanks.

(Roz places the glass beside the Jimbaroo).

Lyle: “He likes you.”

Roz: (Embarrassed) "Oh! How can you tell?"

Lyle: "I just know."

Roz: "I've never seen a Jimbaroo before."

Lyle: "Nobody has ever returned from Swaziland with one. I'm the first one. He'll like it in America. We might even do a little traveling."

Roz: "I hope so. Alright, goodnight again." (She leaves).

Lyle: (He gets into his sleeping bag, turns off the lamp and yawns) "Don't worry. It will be midnight soon."

"Let all the American people be warned that to the really greedy and savage pot-hunter, no bird is sacred, and no bird is safe. But for protective laws mercilessly enforced, the pot-hunters would kill all our song-birds, woodpeckers, tree protectors, shore birds, herons and cranes *in about three years!*" (1)

*Hornaday's American Natural History* book of 1927 presents that dreadful picture of the state of the American air. A victim of that war can be seen clearly in the terror poured on the Carolina Parrot. Their bright red gold and green used to sweep over American land, from the hot swamps of Florida, over rivers, forests and plains and meadows, all the way north to the shores of blue Lake Erie. But as the land was broken and cut up by fences and telegraph poles, roads and railroads, industries, towns and cities, the natural tide of life was dammed. As a result, the settlers' new continent was a world out of balance, suffering extinctions.

So what can you say about a painted bird that has as much as doomed itself against the eventual empire growth of the United States? The ways it knew couldn't go on.

John James Audubon was there to see the parrot before it disappeared. He could capture it in painting and words. Equating this rare bird with the strangling, invasive cockle-bur weed which it fed upon, he allows it to symbolize a threat to civilization.

"The parrot does not satisfy himself with cockle-burs, but eats or destroys almost every kind of fruit indiscriminately, and on this account is always an unwelcome visitor to the planter, the farmer, or the gardener." (2)

Not surprisingly, a terrible reaction lay in store for the parrots. Slaughter. Audubon war coverage:

"The gun is kept at work; eight or ten, or even twenty are killed at every discharge. The living birds, as if conscious of the death of their companions, sweep over their bodies, screaming as loud as ever, but still return to the stack to be shot at, until so few remain alive, that the farmer does not consider it worth his while to spend more of his ammunition. I have seen several hundreds destroyed in this manner in the course of a few hours..." (3)

When the shooting was over, the parrots were almost gone forever, there were only scattered survivors left to vanish. An unnamed mercenary in *Hornaday's American Natural History*, found his way deep into the wetland of the Sebastian River. Carrying a lantern late at night, he was half in water, splashing and shining, looking for the right dead hollow tree. The parrots who roosted there were the last of the line and they were easy to catch. Drowsing, hanging from their beaks and claws to the rough bark, he soon had the lot of them. For a heady price he bagged them and sent them off by freight to die in New York City.

"Birds are not aggressive creatures, miss. They bring beauty into the world. It is mankind rather who insists upon making it difficult for life to exist upon this planet."

—*The Birds* (Alfred Hitchcock, 1963)

During these lost years on Earth—September 14, 1878 to July 6, 1921—a curious shadow of Charlie Chaplin lived, worked and died. Billie Ritchie acted alongside Chaplin in Fred Karno's English music-hall troupe, and when

Chaplin made the move to America, off the vaudeville stage into moving pictures, Ritchie followed.

Although Billie Ritchie have may created the character Chaplin used on his rise to fame (the role in the sketch 'Mumming Birds'), Ritchie appeared to become another Charlie Chaplin on film. He wasn't the only one—so popular was the creation of the baggy tramp, that by 1917 Chaplin felt moved to take the movie imitators to court. In his autobiography, Chaplin asserts, "As the clothes had imbued me with the character, I then and there decided I would keep to this costume, whatever happened." (4) But no mention is made of his peer, Billie Ritchie. In fact, Ritchie contended the image was his. He told interviewers in 1917: "I first used my present make-up in my vaudeville act with my three sisters in 1887…Two years later I again used the same make-up in the character of the street musician in 'Early Birds' while with the Karno company. I claim that I am the originator of this make-up and of the comedy that is associated with the make-up." (5) Most likely the tramp with moustache, cane and bowler became a stock character, but Charlie Chaplin gave the most memorable and lasting performance.

These days it's even difficult to find footage of Billie Ritchie. An introduction to the video remains of *Live Wires and Love Sparks* warns that "the only surviving original print is missing the final few feet of action," (6) then a scowling Billie Ritchie appears. He has on the familiar uniform worn by Chaplin, yet he presents a different soul in there. He's not a doppelganger, he's a Halloween imitation with enough of something original showing through the disguise. Before the film is gone, he's been chased by clowns up onto the roof and off. Lost in the dream, Billie Ritchie is left stranded in the air, at the height of telephone wires, as the film runs out before it's even done.

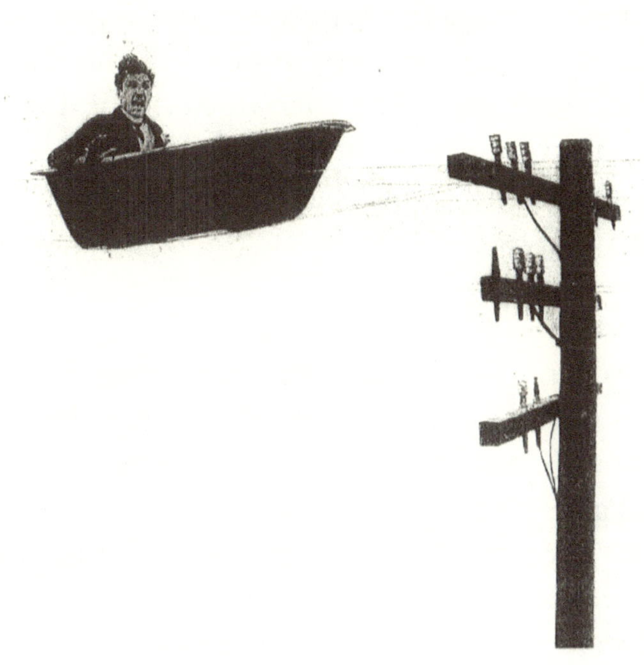

At L-KO studios, Billie Ritchie made films with titles like *Love and Surgery, It Might Have Been Serious, Hearts and Flames, Bill's Blighted Career, The Curse of Work, A Doomed Hero*, and *Life and Moving Pictures*.

Then in 1919, ostriches on the set of his comedy attacked him. He never did recover. Within two years he died from those pains.

The gray details of his career require powers of investigation into the loom of the past 80+ years of history. Following a false lead (perhaps a wrong citation) pointing to the *Fort Wayne Journal-Gazette* of Tuesday, June 8, 1915, I searched in vain for a paragraph on Billie Ritchie. Instead, I was socked to find a comic strip entitled "Flooey and Axel" above the For Rent and Real Estate classifieds of old. There (four years before Ritchie's tragic run-in with the birds), in 4 panels, is a man in black being preyed on by an ostrich.

"The ostrich lays the perfect egg, the largest and most beautiful of all eggs; and in the mind of the Ancients, part of the effluences from the stars which the bird receives must be contained in it. And as we shall see, in medieval times this incomparable egg became one of the liturgical symbols of Christ." (7)

On a Sunday morning, September 12, 1880, the *New York Times* reported 'An Aerial Mystery.' Rising a thousand feet over Coney Island, a man with wings—his legs adapted to flight—was flapping and kicking in the summer thermals. The stark, harpy silhouette against the blue was lifted and powered by "bat's wings and improved frog's legs…The movements made by the object closely resembled those of a frog in the act of swimming with his hind legs and flying with his front legs." (Surprisingly, the *Times* failed to notice the resemblance to Da Vinci's flying machine, which with its bat wings and leg apparatus looked and acted exactly like the "Coney Island monster.") Since August, he, it, whatever, had been seen chopping low over Kentucky and then above St. Louis by a number of citizens. It even tipped its wings at a passing locomotive. New Yorkers were able to look up and notice its "deep black color" and "The face of the man could be distinctly seen, and it wore a cruel and determined expression." The *Times* allowed, "It is without doubt the most extraordinary and wonderful object that has ever been seen, and there should be no time lost in ascertaining its precise nature, habits and, probable mission."

The reporter deduces logically, "Of course the first impulse of the unreflecting mind will be to exclaim that the mysterious flyer is an aeronaut who has invented practicable wings, and is secretly experimenting with them before making his invention public...This has been the invariable practice of these ingenious aeronauts who have claimed to be the inventors of balloons or other apparatus capable of navigating the air. That the mysterious flying man has not followed this custom makes it perfectly clear that he is not a professional aeronaut."

Because this is no ordinary pilot and the tabloid lacks the insight to deal with the unreal (missing the Edgar Allan Poe mind of 1849) the newspaper tries to humor its way to an explanation. There is only one "natural and probable explanation" for the flying man in black...he is a preacher... looking for sermon inspiration in the "crimes and wicked indecencies" of the city below.

The sky exploded and tore apart and out of it floated a white parachute. Hanging by the linen underneath swung a man with one leg—his right leg had broken off as he fell. He sunk through the cloud layer at 4,000 feet, then he saw France, farms, green and yellow fields, and soon there were people on the ground watching him come down. A woman carried pails.

It was a strange arrival to Earth for this master of gravity. Douglas Bader, known in the air as "Dogsbody," was 'the indestructible man,' the source of a "growing and inspiring myth that Bader was bomb-proof, bullet-proof and fireproof." (8)

When he hit land in this war zone, he was taken to a doctor who asked him in English about his missing limb. The doctor even joked, "You seem to have lost both your legs—your real one and your artificial one." (9) The humorous German stitched a cut on the flier's throat, then continued his check-up, moving to the pilot's other leg. That's when the doctor suddenly froze, "staring transfixed at the leather and metal that encased the stump of the left leg. There was a silence…At last he noisily sucked in a breath, and said, 'Ach!' He looked once more at Bader, back at the two stumps and again at Bader, and said in a voice of sober discovery: 'We have heard about you.'" (10)

The Germans weren't the only ones. Look into a London window, Christmas Eve in 1939, where Colin Hodgkinson was in the hospital following a terrible airplane crash. His right leg was gone. His surviving leg was like a statue.

"Then…everything changed. I was thumbing listlessly through the *Sunday Express* when the caption of a short paragraph caught my eye. A young man named Douglas Bader, I read, who had lost both legs in an air crash ten years before had talked himself back into the RAF and was now flying Hurricanes on operational duties." (11)

With such an inspiration to follow, the next day Hodgkinson decided to adapt his legs to flight and lose his remaining leg. After all, it was said that two tin legs may even be an improvement for a flier. The G-forces of air combat that affect and limit a pilot's ability were a result of circulation and he'd "heard some theory that Bader could turn sharper than anyone because he'd lost his legs and blood could not sink that far." (12) While the 1942 sky was being scratched with white scar contrails and burning machines fell from them, Hodgkinson was accepted into Spitfire squadron 131 and given the new name "Hoppy."

Despite overcoming the overwhelming odds of lifting into the air, Hodgkinson remained in terror of falling into the sea. True, survival in the English Channel was ten minutes at most, made even more impossible by the weight of thrashing tin legs. It was this fear (more than anything else in war) that caused him to search for a life-saving flotation solution. Chapter 14 of his autobiography is entitled 'Ping Pong' in honor of that failure.

"I was looking about serenely when, at 27,000 feet, just as we were crossing into France, I was shaken by a series of sharp explosions in the bottom of the cockpit. Jumped! I thought grimly, and immediately threw the Spitfire into a violent evasive action. For a few seconds I twisted and turned, scanning what I could of the sky…Nothing…only the squadron flying impeccably on. More explosions; terrifying, louder than ever. Flak? It must be flak. I banked steeply and glared downwards…My controls were intact, but I was being hit, as a series of further bangs convinced me. The drill for bailing out rushed through my mind: undo straps, pull back hood, invert the aircraft. Then, just before I went through these fatal maneuvers, I remembered the ping-pong balls I had stored in my legs. The rarified atmosphere at nearly 30,000 feet had been too much for them…I decided after that farcical incident that I might know explosions enough without creating my own, and flew for the rest of my service with hollow legs." (13)

"The big birds had a trick of coming in from the ocean and fishing in the lake…The comedian resented these incursions bitterly. He never fished himself, as one of his household pointed out to him, but he said he'd be damned if he would provide free delicatessen for all the feathered drifters on the Coast…He bought a gun, a worn army revolver, for $4.50 in a pawnshop, and crouched for days behind a stump, trying to get a pot shot at the intruders." (14)

Like another Icarus, this time in a straw hat, W. C.

Fields plummeted earthwards. His fall was not fearful, it was fated. The scene from *Never Give a Sucker an Even Break* had been written that way on the back of a supermarket bill in 1941.

This is a fitting place to end, with him dropping carelessly towards Shangri-La. It takes half a minute for him to fall. 30 seconds of black and white clouds, whistling and tumbling. The parade in the sky has gone by—comedians, birds, pot shots and aeronauts.

**Footnotes (Stock Footage)**

"Only he who seeks an oracle will naturally pay attention to the flight of the crow, and he must loudly proclaim his question, addressing the bird at the moment when it flies into the open." (15)

1) *Hornaday's American Natural History*; William T. Hornaday; Charles Scribner's Sons, NY; 12th Edition, 1927; Page 173
2) *Birds of America*; Volume IV; John James Audubon
3) *Ibid.*
4) *My Autobiography*; Charles Chaplin; Simon and Schuster, NY; 1964; Page 146
5) *Motography*, January 6, 1917
6) *Slapstick Encyclopedia Volume 5*; *Chaplin & Company: The Music Hall Tradition*; Kino Video, NY, 1998

7) *The Bestiary of Christ*; D.M Dooling; Arkana, NY; 1992; Page 275
8) *Reach for the Sky: The Story of Douglas Bader, Legless Ace of the Battle of Britain*; Paul Brickhill; W.W Norton & Company Inc., NY; 1954; Page 210
9) *Ibid.*; Page 223
10) *Ibid.*; Page 224
11) *Best Foot Forward*; Colin Hodgkinson; W.W Norton & Company Inc., NY; 1957; Page 89
12) *Reach for the Sky*; Page 201

"Perhaps the greatest 'Captain Kangaroo' memory for yesterday's children, today's adults, is of a Gus Allegretti creation—Mister Moose and the ping-pong balls. I am often asked what word or signal Mister Moose engaged to trigger the fall of those spheres. There were many cues, of course, ranging from knock-knock jokes to rhymes to riddles. I am grateful to Gus for this wonderful addition to the show, but I am able to write these words today because of a change made the first time we performed that ritual. The writer had called for golf balls to fall and I said, 'No!'" (16)

13) *Best Foot Forward*; Page 159-160
14) *W. C. Fields: His Follies and Fortunes*; Robert Lewis Taylor, Doubleday & Company, Inc., NY; 1949; Page 254
15) 'Bird Divination Among the Tibetans', *Sino-Tibetan Studies*, Volume 2; Berthold Laufer; New Delhi; 1987; Page 9
16) *Good Morning, Captain: 50 Wonderful Years with Bob Keeshan, TV's Captain Kangaroo*; Robert Keeshan; Fairview Press, Minneapolis Minnesota; 1996; Page 73

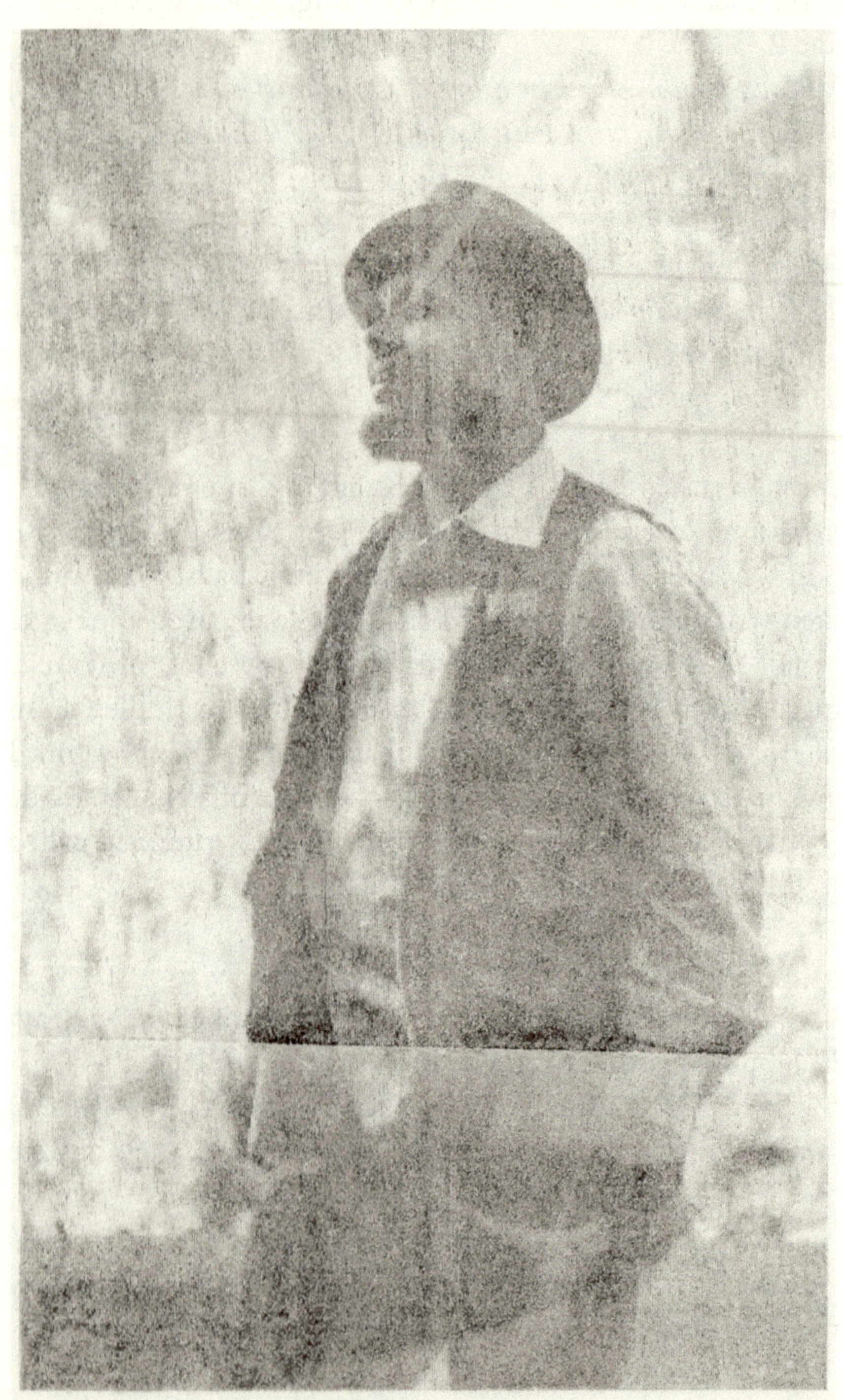

ROBERT HUFF

Birds carried fifteen years away
Like an abandoned nest, put them
To rest somewhere I couldn't see

—Robert Huff, from "Traditional Red."

## *ROBERT HUFF IN BELLINGHAM*

Twenty years is a lot of birds passing overhead and almost enough time to wear away the memory of one who watched below. There is a faint outline of Robert Huff's life in *Contemporary Authors* which is also long out of date. It doesn't even mention his death two decades ago. The four books of poetry published during his life are long out of print. It's as if he's been left in a state of limbo.

I have tried here to track down information on him, writing to artists, professors and students who knew him here in Bellingham, Washington. There are people who helped immeasurably in the making of this. For filling in the rest of the details, I had to rely on my own detective work.

In the summer of 1964, Robert Huff arrived in Bellingham, hired by then-Western Washington State College as an associate professor of English. He filled out a mimeograph Thumbnail Sketch form for recent faculty. Though new to Bellingham, under 'What part of the country do you call home?' he answered: "Pacific Northwest & (Lake Michigan)" For 'Fields of specialization,' he put: "Poetry & Art & Art History." Lastly, to 'Some new faculty members have asked how they might most efficiently find who else shares their special interests' he replied: "I should prefer the time established tendency to attract my friends as the feathers fall.

X (Cock Robin)."

Knute Skinner, who began working for the English department two years earlier, recalls: "At the time Bob was hired, I was teaching only three months a year at Western—as a visiting lecturer, teaching poetry writing, so I had no part in hiring him. I was told by the department chair that they had been looking for a fiction writer but, not having found one, hired a poet instead. And for some time my acquaintance with Bob was limited to my three-month residence—and some correspondence—but we did become friends quickly."

Their friendship can be seen in a short film which was broadcast locally as a television special on Thursday, January 21, 1965 at 10:30 PM on Channel 12. First, the existence of this film is in itself another story of rescue from oblivion. Last summer, Bellingham's TV station KVOS sold and gutted its studio property. Fortunately, the Center for Pacific Northwest Studies was able to acquire and store much of their vast collection of tapes and film reels, including this program called "The Natural World of Poetry."

As the black and white film begins, Robert and Knute are waiting in the living room of a house, in front of a fireplace preparing to read. Huff, wearing a suit coat with sweater and tie, with one foot casually up on the bricks, holds a paperback copy of *Modern Verse*. He coughs, and waits for the camera to track in on him. Then he reads, "Beginning My Studies."

Afterwards, Knute Skinner introduces the show, "You've just heard a poem, read by Robert Huff, written by Walt Whitman that states an important principal for the composition of poetry. And that is, although the poet deals with abstract ideas, he must because of the nature of his craft use concrete imagery. He must use the natural world in his poems, 'the least insect or animal,' as Whitman says."

Now seated at the fireplace, after Knute's reading of Yeats, Robert continues, "The contemporary poet, John Crowe Ransom's poem 'Bells for John Whiteside's Daughter' is especially moving because he is able to infuse the poem with a new life. Although in actuality it presents the typical cliché reaction of most people to the death of a very young child. Particular attention, I think in this poem ought to be paid to the middle section." He reads the poem.

"Bob's written a poem on the same subject, the subject of death," Knute tells us. "This poem, 'Their Suicide,' presents the subject through two points of view. The speakers in the poem are two bachelors who have rescued a man who has attempted to kill himself. While waiting for the doctor to arrive, they find internal difference where the meanings are." Before the smoking fire, Huff and Skinner read the poem together, dramatically, back and forth. The camera dissolves on the log in the fire then opens again on a fern planted next to the fireplace as Knute reads his poem, "The Park" and a few others.

From the sun shaped clock on the wall, the camera pans down to Huff who holds his first book, *Colonel Johnson's Ride*. Opening it, he reads, "Rainbow," a poem that begins:

> After the shot the driven feathers rock
> In the air and are by sunlight trapped.
> Their moment of descent is eloquent.
> It is the rainbow echo of a bird

Huff stands and continues, "The poem 'Rainbow' is one of mine, as are the next three that I shall read. The following poem was written in memory of Theodore Roethke, one of the finest poets in the Northwest, who died in August, 1963." He reads "On the Death of Theodore Roethke," which ends with:

In water and in air
Recall the spirit spare,
Listening as I go
To down of green-winged teal
When the blue martens steal,
By moonlight, speckled snow,
For any afternote
Natural to your throat
That finds me in its flow
Or happens to the stones
Under my falling bones,
Because the earth is so.

Leafing through the book, he continues with "The Dying Dentist" then he turns the pages, pulls out a bookmark and says, "This last poem, as is perhaps very obvious, was written at a rodeo," and he reads, "Brahman."

After a cut, we return to Skinner who announces, "The last poem that we are going to read is another dialogue. This is a well-known poem by A.E Housman entitled 'Is My Team Ploughing.' In this poem one speaker, a dead man, questions his best friend to inquire whether life still goes on." Huff begins, "Is my team ploughing/ that I was used to drive/ and hear the harness jingle/ when I was man alive?" and so they take turns until the short film ends.

Although Huff had landed in Bellingham, it was only for a short time. In 1966, he left to be Writer-In-Residence at the University of Arkansas. Knute Skinner remembered, "Bob was very helpful to me at times, especially in finding accommodation for my family and me. During the year he spent in Arkansas, we rented Bob and Sally's house in Bellingham. I was asked by the department to teach two quarters that year, to help fill in for his absence." I asked Knute about a poem he had written specifically for Robert Huff. "I believe I wrote 'Nothing Ever Lost' during that time. My memory is that I mailed it to him in Arkansas. The poem does address concerns he had, which I shared, chiefly those of confronting memories that may be unpleasant, but which are useful to poetry. Anyway, the reference to the dead friend is to an actual dead friend that Bob mentioned quite a few times. The easy promise refers to a fear he shared that he wasn't living up to his potential as a poet." Simply put, Skinner concludes the poem to his friend with words that define my tribute to Robert Huff as well:

> And if nothing comes of it,
> you have your life story.
> And nothing
> like it or not
> is ever lost.

With a second published book of poetry, *The Course*, Huff returned to Bellingham in 1967. This would be the end of a long migration. Born in 1924, in Illinois, his teaching experience took him to Wayne State University in Michigan, University of Oregon, Fresno State College, Oregon State University, University of Delaware, University of Arkansas, as well as service in the sky over World War Two Europe. Though he had settled in Bellingham, the City Directory provides a record of his restlessness. Beginning with the 1965 listing: "Huff, Robert E (Sally A) prof WWSC h2820 Eldridge," Huff would live in at least six other places over the years until his retirement in 1989.

The 1974 entry is the first time his wife Sally is not mentioned, so it would appear their divorce was around this time. For personal information on these years and more, we await the sharing of his immediate family. I can only share the public face of Huff, mostly as it concerns his work as a teacher and poet.

Samuel Green, who would become Washington State's Poet Laureate in 2007, came to Western in 1970, hoping to work with Huff. In a 2009 interview, he explained, "… there was a teacher I'd heard about, Robert Huff, who was a poet. He was not that well known outside of poetry circles, it seemed to me, but I'd heard that he was wonderful…And Bob Huff was just exactly what I thought he would be. He was the man who knew about poetry in ways I needed to know…Bob taught me about true passionate commitment. He was a man who was deeply in trouble in his own life; one of his marriages was ending when I got here. He was drinking heavily; that was a problem for him, always. But, about poetry there was no bargaining. Poetry had the presumption of importance. It was a central part of his life. It wasn't a pose. It wasn't that he couldn't be melodramatic about it—he could—but it was serious business. Poetry was something you gave yourself to, and you didn't give yourself partly; you gave yourself wholly to it. I hadn't seen that before with people who loved poetry…For Bob it was; it defined him."

Another Huff student and poet, Gaylord Hart wrote to me: "I studied at WWU from 1976-78 getting an MA in English with a creative writing concentration. At the time, there were two poets in the department, Bob Huff and Knute Skinner. I spent most of my time working with Knute since he taught the writing workshops. Bob tended to teach poetry classes, undergraduate, not graduate. I did take at least one poetry class from Bob. This was an undergraduate class for seniors, a 400 level course, but graduate students could get credit for a certain number of these...I remember in Bob's better moments how sensitive he was to the poetry and the writers, how he could latch onto a detail in a poem and make it fresh, bring it alive. While both critics and poets revere the poem, and no doubt appreciate it equally, they don't necessarily appreciate it the same way. Poets see the poem differently, and Bob was a poet. It was this that I admired. And sometimes when he talked about a poem, you could see Bob as a tender man, insightful about the poem, but placing it in a larger context, making connections that seemed obvious once stated, but that were in fact elusive to most readers."

Steven Dolmatz, now a teacher himself, was also a student of Huff's at this same time. He recalls how in class, "he would drift in and out, go on tangents then reel it back in and have great things to say." At these times, Huff was "incisive about criticism, with an unnerving taste and sense of how to create voice out of a poem, how to tighten the writing, get the image and lead the poem. He would close his eyes and go right to it, 'that's the poem.'"

From Robert Huff's first book, *Colonel Johnson's Ride* (1959) his poem "Professor Emeritus" pictures the teacher as an old hunting bird, "huddled in his chair":

> And teaching is a kind of poetry,
> A way of shaping knowledge on the lee
> Side of the world effectively.
> I used to dream of shanghaiing
> All young minds for the sea
> By rolling at them riddles of the kind
> Which have no answers, save the ones we find
> In travelogues big as the Odyssey,
> When I was apt at illustrating tales

With movements like the motion of great whales.

Sam Green found a mentor in Huff, when "as a student, I had no idea what I was doing, I was fumbling and stumbling and Bob just—he would just *push* me. But, mostly he *pulled* me; he just set a pace and an example, and then he watched. He was one of those kinds of teachers, he was brilliant at it...Bob made it very clear that there was a lot to know, and that you had to know it. All of it. There were no shortcuts. If you were going to do this—commit to poetry—then you had a long journey ahead of you, and you might as well get started. And you might as well have the right attitude going in, meaning: you're an apprentice and you're going to stay an apprentice for a long, long while, because there are giants before you and you need to look at those giants."

Huff certainly made them a part of his life. D.H Lawrence, W. B. Yeats, Robert Frost, E. E. Cummings, Wordsworth, Emily Dickinson, Robert Lowell, Carl Sandburg, James Wright, Theodore Roethke were all central to his teaching. And Dylan Thomas, whom Huff describes in a poem as "the buoyantly doomed Welsh bard" must have been a huge influence. Like a burning meteor, his ride is well described in John Brinnin's *Dylan Thomas in America*. Knute Skinner confirmed this, "Dylan Thomas was a big influence. As you probably know already, Bob and Sally named their son after Dylan. Bob was also much influenced by Yeats and Frost and would sometimes get maudlin if he heard either quoted in public—although he liked to quote them himself. They were an ideal he felt he could never live up to."

At the 1961 Bread Loaf Writer's Conference, Lew Turco befriended Huff: "The recently deceased Welsh poet Dylan Thomas was one of the fabled people of our generation, and Bob Huff and I used to have Dylan Thomas sound-a-like contests." And in a 1982 interview, Huff recalled, "I used to be very much influenced by reading mannerisms, trying to present poems say the way Dylan Thomas would have. Thank God I got out of that." But he did have trouble with another well-known influence on Dylan Thomas.

Huff's late-night carousing in town became legendary. A former student told me, "If you lived in Bellingham and enjoyed visiting the taverns, Bob was frequently nearby. Bob was always enjoyable to drink with in the bars."

Unfortunately, this could carry on into Huff's work. Sam Green said, "I remember a particular time he came in [to class], and he'd been drinking all afternoon…Yet when Bob came in that day, everyone was silent. He was clearly emotional. He sat down, and he looked at us, and for a minute he didn't even register, I think, that we were there. Finally, he looked around at us as though we couldn't possibly understand. He locked eyes with me, because he knew that I was at least trying, I think. He said, 'I've been drinking whiskey all day and reading E. E. Cummings. I'm going to read him to you.' And he did, for the entire class period. He read so well, even under the influence. This was serious. Each word found its place in his mouth. I wept hearing him do that. Partly I think it was because I could see the problem (his drinking), but partly because I loved poetry, too, and it was so wonderful to find someone who loved it the way I loved it and more. He read Robert Lowell right after that; he actually recited 'Quaker Graveyard in Nantucket,' and after the end of it he broke into tears."

Gaylord Hart shared a similar memory with me. "He lived the poetry, but he also frequently showed up for class inebriated, and was prone to breaking out in tears in class. When Bob was sober, you could talk poetry with him, have discussions about art and life. He was a kind man, with an infectious smile, and when sober, a quick wit...Bob was unpredictable as a teacher, and for this reason, I think most students stayed away after one course with him. I honestly can't say that Bob's lucid, perceptive moments as a teacher outweighed his inebriated moments. The latter were more frequent, but the former had more weight."

Huff knew well-enough what was happening to address it in his poetry, like "September 1966" which begins and ends with a heron passing above the misty school:

And fogging in this week September's back.
My students, always quick to find me out,
Cannot forgive bad news. I am old hat.
I lock the door, pretend the window's black,
Feel round the bottom drawer and reach my flask...
Perhaps that cloudy heron was a stork,
A nuisance around any chimney top.
All old birds ought to be against the law.

Birds fly from all of Huff's books. Sometimes they are totems, sometimes they are projections of himself, like the hawk in "Early Snow" a cold, gothic poem of a marriage falling apart. There are also bird hunters. Such a poem for his daughter, titled "Rainbow," becomes a hard life lesson.

"Times are economically bad," he typed in a 1975 departmental bibliographic record, "My third book MS has been accepted by two presses which are experiencing financial needs, The Swallow Press and The University of Virginia Press. Because these presses are financially hard put, my MS is also now in the hands of Alfred Knopf, where it is under final consideration this month."

Then on October 28, 1976, the Public Information

Office issued an announcement from the English Department regarding his third book. "This year's winning selection for The Virginia University Poetry Series is 'The Ventriloquist: New and Selected Poems' by Robert Huff, a member of the Department of English at Western Washington State College. 'The Ventriloquist' was selected from hundreds of manuscripts submitted to distinguished writers throughout the country who acted as primary judges. The final judge was Richard Eberhart, who has written an introduction to the volume. The work will be published by The University Press of Virginia next spring." After receiving the Associated Writer's Poetry Series Prize, the book was published in 1977. The book-flap actually sums up all three of Huff's books: "Many of the poems speak with compassion for the individual and praise the outsider; others continue in the best poetic tradition of honoring the dead. There are songs, jokes, simple direct lyrics, satires on fashionable attitudes, and poems that pay homage to writers whose work influenced the poetry of our time and the author's own style." The book also comes with praise from Huff's co-worker, poet Annie Dillard, "Robert Huff writes with a kind of special, pained exultation that makes his poems distinctively fine. His caring for people so dominates his poems that his world is a series of heart's landscapes, moving and mental and real. Huff's is an excellent, controlled voice. He wears well. And, on top of all this, he *swears* well."

Between 1977—1979, Paul Lindholdt organized weekly readings at Fast Eddies, a bar on State Street in Bellingham. "Huff would come in and sit by himself the couple times I remember best, kind of sullen and drinking." As the night wore on, he could be counted on to recite Dylan Thomas, or a "Dream Song" of John Berryman's. Lindholdt continued, "On one occasion my then-wife joined him and they chatted for a while, until he took off his glasses, folded them carefully while regarding her, and then threw them with great force on the opposite wall and said, 'Goddamn, you're beautiful!'"

In 1980, Lynda Schor was hired as Writer-in-Residence to teach two fiction writing workshops for a quarter at WWU. She brought her three kids by train from New York City to Seattle, then by bus to Bellingham. With no car of their own, "Bob used to drive us around, which given how much he drank was kind of crazy…Bob was totally friendly and helpful. He was also a major alcoholic. He had a cute crew cut, and a little paunch. I got the feeling he liked kids. I think he'd recently been divorced. He visited us nearly every evening, brought his own booze, and talked for hours. He never noticed if we had to take our baths and go to sleep. He was not allowed to drive (probably had a few DUIs) so he painted his car so the cops wouldn't notice it, and he kept driving."

Poet Kelly Cherry, who was hired after Schor's term, wrote: "I knew him only for the spring semester of 1981. When sober, he was a delight to talk with. He could be kind, supportive, and helpful. When my little dog ate part of the carpet in my office—while I was teaching a class—and I worried that the university would send both me and my dog packing, he simply moved a file cabinet over the section my dog had eaten…We certainly did talk about poetry, but I don't remember what either of us said. I believe I probably did show him poems I was working on and he published something of mine. But he could also be very mean, usually when drunk. He was enough of a drinker that one didn't always realize he was drunk: one of those drinkers who can seem for the duration of a conversation to be sober enough but then might collapse into a full-on, sloppy drunk. I had experience with that, but I didn't then understand anything about alcoholism...Somehow—maybe there had been a previous accident he'd mentioned to me—I had a foreboding about him and fire..."

This is not surprising. As well as snow, fire is a reappearing, overpowering image in Huff's poetry. Beginning with his first book, there are haunting poems like "The Smoker" and "Firefighter" and "Blue: A bombing mission over Germany April 30, 1943."

Cherry continued, "I badgered him for information about Annie Dillard, who had taught there, though the fiction writer Lynda Schor was my immediate predecessor. During most of our conversations, which took place at the office, he was gentlemanly and interesting." Cherry also added, "I learned from him, not only about poetry but about the poet's obligation to remain free of jealousy and favor. About, in other words, the extent to which the poet must remember she is one of many (the long line of people, and not just literarily inclined people) and not somehow special or apart from them."

As the 1980s progressed, Huff balanced on a blade.

A feature article on Huff in *The Western Front*, from February 12, 1980 touched on this:

But it was a dream that eventually was to lead him to a detoxification center 12 months ago.

Huff lights another Lucky Strike. "All that's in the past now," Huff explains. "I've embraced the contradictions and found a cure for my own time being."

"Today I've got a drawer full of newly written poems,

some of them are children's poems. And I've got new students to teach each quarter."

Skinner continues, "For that year we knew a sober Huff we hadn't known before. It was, in fact, the talk of his friends and acquaintances how much *nicer* he'd become. Not argumentative, not given to unpleasant insults, not given to moods of depression. At the end of the year, however, he began drinking again. He had, in fact, told me he'd been counting the days till he could get drunk again. It was a pity he didn't like himself sober."

The 1975 edition of *Contemporary Authors* had a short sidelight composed by Huff saying that for his poetical training, he was grateful "to the shores of Lake Michigan near Saugatuck, Michigan, and to the forests of the Northwest." As for his interests, he listed them as hunting and fishing, "both of which are rapidly becoming sitting by the sea." In 1982, he updated his entry considerably. "I believe that place (not regionalism) is important to poetry. I am often stimulated by specific reactions to individual detail to recall similarities of appearance from an earlier experience in a different place. I'm frequently moved to make a poem out of comparing this past memory to immediate occurrences. Once in a while I'm led by my natural environment to think about what I have read by gifted writers whose response to the natural world I feel I share. At one time, after losing a big salmon, I sat down on a riverbank and began a poem by talking to a wild flower about animals, fish, myself, and D.H. Lawrence. When it was completed I called it, fairly, 'To a Violet.' But it was about time and place, something very important to writers like Flannery O'Connor and Eudora Welty, whose short stories I find far more poetical than most contemporary poems

I run across in magazines these days. Prosaic poetry seems to be in fashion. With rock music and its lyrics in mind, pray that fashions are always temporary. Amen." Under Avocational Interests, he again listed hunting and fishing, "both of which seem to be turning into bird watching and sitting by the sea."

Throughout the decade, Huff regularly shepherded poetry for the annual Leslie Hunt Poetry Award. This award of $100 was granted to the student with the best previously unpublished poem or group of poems.

Following its debut in 1965, Huff served as advisor for Western's literary magazine, *Jeopardy*. "The editors make all the decisions; I advise. If something is in questionable taste, they might come to me to see if we could get away with it."

He gave a campus reading February 4, 1982, from his three collections and also read poems from two unpublished manuscripts, *Taking Her Sides on Immortality* and *Shore Guide to Flocking Names*. He promised, "The poems will be both light and serious so the audience won't get bored." The accompanying newspaper article also included some insights to his writing. Huff claimed to be "not disciplined enough for a morning schedule," usually writing at night. When confronted by writer's block, "I just stay there until it goes away." Also, "My essential inspiration for writing has been my reaction to the non-human environment and the reactions of others to the natural world around them." Claiming that poets are "economic victims of the times," Huff concludes, "The kind of specialized mentality, aptitude, which leads one to be interested enough in poetry to want to study the craft at the university level very frequently leaves one in situations in which there's little other employment after graduation except doing the same things that teachers do."

He spoke more about writing poetry in a *Bellingham Herald* feature article from the same year, comparing writing to bird-watching: "It begins by learning how to record in detail the appearance of things. It involves the development of a capacity to present at once the actualities of life and suggest the writer's interpretation of things…You can depend on birds. You can depend on their habits, their coloration, their migration patterns—they're so consistent."

He continued, "The importance of *reading* poetry for young college students is to gain an understanding of vivid, concrete language. Student readers and writers of poetry learn very early that emotional states of being and strongly held ideas of liberty, love, fear, hatred, democracy or totalitarianism cannot be communicated in pleasant-sounding combinations of abstractions and generalities. Communication demands an appeal to the senses."

Summer quarter of 1982 found Huff on the panel discussion for the Book of the Quarter. (He had served on a panel previously in 1965 for Theodore Roethke's book, *Words for the Wind.*) The title chosen was *The Collected Poems of Sylvia Plath*. The panel met at Wilson Library.

Huff also had other words for the library. A May 1, 1983 memo from Wilson Library and Corridor Information Services asked the university's faculty and staff to provide a list of publications the library should purchase. Here is Huff's response:

"Attached is a list of my publications. Regarding the three volumes of poetry, the first COLONEL JOHNSON'S RIDE, is out of print; of the second, THE COURSE, there are only a few copies left. I would appreciate it if Wilson Library would purchase two copies of THE COURSE from WSU Press, so that stolen copies might be replaced. I fear also that COLONEL JOHNSON'S RIDE is missing from our library. If it is possible through the help of some highly-in-the-know book dealer we might be able to buy a copy or more of COLONEL JOHNSON'S RIDE from some private library sale. I would be happy to purchase any copies of that book that Wilson Library may find available beyond the library needs. Robert Huff."

Poet and Professor Paul Lindholdt, a student of Huff's and a longtime friend, explained to me, "He didn't pull any punches in the classroom. He just told people exactly what he thought and some would call it blunt and abrasive and even abusive but that's who he was. If I were to choose a single adjective to describe him, it would be 'bluster,' which has more negative connotations today than it does positive, but he managed to bluster in ways that were positive and inspiring as well as overbearing at times."

Although the English Department doesn't keep records of past course descriptions, luckily one survived, making its way to the library Special Collections. The 14 stapled pages include Huff's personal description of three classes he taught for the Winter Quarter of 1983:

ENGLISH 353. 4 cr. MTWR-12.
INTRODUCTION TO POETRY WRITING.
CONTENT: Opportunity for disciplined expressing in writing poetry. Reading of modern poems as models for various approaches to the individual composition of poetry. Original poems by class members presented orally by the writers and discussed and evaluated by the instructor and the class as a whole in weekly workshop sessions.
WRITING ASSIGNMENTS: Approximately nine poems

in which you attempt to avoid excessive reliance on abstractions, generalizations, the jargon of politics and popularized sociology—such as "life style," "involvement," "Awareness," "sensitivity," "viable," "relate to," "alternatives," etc.—and in which you especially try to omit sentimentality (the expression of unwarranted unmotivated emotion) and focus attention on concrete detail.
EVALUATION: Based on improvement and quality of completed assignments.

ENGLISH 421. 4 cr. MTWR-1.
STUDIES IN MAJOR AMERICAN WRITERS: W.C. Williams, Robt. Lowell, Theodore Roethke
CONTENT: Selected readings in Williams, Lowell, and Roethke which focus attention on the influence of the modern movement on each writer. Particular attention will be paid to similarities and differences regarding subject matter, basic intentions, characteristic points of view, imagery, personal idiom, and the development of individualistic styles.
ASSIGNMENTS: Short oral reports. A written summary of major project.
Major Project: An analytical essay dealing with one or two of the three poets.
EVALUATION: Final evaluation based on class participation, reports, project summary, and the major essay.

ENGLISH 504a. 5 cr. W-7-10 p.m. + 1 hr/wk arr.
SEMINAR IN THE WRITING OF POETRY
CONTENT: Individual projects in poetry will be submitted for group discussion. Several recently published volumes of poetry will be studies for examination of originality of styles.
Texts: Philip Larkin—*High Windows*
James Tate—*The Lost Pilot*

Donald Hall—*Kicking the Leaves*
Theodore Roethke—*The Far Field*

1. Is there a particular choice of subject matter and approach to it? Does the subject matter and attitude seem fashionable? original? individualistic?
2. Are any specific elements of poetry emphasized?
3. Is there a definable tone which dominates the book?
4. Is there a reliance of any kind on the work of a writer who is better known, a contemporary or otherwise?
5. Generally speaking, what would you say characterizes the book?
6. Do you feel that your own work is in any way similar?

SUGGESTIONS FOR THOSE WHO ARE TEMPORARILY OUT OF TOUCH WITH THE DELPHIC ORACLE:

1. A childhood memory presented from an adult point of view (retrospective) which relies on dramatic narration and/or several approaches to a single motivating image (either purely descriptive or figurative) or incorporates a series of related images. The effect, frequently of loss, nostalgia, disillusionment, is achieved in part by the contrast between the time of the incident and the time of the telling, the relative innocence of the recalled event as it was initially understood and the sophisticated and insightful vocabulary of the speaker. For examples, see Joyce's highly poetic story "Araby" (Dubliners) and Dylan Thomas' "Fern Hill."
2. A poem which relies for its effect on an occasion, the death of a relative or friend, a marriage, a divorce, a birthday, a first love, a meeting, a parting, perhaps a strong reaction to an event of personal or national or international importance. The field is open. It may be an account of an immediate reaction or a poem of contrasts between appearances, feelings, evaluations of the occasion as first experienced and as first recalled. If the latter, the approach is similar to suggestion 1.

3. A poem which opens with purely descriptive detail and develops into a piece in which, as Theodore Roethke put it, "detail deepens into symbol."

4. A poem which relies heavily on sound effects. See Sitwell, Cummings, Thomas.

5. A poem which excludes any kind of figurative image and depends on the "pure," non-figurative, descriptive image. This is a currently fashionable approach very

—Missing rest of description—

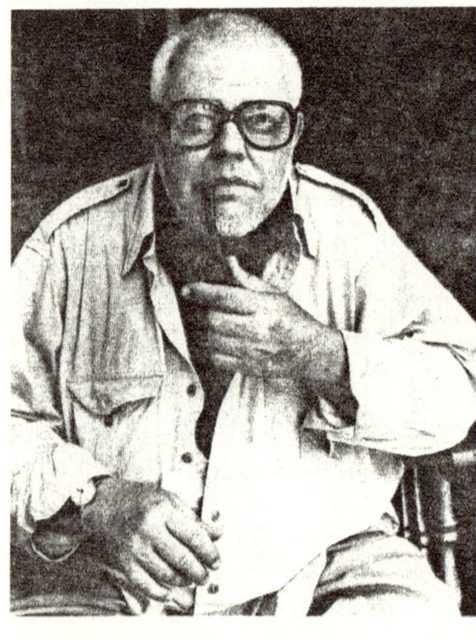

Robert Huff has read at numerous universities and other institutions throughout the country including the Poetry Center of New York and The Library of Congress.

# ROBERT HUFF

Reading Selections from *The Course, Colonel Johnson's Ride, The Ventriloquist, Shore Guide to Flocking Names* and *Taking Her Sides on Immortality.*

"His caring for people so dominates his poems that his world is a series of heart's landscapes."

Annie Dillard

"The best of his poetry speaks to us, our time and our situation, person by person. He makes poetry a form of friendship and reminds us what it is to be cherished in our ice age . . . He is what the good poet is today, hard, honest, warm, hurt, with his teeth on edge. More power to him."

Karl Shapiro

". . . the language exploding into articulations as if to say, 'And I only am escaped alone to tell thee'."

Anthony Hecht

"I like Robert Huff's verse. I find it fresh and vigorous and human and it smells of the earth of America and of its vivid history."

Sean O'Faolain

"When I first read a few poems by Robert Huff I was startled by their bounce, their comedy, their depth of feeling — by their general artistic authority."

James Wright

"The most underrated poet in America."

James Whitehead

"He has the sinew, sound effects, and rhythm of a real poet."

Robert Lowell

AT VILLAGE BOOKS 1210 11th STREET

SUNDAY OCT. 20 7PM

Huff's last published book *Shore Guide to Flocking*

*Names* plays off an actual, popular birdwatcher's field manual title. Comprising ten poems with beautiful illustrations, Huff described it as "a book of poems about birds designed for young people and all readers with a sense of humor."

The manuscript took some years to finally find a publisher. I found first mention of it in an Annual Activity Report dated May 24, 1979, where he writes, "Presently at work on a new book of poems and a bird book for children consisting of a series of poems about shore birds."

*The Bellingham Herald* from September 24, 1982 devoted it's Friday section cover photo to Huff with the feature article, "Robert Huff: His best birdwatching is done with a pen." His *Shore Guide* manuscript is mentioned as "still in search of a publisher."

In 1984, a student at WWU named Steve Colello took Huff's bird manuscript to local publisher and artist Michael Oppenheimer, owner of Fanferon Press. Formerly located on the corner of Dupont and F Street, Fanferon used a monotype press. Handcrafting each page, each poem set one letter at a time, it was a labor of love.

"Robert came to the press a few times," Michael Oppenheimer recalled. "He loved the place. He was totally on board, he loved the idea. I immediately liked him. I liked that he appreciated what was happening, what I was all about and what the press was all about. Steve was learning a lot and Robert was getting the book published. He provided us a great deal of trust and let us do the book. I don't remember any issues with him, he was very appreciative. We actually sold some books. The agreement was he would sell the books and I would get my expenses paid and then he would take the rest."

On September 28, 1985, Huff sent a memo to Western's Public Information office. The Subject Line was

"Another Poetry Reading (hopeless attempt to sell SHORE GUIDE TO FLOCKING NAMES)." He announced the forthcoming reading of his new book, adding, "Enclosed you'll find an inscribed, signed, beat-up copy of SHORE GUIDE all for you, a bribe for delivering your press release by hand to *Western Front* and begging them to give the reading some kind of notice with photo. Last spring they gave me diddly on announcement, then sent a reporter and photographer to Fairhaven for the reading and printed ZERO of the results. So let's give this one a new whirl."

*The Western Front* did announce the local reading of Huff's latest book at Village Books on Sunday, 7 PM, October 20, 1985. The same article also included a few words from Huff extolling bird-watching, finding migratory ones the most attractive for him and adding: "I was fortunate as a child, raised in a rural area outside Chicago. I started to write quite young, mostly abstract work. My idol was Carl Sandburg. He still is…I spend about three days a week at nearby lakes and get a lot of my inspiration from nature… There is always the danger of sentimentalizing, but birds just do the things they were born to do and exist and perpetuate themselves."

Village Books owner, Chuck Robinson has a video recording from this time. "It hasn't been played in years," Chuck warned me, "so I hope it is still viewable." Amazingly, it was. It's a twenty minute segment of a locally produced 1985 cable TV program called *The Reading Room*, hosted by Greg Cornia. Huff sits heavy as an old owl in a chair beside a table, coffee cups and a white lamp, a cut-out blue city silhouette in the background.

Greg Cornia: "Let's move on to your poetry. There's one poem that we talked about that I felt captured quite a bit of what you do in one line and that's 'The Dying Dentist.' Could we start right off with a reading? It's an early poem that you did many years ago, more than we'll admit."

Robert Huff: "Yeah, well we needn't worry about that. It's hopeless, I've tried. This poem was written with my father in mind." (RH reads "The Dying Dentist.")

GC: "There's one line in there that I had you read that for because it says 'man, beast, and bird are after all, all one,' and I think that typifies so much of your poetry. If there's a theme to your poetry, that's it, but that's not necessarily your line. I think that's something you said comes from—"

RH: "It's one of the few things I share with D.H Lawrence."

GC: "Okay. And that's very autobiographical?"

RH: "Yes, in a way it is. My father was determined to have an office on the 33rd floor of the Pittsfield Building in Chicago. And he did. But in a way he paid the price for that elevation."

GC: "It was first published in *Colonel Johnson's Ride*. There's another poem in here that I'd like you to read because we'll make a circle that comes back to it. That's 'Cormorants' and in your latest publication we have 'Cormorant.'"

(RH reads "Cormorants.")

GC: "A lot of your work has animal images or birds or animals in it. Where do those images come from? What is the inspiration for this?"

RH: "Oh, one really is hard put to be sure about things like that but I was in a way fortunate when I was very young. My parents lived part of the year in Chicago and part of the year on Lake Michigan in a little town called Saugatuck, so I would transfer from one school to another every year. It gives a growing up person a chance to make certain decisions. And I chose the rural side."

GC: "Is that what brought you to the Northwest?"

RH: "Yes, actually it is. I turned down a job at Miami University in Oxford, Ohio to come to the University of Oregon. I was so eager to get a hold of one of those big salmon."

GC: "Where did your original impetus to write poetry come from?"

RH: "I think that people who write poetry began writing from one of two impetuses. If they're fortunate they began writing because of an inherent need to praise certain aspects of the world in which they're born. And the other part of it is making the most of adversity as time passes. And perhaps the most gifted and most fortunate poets are able to do both of those things as they age. The poem I had in mind is a poem by William Butler Yeats. This is one of Yeats' later poems and as he aged, as he began to feel his physical strength waning, he was making the most of adversity by rejecting the world that he had led in his youth and embracing the abstract, the spiritual and this poem is his way of creating in his own mind a heaven for artists."

(RH reads W.B Yeats' "Sailing to Byzantium.")

GC: "I'd like to move on a little in your own life. You ended up being in the service for a little while and you came back and out of that came a poem that I found as powerful as any I'd read of yours."

(RH reads "Hen" from *The Course.*)

RH: "Perhaps I'd been reading Wordsworth, although I'm not sure."

GC: "Was that a pretty personal poem coming out of the service?"

RH: "Yes, that poem was written a considerable number of years afterward. I changed the towns around. I had a lot of experience working for the General Motors Acceptance Corporation attempting to collect bills. I was called a Field Representative. I was scared to death. I had to bolster myself up with a little Dutch courage and a very large cigar when I would visit some of the establishments where my unpaid bill people were working. And for some reason many of them worked in these poultry killing shops. That's where it came from."

GC: "Real quickly, before we go on a break, you're doing something very few modern poets are doing. You're writing rhyming verse. What prompts that?"

RH: "Well, I don't know. Perhaps it's the influence of writers like W.B Yeats, Henry Reed, some of Theodore Roethke. I've always liked to rhyme. I realize it can be a crutch because it's enjoyable to hear musically pleasant things even if the foolish old poet has nothing to say."

GC: (After a recital of 'Cormorant,' GC holds up *Shore Guide to Flocking Names*) "This is a great little volume of poems and they're all about birds. What prompted that?"

RH: "I can't remember actually. I wanted to write a poem which I hoped would have appeal for both young and old readers. I suppose it's because I'm somewhat of an ardent bird watcher and I had been using Roger Tory Peterson for so many years, I decided to write a series of poems based upon some of the birds that I enjoy watching, and I manipulated that title around too. I picked out some of these birds that I thought had humorous names."

GC: "It becomes a humorous volume. The limerick cadences add to the humor. It becomes very fun to read, kind of an updated *Mother Goose*. Could you read from a poem in progress?"

RH: "Well, I think it might be appropriate since I seem to be the Birdman of the Area to read a poem from this new manuscript." (He picks up *Taking Her Sides on Immortality*, bound in a black folder stuffed with bookmarks) "It's about a bird but it's completely different from the way I handled the subject matter in *Shore Guide to Flocking Names*. I had come across a bird by one of the nearby lakes. It was afflicted with something. I think it was more than lead poisoning. Since I've hunted for so many years, I thought I would try to write the poem from the bird's point of view. (RH reads "Mallard Dying" to end the show.)

It's so fortunate to be able to watch Robert Huff. This long-hidden video, taken with the earlier 1965 TV program, shows that Huff never lost his power of presence and poetry.

Another reading from his new book occurred at Western, on February 13, 1986. The announcement in the school paper reads: "Robert Huff, of the English Department, will give a presentation titled 'Shore Guide to Flocking Names: Time Yet for a Hundred Indecisions,' at noon Thursday, in the library presentation room. The presentation is part of the Bureau of Faculty Research's lecture series." What wouldn't have escaped Huff's notice had he read the paper is the adjacent large illustrated ad of W.C. Fields hawking sandwiches. Huff had praised Fields in his poem, "The Poet as W.C. Fields Observes a New Face in the Audience May 14, 1970" which he set at a poetry reading in a platinum aviary.

In fact, the publication of his fourth book gave Huff the steam for a number of readings beginning with a May 23, 1985 reading at Fairhaven College. Later, from an announcement on April 22, 1986 comes "'Poetic Metaphor: The Joy of Making the Most of Adversity' is the title of a talk tonight by Robert Huff 7-9 pm. in the Wilson Library Presentation Room." The next month, the Public Information Office gave notice of: "A free reading for 7 pm. Wednesday May 21 at Fairhaven College," adding, "He will be on leave from WWU next year to travel and work on a sixth collection of poems at the MacDowell Colony in Peterborough, New Hampshire." His final performance on campus was "A free reading at the Wilson Library Presentation Room at 8 pm. Thursday May 25, 1989, reading poems from *The Course, Colonel Johnson's Ride, The Ventriloquist, Shore Guide to Flocking Names*, and *Taking Her Side on Immortality*."

From the beginning, readings had always been an integral part of Huff's poetry experience. In a 1966 article in Western's college paper, Huff explained the importance: "In one way or another all poetry is primitive; it is involved with sound which must be heard and doesn't always have to be understood as we know informational prose. Poetry has to be read aloud if we want the whole of it. When we hear the poem, the experience which generated the poem is born again. Much good poetry is a combination of controlled ranting and rhythmically balanced meditation."

He recited poetry all over America and made it a big part of his life in Bellingham and locally too. Just down the road from Bellingham, the Mt. Vernon newspaper, *The Skagit Argus Marquee*, printed an interview with him on Tuesday, March 19, 1985:

Since many are confused by what modern poetry is or isn't Huff paused when asked for a definition of poetry.

It had apparently been a while since anybody had asked him such a basic question.

In a thoughtfully slow reply, Huff said, "Poetry is an artistic form of verbal expression which emphasizes patterns of sound and imagery so that at its best it is capable of communicating thematic content and functions as an art object in itself."

Those of us without a masters degree in literature might interpret that as 'poetry is a painting in words,' a work of moving and somehow musical art.

Huff said the best way to begin appreciating this more modernistic and highbrow form of poetry might be to listen to 'spoken word' recordings that are available in most libraries.

Two paperback books Huff suggests to those who want to start their journey into this sometimes confusing art form are "Major British Poets" and "Major American Poets."

Reciting the opening lines of "Rainbow" from memory, Paul Lindholdt told me of a day with Huff in the fall of 1987. "He invited me to go hunting with him and he said I'm so old and feeble you'll probably have to hold me up." They took a trip north of Bellingham to Lake Terrell to go water-fowling. "Not pleasant to remember, but he got careless with a shotgun as though he was testing my trust and swung it right across my midsection at one point. The way I grew up with guns and hunting that was just absolutely forbidden, but I knew him well enough that it was like he was testing me. Nothing came of it, we continued on."

A local high school teacher who was a student of Huff's in the late 1980s shared this vision: "I had Huff for two classes: a modern American poetry class and a poetry writing class. I broke stride with standard opinion and thought he was an outstanding professor. He didn't realize it, but he was a gifted teacher. He talked about how much he hated teaching, how he was already long retired but the administration didn't know, and how he wasn't a good teacher. He said the only thing teaching did for him was to keep him from being homeless. He had an amazingly broad swath of knowledge for American poetry. He knew what was going on currently too—introduced me to Mary Oliver, Komunyakaa, Miller Williams, Donald Hall...He could pick up a piece of cold copy and you'd think he read it a dozen times, what a talented reader. I thought he was great—I just wanted to bring popcorn and watch. Often he was noticeably tipsy—or well beyond tipsy. Sometimes clearly shitfaced. He'd read a beautiful poem and cry. I heard him read something once by Amy Lowell, cried afterword, pounded a table, and said I defy you to find any son of a bitch today who can write a poem like that. Don't get me wrong—he wasn't drunk all the time. But much more so during the poetry writing class—that was at night. And it was often the case during that class. I certainly learned much more about poetry from those two classes than from eight or ten others I've taken over the years. And discounting the alcohol, I can only think of one teacher who had influenced and impacted my teaching more than Huff. Right before he retired, he gave a reading at Western. I recall that he followed the protocol that is today much ignored: he started and finished his reading with poems by other poets. That used to be the standard."

Poet Jason Graham has a vivid memory from 1988: "I met Huff back when I was a freshman at WWU. I was trying to get into his poetry class. He only addressed me from a lateral view, with grunts. 'Class is full.' I said, 'You knew my dad, Mike Graham, around 65'—he said you're a great poet.' Another askance look. And that was all. I should add, Huff was heavily seated in his office when the aforementioned, 1-sided conversation took place. He was wearing some soiled beige-whites, a la George C. Scott's portrayal of Ernest Hemingway in the film *Islands in the Stream* which was a weird adaptation of *The Old Man and the Sea*. Huff was an amazing poet. One of my favorite Huff poems appeared in *Jeopardy* magazine, 'Will Rogers to Wiley Post.' It's a beauty."

On his recommendation, I tracked down this poem, which appeared in the Spring 1990 issue, along with another yet-to-be compiled poem, "Documentary: In Memory of James Wright." In the Contributor's Notes at the end, following a list of Huff's publications and accolades, comes, "He is also one of our poets in residence at WWU, is newly retired, and missed by many."

Huff retired in June, 1989. His final years were lived with his wife Jane in Sandy Point, just north of Bellingham, on a turn of land visited by shorebirds.

So this night ends a visionary day
Between the bait and an abandoned nest
a great horned owl by starlight, signaling,
approaches, and I learn to realize
the wisdom of my own sharp, wintry thorn.

—from "December 21, 1970"

On Friday, August 13, 1993, the headline of *The Bellingham Herald* reported a robbery shooting at Fountain Hardware. The next day, that news was still headlining—'It seems like a nightmare'—but directly beneath that story is 'Former WWU professor dies in fire at Sandy Point.' It's an awful thing to read. While sitting deep in his chair on Friday night, Robert Huff's cigarette lit him on fire and the inferno took his life. Three days later the obituary gave notice that "At his request, no services will be held. His body will be cremated," and "Memorials may be made to the Audubon Society."

Codicil

No wake, please,
service or
funeral.
The ashes
at all cost
are to be

delivered
directly
into the
hands of near
survivors
who shall (if
need be) bribe
morticians
until what
was so loud
is partly
toward its still
patch of deep
sound beside
a stream in
the Union
Creek District
of the green
Rogue River
National
Forest, tucked
below one
or two clumps
of daisies—
which ought to
take—or if
not, any
fern that thrives
in shady
light will do
the trick at
least as well
or better.

I first became aware of Robert Huff without even knowing it. Working at the Western library one day, I saved an LP from the Discard Shelves. The title of the album was *The Sounds of Pacific Northwest Poetry* and without realizing it yet, tracks 8-10 on Side Two held the voice of the man who would urge me on in the writing of this. After reading Huff's poetry, I went looking for a biography beyond the brief words written on his bookcover flaps. So I went back to that long row of Discard Shelves at the library. The entire run of *Contemporary Authors* awaits its doom there. Western's library is in the process of ridding itself of books, of paper, and as physical evidence disappears from the shelves, this story of Robert Huff feels closely related. Specifically, it is the story of loss.

Why haven't his books been reprinted? There are several mentions of two manuscripts *Taking Her Sides on Immortality* and *Beginning in Winter* which have yet to be published. The first one I tracked down to a special collections library in New Hampshire. The curator there told me, "*Taking Her Sides on Immortality* is an 86 page typescript with a very positive blurb at the beginning by Annie Dillard but no contents page...We don't own the copyright on Huff's work, I'm afraid, and I don't know who does. In a horrible coincidence, we were writing the note for the collection and about to contact him for information the very same week that he died in the house fire."

Reflecting on Huff's legacy, Sam Green said, "One of the things I love about Bob Huff is that he left us a lot of poems...I love the fact that he left this body of work behind for us. And I would want to make sure that more people read it." For me his presence is felt strongly. He is still a part of this place—the mountains, rain-blown ocean air, forest and all those birds. Finally, I can't think of any better way to finish this, than how Robert Huff himself said farewell to many an evening or poetry reading, with a recital of one of his favorite poems. "Mr. Flood's Party" by Edwin Arlington Robinson begins:

> Old Eben Flood, climbing alone one night
> Over the hill between the town below
> And the forsaken upland hermitage
> That held as much as he should ever know

It's easy to see why Huff would identify with this poem, set on a path like the one he took many times himself, going up the hill from the lights of Bellingham to the university in the trees. And even after twenty years it isn't hard to hear that voice of Robert Huff, climbing with old Eben Flood, stopping to praise the bird above a moonlit town, enduring adversity to the very end:

> "For auld lang syne." The weary throat gave out,
> The last word wavered; and the song being done,
> He raised again the jug regretfully
> And shook his head, and was again alone.
> There was not much that was ahead of him,
> And there was nothing in the town below—
> Where strangers would have shut the many doors
> That many friends had opened long ago.

**Sources:**

*The Western Front* online collection
*The Bellingham Herald*
Sam Green interview with Tamara Belts, WWU Oral History Program, conducted February 5, 2009.
Lew Turco's online site, *Poetics and Ruminations*, "A Memoir of Robert Huff," April 20, 2011.
Wilson Library Special Collections, WWU
The Center for Pacific Northwest Studies, WWU

Correspondence with:
Knute Skinner, Sam Green, Gaylord Hart, Steven Dolmatz, Lew Turco, Paul Lindholdt, Lynda Schor, Kelly Cherry, Michael Oppenheimer, Chuck Robinson, Jason Graham, Roland Goodbody

Also thanks to Robert Bussard, Tamara Belts, Peter Smith, Eric Mastor, Tony Kurtz, Rob Cheesman, Larry Smith

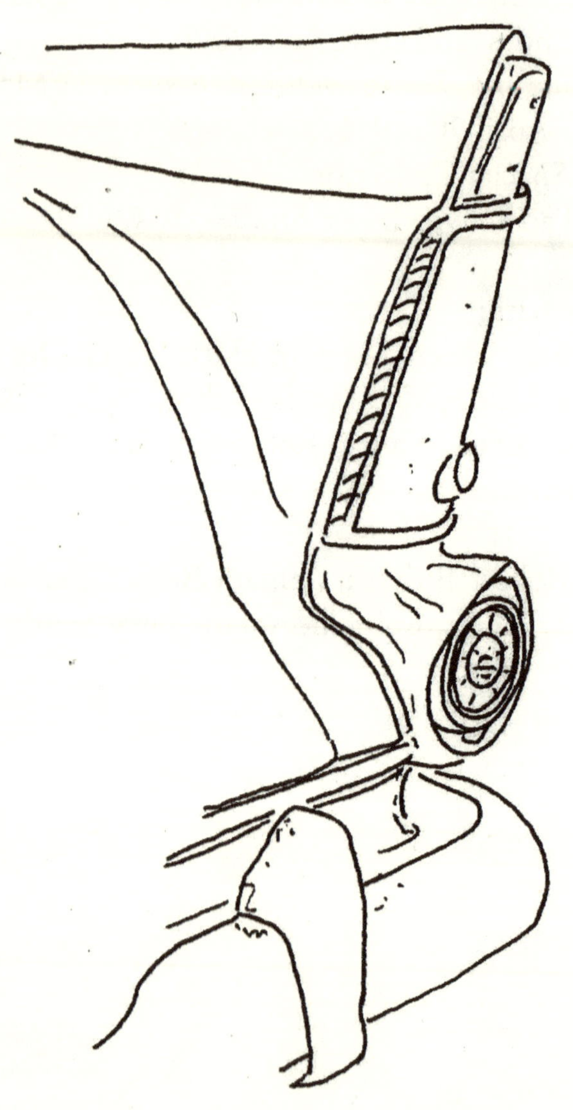

[A Super-8 movie. Set in summer of 1945]

Clouds.
Steam clouds from a factory drift over town.
Camera zooms into steam.
Camera pulls back from steam and it is a boiling pot of water on stove.
Pulling back further reveals a shaking hand holding uncooked spaghetti.
Sound: water boils and the quiet, reed-like shaking of pasta stalks.
Title appears:

***LITTLE ITALY***

Sound of knock on door.
The hands shove spaghetti back in cupboard on shelf, slams cupboard door shut.
Door opens to reveal a Japanese man in black clothes.
Spaghetti lets him inside and closes the apartment door.
Japanese man: "I am the last messenger. It is very important that I speak to you."
Spaghetti points at a chair, while he seats himself in another chair to listen.
The Japanese man reaches in his pocket and takes out a rolled up parchment tied with a ribbon.
Spaghetti hears the water boiling in the kitchen and offers: "Would you like some tea?"
Japanese man: "Yes please."
Spaghetti gets up and goes to the kitchen.

He opens a cabinet and takes out two cups, a box of tea, and sets them on the counter.
Then he gets a matchbox off the shelf.
He opens it and pours some powder into one of the cups.
The cup has a broken, taped handle.
Spaghetti drops teabags in each cup and pours hot water from pan.
He carries the two cups back to the other room.
He passes the broken cup to the Japanese man.
Spaghetti: "Be careful of the handle."
Japanese man: "Thank you."
Spaghetti: "You're welcome." Pause. "You are taking a risk coming here. You're lucky if nobody saw you."
Japanese man: "It is not difficult to be unseen." He takes sip of tea. "Now if you please." He holds out the scroll to Spaghetti. "This is for you."
Suddenly the Japanese man's body slumps out of the chair.
The cup of tea falls from his hand and hits the floor. The handle is broken free again.
Spaghetti calmly sips from his tea then leans down and sets his cup next to his chair.
He walks over to the Japanese man and grabs his ankles.
Spaghetti drags him across the floor, over to a closet.
He opens the door and pulls and heaves the Japanese man inside.
Other shoes and legs, tangled bodies, can be seen briefly.
Spaghetti shuts the door.

BLACK

Camera fades in to the sound of a popular Italian dance song.
Cigarette smoke surrounds Spaghetti's face and clears.

Spaghetti is in a little Italian restaurant.
He stares out the window at the sky.
A waitress appears next to him.
She holds a notepad and sighs at him: “One of these days it’s going to happen.”
After a moment, he replies: “The usual please.”
She rolls her eyes.
He doesn’t take his eyes from the sky.
He says: “Grilled cheese and a cola.”
She can’t write it. She gestures the pen at him like a sharp knife.
Exasperated, she asks: “Why don’t you ever order spaghetti?”
She looks over her shoulder at the cook framed in the kitchen window.
Waitress: “He never orders our spaghetti!”
Spaghetti is watching the sky.
A seagull wheels in the clouds.
The camera follows the bird as it turns.
The Italian song is the only sound.
The bird turns into an airplane, a bomber flying overhead.

The song has ended and Spaghetti enters his apartment with a police officer.
Policeman: “So help me, you better be telling the truth.”
Spaghetti stops at the closet, opens the door and pulls the lightbulb string.
Clothes on hooks and hangers and some shoes placed in a neat line.
Policeman, furious: “I don’t believe it!” He steps back and sees something on the table.
A model airplane, half built, surrounded by parts and paper directions.

The policeman storms over to it, pours glue over the kit and snaps it in Spaghetti's face.
Policeman: "You're a liar!" A broken airplane wing is stuck to Spaghetti's nose. "Like Pinocchio!"
Spaghetti raises his hands to cover his face.

Cut.

The crackling start of a record.
The music is "Ave Maria."
Fade in, time has passed.
Spaghetti is alone in his apartment.
The table is covered with the mess of broken airplane parts.
Spaghetti has a bandaged nose.
He lays a handful of scrolls on the table.
He unwraps one and weights the corners down.
It is part of a map.
The record starts to skip.
Spaghetti unrolls the next scroll and all the rest.
Like puzzle pieces, he fits them together.
When they are assembled, it makes sense to him.
A road travels out of town, to a mountaintop where an X is marked.

Fade out.

Sudden comic Italian opera music.
Spaghetti and another man stand next to a car parked under bare trees in front of a cold looking house. A 'For Sale' sign is stuck on the car window. They haggle. The owner shakes his head no, holds up his hands. Spaghetti begs, relents, and finally reaches into his pocket and gets his wallet. He counts

out some bills. Then more. And more. Then he shakes everything out of it, into the hands of the car owner.

Postcard scene. That car is driving up a road to the cloudy mountain.

WHITE

Spaghetti, knee deep in snow. He has a compass in his hand and the taped together scrolls rolled under his arm. He stops at a spot and looks around. Nothing but snow.
Slowly, he sits down in the white and stares at the distant city.
Close up of his face as he turns around.
Six Japanese men approach him.
One of them calmly points.
Spaghetti turns to look at the city and there is a bright flash of light on his face.
A thundering rumble.
Spaghetti closes his eyes tightly and keeps them closed.

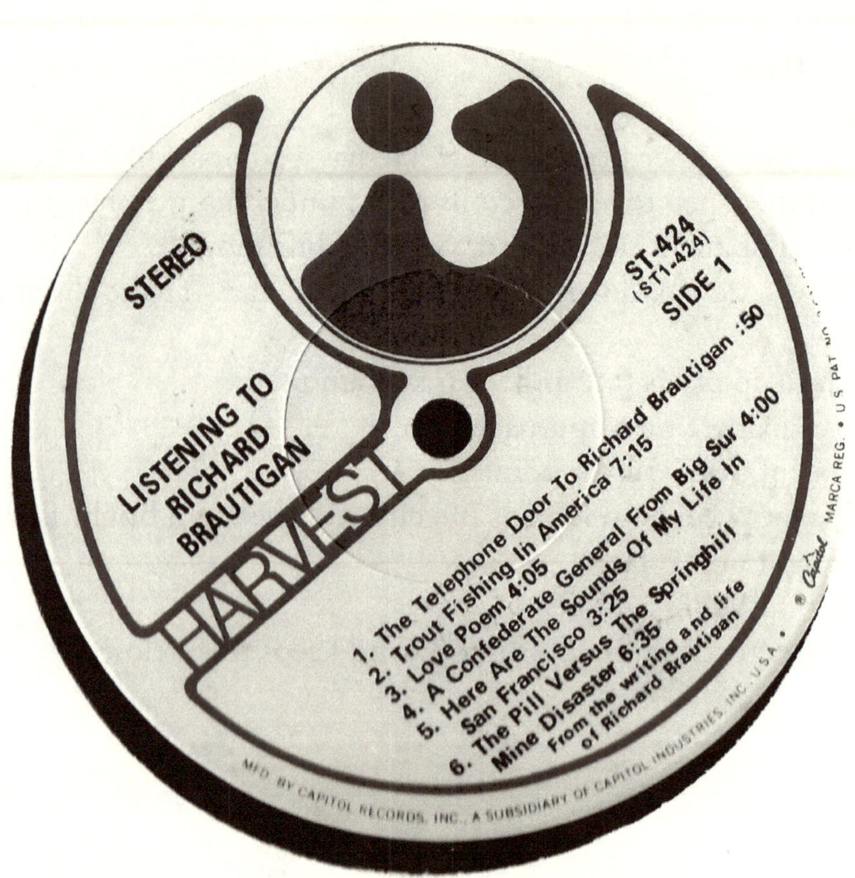
STEREO
ST-424
(ST1-424)
SIDE 1
LISTENING TO
RICHARD
BRAUTIGAN
HARVEST
1. The Telephone Door To Richard Brautigan :50
2. Trout Fishing In America 7:15
3. Love Poem 4:05
4. A Confederate General From Big Sur 4:00
5. Here Are The Sounds Of My Life In
San Francisco 3:25
6. The Pill Versus The Springhill
Mine Disaster 6:35
From the writing and life
of Richard Brautigan
MFD. BY CAPITOL RECORDS, INC., A SUBSIDIARY OF CAPITOL INDUSTRIES, INC. U.S.A.
Capitol
MARCA REG.

On Saturday morning, January 7, 2012, I went to Seattle to meet John Barber. John is editor of *Richard Brautigan, Essays on the Writings and Life* (2007) as well as curator of the comprehensive online site, *Richard Brautigan Bibliography and Archive* at: www.brautigan.net.

Down in the boiler room of the Fairmont Hotel is a narrow crowded café. We found a little table and he allowed me to record this interview. I was a little worried that later on I wouldn't be able to hear him over the espresso machines steaming and clunking, cups and plates clattering, all the forks falling on the checkerboard floor, a weird pinball sound, conversations all around, the big band soundtrack CD with a crazy "In the Mood" track skipping in the background, fading for a while then reappearing.

Setting a copy of *An Unfortunate Woman* between us, I stopped at page 70, where Brautigan's journal suddenly wonders what happened to time, as it jumps from San Francisco into a blur. I asked John if perhaps that missing time could be filled in:

That was in the Spring of 1982. He had actually been contracted to be a visiting professor in the English department prior to that and he started in April. During early March, he was traveling and the English department at Montana State University was writing him letter after letter saying, "Are you coming, we really need to know?" and he signed the contract on the very last day that he could and returned it.

He had a ranch in Paradise Valley, just south of Livingston. He was also given an apartment in the married student housing dorm at Montana State University. It was a high-rise sort of dorm. He also stayed in a very inexpensive motel in Bozeman that I showed him. $9.95 cents a night. He would often phone me and say, "Come and pick me up and let's go to Bozeman and I'll buy your drinks." So I would drive fifty miles to his ranch to pick him up and then fifty miles back to Bozeman, and then he insisted on closing down every bar, every possible opportunity for drinking. Main Street Bozeman had a number of them, but he had two or three favorites. He really liked the Eagles' Nest, the VFW bar.

*Was he known there?*

He was known everywhere. He was, however, very hard to be around because he was always drinking and always had a lot to drink. And people that are always drinking can be very tiring. He would frequently just get up and go sit down at a table with strangers and start talking to them and ask them really pointed, embarrassing questions and then argue with them about their answers to the point where they broke down or got really uncomfortable. So he was fairly obnoxious and people knew that and some people didn't like it so much. Despite that, he would come and hang out in Bozeman searching for what he called "the great American good time," and I would provide the transportation back and forth. One time, I gave him a ride in a yellow school bus and he writes about that.

*He thanks you in this book. And you stopped at the grocery store for him too. What did you get?*

I think we got some wine and spaghetti.

*I think he mentions he got lots of lettuce. He wanted to make a salad.*

That could be. I don't remember exactly, but I remember we got two or three plastic bags full of groceries. And then we got back on the bus and I drove him, dropped him off in front of his house.

*Why were you driving a school bus?*

My job was working for a tour bus company based in Bozeman. That was the way I was putting myself through school. When working with a local or smaller group, I would drive a school bus as opposed to the big tour buses. There was a girl scout camp up the Yellowstone River from where Richard Brautigan lived and I was going to pick up a group camped there and bring them back to Bozeman. I had to drive right by his house to get to this campground. The night before my trip he was in town, so I just said, "Look, I'm going this way tomorrow and if you don't have any problem riding a school bus I can give you a ride."

*Did he sit right up in the front with you?*

Yes, he sat in the front seat of a school bus.

*Could you talk about how you found Richard Brautigan as a teacher?*

It was a creative writing class. The very first thing that he said was, "If you want to learn to write, I can't teach you. That's something you're going to have to do through your own process." And although he didn't talk about it, it was clear that he had been through his own process to learn how to write, which is pretty well documented. He started with poetry, so he could learn how to put words together to make a sentence, and then having felt success at writing a sentence, he felt he could take on a novel. So he said, "Instead of teaching you how to write I can give you the benefit of my experience in the publishing world. I can talk to you about those sorts of things and I can respond to your writing and give you some feedback."

He would stand in front of the classroom, or lean against the table in front of the classroom because he had a broken leg that his doctor had decided not to put in a cast. He was walking around with a broken leg using a cane. He was dressed entirely in blue denim, blue denim jeans and a blue denim farm jacket, worn brown cowboy boots and a black wool felt Elmer Fudd hat, with flaps that were up and tied across the top. And of course, his signature glasses, long blonde hair and the signature long droopy moustache. He looked very much like his photograph on the front of one of his early novels.

The class met once a week and each meeting was a workshop where we shared our writings with each other. Brautigan responded with encouragement. At the end of each class he would provide a writing prompt and we would go off for a week and work on this prompt. One of the prompts that I remember was to go someplace on the campus that you haven't been before and write about what you see and what you experience there. We would write about it and then come back and go around the room, each of us reading what we had written and then everyone in the class would respond. Brautigan's response was always, "I like that. That's very interesting. Keep writing." He would never say something like, "Well maybe you should shift paragraph two and three or it seems like something's missing where you try to make a transition between these two ideas—" He would never say that. His written comments were always very short, "this is good, keep writing," and then that was the end of it.

There was one assignment where we could write something longer and I wrote about the time that I had spent on steamboat hotels going up and down the Mississippi River and he called me to say, "I'm sitting here with [girlfriend at the time] and we're reading your paper and just rolling on the floor in laughter. I wanted you to know that this is really great. When I finish this, if you like, I'm going to share it with my agent and see—" and I thought Ohhh!—and nothing ever came of it. Still, it was pretty exciting that he called me to say that he liked what I was doing.

At the end of the very first class meeting, after everyone had left, I walked up to him and I said, "I would like to be friends with you outside of class." He looked at me, he had this long hook-like nose, and he looked at me down his nose and I thought he was thinking, "Well, I've been approached by a lot of groupies but never by a male"...Just this kind of long pause...and then he said, "Let's go to the Eagles' Nest and have a drink and talk about it, but I think I would like that." So I gave him a ride to the Eagles' Nest and we had lots of drinks and that was it. That was the start of the friendship.

*Didn't he have a white car?*

He had a car that had been given to him by Greg Keeler. It was in his barn. He also had an abandoned car, this rusting thing that he would sit on. It was fabulous. You would sit on it, leaning up against the windshield and look at the Absaroka Mountains. They were snow covered year round so you were lying out there in the sun and looking at these huge soaring mountains that are, in my experience, the most magnificent mountains in the country. The other car was in his writing barn, just sitting there. He never drove, he never learned to drive, I don't think he ever drove anything.

He really didn't talk about anything that had to do with him personally and I made a point of not pushing this information. He never talked about his childhood, he never said anything about his family, he never said anything about San Francisco or Japan.

*Would he talk about what he was writing?*

He was working on *An Unfortunate Woman* while the class was going on. He told me several times during the class period that he was working on the book and that he had written x-number of chapters and it was very sad, about a friend who was dying. He never said anything to me about it, he just frequently mentioned that his friend was dying. He never gave his friend a name, but that was very typical. Throughout all of his books there's a nameless narrator. He never uses names for anybody. *My friend*, or *a friend*, and I think this is part of what we can point to, to say that much of the content in Brautigan's books is fictionalized autobiography.

One afternoon he called and said, "My friend just died, bring a bottle of whiskey and come over." And so I did. I spent the evening with him and it was an amazing experience. The next day I said, "I wrote about our experience in my journal," and he got very upset I had written about a private experience that we had shared together. On one hand, I can understand that. On the other hand he was a writer and he kept a journal and he wrote about things that happened to him during the day, so I thought okay, it's a private thing, but at the same time he's hypocritical being upset with me for doing something that he would have done as a writer. He concluded by saying, "If you ever show that to anybody before I'm dead, I will haunt you for the rest of my life." And I did and he does. So I guess that's fair.

He never showed me anything that he was working on. The only times that he talked about his own work, was the first time I went to his house, he had just received a box of copies of *So The Wind Won't Blow It All Away* from his publisher. He gave me a copy and, he was kind enough to sign it. So he said something about his book there. I had other copies of his books which later I brought to him and he was gracious enough to sign, but he never talked about them. Another time, I told him that I would really like to get copies of his earliest books—

Waitress: Did you guys order three cheese croissants?

JB: No, we didn't, I'm sorry.

*Three, no less.*

She's only holding two…He told me in response, "Well they're out of print. They're very hard to get, and they're very expensive." I didn't know it at the time, but he was being absolutely truthful with me. His earliest books ARE out of print and they ARE hard to get and they ARE very expensive. He had a few of his books in translation that were on the bookshelf in his living room, but other than that his house was very sparsely furnished, just minimal furniture. Nicely done though, he had taken this Montana ranch house, brought carpenters and redwood lumber from

Bolinas and redone the inside of his house. It was really fine, detailed finished carpentry. And a guesthouse which was an old smokehouse next to the main house had been completely redone with this redwood lumber. The backyard of his house was overgrown, the front was mowed. I don't know who mowed it, but the back part of the place was grown up, the weeds were waist high and there were deer. Away from the house was a grove of cottonwood trees. When they bloomed they dropped white fluffy seeds that floated around and collected on the porch, turning into a giant ball. The chicken coop was there but there were no chickens. It didn't look like chickens had been there in quite a while.

*Was writing your story about him really how it ended between you?*

That was part of it. We had a disagreement and he told me to go away, to never see him again. I saw him once more after that, on the sidewalk, in Bozeman. I walked up to him and he was very surprised. It was as if he had seen a ghost. I said, "Look, I don't want our friendship to end this way. I'm very sorry. I'm sorry for my part in the disagreement and I apologize and I hope that we can still be friends." He replied, "I don't know. I'll have to think about it. I'll let you know." And then I wrote once after that and again apologized, "I was thinking of you and I wanted to apologize again." I sent the letter to his Livingston address. It was forwarded to him in Japan. I got a letter in reply from Japan. It was very short. He said, "Forget the past. It ain't worth it. Let's try to get together when I'm back in Montana. I would like that." And that was the last thing that I ever heard from him. He never contacted me, never got in touch. I actually had a premonition, a thought that sometime I would open the paper and learn that Richard Brautigan was dead. Sure enough, I did, and he was.

Generally speaking when an author dies, his or her literary career continues going in the same direction that it was going at the time of their death. If it's down, that's the way it goes. If it's up, then death just helps it because now there's a reason to republish everything. Richard Brautigan's literary career has been totally the opposite of this. Despite the fact that his literary career was trashed at the time of his death, he continues to attract an incredible following of readers. Everyday somebody discovers Richard Brautigan for the first time and claims him as his or her favorite writer.

As an author, he was extremely courageous because every book that he wrote was not a sell-out, not a cop-out—he did what he wanted to do. It took him twenty-something publishers to get *Trout Fishing in America* published, but he did and it sold over a million copies. Each of his other books is a particular vision. I don't think that credit is given for that in a world where we expect certain packages.

Richard Brautigan very much enjoyed a public persona and he created one for himself. He would look in the windows of stores and criticize rock stars posing on the covers of their albums, yet he would do exactly the same thing for his own books. He controlled everything about his early books, even the photographer that would take the picture for the cover and the typeface and the page formatting. It was totally unusual in America at that time for an author to have complete control over their books. And he did.

That's why the first omnibus, the three volumes have three different type settings reproduced, as he says, in the likeness of the original. That was all part of what he was controlling. So he's criticizing people for being on the covers of their record albums, yet he's posing like a rock star on the covers of his books, and always with a different woman. He was purposely mysterious about his background and he was using that mystery as a way to market himself, promote interest in himself, as this kind of Emily Dickinson-like character from a parallel universe that's speaking in telegrams, using language that William Carlos Williams would approve of. He cultivated this mystery about himself, but at the same time he walks around being a public person promoting himself and his books. There is a story that he saw someone in a bookstore looking at one of his books and he said, "Steal that book. Take it home. That's my book. It's a good one."

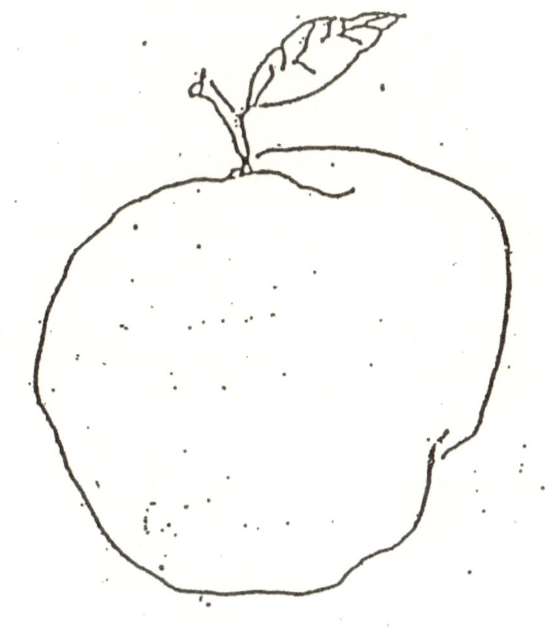

# *ELBOWS & KNEES*

## *Essays & Plays*

Written by Allen Frost

2003-2013

## Books by Good Deed Rain

*Saint Lemonade*, Allen Frost, 2014. Two novels illustrated by the author in the manner of the old Big Little Books.

*Playground*, Allen Frost, 2014. Poems collected from seven years of chapbooks.

*Roosevelt*, Allen Frost, 2015. A Pacific Northwest novel set in July, 1942, when a boy and a girl search for a missing elephant. Illustrated throughout by Fred Sodt.

*5 Novels*, Allen Frost, 2015. Novels written over five years, featuring circus giants, clockwork animals, detectives and time travelers.

*The Sylvan Moore Show*, Allen Frost, 2015. A short story omnibus of 193 stories written over 30 years.

*Town in a Cloud*, Allen Frost, 2015. A three-part book of poetry, written during the Bellingham rainy seasons of fall, winter, and spring.

*A Flutter of Birds Passing Through Heaven: A Tribute to Robert Sund.* 2016. Edited by Allen Frost and Paul Piper. The story of a legendary Ish River poet & artist.

*At the Edge of America*, Allen Frost, 2016. Two novels in one book blend time travel in a mythical poetic America.

*Lake Erie Submarine*, Allen Frost, 2016. A two week vacation in Ohio inspired these poems, illustrated by the author.

*and Light*, Paul Piper, 2016. Poetry written over three years. Illustrated with watercolors by Penny Piper.

*The Book of Ticks*, Allen Frost, 2017. A giant collection of 8 mysterious adventures featuring Phil Ticks. Illustrated throughout by Aaron Gunderson.

*I Can Only Imagine*, Allen Frost, 2017. 5 adventures of love and heartbreak dreamed in an imaginary world. Cover & color illustrations by Annabelle Barrett.

*The Orphanage of Abandoned Teenagers,* Allen Frost, 2017. A fictional guide for teens and their parents. Illustrated by the author.

*In the Valley of Mystic Light: An Oral History of the Skagit Valley Arts Scene,* 2017. Edited by Claire Swedberg & Rita Hupy.

*Different Planet,* Allen Frost, 2017. A collection of four science fiction adventures featuring reincarnation, robots, talking animals, outer space and clones. Cover & illustrations by Laura Vasyutynska.

*Go with the Flow: A Tribute to Clyde Sanborn.* 2018. Edited by Allen Frost. The life and art of a timeless river poet.

*Homeless Sutra,* Allen Frost, 2018. Four stories: Sylvan Moore, a flying monk, a water salesman, and a guardian rabbit.

*The Lake Walker,* Allen Frost 2018. A little novel set in black and white like one of those old European movies about death and life.

*A Hundred Dreams Ago*, Allen Frost, 2018. A winter book of poetry and prose. Illustrated by Aaron Gunderson.

*Almost Animals*, Allen Frost, 2018. A collection of linked stories, thinking about what makes us animals.

*The Robotic Age*, Allen Frost, 2018. A vaudeville magician and his robot track down ghosts. Illustrated throughout by Aaron Gunderson.

*Kennedy*, Allen Frost, 2018. This sequel to *Roosevelt* is a coming-of-age fable set during two weeks in 1962 in a mythical Kennedy-land. Illustrated throughout by Fred Sodt.

*Fable*, Allen Frost, 2018. There's something going on in this country and I can best relate it in fable: the parable of the rabbits, a bedtime story, and the diary of our trip to Ohio.

*Elbows & Knees: Essay & Plays*, Allen Frost. 2018. A thrilling collection of writing about some of my favorite subjects, from B-movies to Brautigan.

www.ingramcontent.com/pod-product-compliance
Lightning Source LLC
Chambersburg PA
CBHW032026050726
47590CB00006B/2316

* 9 7 8 1 6 4 4 6 7 4 6 5 9 *

composition STUDIES

Volume 51, Number 2
Fall 2023

## Contents

## Book Reviews

## Editorial Introduction: What Is Good Writing?

Following our spring issue's Where We Are on AI and Writing, and on the heels of many new publications, conference presentations, departmental workshops, and thinkpieces on generative language technologies, we noticed something: our discipline has a propensity to discuss generative AI in terms of what it means for students and student writing before we figure out what it means for...well, us. That is true here at the journal, too. We have spent little time on what generative AI would mean for the staff and readership of *Composition Studies*—that is, for us as academic writers, readers, reviewers, editors, and publishers.

In response to this observation, we found ourselves wondering: What would it mean to explore what generative AI means for professional academic writers (instead of jumping immediately to thinking about students)?

We've come at this question sideways a few times before. Our spring 2023 editorial asked "why write?" With that question, we meant to imply, among many other things, something like "why write when AI can write for you?" But there's more to it than just the question of why we write, though that is an important question. There is also the question of how we judge and interpret quality and efficacy with respect to meaning in writing. (And though we might resist judging, we do.) Secondly, we've come at the question of good writing sideways in our research. In presentations and workshops on the Teaching for Transfer curriculum, we are often asked: is the writing that students are transferring...good? To be truthful, we have often found these questions puzzling—as if good writing could be evaluated separately from the contexts from which it emerges and into which it transfers. Nonetheless, the question persists.

So when our observations about AI and writing raised old questions anew—how we imagine that we understand what good writing looks like; whether we understand how to create good writing; and whether we understand how to teach toward good writing—we thought we'd come at it sideways.

To explore what good writing is, then, we conducted a small and by now very-common textual experiment. To start, we fed ChatGPT 3.5 two different prompts, which are below alongside excerpted sections of ChatGPT's responses. (We chose ChatGPT simply because it's the most popular generative language model currently.) In conducting this experiment, we were interested not only in what it would produce–and what our responses to that would be–but also to explicitly explore whether some or all of those responses were what we would consider good writing.

*Composition Studies 51.2 (2023): 9–17*

## An Editorial Experiment in Genre

*Prompt 1*

"Write an editorial introduction for a composition studies journal."

*Response 1*

Title: Redefining Composition Studies: Exploring Multimodal Approaches and Digital Literacies

This editorial aims to highlight the evolving nature of Composition Studies and the growing significance of multimodal approaches and digital literacies in the field.

This reads like a straight old-school thesis.

While the importance of written communication remains undeniably significant, it is essential for Composition Studies to acknowledge that communication in the 21st century is multimodal. In our increasingly digital world, individuals communicate through not only text but also images, videos, audio, and other visual and spatial modes.

I think people may not realize this as much as they should. These sentences show just how much this sentiment is both a) still unrecognized and b) a commonplace.

Digital literacies encompass a wide range of skills, including the ability to critically evaluate online information, create and curate digital content, collaborate in virtual spaces, and use digital tools effectively.

This is a simplified if straightforward definition. Some version of this is probably on 1000 educational webpages, from academics departments to libraries and so on.

This shift can be daunting, but it is essential for educators to embrace the potential of digital tools and media to enhance learning outcomes and engage students.

Fair enough, but we don't always use digital tools or understand how to. So here is what the limit of AI: what does this even mean in practice?

Composition Studies no longer exists in isolation.

I mean, lol, OK? This is true, but just laughable cliche to the max.

Educators must ensure that all students have access to the tools and resources necessary for effective digital literacy development.

Easier said than done yet again! What does it mean that all students have access because this is a hard one to accomplish. More empty assertion without anything that would work toward making it true.

Multimodal approaches and digital literacies are reshaping the way we think about communication and writing instruction.

The cliche, lol! But, also, this reads like a draft sentence from my dissertation circa 2011. /embarrassed

Through this journal and others like it, we hope to foster the exchange of ideas and research that will continue to shape the future of *Composition Studies.*

"And others like it"–genre fail. But also, pretty circular logic here.

*Prompt 2*

"Write an editorial for a journal called *Composition Studies* that is dedicated to the range of professional practices associated with rhetoric and composition: teaching college writing; theorizing rhetoric and composing; administering writing related programs; preparing the field's future teacher-scholars. The editorial you write should be no more than 500 words and appropriate for the fall 2023 issue of the journal."

*Response 2*

Title: Navigating the Dynamic Landscape of Rhetoric and Composition

As we usher in the Fall 2023 issue of *Composition Studies*, we find ourselves at the heart of an ever-evolving landscape of rhetoric and composition. This journal has long been dedicated to the multifaceted professional practices associated with our field,

It's a bit self-aggrandizing, but it reads like something we would write. Not sure whether to be impressed or embarrassed.

With each passing issue, we continue to celebrate and interrogate the complex, nuanced nature of our discipline.

This sounds very much like us. And it's true. Yikes.

In this issue, you will find insights into innovative teaching methods, the integration of technology into the writing classroom, and the exploration of inclusive practices that prioritize the voices of all students.

This is totally untrue…but well said. lol.

Rhetoric and composition theory, the intellectual bedrock of our field, continues to develop and diversify. We encourage our readers to embrace the rich theoretical tapestry that defines our discipline and engage in dialogue with fellow scholars.

What a weird first sentence. The second is a sentiment we've expressed, but.. the bedrock tapestry? Holy mixed metaphors.

We hope this issue serves as a catalyst for meaningful conversations, sparks intellectual curiosity, and inspires you to continue your vital work in rhetoric and composition. Your participation enriches our field, and together, we chart the course for the future.

This is true. And also sort of how we would probably write it. We are choosing to laugh rather than cry, right?

## Reactions and Ruminations

### *Writing as/with technology*

We find ourselves continually thinking of ChatGPT as a technology. If we think of writing as requiring technology and as a technology itself (a la Dennis Baron in *A Better Pencil*), then it's not impossible that writing could become an obsolete technology—at least in the forms we know it currently—much like an inkwell or an abacus. If we think of writing as a technology that structures thought (a la Walter Ong), we might wonder what could replace it. Would something like prompt engineering—which is the reiterative process we engaged in very briefly in our experiment—structure or restructure thought in ways that are better and worse than writing as is currently configured? Put bluntly: what would change about thinking if writing, with and as a technology as we know it, changed dramatically?

### *within dynamic situations*

In the time took to conduct our experiment, reflect on it, and write it up, the variables have changed yet again: Google Docs–in which we compose these editorials–has just added an AI assistant that is lurking in the left-hand pane, every moment, offering to "Help me write."

*full of definitions and disagreement*

ChatGPT believes—well, ChatGPT stated given a certain prompt at a certain time—that "Good writing is like a well-crafted painting: it draws you in with its clarity, creativity, and ability to convey ideas effectively." Certainly, we believe in writing as techne and poiesis. But, clearly, we disagree that clarity, creativity, and communication are the only ways to judge the quality of texts.

*with post-hoc attention to the ethics of experimentation.*

Ethically speaking, we conducted this experiment with knowledge of—and therefore in some ways despite—knowing that large language models like ChatGPT require an inordinate amount of resources to train, operate, and query. (An inordinate amount that increases enormously with every new training model.) Our hope is that investigating a technology like ChatGPT this way might lead to less use of the technology overall; even so, this editorial participates in some small way in that resource use. What's more, we do not explore here how a definition of "good writing" might require—in the first place—to take into account the resource use of the technologies required to create that writing. Indeed, it might.

## Conclusion: So, Like, What Is Good Writing?

In returning to the central question of what generative AI would mean for professional academic writers, we are met with a flood of other related questions.

What would it mean if we had written this entire editorial with generative AI? Would it have been *de facto* bad writing because it was machinic writing? Would it have been bad because it missed the mark on many generic conventions of an editorial, or because it constructed mixed and contradictory metaphors, or because it reiterated commonplaces and cliches?

What would it mean if we wrote the summaries of the journal's content (in the In This Issue section that follows) with AI? Would it be OK–and for whom–if our reviewers used generative language models to create anonymous reviews for article submissions? What if we used it to rate book review and course design proposals?

What would it mean if we used it to write the decision letters—those accept, revise & resubmit, and rejection notes—that go back to authors?

(And then: What of the genres and genre sets of the discipline? How about using it to tailor a job application letter? What about to draft a template for a letter of recommendation?)

Could ChatGPT, in any of those contexts, produce "good writing"? We think not.

But: Why not?

## In this Issue

### *At a Glance*

This issue's At A Glance is "Ameliorating Violence in Composition: A Need for Vigilance" by Scott Gage and Kristie S. Fleckenstein. In this graphic, the authors draw together the insights from their edited collection, *Violence in the Work of Composition: Recognizing, Intervening, Ameliorating*, for a cleverly designed triad that links nine dynamics of violence across the discipline: three types of violence, three spaces of violence, and three ways of responding to–and, thereby ameliorating–violence in composition.

### *Aricles*

Qianqian Zhang-Wu, Alison Stephens, and Neal Lerner's "Meaningful Writing Projects Among Multilingual Undergraduate Writers: Personal, Practical and Developmental" extends the results of *The Meaningful Writing Project* by exploring "the meaningful writing experiences" of 325 multilingual students. The qualitative study discovered that students find their writing more meaningful when it's connected to their "identities, histories, and aspirations," which leads the authors to offer five premises about meaningful writing and dispositions that help students see value in their writing.

In "Building Bridges and Changing the Story: Recognizing Funds of Knowledge in Summer Bridge Programs," Maria Conti Maravillas reports on a qualitative study of summer bridge program websites. Through a detailed survey, Conti Maravillas finds that bridge program sites provide a partial but promising orientation to funds of knowledge discourse. Conti Maravillas challenges compositionists to engage their student affairs and academic support colleagues by using this partial engagement with funds of knowledge discourse as a tool for facilitating fuller collaboration, not only on websites but also in program design and implementation.

Cynthia A. Cochran, Rebecca Day Babcock, and Aliethia Dean's "Writing about Writing: A Snapshot in Time" searches for the range and depth of understandings of Writing About Writing (WAW) through surveying more than 30 faculty who teach the curriculum. What they find is multifaceted: a dispersed but coherent set of definitions and conceptual understandings of WAW; a clear set of course foci for WAW; an emerging but diversified canon of readings for teaching WAW; and a mappable set of classroom activities, course goals, and writing assignments that demonstrate how WAW is enacted in writing classrooms in the US and Canada.

Brad Jacobson and Rachael Shah argue for a Deweyan "democratic design" approach to program leadership in "Building Our Ideals into Program Structures: Democratic Design in Program Administration." Using a case study approach, they outline three principles–stakeholder leadership, political vision, and epistemic equity–that can be applied across a variety of programmatic opportunities. Jacobson and Shah argue that democratic design helps leaders in composition studies align their values with program design and administration.

*Course Designs*

A. Kay Emmert, Andrew Moss, David Morris, and Andrew Bowman's course, "Principles of Business Communication," brings together two branches of technical and professional communication through an ecological, social justice-based frame for contemporary students. The goal of the course is for students to apply professional communication to workplace writing contexts. In redesigning this course through a broad writing pedagogy lens, the authors come to three conclusions about productive course revision: 1) it "begins with taking stock of everyone and everything in the ecological frame, including students, instructors, program administrators, advisors, and other departments;" 2) it "must continue beyond a single revision;" and 3) it "provides a professional development opportunity" that must be balanced "with a sense of what labor we could consider part of instructional duties and what labor we would need to compensate fairly."

Before teaching "Introduction to the Theories and Practices of Composition Teaching," Antonio Byrd and Virginia M. Schwarz wondered how to create a course that engaged graduate students from across English disciplines but avoided an introduction to the field that "reified whiteness." They formed a cross-institutional partnership and created "anti-oppressive, inclusive" introductory composition graduate courses for their individual universities. By adopting a "social justice theme and humanizing course content" Byrd and Schwarz prioritized equity, inclusion, and diversity while still attending to course coverage. The cross-institutional partnership helped these two teacher-scholars to see "graduate education as a site to amplify and actualize the social justice commitments of the field."

*Where We Are: Ungrading*

This issue's Where We Are focuses on ungrading, an assessment approach popularized by *Ungrading: Why Rating Students Undermines Learning (and What to Do Instead)*, a 2020 edited collection by Susan Blum. As Megan Von Bergen's contribution sketches out, ungrading has a longer history and joins—but is not co-identical with–assessment practices like contract grading, labor-based grading, and even portfolio grading, all of which have received much attention in the discipline as equity-oriented alternatives to traditional grading. Ungrading's popularity is also linked to the COVID-19 pandemic, as Ellen C. Carillo makes clear (and as will be explored more in a forthcoming *Pedagogy: Critical Approaches to Teaching Literature, Language, Composition, and Culture* special issue on the same topic), perhaps because it reduces stress and complements movements in generative AI technologies. Conversely, Hannah Davis' contribution to this WWA stages a comparative self-study, testing ungrading against other assessment mechanisms. She finds that "even in the ungraded section of my course, students' summative self-assessments were more likely to be performative, used to prove or justify a desired grade," which complicates the relationship between reflection, self-assessment, and engagement-based grading. Finally, Maggie Fernandes, Emily Brier, and Megan McIntyre argue against the discourse of ungrading, for two reasons: first, because, in their words, we are still assigning grades in the end (and students know that) and, second, because discourse on ungrading "flattens the critiques of normative and oppressive writing assessment that our field has challenged for decades" especially with respect to "linguistic diversity and disability justice." In other words, ungrading discourse needs, at the very least, a deeper sense of the disciplinary efforts that predate it.

We hope you enjoy these four provocative pieces on an exciting, complex, and contested assessment practice.

*Book Reviews*

This issue's book reviews cluster around three areas of crucial interest to the discipline: multi- and translingual writers; methods and methodologies; and investigations of the discipline's past and future.

Scholars and teachers interested in multilingual and transnational writers will find reviews of four volumes that take up those topics from different perspectives. These books highlight how multilingual writers of all kinds have contributed to writing research writ large; how translingual approaches to teaching differ across continents; how American institutions of higher education can better support international, multilingual students; and how writing program development and administration functions in particular multilingual contexts.

Similarly, this issue includes a trio of reviews of books that highlight new and established methods and methodologies in writing research. The books reviewed overview not only specific research methods—like lifelong and lifewide literacy research, archival research, and collaborative storying research–but also how those methods function in teaching and professionalization contexts.

*Desegregation State* provides a historical study of the "systemic ways writing programs were informed by desegregation policies" in Georgia between 1970 and 1988. Both the review and the book make clear that the discipline has much to learn about its racialized past from historical study and much to learn about its racialized present, too. Our hope is that the reviews on translingual and multilingual writers, along with the At A Glance for this issue, will go some way toward learning those lessons and ameliorating their historical and contemporary harms.

Finally, this issue contains the list of *Composition Studies* Reviewers for 2022, which usually appears in our spring issue. We all—journal staff and authors together—remain indebted to and grateful for our colleagues who devote their time, energy, and attention to providing reviews of article submissions.

MD & Kt
Boston and Orlando
November 2023

# At a Glance

## Ameliorating Violence in Composition: A Need for Vigilance

*Scott Gage and Kristie S. Fleckenstein*

Violence is a constant presence circulating around and through the work of composition. A force circumscribing the capacity of individuals and communities to thrive and flourish, violence inflicts harm in three interconnected ways: (1) physically (direct violence), (2) systemically (structural violence), and (3) communally (cultural violence). We all, as teachers, scholars, and administrators, contend everyday with these forms of violence across disciplinary sites and practices. The contributors to *Violence in the Work of Composition: Recognizing, Intervening, Ameliorating* reveal both violence's ubiquity and its seeming intractability. But, at the same time, they also reveal hope in perceiving and responding to such instances of harm, not just once but over and over again as the situation demands. These compositionists point us to three responses to violence that may blunt its force, however temporarily: (1) recognizing (seeing violence as violence), (2) intervening (resisting and disrupting violence), and (3) ameliorating (committing to violence's long-term cessation). These strategies cannot be a one-time effort if we are to redress violence's relationship with composition. Rather, the strategies require persistence and vigilance. Without that, violence will continue to shape and limit the horizon of possibility in our classrooms, programs, and writing centers.

*Composition Studies 51.2 (2023): 18–19*

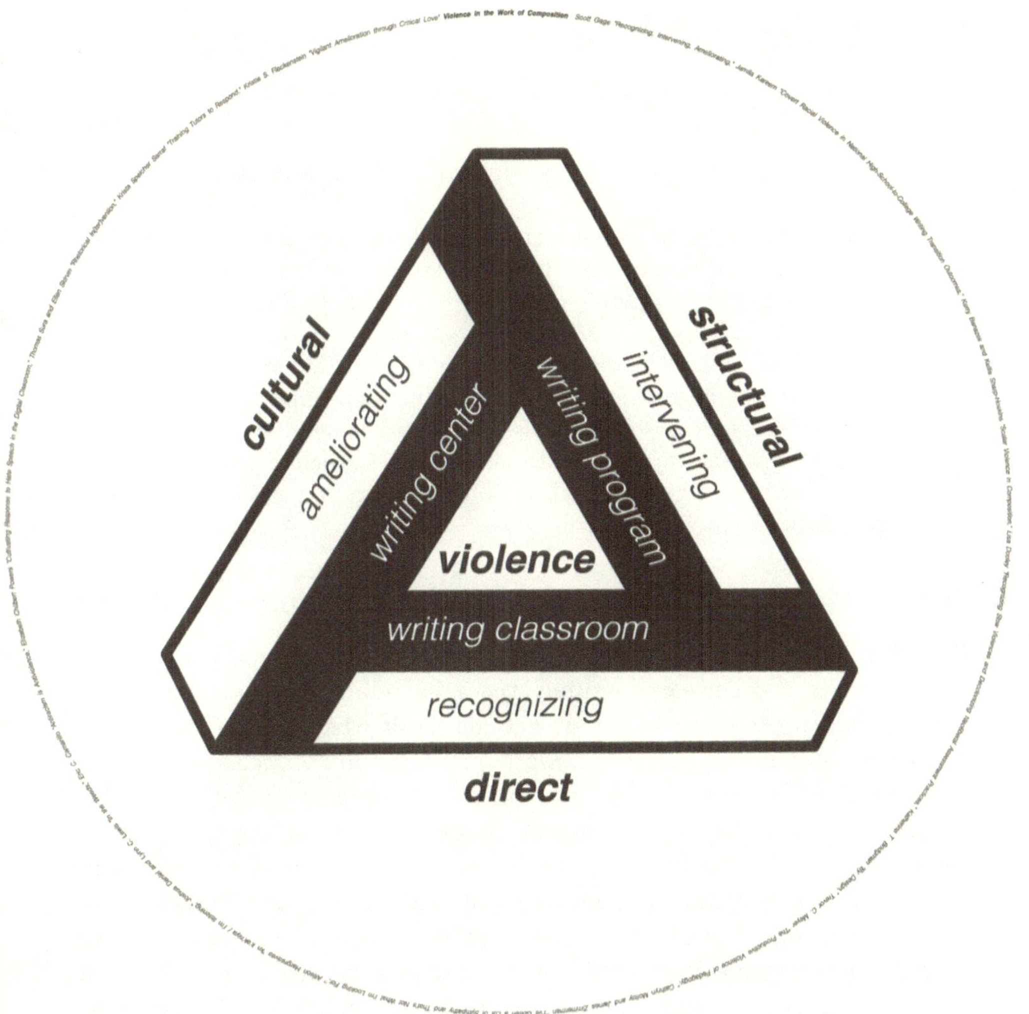


*Composition Studies 51.2 (2023): 18–19*

# Articles

## Meaningful Writing Projects Among Multilingual Undergraduate Writers: Personal, Practical and Developmental

*Qianqian Zhang-Wu, Alison Stephens, and Neal Lerner*

Our research explores the meaningful writing experiences of 325 undergraduate students who self-identify as multilingual. Through qualitative coding of open-ended survey data, we found that respondents considered their writing meaningful when it allowed them to make personal and relevant connections and learn new skills and strategies. Our findings are aligned with the results of *The Meaningful Writing Project*, suggesting that the ways all students find their writing meaningful are interwoven with their identities, histories, and aspirations. After presenting our analysis of multilingual students' responses, we posit several conditions for teaching writing across the curriculum that allow complex, mobile language users to exercise their personal, social, and linguistic resources and have the opportunities for meaningful writing experiences.

---

Recent statements from professional organizations describing student outcomes of college-level writing classes, including classes for multilingual students, largely offer teacher-driven criteria of what "success" might look like. For instance, in "The Framework for Success in Postsecondary Writing" (Council of Writing Program Administrators, National Council of Teachers of English) and the "WPA Outcomes Statement for First Year Composition" (Council of Writing Program Administrators), we are told students should develop "habits of mind," "knowledge of conventions," and "integrate their own ideas with ideas of others," among other outcomes. These teacher-driven constructs are seemingly generic, assumed to be applicable to all students, no matter the language and personal assets that students bring to our classrooms, labs, writing centers, and other learning spaces. A notable absence is the idea that students should find their writing to be meaningful.

In contrast and in response to these initiatives, Michele Eodice, Anne Ellen Geller and Neal Lerner (*The Meaningful Writing Project*) introduced the student-driven construct of meaningful writing. To challenge the traditional top-down ways of writing assignment design and instruction, Eodice et al. (*The Meaningful Writing Project*) centered students' perspectives to understand their needs as developing writers. Based on surveys and interviews with over 700 seniors across three institutions, they conclude that undergraduates find writing meaningful when they have opportunities "to tap into the power of personal connection; immerse themselves in what they are thinking, writing, and researching; experience what they are writing as applicable and relevant to the real world; imagine their future selves" (Eodice et al. "What Meaningful Writing Means").

While the pedagogical and research importance of the Meaningful Writing Project (MWP) has resonated for many readers, Eodice et al.'s study (*The Meaningful Writing Project*) focuses on all students' without paying specific attention to multilingual writers. Yet, with the increasing internationalization of higher education and a more diversified domestic student body, American college campuses have evolved into "fundamentally multilingual spaces" (Conference on College Composition and Communication). As a result, centering linguistic diversity and multilingualism is essential to understanding students' writing experiences (Donahue; Halasek, Clinnin, and Selfe; McCorkle).

In the research we report on here, we follow Mary Hedengren's urging in her review that "more research in writing studies should follow the example of *The Meaningful Writing Project*, laying aside our teacher-based assumptions and instead reaching out to a wide variety of students to discover insights into their college experience" (256; see also Baker and Wright; Canagarajah). Our research seeks to uncover the perception of meaningful writing experiences of students who identify as multilingual at a private R1 university in the northeast United States.

Our study hinges on the intersection of two terms: multilingualism and meaningful writing. Contrary to common administrative practices that conflate the terms multilingual student with international student or second-language learner, we take multilingualism as a self-reported construct (see the Methods section for more on how students reported language identity). Following Yuko Butler's definition of multilingual writers as "individuals or groups of people who obtain communicative competence in more than one language, with various degrees of proficiencies, in oral and/or written forms, in order to interact with speakers of one or more languages in a given society," multilingual in our research is not a concept determined by students' levels of proficiency in various languages (112). Instead, we consider multilingual a self-reported construct, reflecting the fluidity and complexity of students' languaging practices and linguistic identities. As for the term *meaningful*, our intent is to be faithful to the impetus for the MWP: Rather than pre-define *meaningful* for students taking our survey, we aimed to highlight students' agency and voices (Horner and Tetreault; Kiernan, Meier, and Wang) to create a student-driven construct of the word.

As such, we started with a descriptive question: What do multilingual students describe as meaningful writing projects? We found that perceptions of meaningful writing across our study participants were largely consistent with college seniors in the original MWP (Eodice et al. *The Meaningful Writing Project*). Moreover, since our respondents reported meaningful writing experiences from across the curriculum, our findings are not only relevant for composition specialists (who might already recognize diverse students' linguistic assets) but also for faculty who teach writing in the disciplines, where deficit views of multilingualism may persist. Based on the responses from linguistically diverse students that we analyze in this article, we posit several teaching and learning premises for meaningful writing in an increasingly fluid higher education context.

## The Meaningful Writing Project

Because our study is based, in part, on *The Meaningful Writing Project* (Eodice et al.), we offer a brief overview of the MWP's methods of data collection and analysis. One component of the MWP was a survey distributed in spring 2012 to seniors at three U.S. research institutions. The survey asked students the following open-ended question:

> Think of a writing project from your undergraduate career up to this point that was meaningful for you and answer the following questions: What was the writing project you found meaningful? (Please describe it.) What made that project meaningful for you? (Eodice et al. *The Meaningful Writing Project* 9)

Based on 707 survey responses, Eodice et al. developed 22 codes to describe the data, four of which occurred most frequently–when students:

1. described a "personal connection" to the topic they were writing about or to their identities as writers and students,
2. saw their meaningful writing as applicable or relevant to their presents and/or futures,
3. described the content they were learning itself as a meaningful experience,
4. found the process of research and writing a primary contributing factor to a project's meaningfulness (*The Meaningful Writing Project* 4).

Based on these findings, Eodice et al. conclude that for faculty "to make writing agentive, relevant, and consequential, projects can be designed to cultivate personal connections, relations to future selves, and the disposition for lifelong learning" (*The Meaningful Writing Project* 130).

The MWP offered an emic understanding of how students engage with their writing in meaningful ways, representing a shift in viewing student writing via "outcomes" research (e.g., solely looking at students' written products) to viewing student writing in terms of the "incomes" (Guerra) they bring to their learning and how opportunities for agency and engagement might be cultivated through meaningful writing. While MWP's findings were limited to a relatively small sample size within three particular institutions, its conclusions have resonated with readers interested in shaping writing instruction to make students' experience of learning more meaningful. As Jeanine Williams notes in her review of the book, MWP is "a useful work for anyone who wishes to connect an assignment to the greater scope of their students' lives and provide a college experience that resonates beyond the classroom" (63). Yet, despite its importance as an insightful framework to understand writing pedagogy from learners' perspectives, the MWP focused on college seniors in general. It remains unclear whether those findings hold true for multilingual writers. In this study, we focused the MWP lens on self-identified multilingual students at our university.

## Methods

### *Research Context*

This study occurred at Northeastern University (NU), a private research-intensive university in the northeastern United States that saw the percentage of international undergraduate student enrollment increase from 9.7% to 16.8% from 2009 and 2019, making NU one of the top international-student host institutions in the US. (Pseudonyms are assigned throughout to protect privacy.) In our institutional context where student mobility and multilingualism is the norm, the idea of "superdiversity" (Vertovec) is particularly applicable. The prefix super- was added to highlight "the sense of superseding" and to depict "what is 'above and beyond' what was previously there" (Meissner and Vertovec 545). Superdiversity transcends the simple concept of viewing diversity in its plural form, but instead emphasizes the intersectionality and complexity of the interactions of all factors related to mobility (Blommaert; Horner et al.). Mya Poe and Qianqian Zhang-Wu point out that thanks to global mobility, most college students either come from multilingual households or grow up exposed to rich linguistic diversity. These students' linguistic capabilities are often messily aligned with their nationalities and ethnicities ("Confronting Superdiversity"; Zhang-Wu). In short, traditional terms like *ELL* and *international* to describe multilingual students are not adequate to capture the complex language identities of our students.

Consider, for example, Anjali who is an accounting major originally from India who grew up in Israel and New York. Anjali speaks Hindi, Hebrew, Spanish, and English. Or Xue, a computer science major who was born in Shenzhen, China. After moving between Hong Kong and Bejiing as a child, he continued primary school in Athens and Paris and later completed secondary school in Japan, Shenzhen, and the United States. Xue speaks Mandarin, Cantonese, English, Greek, Japanese, and some French. The lives of these students, among many more, typified our need for more nuanced approaches to acknowledge multilingualism in our institutional context and look beyond rigid terms such as *second-language learners*.

Our university, however, did not always meet this changing demographic with an asset-oriented mindset. During a period of large increases in international student enrollment, a 2012 Faculty Senate report stated that "faculty and advisors have noted an increasing number of cases where individual student success is limited by English language understanding/ability" and called for "a diagnostic screening for entering students for whom English is not a native language." We need to note that the authors of this report did not consult with Writing Program faculty with expertise in multilingual writing (nor, as far as we know, was diagnostic screening ever implemented). Nevertheless, several Writing Program faculty recognized the need to better understand the changing demographic of our students and to respond to this deficit-oriented institutional mindset.

As a result, we engaged in several years of IRB-approved data collection via undergraduate surveys beginning in 2013 to understand multilingual students' writing experiences in our super diverse context (for findings of our program-based multilingual surveys over the past decade, see "Confronting Superdiversity" and "Confronting... Again"; Gallagher and Noonan; Poe and Zhang-Wu).

### *Our Survey*

In our 2018 iteration of the survey, recognizing the importance of a student-centered approach to inform writing pedagogy, we added a question to investigate the construct of meaningful writing that has become the basis of the present study. Specifically, in addition to 34 questions tapping into students' linguistic identities (e.g., languages spoken in the home), histories (e.g., languages spoken in school) and practices (e.g., preferred language after graduation), we added an open-ended question identical to the central question in Eodice et al. (*The Meaningful Writing Project*): "Think of a writing project [. . .] that was meaningful [. . .] What made that project meaningful for you?"

We distributed our survey to 5,382 NU undergraduates who had completed the second course in our required writing sequence, Advanced Writing in the Disciplines (AWD). For context, NU requires that students take at least four designated "writing-intensive courses," (first year writing, advanced writing, and two courses in their majors); most students will take AWD in junior or senior year, and thus have likely engaged nearly all of the required writing coursework. We received 1,153 survey responses, a response rate of 21%. We posed two questions to find a population of multilingual students for the purposes of our study: Are languages other than English spoken in your family home? Even if languages other than English are not often spoken in your family home, do you consider another language to be important to your ethnic and/or cultural identity?

A total of 488 respondents answered "yes" to one of these questions; together, they named 84 different languages that were spoken in the home or important to their ethnic/cultural identity (see Appendix). Of these, 325 students offered responses to our meaningful writing question, and these data constitute the corpus for the analysis that follows.

### *Analysis*

To analyze students' description of their meaningful writing experiences, we followed the tradition of qualitative coding, ensuring reliability and validity through a recursive process of description, negotiation, and confirmation (Saldaña). It's important to note that we did not simply apply the codes developed in the original MWP research (Eodice et al. *The Meaningful Writing Project* 157); instead, we decided to approach coding through an emic perspective, based on what we saw in each response, and thus our goal was to develop a code book specific to our data.

Following Cheryl Geisler's recommendation, we applied a single code to each response, determining in each case which code or reason the student offered for why the project was meaningful seemed most emphasized. To establish our codes, we first separately and then collectively developed codes that offered preliminary descriptions of the data, and then went through several rounds of applying those codes to a randomly selected number of responses. Once our level of agreement was acceptable, we determined a final code book (see Table 1). We then assigned each student's response to two of our research team members to code independently. Next, we compared coding results. In cases of discrepancies, we negotiated an agreed-upon code or we used a third reader to determine the final code.

Table 1. Codebook with Results

| Code | Description | Example | Count | % of Total |
|---|---|---|---|---|
| **PERS** | Writing to share personal experience, note personal growth, or express connection to the subject | "Doing a research paper on educational systems... was a very personally interesting topic for me. It focused on an issue which directly concerns my dad's home country." | 113 | 34.8% |
| **PRAC** | Writing for practical reasons—for major or work | "In my advanced writing class creating a flyer ... was meaningful because that is something that I could be doing in the real world." | 70 | 21.5% |
| **IMPRO** | Writing to improve—challenging yet helpful | "I found it meaningful because of the amount of work involved in preparing the project and for the quality of work I feel I produced. Combining hard work with good work leads to meaningful work." | 51 | 15.7% |
| **NEW** | Writing as a novel experience (possibly creative/ fun projects) | "One project that stood out to me was writing a buzzfeed article. I thought that was completely different than the other projects I've done." | 28 | 8.6% |
| **REQ** | Writing to meet a requirement (not enjoyable or meaningful) | "I write only to satisfy requirements. I don't find it particularly enjoyable." | 16 | 4.9% |
| **CHANGE** | Writing to change someone's mind | "In a class I'm currently taking, an assignment included writing a letter to an individual to hopefully affect some kind of change and be a disabilities advocate. . . . Working on your writing skills does not only mean improving your ability to write an essay, but also... encourage[s] meaningful conversation." | 10 | 3.1% |

| Code | Description | Example | Count | % of Total |
|---|---|---|---|---|
| TEACH | Teacher-student relationship noted | "In my first year writing class I wrote an oped piece. . . . I found the project meaningful because my professor gave me thoughtful feedback on writing that I had put effort into." | 9 | 2.8% |
| INSUFFICIENT INFO | Not enough information provided | "Zika virus project." | 28 | 8.6% |
| TOTAL | | | 325 | 100% |

## Findings

Multilingual students in our study find writing meaningful when offered opportunities to fulfill personal, practical, and developmental goals. Such perceptions are consistent with the cross-institutional undergraduate population analyzed by Eodice et al. (*The Meaningful Writing Project*), lending evidence that meaningful writing is a robust construct, one that intersects multiple identities and centers all students' desires for agency and consequential learning.

### *Meaningful Writing for Multilingual Students: Personal, Relevant, Developmental*

As shown in Table 1, we found that nearly three quarters of the self-identified multilingual students in our study found their writing meaningful when it offered a way to:

1. share personal experience or experience growth or express a personal connection to the topic;
2. see their writing as practical or relevant or connected to their majors or their future professional identities; and
3. offer a means to improve a skill or strategy or learn a new way of writing.

These three codes connect strongly to the "personal connection," "applicability/relevance," and "content learning" codes that were most frequent in the Eodice et al.'s MWP study (*The Meaningful Writing Project*). We next offer examples of each of these frequently occurring codes. To note, we have omitted linguistic identifiers when providing excerpts to avoid reductively correlating findings with particular language backgrounds. We direct our readers instead to the multilingual context of our respondents (see Appendix).

*Code "PERS"*

The largest set of student responses (34.8%) fell under PERS (personal). This echoes findings from previous research, indicating the importance of writing in facilitating personal reflection (e.g., Leonard; Vieira) and identity expression (e.g., Canagarajah; Cox) among multilingual writers. Students' responses highlighted writing projects where they had choice and were "able to relate" or establish "a real connection" between their meaningful writing projects and their identities. Occasionally, these responses talked about popular culture–such as writing about *Lord of the Rings*—but more prevalent themes included times when students found projects meaningful when their identities were closely tied to that writing, such as when they wrote of familial history, when they were able to investigate subject matter tightly linked to their own identity, or when they were able to construct a version of themselves in their writing. As one student wrote, "I [. . .] ended up with an extremely personal piece about my grandparents, who are Cuban refugees and struggled to learn, read, and write English here." Similarly, another student wrote about a historical project that was meaningful "because it connected to my family's own history of being Jewish Americans living in Georgia at the same time the case took place." In these cases, writing became meaningful when thus far invisible threads of their linguistic and cultural identity were pulled to the surface through the writing project.

Heritage was not the only identity connector, however. For instance, an engineering student found writing meaningful when it allowed her to connect her professional identity as an engineer and personal identity as a Black woman:

> The writing project that was the most meaningful… is a compiled project over the system about Black Women in STEM. [. . .] I am a Black woman, I'm from Ethiopia, so the significance of this project is very personal to me.

This type of meaningful writing relates to another theme in the PERS code, where multilingual writers valued the opportunity to showcase themselves. For example, a student found filling out a pre-med application packet particularly meaningful because:

> The process allowed me to evaluate my life and academic experiences and paint them in a manner that would convince the committee [. . .]. It was incredibly meaningful because it introduced me to the

style of really writing in a way that would showcase my personality, experiences, and determination.

While researchers have investigated the construction of the self in multilingual writers' autobiographical and creative writing (e.g., Yang; Hanauer), we extend this work by showing a correlation between personal writing experiences and the learners' sense of value. Our results echo Eodice, Geller, and Lerner's findings in "The Power of Personal Connection," where students draw on internal (e.g., writerly identity and development) and external (e.g., family, community, peers) factors to make writing meaningful.

*Code "PRAC"*

PRAC (practical and relevant) was our second most frequently occurring code, capturing 22% of the total responses. PRAC was assigned when students described writing with a real-world impact—writing that transcends the classroom and connects to broader social and professional interests. This code is similar to Eodice et al.'s "APP+" code, one that accounts for students finding writing projects meaningful when they were applicable, relevant, authentic, or real world (*The Meaningful Writing Project*).

One student wrote about "creating a flyer that targeted a specific audience. It was meaningful because that is something that I could be doing in the real world." In some responses, students found meaning in the opportunities connected with their intended careers post-graduation. One student wrote, "I have prepared a poster, abstract, and scripts for the American Chemical Society meeting in Boston. It is meaningful because it is important to my career as a scientist." We note that these writing projects cut across multiple genres and multiple fields, reflective of the complexity of writing in the "real world" (Brandt). But in each case, students expressed a clear connection between what they chose as meaningful and what they expected to be doing as professionals.

Students also considered writing projects meaningful when they were applicable to their coursework or majors. We distinguish codes PRAC from PERS by observing that students in this category saw the practicality of their meaningful writing projects in a shorter time frame; these projects had connections to other courses they might be taking or to their studies as a whole, as in the following response: "Lab reports in engineering classes helped me practice communicating technical data and conclusions/actions based on that data."

Finally, students found writing projects meaningful when they were relevant to issues with which they were deeply involved. While not occurring as frequently as other responses within this category, several students noted the "practicality" of their projects as related to concerns they had for justice or equity or topics for which they expressed passion. One student told us that they "designed a mock 'app' with a group about personalized medicine," which they found meaningful because it was "definitely a cool and meaningful experience to see how the class material I was learning could be meaningfully applied, even in a mock setting!"

Overall, responses coded as PRAC described writing projects that were: (1) applicable to their future careers/future identities or disciplinary fields, (2) applicable to their coursework or majors; (3) relevant to their current concerns or issues with which they were deeply involved.

### *Code IMPRO*

We coded 51 responses (15.7%) IMPRO (improvement), where students felt that some aspect of their knowledge and/or skills improved. Some responses were marked by the intensity of the work ("it was the most amount of writing and research I have ever done"). Other responses were characterized by gratitude: "I have worked a lot with scientific research writing in my present co-op and am very grateful for the opportunities to expand my knowledge and skills in that field." Many in this coding category saw what they were learning as not merely for practical gain or applicability, but for satisfaction from a learning opportunity. As one student described, "I felt extremely accomplished after I was finished with it."

### *The Absence of Meaningful Writing*

Not every student who filled out our survey and the MWP question reported having had a meaningful writing experience. In these responses, which we coded REQ (required), 16 out of 325 respondents (4.9%) mentioned that they did not find any writing meaningful, as in this response: "There wasn't anything that was meaningful, all the assignments were just required." This finding was consistent with Eodice et al.'s MWP as a whole, in which 4% of students filling out the survey reported no meaningful writing experiences as undergraduates (*The Meaningful Writing Project*).

Two students specified particular definitions of meaningful: "None of my writing assignments have been particularly meaningful. Some of them have been interesting to research or had interesting topics, but I wouldn't call any of them meaningful." In this case, the participant distinguished between the concepts of interesting and meaningful, associating meaningful writing with important events and ideologies in life. This illustrates the dynamics of meaningful writing: An assignment from a particular class might lead to a meaningful writing experience for one student in that class, but not for all. What seems essential are the ways an assignment might offer "expansive framing" (Engle et al.) or the opportunities for students to make personal or practical connections or explore the possibilities for improvement or knowledge making.

## Discussion

As we consider the pedagogical implications of our study, we must note the sheer variety of locations and instances of meaningful writing—derived, perhaps, from the superdiversity of our multilingual population and the "dynamic, embodied, and deeply distributed" (Fraiberg 168) contexts in which they write. While we cannot dictate when and where meaningful writing happens, we can describe several premises about meaningful writing and dispositions towards students that can create opportunities for students to see value in their writing processes or products.

*1. Meaningful writing is likely to happen when students are invited to connect their experiences and aspirations to course content.*

Our study, particularly our findings for responses we coded PERS, points to the importance of moving away from deficit thinking, i.e., "students cannot," "students are unprepared," "languages other than English get in the way of learning to write." As other scholars have pointed out, embracing an asset orientation to multilingual students is essential for recognizing students' agency and ongoing re-creations of their identities in writing (e.g., Guerra; Mori; Scotland; Shapiro and MacDonald; Yang). We saw repeatedly in our survey students describing writing projects that offered pathways to connect their interests and histories with course content, such as the following:

> A writing project I found meaningful was the academic autobiography I completed in Advanced Writing. This project really helped me examine why I chose my major and what drives me in motivating me. I also ended up doing a lot of interesting research on theorists in my field that I previously knew next to nothing about. (PRAC)

Some assignments are more suitable for these kinds of opportunities than others; however, even in relatively rigid and prescribed genres, incorporating informal writing alongside more formal tasks can invoke students' connective thinking and motivation that are essential to meaningful writing (Hill and Shooshanian).

*2. Meaningful writing is likely to happen when students are entrusted with choice.*

Students regularly emphasized some version of the following: "I had a lot of freedom to choose the topic" (PERS). This echoes the work of other multilingual writing scholars who have for some time observed the generative effects of personal and identity-based writing projects that help multilingual students recognize their linguistic assets and develop their agency as writers (e.g.,

Bizzaro and Baker; Hanauer; Shapiro et al.). It is also consistent with Eodice et al.'s MWP finding that the possibility of "choice" occurred in nearly one third of all responses (*The Meaningful Writing Project* 36). We echo existing calls for agency and choice in topic, but we also caution against a reductive assumption that personal writing is always meaningful. While many students in our survey appreciated opportunities to explore their cultural/linguistic histories and to experiment with novel forms, some respondents explicitly stated that "creative/personal" writing or even "interesting" topics were not necessarily meaningful.

We observe instead that students who feel committed to a topic and its outcomes are by extension more likely to be committed to their readers. One student mentioned, "I was very ... *committed* to writing exactly how I felt about the topic. I wanted other people reading my paper to be able to understand my thoughts and ideas" (PERS). The student highlighted "commitment" and used it to trace a compelling relationship to their audience. Topic choice, then, may create opportunities for meaning when students can imagine themselves within a community of readers and writers who share a common goal (Scotland).

*3. Meaningful writing often occurs when students can imagine connections between their past and future selves.*

In some cases, this outcome occurs when students can conceptualize a sequence in their skills. Sometimes, students described the process as an apotheosis, as one Economics major did when describing a paper as a culmination of learning: "I finally put my education to work by writing a paper based on data and statistics" (PRAC). Other students connected past and future selves while writing from a threshold (e.g., applying to graduate school or returning from internship). One student described an application for a prestigious scholarship, emphasizing the challenge of writing about "everything I had ever accomplished in my life" (PERS). This student emphasized the arduousness of the writing process, a theme that we elaborate on in the following observation.

*4. Meaningful writing can happen when students are faced with a challenge and able to construct a resolution.*

Here, we separate the concept of writing being enjoyable from it being meaningful, with each essentially functioning as a subset of the IMPRO code we described above. For example, one student contends, "The lit review ... was probably most meaningful. While I didn't like it, I feel that it helped me better understand how to conduct research and apply it to my writing." Students regularly discussed the importance of intellectual rigor in their meaningful assignments, such as when a health sciences major talked about a paper on drug prices that was "the most applicable" paper of her undergraduate career yet "the hardest to write." Challenges happened in students' disciplines and also in required writing courses. As one student put it, "The project was difficult and took a long time to complete, but I value it because of the depth of the paper and the lessons I learned along the way." In other words, students may struggle with writing, but they found meaning in the trajectory of improvement. As a result, one application for faculty who work with multilingual writers may be to avoid watering down writing-intensive assignments. Easier projects do not make an assignment more memorable or meaningful. Moreover, 2.8% (9 out of 325) of our respondents specifically mentioned instructor guidance: "I got feedback from my professor on a higher level" or "My professor was also extremely helpful . . . and I felt I got better as a writer" (see "TEACH" code in Table 1). For these students, the relational aspect of going through a difficult writing task perhaps helped make the experience meaningful.

*5. Meaningful writing did not happen in a specific location.*

We were pleased to find that 43% (141 out of 325) of our population mentioned our required Writing Program courses as the sites of their meaningful writing. While that finding might speak to the paucity of writing opportunities in their other classes, we are reminded of the potential impact of required writing. Rather than a mere hurdle to overcome, required writing courses might represent opportunities to put into place the elements for meaningful writing to occur.

However, we also saw many occasions outside of writing courses where students found meaning. Meaningful writing happened in internships, capstone projects, and courses in fields as varied as biology, management, and civil engineering—and, of course, meaningful writing happened nowhere for students who didn't find any writing meaningful. As a result, one premise that we hold as writing faculty is that meaningful writing happens in unpredictable sites across the curriculum and in the workplace. This conclusion reinforces the centrality of writing in subject courses and professional settings, even if it appears as a hidden curriculum (Gere). Consequently, faculty who are not writing specialists are also responsible for preparing multilingual students as writers in the disciplines (e.g., Zhang-Wu). The pedagogical implications of meaningful writing, then, apply not just to faculty who already identify as writing teachers but to faculty in the disciplines and advisors, mentors, and coaches who support students in their professional goals (Cox; Gere et al.; Zawacki and Cox).

## Conclusion

In this article, we have established connections between multilingual writers and meaningful writing to highlight the role of students' autonomy and self-definition in writing contexts. We have also shown that multilingual students at our institution found writing meaningful in ways consistent with Eodice et al.'s *Meaningful Writing Project* findings for a more general student population, indicating that the original construct of MWP continues to hold true for students from culturally, racially and linguistically diverse backgrounds. In essence, the "power of personal connection," a key concept of the MWP, is driven by students' desires to learn, and those desires span language categories and institutions. What is most important, in our view, is that writing researchers and teachers adopt a view of student learning based on students' incomes (Guerra), assets (Shapiro and MacDonald), capital (Mori) or the experiences, desires, and goals students bring to any learning situation, but particularly to those in which writing is central.

That is not to say that students' linguistic identities are not important on the surface. While we found few salient differences in how these different populations perceived meaningfulness compared to the more general population in Eodice et al. 's MWP (*The Meaningful Writing Project*), we believe that is a consequence of the student-driven construct of meaningful writing. This asset-based approach invites students to make personal connections and apply practical goals to their writing tasks, an approach that is similarly generative for linguistically diverse groups of learners. This conclusion is significant for any faculty who support writing in the disciplines and must advocate for diverse students' linguistic assets with faculty and counter prevalent deficit mindsets when it comes to multilingual writers.

Focusing on self-identified multilingual students' perceptions of their meaningful writing experiences both within and beyond college composition classrooms (i.e., during content-area learning such as lab reports and social interactions such as internship), our study sheds important light on writing pedagogy across the curriculum. Because no content-area knowledge can be expressed without language, all disciplinary faculty members are in essence also writing teachers (Zhang-Wu; Zhang-Wu and Brisk). Echoing the student-centeredness of the MWP and the approach of many multilingual-student specialists (e.g., Donahue; Shapiro et al.), we call for higher education teachers both within and beyond the writing program to pay attention to multilingual students' own articulation of their identities and meaning-making at various points of their careers, and how they describe their strategic use of multiple languages in their personal, academic, and professional lives.

## Limitations and Future Directions

Our exploratory study is limited due to its highly contextualized nature and site-specific findings. We have tried to mitigate this limitation by comparing our results to the wider Meaningful Writing Project and have found that students who self-identify as multilingual define meaningful writing in ways similar to the respondents in the broader MWP. Nevertheless, our intention is not to offer a prescription for designing meaningful writing assignments at the college level, but to foreground the needs of multilingual writers through a student-centered approach and examine the intersection of meaningful writing and multilingualism.

Our study has raised many questions that need to be explored by future research: Do multilingual college students' conceptions of meaningful writing change over the course of their undergraduate and graduate careers? Are multilingual students' perceptions of meaningful writing at odds with writing faculty constructions of meaningful writing? What methodological approaches will help researchers trace the emergence of meaningful writing with multilingual students in diverse contexts? Finally, while our study focuses on multilingual students' perceptions of meaningful writing, what exactly do meaningful-writing informed curricula look like in college composition classrooms as well as content-area instructions across the disciplines?

Offering all students opportunities to have meaningful writing experiences should be the goal of any class in which writing plays a role (as well as non-classroom contexts such as professional internships, laboratories, and community settings). More broadly, offering students opportunities for meaningful learning is at the heart of our educational enterprise, and multilingual students bring considerable assets to their writing—their languaging practices are often fluidly deployed as assets and blended between multiple systems (e.g., Canagarajah; García; Horner et al; Jørgensen.). Canagarajah has reminded us that when teaching multilingual writers, rather than "impos[ing] a one-size-fits-all pedagogy," teachers need to constantly learn from students and "develop teaching practices from the strategies learners themselves use" (415).

In sum, our study contributes to The Meaningful Writing Project framework by drawing attention to the importance of personal, practical and aspirational aspects in meaning-making among learners from culturally, racially and linguistically diverse backgrounds. Following a long tradition of student-centered learning, we see students—their histories, linguistic resources, hopes, and aspirations—as central to our work, and as a starting point for constructing learning contexts that are truly meaningful.

## Appendix: Languages/Dialects Cited by Multilingual Students at NU (2018)

| Language | Total Frequency | Language spoken in family home | Language not spoken in the home but important to ethnic/ cultural identity |
|---|---|---|---|
| Chinese<br>*Mandarin*<br>*Other dialects (Cantonese, Taiwanese, Fuzhounese, Shanghainese, Teochew, Hok-kien)* | **123**<br>*79*<br>*44* | 102<br>*68*<br>*34* | 20<br>*11*<br>*10* |
| Spanish | **86** | 60 | 26 |
| Italian | **33** | 13 | 20 |
| Korean | **30** | 28 | 2 |
| French | **29** | 16 | 13 |
| German | **29** | 19 | 10 |
| Hebrew | **26** | 4 | 22 |
| Russian | **23** | 23 | 0 |
| Hindi | **17** | 13 | 4 |
| Arabic | **14** | 13 | 1 |
| Japanese | **12** | 6 | 6 |
| Vietnamese | **11** | 11 | 0 |
| Gujarati | **9** | 9 | 0 |
| Haitian Creole | **7** | 6 | 1 |
| Greek | **7** | 6 | 1 |
| Portuguese | **8** | 8 | 0 |
| Yiddish | **7** | 0 | 7 |
| Gaelic | **6** | 0 | 6 |
| Marathi | **6** | 6 | 0 |
| Punjabi | **6** | 6 | 0 |
| Polish | **5** | 4 | 1 |

| Language | Total Frequency | Language spoken in family home | Language not spoken in the home but important to ethnic/ cultural identity |
|---|---|---|---|
| Tamil | **5** | 4 | 1 |
| Albanian | **4** | 3 | 1 |
| Bengali | **4** | 4 | 0 |
| Hungarian | **4** | 3 | 1 |
| Tagalog | **4** | 2 | 2 |
| Telugu | **4** | 3 | 1 |
| Twi | **4** | 3 | 1 |
| Urdu | **4** | 4 | 0 |
| Armenian | **3** | 3 | 0 |
| Finnish | **3** | 1 | 2 |
| Igbo | **3** | 2 | 1 |
| Khmer | **3** | 3 | 0 |
| Thai | **3** | 2 | 1 |
| Turkish | **3** | 3 | 0 |
| **Other languages cited (≤ 2 occurrences)**<br><br>Afrikaans, Akan, Amharic, American Sign Language, Assamese, Bafang, Bahasa Indonesia, Bisaya, Braille, Cape Verdean Creole, Creole, Croatian, Ewe, Fante, Farsi, Flemish, Ga, Hausa, Hawaiian, Ilocano, Kannada, Kazakh, Kichwa, Lithuanian, Malayalam, Norwegian, Patois, Persian, Pidgin English, Romanian, Serbian, Serbo-Croatian, Sindhi, Sinhalese, Swahili, Swedish, Tirolerisch, Tongan, Ukrainian, Welsh, Zulu | | | |

## Works Cited


Baker, Colin and Wayne E. Wright. *Foundations of Bilingual Education and Bilingualism.* Multilingual Matters, 2021, doi:10.21832/baker9899.

Benda, Jonathan, Michael Dedek, Kristi Girdharry, Chris Gallagher, Neal Lerner, and Matthew N. Noonan. "Confronting Superdiversity in U.S. Writing Programs." *The Internationalization of U.S. Writing Programs*, edited by Shirley Rose and Bud Weiser. Utah State UP, 2018, pp. 79-96.

Benda, Jonathan, Cherice Escobar Jones, Mya Poe, and Alison Y. L. Stephens. "Confronting Superdiversity Again: A Multidimensional Approach to Teaching and Research Writing at a Global University." *Writing Across Difference: Theory and Intervention*, edited by James Rushing Daniel, Katie Malcolm, and Candice Rai. Utah State UP, 2022, pp. 218-237.

Bizzaro, Patrick and John Baker. "The Poetic and the Personal: Toward a Pedagogy of Social Equity in English Language Learning." *Teaching English in the Two-Year College*, vol. 42, no. 2, 2014, pp. 172-186.

Blommaert, Jan. "Citizenship, Language, and Superdiversity: Towards Complexity." *Journal of Language, Identity & Education*, vol. 12, no. 3, 2013, pp. 193-196, do i:10.1080/15348458.2013.797276.

Brandt, Deborah. *The Rise of Writing: Redefining Mass Literacy*. Cambridge UP, 2015, doi:10.1017/cbo9781316106372.

Butler, Yuko Goto. "Bilingualism/Multilingualism and Second-Language Acquisition." *Blackwell Handbooks in Linguistics: Handbook of Bilingualism and Multilingualism*, edited by Tej K. Bhatia and William C. Ritchie. Blackwell, 2012, pp. 109-136, doi:10.1002/9781118332382.ch5.

Canagarajah, Suresh. "Codemeshing in Academic Writing: Identifying Teachable Strategies of Translanguaging." *The Modern Language Journal*, vol. 95, no. 3, 2011, pp. 401-417, doi:10.1111/j.1540-4781.2011.01207.x.

Conference on College Composition and Communication. *CCCC Statement on Second Language Writing and Multilingual Writers*, 2020, cccc.ncte.org/cccc/resources/positions/secondlangwriting. Accessed 24 Feb. 2022.

Council of Writing Program Administrators. *WPA Outcomes Statement for First-Year Composition*, 2019, wpacouncil.org/aws/CWPA/pt/sd/news_article/243055/_PARENT/layout_details/false. Accessed 24 Feb. 2022.

Council of Writing Program Administrators, National Council of Teachers of English, and the National Writing Project. *Framework for Success in Postsecondary Writing*, 2011, wpacouncil.org/aws/CWPA/asset_manager/get_file/350201?ver=7548. Accessed 24 Feb. 2022.

Cox, Michelle. "Identity, Second Language Writers, and the Learning of Workplace Writing." *Reinventing Identities in Second Language Writing*, edited by Michelle Cox, Jay Jordan, and Christina Ortmeier-Hooper. National Council of Teachers of English, 2011, pp. 75-94.

Donahue, Christiane. "The 'Trans' in Transnational-Translingual: Rhetorical and Linguistic Flexibility as New Norms." *Composition Studies*, vol. 44, no. 1, 2016, pp. 147-150.

Engle, Randi. A. et al. "How Does Expansive Framing Promote Transfer? Several Proposed Explanations and a Research Agenda for Investigating Them." *Educational Psychologist*, vol. 47, no. 3, 2012, pp. 215-231, doi:10.1080/00461520.2012.695678.

Eodice, Michelle, Anne E. Geller, and Neal Lerner. *The Meaningful Writing Project: Learning, Teaching, and Writing in Higher Education*. Utah State UP, 2016, doi:10.7330/9781607325802.

Eodice, Michelle, Anne E. Geller, and Neal Lerner. "The Power of Personal Connection for Undergraduate Student Writers." *Research in the Teaching of English*, vol. 53, no. 4, 2019, pp. 320-339.

Eodice, Michelle, Anne E. Geller, and Neal Lerner. "What Meaningful Writing Means for Students." *Peer Review*, vol. 19, no. 1, pp. 25-29.

Fraiberg, Steven. "From Activity to Mobility Systems: Tracing Multilingual Literacies on the Move." *Transnational Writing Education: Theory, History, and Practice*, edited by Xiaoye You. Routledge, 2018, pp. 156-169.

Gallagher, Chris and Noonan, Matt. "Becoming Global: Learning to 'Do' Translingualism." *Crossing Divides: Exploring Translingual Writing Pedagogies and Programs*, edited by Bruce Horner and Laura Tetreault. UP Colorado, 2017, pp. 161-178, doi:10.7330/9781607326205.c009.

García, Ofelia. "Education, Multilingualism and Translanguaging in the 21st Century." *Social Justice through Multilingual Education*, edited by Tove Skutnabb-Kangas, Robert Phillipson, Ajit Mohanty, and Minati Panda. Multilingual Matters, 2009, pp. 140-158, doi:10.21832/9781847691910-011.

Geisler, Cheryl. "Coding for Language Complexity: The Interplay among Methodological Commitments, Tools, and Workflow in Writing Research." *Written Communication*, vol. 35, no. 2, 2018, pp. 215-249, doi:10.1177/0741088317748590.

Gere, Anne Ruggles. "Kitchen Tables and Rented Rooms: The Extracurriculum of Composition." *College Composition and Communication*, vol. 45, no. 1, 1994, pp. 75-92, doi:10.2307/358588.

Gere, Anne Ruggles,et al. "Rewriting Disciplines: STEM Students' Longitudinal Approaches to Writing in (and Across) the Disciplines." *Across the Disciplines*, vol. 15, no. 3, 2018, pp. 63-75, doi:10.37514/atd-j.2018.15.3.12.

Guerra, Juan. "Cultivating Transcultural Citizenship: A Writing Across Communities Model." *Language Arts*, vol. 85, no. 4, 2008, pp. 296–304.

Hanauer, David I. "Meaningful Literacy: Writing Poetry in the Language Classroom." *Language Teaching*, vol. 45, no. 1, 2012, pp. 105-115. doi:10.1017/S0261444810000522.

Hedengren, Mary. "What We Mean When We Say 'Meaningful' Writing: A Review of *The Meaningful Writing Project*." *The WAC Journal*, vol. 29, 2018, pp. 252-56. doi:10.37514/WAC-J.2018.29.1.13.

Hill, K. Dara, and Alexandra Shooshanian. "An In-service Teacher's Use of Code-meshing Pedagogies: Cultivating Formal and Informal Contexts for Writing Development in a Clinical Setting." *Journal of Language, Identity & Education*, 2021, pp. 1-17. doi:10.1080/15348458.2020.1863807.

Horner, Bruce,et al.. *Mobility Work in Composition*, Utah State UP, 2021. doi:10.7330/9781646420209.

Horner, Bruce, and Laura Tetreault. "Translation as (Global) Writing." *Composition Studies*, vol. 44, no. 1, 2016, pp. 13-30.

Jørgensen, J. Norman. "Polylingual Languaging Around and Among Children and Adolescents." *International Journal of Multilingualism*, vol. 5, no. 3, 2008, pp. 161-176, doi:10.1080/14790710802387562.

Kiernan, Julia, Joyce Meier, Joyce, and Xiqiao Wang. "Negotiating Languages and Cultures: Enacting Translingualism through a Translation Assignment." *Composition Studies*, vol. 44, no. 1, 2016, pp. 89-107.

Leonard, Rebecca Lorimer. "Traveling Literacies: Multilingual Writing on the Move." *Research in the Teaching of English,* vol. 48, no. 1, 2013, pp. 13-39.

McCorkle, Ben, Kay Halasek, Kaitlin Clinnin, and Cynthia L. Selfe. "Negotiating World Englishes in a writing-based MOOC." *Composition Studies*, vol. 44, no. 1, 2016, pp. 53-71.

Meissner, Fran, and Steven Vertovec. "Comparing Super-Diversity." *Ethnic and Racial Studies*, vol. 38, no. 4, 2015, pp. 541-555, doi:10.1080/01419870.2015.980295.

Mori, Miki. "Writing and Achievement at University as Individualistic or Social Practices: Two Latino Undergraduates' Contrasting Approaches to Academic Success." *Journal of Language, Identity & Education,* vol. 18, no. 2, 2019, pp. 126-140, doi:10.1080/15348458.2018.1528546.

Poe, Mya, and Qianqian Zhang-Wu. "Super-Diversity as a Framework to Promote Justice: Designing Program Assessment for Multilingual Writing Outcomes." *Composition Forum*, vol. 44, 2020, pp. 1-15.

Saldaña, Johnny. "Coding and Analysis Strategies." *The Oxford Handbook of Qualitative Research*, edited by Patricia Leavy. Oxford UP, 2014, pp. 581-605, doi:10.1093/oxfordhb/9780199811755.013.001.

Scotland, James. "Using Texts Which Address Local Issues to Create a Discursive Space within an Undergraduate Writing Course." *Journal of Language, Identity & Education*, vol. 19, no. 4, 2020, pp. 260-274, doi:10.1080/15348458.2019.1655425.

Shapiro, Shawnaet al. "Teaching for Agency: From Appreciating Linguistic Diversity to Empowering Student Writers." *Composition Studies*, vol. 44, no. 1, 2016, pp. 31-52.

Shapiro, Shawna, and Michael T. MacDonald "From Deficit to Asset: Locating Discursive Resistance in a Refugee-Background Student's Written and Oral Narrative." *Journal of Language, Identity & Education,* vol. 16, no. 2, 2017, pp. 80-93, doi:10.1080/15348458.2016.1277725.

Vertovec, Steven. "Super-Diversity and Its Implications." *Ethnic and Racial Studies*, vol. 30, no. 6, 2007, pp. 1024-1054, doi:10.1080/01419870701599465.

Vieira, Kate. *Writing for Love and Money: How Migration Drives Literacy Learning in Transnational Families*. Oxford UP, 2019.

Williams, Jeanine. "Book Review: *The Meaningful Writing Project: Learning, Teaching, and Writing in Higher Education.*" *Scholarship and Practice of Undergraduate Research*, vol. 1, no. 2, 2017, p. 63.

Yang, Shizhou. "Potential Phases of Multilingual Writers' Identity Work." *Transnational Writing Education: Theory, History, and Practice*, edited by Xiaoye You. Routledge, 2018, pp. 115-137.

Zawacki, Terry Myers, and Michelle Cox, eds. *WAC and Second-Language Writers: Towards Linguistically and Culturally Inclusive Programs and Practices.* The WAC Clearinghouse and Parlor P, 2014, doi:10.37514/PER-B.2014.0551.

Zhang-Wu, Qianqian. *Languaging Myths and Realities: Journeys of Chinese International Students.* Multilingual Matters, 2021.

Zhang-Wu, Qianqian, and Maria E. Brisk.'I must have taken a fake TOEFL!': Rethinking Linguistically Responsive Instruction Through the Eyes of Chinese International Freshmen." *TESOL Quarterly*, vol. 55, no. 4, 2021, pp. 1136-1161.

# Building Bridges and Changing the Story: Recognizing Funds of Knowledge in Summer Bridge Programs

*Maria Conti Maravillas*

Positioned at the crucial point of access to higher education, summer bridge programs often serve students of color and multilingual learners as well as first-generation and low-income students. Bridge programs, which frequently include first year composition courses, represent an underexplored entry point for collaborations between academic and student affairs. In this qualitative research study, twenty-two summer bridge program websites were systematically coded and analyzed to assess the extent to which bridge program website discourse incorporates funds of knowledge, which are the resources and experiences that diverse groups of students bring to university spaces (Moll et al.). The results from this study indicate that bridge programs provide models for integrating aspirational knowledge and familial knowledge, two funds of knowledge areas, into academic coursework and departmental programming, particularly into the work of writing programs. Composition scholars are uniquely positioned to share their expertise regarding linguistic knowledge and resistant knowledge with their bridge program colleagues. This article suggests that campus partnerships between academic and student affairs can create meaningful institutional change to better support diverse groups of students.

---

While squinting against the harsh desert sun streaming through the window, I began returning the classroom to its original state. I had just finished my first day of teaching composition in a summer bridge program for incoming students at my institution. I saw one student standing off to the side. Haseya hesitantly met my smile and stepped forward.[1]

"Miss, I want you to know that I'm a Navajo student." As we began talking, Haseya explained that she had only ever attended school on the reservation and that she was worried about the workload at a four-year university. We began meeting regularly after class to discuss assignments. She asked questions about the difference between a personal narrative and a research paper because she had never encountered a research paper before. She wanted to know if her ideas in her first language translated clearly into English and if her writing was college-level. She spoke about not wanting to let her family down.

As I came to know the other students, I was surprised to find that Haseya's experiences were not unique. The students I worked with had little relevant experience with academic research, which was a required component of the summer bridge program. They expressed low confidence in their writing and exchanged personal stories of the ways in which teachers had shamed them for using Spanish in school. Over half of the students were multilingual. Many were the children of immigrants, immigrants themselves, or Generation 1.5 learners, students with "life experiences that span two or more countries, cultures, and languages" (Roberge 4). They wrote about achieving their dreams of college graduation to honor the sacrifice of their families. I did my best to counter students' deficit views of their own intelligence and abilities. I sensed that there were ways to integrate linguistic and cultural knowledge more meaningfully into course themes and assignments, but I felt unsure about how to do so.

Composition programs are enmeshed in the work of bridge programs, which serve incoming first year students at the point of access to higher education. Bridge programs usually include several weeks of accelerated coursework, study skills workshops, and social activities as well as a residential component in the summer before a student's first semester. They provide "intensive" introductions to "college expectations and the cultural contexts of the institution" (Gonzalez Quiroz and Garza 103). These programs may be housed in student affairs, new student and transition offices, diversity and inclusion offices, or institution-specific TRIO programs funded by the U.S. Department of Education, such as Upward Bound. Summer bridge programs can serve as the first component of a more comprehensive initiative that encompasses advising, tutoring, career preparation, and study skills workshops. Across the country, first year composition is a frequent component of bridge program coursework. Writing studies instructors may teach in their institution's bridge program, and a student's first college writing experience may be in a bridge program composition course. Yet little published research in writing studies focuses on bridge programs, even though these programs represent an exciting and underexplored entry point for bridge-building between academic and student affairs.

Bridge programs typically serve diverse groups of students, such as students of color, first-generation students, multilingual learners, and low-income students.[2] Diverse student populations are often categorized by colleges and universities as "at risk" due to their low retention and graduation rates (Rios-Aguilar and Kiyama, "Introduction" 4). Institutional and cultural stereotypes have popularized claims that these students lack motivation and family support, are lazy, or are academically underprepared (Mora and Rios-Aguilar 152). This at-risk discourse stems from deficit models of learning and assumptions about students and permeates the work of higher education institutions.

In seeking to remedy student deficits, higher education institutions miss an opportunity to tap into the resources that students already possess. Students from diverse groups bring specific strengths and resources, or "funds of knowledge," to university spaces (Moll et al.). The term funds of knowledge became widely known in educational circles after anthropologists and education researchers at The University of Arizona partnered with K-12 teachers to interview Mexican-American and Pascua Yaqui families. The researchers found many different funds of knowledge such as cultural knowledge and the ability to move back and forth between multiple languages. They argue that instructors should incorporate these knowledge areas into the curriculum to help students make connections between their prior experiences and course content.

Several pedagogies from writing studies share key features with the interdisciplinary funds of knowledge framework. These pedagogies include translanguaging (Horner; Parmegiani), student-led ethnography (Murie et al.), storytelling (Mlynarczyk and Babbitt; Parmegiani), students' right to their own language (Gilyard and Richardson), code-meshing (Young), hybrid literacies (McCrary), and anti-racist pedagogies (Condon and Young), among others. While these approaches are not specifically identified as funds of knowledge, many operate from an epistemological stance that views students as valuable repositories of knowledge. Instructors employing these and similar pedagogies have found ways to incorporate students' prior experiences and expertise into assignments and course themes.

For example, Qwo-Li Driskill outlines a pedagogy that utilizes a "decolonial skillshare" method in which "students are asked to not only learn *about* indigenous rhetorics but to learn indigenous rhetorics through linguistic, embodied, and material practices" (58). As both learners and teachers, students engage in embodied practices surrounding indigenous languages, wampum records, and woven baskets. This pedagogy honors the knowledge and skills that students bring to university spaces from their home communities. As another example, Kelly Medina-López uses an anti-racist pedagogy in her "Corrido-ing Composition" assignment, which asks students to compose *corridos* (Mexican folk ballads) "while considering genre, language, audience, community and cultural epistemologies, information literacy, and knowledge production all within the very real contexts of institutional power dynamics and 'what counts' as university writing" (Summerhill et al. 124). Because students draw on cultural knowledge to compose their *corridos*, this assignment is aligned with the funds of knowledge framework.

However, these pedagogical approaches stop short of acknowledging students' funds of knowledge directly, which may make it more difficult for students to see their prior experiences as true strengths. In addition, these pedagogies typically only focus on one or two funds of knowledge areas, but the funds of knowledge framework provides a multifaceted model for students to understand their strengths across many areas, from linguistic expertise to cultural experiences and community knowledges. More instructors would become aware of funds of knowledge pedagogies if they were incorporated into the scholarly conversation surrounding writing studies. As an example, Genesea M. Carter employs the dual frameworks of funds of knowledge and discourse communities in a digital literacy map assignment. In this project, students choose four communities in which they are insiders. Drawing on their prior knowledge, they create maps that visually represent the literacies of those communities. There is a need for more scholarship like this in writing studies that directly engages the funds of knowledge framework. In the context of the wider university, much work remains to bring various program structures to their full potential in terms of emphasizing students' prior knowledge.

As I prepared to teach a second bridge program composition course the following summer, I considered a funds of knowledge framework to better recognize the prior experiences and resources of my students. I designed the course around the theme of language varieties, which allowed me to incorporate linguistic knowledge as one approach to funds of knowledge. However, I saw the need for models of composition courses that incorporated multiple approaches to funds of knowledge in a single course. Thinking about bridge programs across the country, I also wondered about the extent to which they reflected a funds of knowledge orientation to students, especially considering the at-risk discourse surrounding diverse student populations in university spaces.

This frustration served as the exigency for this research project. I conducted a study of the website descriptions of twenty-two summer bridge programs across the United States; I focused on websites because they can reveal the discourses that shape programs and institutions (Barrios; Knight et al.; Pack Sheffield). Despite the dearth of scholarly attention on program websites, they are "important institutional spaces that serve as interfaces to particular values, beliefs, and practices" (Knight et al. 192). What is included or excluded from a program's website communicates information about the values and assumptions undergirding the program, department, college, or institution. In examining program websites, this study focuses on how students in bridge programs are represented to a range of potential audiences, including students and their families, faculty and staff, university administration, donors, and accrediting agencies. My research offers a method for becoming critically aware of online representations of students.

The goal of this study was to explore connections to funds of knowledge concepts across a range of bridge programs. Results from this study identify several funds of knowledge areas where composition programs and other academic affairs units can learn from student affairs initiatives such as bridge programs. Conversely, there are several funds of knowledge areas regularly employed by academic affairs that could be more thoroughly incorporated into bridge programs. Ultimately, this article argues for a model of institutional change-making that draws on shared expertise between academic and student affairs to better serve students.

## Coding Funds of Knowledge

I used systematic qualitative coding to analyze website descriptions of bridge programs to examine how they position themselves and the students who participate in their programs. My research is guided by the following question: In what ways do website descriptions of bridge programs at a range of institutions reflect funds of knowledge approaches to first year students and the support their programs provide? To answer this question, I analyzed twenty-two publicly-available summer bridge program websites across sixteen different institutions (some institutions had multiple programs that met the data set criteria for this study listed below). I limited this study to my institution at the time and its fifteen peer institutions, as specified by the Arizona Board of Regents' Approved University Peer List, so that I could examine programs operating in institutionally similar ways ("Peer Institutions"). Thirteen of the sixteen institutions had at least one bridge program that met the data set criteria, and about half of them had more than one. All are listed as "Doctoral Universities: Very High Research Activity" by the 2018 version of the Carnegie Classification of Institutions of Higher Education ("Institution Lookup"), and they are all large universities, with student populations ranging from 29,911-59,837.[3] They are all listed as "4-year or above," "public," and "full-time." I narrowed my search to institutions and programs that satisfied the following conditions:

1. are exclusively for incoming first-time, first year undergraduate students at the university they will attend in the semester immediately following the program;
2. occur in the summer between high school graduation and the subsequent fall semester;
3. include an on-campus residential option or requirement;
4. include academic courses taught on campus for more than one week; and
5. have their own websites or sections on official university websites.

The appendix details the twenty-two bridge programs in the data set. Twelve of the twenty-two programs, just over half of the data set, are for student populations deemed "diverse," a designation that varies by institution. The other ten programs in the data set may serve diverse student groups without explicitly naming this on their websites. Eighteen of the twenty-two programs in the data set offer first year writing as a mandatory or optional course.

I drew on provisional coding, which establishes a list of codes generated from the study's conceptual framework, research questions, or previous research findings prior to data collection (Saldaña 168). Since my research question focused on funds of knowledge, I used Tara J. Yosso's article "Whose Culture Has Capital?: A Critical Race Theory Discussion of Community Cultural Wealth" to develop the codes. Yosso argues that funds of knowledge are forms of community wealth which can be strategically employed by diverse communities (77). She synthesizes the work of cultural studies scholars over the past several decades into distinct funds of knowledge categories. While Yosso's article is widely cited among scholars who focus on culturally-relevant pedagogies, Cecilia Rios-Aguilar and Judy Marquez Kiyama argue that Yosso's community wealth categories should be understood as categories of knowledge rather than as types of capital since utilizing funds of knowledge outside one's home community does not always yield economic benefits ("A Complimentary Framework" 18). Therefore, I rendered Yosso's categories in this research as knowledge categories (e.g., "aspirational capital" becomes "aspirational knowledge"). I created codes for four of Yosso's categories (see Table 1 for excerpted codebook):

- aspirational knowledge: the ability to dream of a different future despite barriers (Yosso 77)
- familial knowledge: kinship bonds that serve as models for "caring, coping, and providing" (77-79)
- linguistic knowledge: the ability to communicate in multiple languages or styles (78)
- resistant knowledge: skills developed through opposition to inequity and oppressive structures (80).

Table 1. Excerpted Codebook

| Code | Description | Example or Starting Point |
|---|---|---|
| Aspirational Knowledge | Supporting students' future goals and dreams despite potential barriers | Example: "AAP encourages students to explore their talents and abilities, to believe in themselves and "to aspire to academic and professional excellence." |
| Familial Knowledge | Recognizing how kinship bonds can support student success | Example: "The parents of Millennium Scholars are vital to the program's success." |

| Code | Description | Example or Starting Point |
|---|---|---|
| Linguistic Knowledge | Acknowledging the intellectual and social skills required to communicate in more than one language and/or style | Not present in the data set |
| Resistant Knowledge | Allowing space for diverse groups of students to counter societal messages and structures that devalue them | Starting Point: "Connections with peers who looked like me" |

I examined the entire written text from each website line-by-line to track patterns.[4] Table 1 provides a description of each code and an example. Because none of the bridge program websites in the data set included a code for linguistic knowledge or resistant knowledge, the table identifies a starting point for where resistant knowledge can be better incorporated.

## Learning from Student Affairs Professionals: Aspirational Knowledge and Familial Knowledge

Despite their shared commitment to student support, student and academic affairs professionals frequently operate in separate spheres. Instructors and staff working in one area are often unaware of the work being done in another area on campus. An increased level of collaboration between student affairs and academic affairs begins with honoring the expertise of each group. Bridge programs in this study provide models for integrating aspirational knowledge and familial knowledge into academic coursework and departmental programming. Eight programs in the data set had at least one aspirational knowledge or familial knowledge code.

### *Aspirational Knowledge: Recognizing Students' Potential*

Bridge program references to aspirational knowledge, "the ability to maintain hopes and dreams for the future, even in the face of real and perceived barriers" (Yosso 77), emphasize students' academic and career goals. For example, the webpage for the Summer Bridge Experience at The Ohio State University claims the program is "designed to assist Young Scholars reach [*sic*] their full potential and achieve their academic and career goals through personal, professional, and leadership development" ("Summer Bridge Experience"). Instead of focusing on skills or knowledge that students lack, programs emphasizing aspirational knowledge imply an understanding of students as motivated and goal-oriented.

The Freshman Summer Program at the University of California, Los Angeles is the only other program in the data set that uses the word "potential" ("Freshman Summer Program"). This program is housed in the Academic Advancement Program (AAP). According to the website, "AAP programs and services are linked together by an underlying belief that all AAP students have earned their academic right to be at UCLA and have demonstrated the academic potential to excel at, and graduate from, UCLA" ("Freshman Summer Program"). By referencing students' education as a right and asserting that student participants will graduate, the bridge program makes the implicit argument that they are prepared to overcome challenges. To honor aspirational knowledge, other student success and academic programs should explicitly reference student potential in their programmatic materials.

Another bridge program makes an overt connection to students' dreams and goals through an unlikely ally—corporate partnerships. The Successful Transition and Enhanced Preparation for Undergraduates Program (STEPUP) Summer Bridge Program at the University of Florida is "the [engineering] college's first summer-bridge transition program targeting freshman engineering students, with a particular focus on underrepresented student populations (i.e. Women, African-Americans, Hispanic/Latinx and Native-American students)" and first-generation learners ("Successful Transition"). Students benefit from engineering facility tours, research mentorship by a corporate sponsor, and an alumni speaker series. While corporate sponsorship of bridge programs might seem suspect, STEPUP honors students' aspirations by helping them navigate barriers to fulfilling their goals. For first-generation engineering students, these barriers can include unfamiliarity with potential careers, a lack of procedural knowledge in finding internship and job opportunities, and the lack of personal contacts who are engineers. STEPUP's website discourse provides a useful counter to the banking model of education, described by Paulo Freire as one that views students as empty "receptacles" needing "'to be filled'" (72). Instead of viewing students as "empty vessel[s]" (79) without aspirations, or treating their goals as irrelevant, the website discourse positions students as capable and goal-oriented. STEPUP provides specific contacts and information designed to help students realize their professional goals.

These approaches toward aspirational knowledge employed by student affairs professionals offer a useful model for academic affairs, particularly composition programs. Academic departments and individual instructors can connect what they do to students' own aspirations and goals if they are not already doing so. Most students arrive at higher education with motivations and dreams—they are not blank slates. Yet composition instructors and administrators do not always design assignment options and programmatic pathways around these aspirations. Given the vast potential to connect with students on a deeper level through aspirational knowledge, this funds of knowledge area should be incorporated more broadly into writing studies programs. Assignments can be designed so that students can tailor them towards their individual goals, research interests, and areas of expertise. In addition, composition programs can collaborate with writing centers to offer workshops on personal statements, application writing, and other goal-oriented writing to better support students' aspirational knowledge. By learning from our colleagues in student success, we can better integrate aspirational knowledge across academic courses, programs, and departments.

*Familial Knowledge: Integrating Students' Support Networks*

Alongside aspirational knowledge, familial knowledge offers a useful strategy for integrating students' assets into bridge programs. Familial knowledge involves "recognizing how kinship bonds can support student success" and can involve both biological and non-biological support networks. The Millennium Scholars Program, which houses Summer Bridge at The Pennsylvania State University, emphasizes family involvement: "The parents of Millennium Scholars are vital to the program's success. We expect and encourage parent engagement from Interview Weekend until graduation" ("Summer Bridge"). By deeming families "vital to the program's success," the Millennium Scholars Program comes the closest of the programs in this study to recognizing families' funds of knowledge in its website discourse. Parents are given a venue to network with one another and to assist with events.

On the other hand, these roles may preclude participation in ways that more clearly draw on families' experiences. Luis Moll et al. examine the various "household" areas of knowledge present in communities of color in Tucson, Arizona such as agriculture and mining (soil and irrigation systems, timbering), material and scientific knowledge (masonry, architecture), economics (renting and selling, loans), medicine (herbal knowledge, folk medicine), and household management (budgets, cooking, appliance repairs) (73). Presentations by students' families as a part of bridge program curricula could demonstrate real-life applications of disciplinary expertise and familial funds of knowledge. Composition courses in bridge programs could ask students to write reflections on familial knowledge, particularly as it relates to an expansive definition of multiliteracies. Instructors can intentionally design assignments that make connections to the literacies that students bring with them to university spaces. Student affairs and academic affairs professionals can draw on students' familial knowledge where they are not already doing so, and collaborations between both areas may yield new possibilities.

### *Learning from Academic Affairs: Linguistic Knowledge and Resistant Knowledge*

While bridge programs provide examples for academic programs to recognize and integrate aspirational knowledge and familial knowledge into their work, academic departments can claim different areas of expertise related to funds of knowledge. Composition professionals are particularly well-suited to share their expertise in linguistic knowledge and resistant knowledge with bridge programs and other student success initiatives. As none of the bridge program websites in the data set included a code for linguistic knowledge or resistant knowledge, I provide examples of how bridge programs can better incorporate these funds of knowledge areas.

### *Honoring Linguistic Knowledge*

Many bridge programs serve students who speak more than one language or who speak non-dominant varieties of English such as African American Vernacular English (AAVE) and Chicano English. Drawing on bilingual education research, Yosso frames linguistically-based funds of knowledge as "the intellectual and social skills attained through communication experiences in more than one language and/or style" (78). In their everyday lives, multilingual students "develop and draw on various language registers, or styles, to communicate with different audiences" (79). Due to their experiences of moving back and forth between standardized English, non-dominant varieties of English, and other languages, diverse student populations may already possess intuitive knowledge in audience awareness and rhetorical decision making, skills which are referenced in the Council of Writing Program Administrators' Outcomes Statement for First Year Composition.

Despite the academic strengths of this linguistic flexibility, none of the bridge program websites mention the fact that students bring linguistic knowledge to their programs. Instead, they refer to the bridge program's ability to confer linguistic and communication skills to students. Two programs in the data set are designed for international students and specifically address language use. The International Student Summer Institute at the University of Wisconsin-Madison has the goal of "helping students improve their academic English skills" and easing the "transition to American university life" and academic culture ("International Student Summer Institute"). One of the courses, English as a Second Language 113: Academic Reading and Writing, seeks to help students improve "speaking, reading, writing, and listening skills that are essential to academic success at UW-Madison" ("International Student Summer Institute"). Similarly, Summer Start at University of California, Davis lists a series of writing courses designed for "undergraduate students whose native language is not English" ("Summer Start"). This program offers "opportunities to strengthen language skills and intercultural competencies so that they [students] are better prepared to be a full citizen of the university" ("Summer Start"). Though not an international student program, Early Fall Start at University of Washington also addresses the particular academic needs of international students with "special courses for students who want to improve their English language skills" ("Early Fall Start").[5] The website discourse of these bridge program courses emphasizes a desire to help students gain experience and skills with the kind of standardized English that is valued in higher education institutions; this is certainly helpful, especially for international learners. Bridge programs in the data set that are not designed for international students also describe how their programs develop linguistic and communication skills. However, the website discourse of all programs in the data set stops short of recognizing the versatile linguistic knowledge that diverse groups of students bring with them to university spaces.

Scholars in writing studies can draw on decades of rich disciplinary conversation regarding linguistic knowledge. The 1974 Conference on College Composition and Communication position statement, *Students' Right to Their Own Language (SRTOL),* called for attention to the multiple valid ways that students communicate beyond standardized forms of English, including non-dominant varieties. Although not part of this study's data set, the ESL program at the University of Massachusetts Boston emphasizes an asset-based approach to students' varied language use. The website description for their program serves as a model for how programs can adopt a funds of knowledge stance towards linguistic knowledge:

> Our work in the ESL program is founded on the knowledge that cultural, linguistic, and rhetorical composing processes work together when multilingual students produce writing. . . . the ESL program is committed to racial equity, diversity, inclusiveness, multilingualism, multiculturalism, and individuals' language rights. Thus, we, the ESL program administrators and faculty, believe that our students' multilingual and multicultural repertoires are invaluable assets that promote and enrich the linguistic landscape of the institution and the sociocultural development of all our student body. ("Undergraduate ESL Program")

Bridge programs and writing programs can help students develop this asset-based understanding of the varied ways in which they use language. The statement moves beyond articulating the impact of linguistic knowledge on individual students; instead, it claims that students' multilingualism enriches the institution as a whole and promotes the "sociocultural development" of the entire student body. Thus, the wider university community stands to benefit when linguistic knowledge is recognized and supported. While scholars in writing studies have begun to answer the *SRTOL's* call to honor linguistic knowledge (Canagarajah; Lu and Horner; Young), additional scholarship and resources are needed to shift faculty and staff, administration, politicians, and the general public toward understanding students' varied language use as an asset.

As a beginning step toward this story-changing work (Adler-Kassner 29), composition scholars should seek to partner more intentionally with their colleagues in bridge programs if they are not already doing so. Student support staff should be invited to writing program workshops and professional development sessions. Due to their expertise in linguistic knowledge, writing studies scholars can serve as key ambassadors of this funds of knowledge area. Instructors can share reflection prompts that ask students to analyze their own approaches to language. Bridge program staff may find activities for teaching students about language varieties to be particularly relevant to their own program curricula. Discussions about language diversity across traditional university boundaries have the potential to initiate institutional change.

### *Resistant Knowledge and Social Belonging*

In addition to linguistic knowledge, academics also have expertise in resistant knowledge—academic critique often involves an interrogation of power structures and societal messages. Composition scholars can draw on the work of scholar-activists such as Linda Adler-Kassner, Ellen Cushman, Linda Flower, Paulo Freire, bell hooks, and many others to frame their approaches to resistant knowledge. Diverse groups of students have access to family and community experiences of resistance to racism, identity stereotypes, and inequity. They may arrive at university spaces well-versed in "cultural knowledge of the structures of racism and motivation to transform such oppressive structures" (Yosso 81). While none of the bridge program websites in the data set included a code for resistant knowledge, their discussions of peer relationships and social belonging offer a starting point for this funds of knowledge area.

Rooted in developmental psychology's connection between intellectual and personal development (Boylan and Bonham 59), bridge programs focus on supporting the whole student to develop "personal and academic" skills needed for a positive college experience (vi). Bridge program websites in the data set frequently cite higher education scholar Vincent Tinto's theoretical model for integrating students academically, socially, and culturally into university life. Tinto's foundational text, *Leaving College: Rethinking the Causes and Cures of Student Attrition,* asserts that students need to develop strong academic and personal connections to successfully transition to the institution. Peer connections are a crucial component of this transition. Bridge program websites in the data set use student testimonials to highlight the relationships students could develop with their peers. One student from the Special Transitional Enrichment Program at University of California, Davis said, "After I went through my first day I went to sleep comfortable because throughout the day I had shared my story with people that were complete strangers to me" ("Special Transitional Enrichment Program"). This type of sharing aligns with Tinto's understanding of the social integration that facilitates a "sense of belonging" and "the sense that they are part of a larger community" ("Through the Eyes" 258), which he identifies as critical factors for student persistence (*Leaving College* 120).

One type of peer connection is particularly relevant to resistant knowledge as it relates to diverse groups of students—the opportunity to make friends with peers who share their demographic characteristics. For example, a student from Ohio State's Summer Bridge Experience comments on the "chance to make friends that are more like myself" ("Summer Bridge Experience"). Similarly, a Special Transitional Enrichment Program student at University of California, Davis, refers to the program as "an awesome three weeks that helped me form connections with peers *who looked like me*, and made me feel welcomed in the University" (emphasis added). Both programs primarily serve first-generation, low-income students. Given that U.S. society is stratified by race, ethnicity, and socioeconomic class, first-generation and low-income students in bridge programs are more likely to be students of color as well. Tinto argues that there should be "sufficient numbers of students of similar backgrounds on campus to allow for the development of self-sustaining student communities" ("Through the Eyes" 261). His use of "self-sustaining" implies a funds of knowledge orientation, one that views students as integral to establishing support networks with each other.

These student support networks within bridge programs have the potential to function as manifestations of Nancy Fraser's private "enclaves," spaces where marginalized groups can withdraw from larger groups and gather together. The notion of private enclaves is related to her term "subaltern counterpublics," which are "discursive arenas where members of subordinated social groups invent and circulate counterdiscourses, which in turn permit them to formulate oppositional interpretations of their identities, interests, and needs" (Fraser 67). In bridge programs, groups of students who have little discursive power in general can collectively push back against stereotypes they face in the university and in society. Bridge programs can acknowledge enclaves as a specific programmatic benefit. In doing so, diverse student groups could center student-generated knowledge, such as strategies for dealing with microaggressions, responding to institutional racism, and navigating imposter syndrome.

Making space for these strategies in curricula and activities would allow bridge programs to take supporting the whole student to the next level.

Composition scholars have expertise in employing a critical lens in their research, and student success programs can use their approach as a model for emphasizing resistant knowledge in their programs. Writing studies scholars can identify research that helps their bridge program colleagues advocate for resistant knowledge approaches to stakeholders such as university administrators, grantmakers, and other funders. Composition instructors who teach in bridge programs can design course curricula around themes of social belonging and imposter syndrome. They can create assignments that allow diverse groups of students to speak back to deficit-based societal messages. By incorporating resistant knowledge more thoroughly in their collaborations with bridge programs, writing studies professionals can use their expertise to support student persistence and retention.

## Funds of Knowledge Applications and Future Directions

Bridge programs provide models for integrating aspirational knowledge and familial knowledge into academic coursework and departmental programming, especially in terms of writing programs. Composition scholars and programs are uniquely positioned to share their expertise regarding linguistic knowledge and resistant knowledge with bridge programs. The funds of knowledge framework has the potential to reshape curricula, programs, and retention initiatives if administrators, instructors, and student staff work together. I developed a heuristic (see table 2) for integrating funds of knowledge into academic and student success programs. For each stakeholder group, the heuristic addresses generative questions for interrogating assumptions about students as well as practical questions of application. As a tool for reflexivity, this heuristic can be adapted to the specific contexts of local programs as one way to begin story-changing work, which "proceeds incrementally" (Adler-Kassner 131) and "is most effectively enacted at the local level" (184). It offers a starting point for academic and student success programs to assist students in naming and claiming their prior experiences as valuable in university spaces.

Table 2. Heuristic for Integrating Funds of Knowledge

| Stakeholder | Generative Questions | Practical Questions |
|---|---|---|
| Administrators | What obstacles have students at your institution successfully negotiated to arrive at college?<br><br>How much do you know about the varying prior educational experiences of students from diverse groups? | How can staff professional development, placement mechanisms, student learning outcomes, and assessment account for students' prior knowledge?<br><br>In what ways could program materials use discourse that emphasizes students' assets instead of their deficits? |
| Instructors | What are your assumptions and expectations about what the ideal student is like?<br><br>In what ways do students' prior educational experiences inform their evolving understanding of the bridge program and institution they attend? | What course themes, assignments, and activities prompt students to recognize their own funds of knowledge?<br><br>How do you address grammar, expression, and mechanics in your course? |
| Student Staff (Tutors, Resident Assistants, Peer Mentors, etc.) | What prior knowledge areas do you possess that aren't always recognized in academic spaces?<br><br>What were your personal experiences in adjusting to college? | What multiple forms of intelligence can you acknowledge in other students?<br><br>In what ways can you feature students' aspirational, linguistic, and cultural knowledge in social and academic activities? |

In the introduction to their edited collection, *Retention, Persistence, and Writing Programs,* Ruecker et al. argue that writing studies scholars should engage with institutional, regional, and national retention conversations to keep the focus on student learning (9). They contend that while "first-year composition has long been employing some of the best practices validated by retention research . . . we often fall short of connecting our work to the bigger picture of student success" beyond composition courses (15). Participating in this work is important as enrollment, retention, and graduation rates will remain institutional metrics of success. Empirical data does link participation in a bridge program with higher retention rates, but current data is limited in scope (Cabrera et al.; McCurrie). More research is needed to demonstrate the ways in which funds of knowledge approaches can yield increases in enrollment, retention, and graduation rates.

Additional research may focus on other types of institutions beyond large, four-year, public research universities to see whether this study's findings are more broadly applicable. In addition, bridge program websites offer a limited view of what happens in these programs since these public-facing narratives must appeal to potential students and their families as well as to upper-level administrators who make funding decisions. While program websites can reveal latent assumptions, they "are created and live within institutional and infrastructural hierarchies, and these hierarchies are often invisible to us" (Knight et al. 190). Individual programs do not always have the funds or personnel to create and manage an online presence (196). Content and design can be dictated by a webmaster elsewhere in the institution, such as a university relations office or through a centralized information technology unit (196). In response to this limitation, future research projects can offer a deeper understanding of how bridge programs operate in practice.

Surveys, interviews, and focus groups of instructors who teach writing courses in bridge programs could yield more data about bridge program courses, particularly composition. While these courses were an original focus of this research, there was not enough consistent information across the data set to make claims about the teaching of writing in these programs. Information about course assignments and themes could yield valuable insights regarding the extent to which a funds of knowledge orientation is present, if at all, in these courses. In addition, surveys, interviews, and focus groups of writing program administrators and bridge program leaders would be particularly valuable in mapping the existing relationships between composition programs and bridge programs at a range of institutions.

Research examining the alignment of composition course assignments with funds of knowledge areas would be especially generative as this framework can contribute much to writing studies. Imagine the potential of funds of knowledge to restructure composition placement mechanisms. Policies for writing courses and programs that draw on funds of knowledge would recognize linguistic knowledge as a strength, rather than as a deficit. Instructor professional development could give rise to curricula that honors students' prior experiences as strengths.

As composition scholars and programs embrace public diversity and inclusion missions, collaborating with our colleagues in bridge programs already engaged in this work is essential. Writing studies instructors could attend bridge program professional development sessions and events, and composition programs could invite bridge program professionals to their own events and workshops. Collaboration across areas with a shared commitment to student support is a crucial step toward meaningful institutional change. These types of bridges between academic and student affairs can allow both to partner with students in changing the story.

## Acknowledgments

Thank you to Susan Miller-Cochran, Aimee C. Mapes, and Amy C. Kimme Hea for their guidance of this project in its early stages and to Joyce Olewski Inman, Shane Wood, and *Composition Studies* reviewers and editors for their feedback. I am grateful to my family, to the bridge program students and staff who have impacted me, and to Terrence Portis for showing me how to meet students with compassion.

## Notes

1. Name has been changed.

2. While students can be diverse in many ways, I use these particular identity categories as they are the most common across this study's data set.

3. The exception is University of California, Merced, which is listed as "Doctoral Universities: High Research Activity" and has 7,967 students.

4. I copied the full text of bridge program websites in the dataset as they existed in July 2018. Pages may have since changed. Images, videos, and page design are beyond this project's scope.

5. Early Fall Start is part of University of Washington's Continuum College. I included this program because it meets the criteria and reveals how one university responds to diverse student populations at the point of access.

## Appendix: Programs in the Data Set

Michigan State University: (1) Engineering and Science Success Academy, (2) TRIO Excel Summer Program

The Ohio State University: (1) Louis Stokes Alliance for Minority Participation (LSAMP) STEM Bridge Program, (2) Summer Bridge Experience

The Pennsylvania State University: (1) Learning Edge Academic Program, (2) Summer Bridge

The University of Arizona: (1) New Start Summer Program, (2) UAdvantage First Year Experience (discontinued)

University of California, Davis: (1) Special Transitional Enrichment Program, (2) Summer Start

University of California, Los Angeles: (1) College Summer Institute, (2) Freshman Summer Bridge Program, (3) Freshman Summer Program

University of California, Merced: UC Merced Summer Bridge First-Year Program

University of Florida: The Successful Transition and Enhanced Preparation for Undergraduates Program (STEPUP) Summer Bridge Program

University of Maryland, College Park: Summer Bridge Program for Scientists and Engineers

The University of North Carolina at Chapel Hill: Summer Bridge Program

The University of Texas at Austin: Summer Bridge

University of Washington: Early Fall Start

University of Wisconsin-Madison: (1) International Student Summer Institute, (2) Mechanical Engineering Summer Launch, (3) Summer Collegiate Experience

## Works Cited


Adler-Kassner, Linda. *The Activist WPA: Changing Stories about Writing and Writers.* Utah State UP, 2008.

Barrios, Barclay. "Reimagining Writing Program Web Sites as Pedagogical Tools." *Computers and Composition*, vol. 21, no. 1, 2004, pp. 73-87. https://doi.org/10.1016/j.compcom. 2003.08.019. Accessed 26 Aug. 2018.

Boylan, Hunter R., and Barbara S. Bonham, eds. *Developmental Education: Readings on its Past, Present, and Future.* Bedford/St. Martin's, 2014.

Cabrera, Nolan L., et al. "Can a Summer Bridge Program Impact First-Year Persistence and Performance?: A Case Study of the New Start Summer Program." *Research in Higher Education*, vol. 54, no. 5, 2013, pp. 481-98. https://doi.org/10.1007/s11162-013-9286-7. Accessed 15 Aug. 2018.

Canagarajah, Suresh. *Translingual Practice: Global Englishes and Cosmopolitan Relations.* Routledge, 2013.

Carter, Genesea M. "Mapping Students' Funds of Knowledge in the First-Year Writing Classroom." *Journal of Teaching Writing*, vol. 30, no. 1, 2015, pp. 25-54. https://journals.iupui.edu/index.php/teachingwriting/article/view/20757. Accessed 28 May 2023.

"College Summer Institute." *University of California, Los Angeles*, newstudents.ucla.edu/college-summer-institute/about/. Accessed 1 July 2018.

Condon, Frankie, and Vershawn Ashanti Young, editors. *Performing Anti-Racist Pedagogy in Rhetoric, Writing, and Communication.* The WAC Clearinghouse, 2017. Accessed 30 May 2023.

Conference on College Composition and Communication. *Students' Right to Their Own Language (SRTOL).* CCCC, 1974. cccc.ncte.org/cccc/resources/positions/srtolsummary. Accessed 1 July 2018.

Council of Writing Program Administrators. "WPA Outcomes Statement for First-Year Composition (v3.0)." https://wpacouncil.org/aws/CWPA/asset_manager/get_file/350909?ver=3890. Accessed 10 July 2018.

Cushman, Ellen. "The Rhetorician as an Agent of Social Change." *Writing and Community Engagement: A Critical Sourcebook*, edited by Thomas Deans, Barbara Roswell, and Adrian J. Wurr, Bedford/St. Martin's, 2010, pp. 235-253.

Driskill, Qwo-Li. "Decolonial Skillshares: Indigenous Rhetorics as Radical Practice." *Survivance, Sovereignty, and Story: Teaching American Indian Rhetorics*, edited by Lisa King, Rose Gubele, and Joyce Rain Anderson, UP of Colorado, 2015, pp. 57–78. Accessed 31 May 2023.

"Early Fall Start." *University of Washington*, www.earlyfallstart.uw.edu/. Accessed 1 Jul. 2018.

"Engineering and Science Success Academy." *Michigan State University*, www.egr.msu.edu/dpo/programs/essa. Accessed 1 July 2018.

Flower, Linda. "Going Public in a Disabling Discourse." *The Public Work of Rhetoric: Citizen-Scholars and Civic Engagement*, edited by John M. Ackerman and David J. Coogan, The U of South Carolina P, 2010, pp. 137-56.

Fraser, Nancy. "Rethinking the Public Sphere: A Contribution to the Critique of Actually Existing Democracy." *Social Text*, vol. 25/26, 1990, pp. 56-80. https://doi.org/10.2307/466240. Accessed 26 Mar. 2019.

Freire, Paulo. *Pedagogy of the Oppressed*. 1968. Translated by Myra Bergman Ramos, The Continuum, 2000.

"Freshman Summer Bridge Program." *University of California, Los Angeles*, www.ceed.ucla.edu/bridge/. Accessed 1 July 2018.

"Freshman Summer Program." *University of California, Los Angeles*, www.aap.ucla.edu/units/_new-student-programs/. Accessed 1 July 2018.

Gilyard, Keith, and Elaine Richardson. "Students' Right to Possibility: Basic Writing and African-American Rhetoric." *Insurrections: Approaches to Resistance in Composition Studies*, edited by Andrea Greenbaum. State U of New York P, 2001, pp. 37-51.

Gonzalez Quiroz, Alicia, and Nora R. Garza. "Focus on Student Success: Components for Effective Summer Bridge Programs." *Journal of Hispanic Higher Education*, vol. 17, no. 2, 2018, pp. 101-11. https://doi.org/10.1177/1538192717753988. Accessed 24 Aug. 2018.

hooks, bell. *Teaching to Transgress: Education as the Practice of Freedom*. Routledge, 1994.

Horner, Bruce. "Relocating Basic Writing." *Journal of Basic Writing*, vol. 30, no. 2, 2011, pp. 5-23. https://wac.colostate.edu/docs/jbw/v30n2/horner.pdf. Accessed 20 Aug. 2018.

"Institution Lookup." *The Carnegie Classification of Institutions of Higher Education*, carnegieclassifications.iu.edu/classification_descriptions/undergraduate_profile.php. Accessed 1 July 2018.

"International Student Summer Institute." *University of Wisconsin-Madison*, summer.wisc.edu/intl-summer-institute/. Accessed 1 July 2018.

Kiyama, Judy Marquez, and Cecilia Rios-Aguilar, editors. *Funds of Knowledge in Higher Education: Honoring Students' Cultural Experiences and Resources as Strengths*. Routledge, 2018.

Knight, Aimée, et al. "About Face: Mapping Our Institutional Presence." *Computers and Composition*, vol. 26, no. 3, 2009, pp. 190-202. https://doi.org/10.1016/j.compcom. 2009.05.003. Accessed 20 Aug. 2018.

"Learning Edge Academic Program." *The Pennsylvania State University*, summersession.psu.edu/first-year-students/leap-program. Accessed 1 July 2018.

"LSAMP STEM Bridge Program." *The Ohio State University*, odi.osu.edu/ohio-state-lsamp-scholars/lsamp-stem-summer-bridge-program.html. Accessed 1 July 2018.

Lu, Min-Zhan, and Bruce Horner. "Translingual Literacy and Matters of Agency." *Literacy as Translingual Practice: Between Communities and Classrooms*, edited by Suresh Canagarajah, Routledge, 2013, pp. 582-607.

McCrary, Donald. "Represent, Representin', Representation: The Efficacy of Hybrid Texts in the Writing Classroom." *Journal of Basic Writing*, vol. 24, no. 2, 2005, pp. 72-91. https://wac.colostate.edu/docs/jbw/v24n2/mccrary.pdf. Accessed 1 July 2018.

McCurrie, Matthew. "Measuring Success in Summer Bridge Programs: Retention Efforts and Basic Writing." *Journal of Basic Writing*, vol. 28, no. 2, 2009, pp. 28-49. https://wac.colostate.edu/docs/jbw/v28n2/mccurrie.pdf. Accessed 20 Aug. 2018.

"Mechanical Engineering Summer Launch." *University of Wisconsin-Madison*, www.engr.wisc.edu/department/mechanical-engineering/academics/mechanical-engineering-summer-launch/. Accessed 1 July 2018.

Mlynarczyk, Rebecca Williams, and Marcia Babbitt. "The Power of Academic Learning Communities." *Journal of Basic Writing*, vol. 21, no. 1, 2002, pp. 71-89. https://wac.colostate.edu/docs/jbw/v21n1/mlynarczyk.pdf. Accessed 24 Aug. 2018.

Moll, Luis, et al. "Funds of Knowledge for Teaching: Using a Qualitative Approach to Connect Communities and Classrooms." *Funds of Knowledge: Theorizing Practices in Households, Communities, and Classrooms*, edited by Norma González, Luis C. Moll, and Cathy Amanti, Lawrence Erlbaum Associates, 2005, pp. 71-87.

Mora, Juana, and Cecilia Rios-Aguilar. "Aligning Practice with Pedagogy: Funds of Knowledge for Community College Teaching." *Funds of Knowledge in Higher Education,* edited by Kiyama and Rios-Aguilar, Taylor and Francis, 2017, pp. 145-59.

Murie, Robin, et al. "Building Academic Literacy from Student Strength: An Interdisciplinary Life History Project." *Journal of Basic Writing*, vol. 23, no. 2, 2004, pp. 70-92. https://wac.colostate.edu/docs/jbw/v23n2/murie.pdf. Accessed 29 Aug. 2018.

"New Start Summer Program." *The University of Arizona*, newstart.arizona.edu/. Accessed 1 July 2018.

Pack Sheffield, Jenna. *Writing Program Administration and Technology: Toward a Critical Digital Literacy in Programmatic Contexts.* 2015. The University of Arizona, PhD Dissertation. https://repository.arizona.edu/handle/10150/556599. Accessed 24 Aug. 2018.

Parmegiani, Andrea. "Bridging Literacy Practices Through Storytelling, Translanguaging, and an Ethnographic Partnership: A Case Study of Dominican Students at Bronx Community College." *Journal of Basic Writing*, vol. 33, no. 1, 2014, pp. 23-51. https://wac.colostate.edu/jbw/v33n1/. Accessed 22 Aug. 2018.

"Peer Institutions." *Arizona Board of Regents*, 19 Feb. 2009, www.azregents.edu/arizonas-public-universities/peer-institutions. Accessed 1 July 2018.

Rios-Aguilar, Cecilia, and Judy Marquez Kiyama. "A Complimentary Framework: Funds of Knowledge and the Forms of Capital." *Funds of Knowledge in Higher Education,* edited by Kiyama and Rios-Aguilar, Taylor and Francis, 2017, pp. 7-24.

—. "Introduction: The Need for a Funds of Knowledge Approach in Higher Education Contexts." *Funds of Knowledge in Higher Education,* edited by Kiyama and Rios-Aguilar, Taylor and Francis, 2017, pp. 3-6.

Roberge, Mark. "A Teacher's Perspective on Generation 1.5." *Generation 1.5 in College Composition: Teaching Academic Writing to U.S.-Educated Learners of ESL,* edited by Roberge, Meryl Siegal, and Linda Harklau, Routledge, 2009, pp. 2-24.

Ruecker, et al. "Introduction: Retention, Persistence, and Writing: Expanding the Conversation." *Retention, Persistence, and Writing Programs,* edited by Todd Ruecker, Dawn Shepherd, Heidi Estrem, and Beth Brunk-Chavez, Utah State UP, 2017, pp. 3-18.

Saldaña, Johnny. *The Coding Manual for Qualitative Researchers.* Sage, 2009.

"Special Transitional Enrichment Program." *University of California, Davis,* opportunity.ucdavis.edu/programs/step. Accessed 1 July 2018.

"The Successful Transition and Enhanced Preparation for Undergraduates Program (STEPUP) Summer Bridge Program." *University of Florida,* www.eng.ufl.edu/students/students/star-office/stepup/. Accessed 1 July 2018.

"Summer Bridge." *The Pennsylvania State University,* www.millennium.psu.edu/the-scholar-experience/. Accessed 1 July 2018.

"Summer Bridge." *The University of Texas at Austin,* diversity.utexas.edu/academic-center/summer-bridge/. Accessed 1 July 2018.

"Summer Bridge Experience." *The Ohio State University,* odi.osu.edu/ysp/ysp-for-scholars/summer-bridge-experience.html. Accessed 1 July 2018.

"Summer Bridge Program." *The University of North Carolina at Chapel Hill,* summerbridge.unc.edu/. Accessed 1 July 2018.

"Summer Bridge Program for Scientists and Engineers." *University of Maryland,* cmse.umd.edu/bridge. Accessed 1 July 2018.

"Summer Collegiate Experience." *University of Wisconsin-Madison,* cae.ls.wisc.edu/summer-collegiate-experience/. Accessed 1 July 2018.

"Summer Start." *University of California, Davis,* summerstart.ucdavis.edu/. Accessed 1 July 2018.

Summerhill, Daniel, et al. "Confronting the Comp Classroom: Implementing Anti-Racist Pedagogy and Navigating Opposition." *WPA: Writing Program Administration,* vol. 44, no. 3, 2021, pp. 121-27. https://wpacouncil.org/aws/CWPA/asset_manager/get_file/604422?ver=3. Accessed 28 May 2023.

Tinto, Vincent. *Leaving College: Rethinking the Causes and Cures of Student Attrition.* 2nd ed., U of Chicago P, 1993.

Tinto, Vincent. "Through the Eyes of Students." *Journal of College Student Retention: Research, Theory and Practice,* vol. 19, no. 3, 2017, pp. 254-69. https://doi.org/10.1177/1521025115621917. Accessed 28 Mar. 2019.

"TRIO Excel Summer Program." *Michigan State University,* nssc.msu.edu/programs/triosssprogram/index.html. Accessed 1 July 2018.

"UAdvantage First Year Experience." *The University of Arizona,* thrive.arizona.edu/uadvantage. Accessed 1 July 2018.

"UC Merced Summer Bridge—First-Year Program." *University of California, Merced,* summer bridge.ucmerced.edu/. Accessed 1 July 2018.

"Undergraduate ESL Program." *University of Massachusetts Boston.* www.umb.edu/academics/ vpass/academic_support/academics/esl. Accessed 1 July 2018.

Yosso, Tara J. "Whose Culture Has Capital?: A Critical Race Theory Discussion of Community Cultural Wealth." *Race, Ethnicity, and Education,* vol. 8, no. 1, 2005, pp. 69-91. https://doi.org/10.1080/1361332052000341006. Accessed 1 Aug. 2018.

Young, Vershawn Ashanti. "Should Writers Use They Own English?" *Iowa Journal of Cultural Studies,* vol. 12, no. 1, 2010, pp. 110-17. https://doi.org/10.17077/2168-569X.1095. Accessed 28 May 2023.

# Writing About Writing: A Snapshot in Time

*Cynthia A. Cochran, Rebecca Day Babcock, and Aliethia Dean*

Writing about writing (WAW) pedagogy is becoming a dominant approach to teaching writing, yet lacks descriptive empirical studies. In response to this deficit, we surveyed postsecondary instructors using WAW in the US and Canada to discover how they define WAW conceptually (what they think) and operationally (what they do). We used grounded theory to code data and inform our analysis of surveys, interviews, and course materials, including reading and writing assignments. Participants defined WAW as a movement, a pedagogical approach, and a subject matter whereby students read disciplinary literature in writing studies, use writing to investigate and understand writing and writing processes (especially their own), and develop metacognition about writing (including for transfer). The course subject or focus was writing itself, disciplinary content of writing studies (including research), and students' own reflective awareness. Instructors used a range of readings to teach disciplinary content and research methods in writing studies. Classroom activities included practicing and reflecting on writing and researching writing. Assignments focused on the topic of writing including rhetorical analysis and real-world writing tasks, often emphasizing reflection and metacognition.

---

"What I would loathe to see . . . is someone come out with a rule book on writing-about-writing with a step-by-step outline to follow. We need to be much more open and allow our teaching to be much more situated than that." – Christina Grant

Writing about Writing (WAW) pedagogy is gathering attention in research and practice, yet descriptive empirical studies are lacking outside of self-reports, and few empirical investigations focus on how instructors themselves conceptualize and enact WAW. The lack of such empirical studies limits our understandings of WAW in practice and our ability to define WAW with respect to how it is enacted in writing classes. The study we report on here aims to fill that gap: to determine WAW's operational and conceptual definition based on information gathered from a broad group of practitioners. That said, a brief overview of WAW is warranted, at least to anchor our discussions of WAW texts and case studies that contextualize the study. WAW is an approach to composition using writing assignments based on primary research on writing, students' literacy experiences, and course readings that include writing studies and non-academic texts about writing (e.g., famous writers' writing memoirs or laypeople's autobiographies on writing and literacy). WAW adheres to the idea that, as writing experts, faculty should teach their expertise. To investigate actual practice in WAW and establish a descriptive (rather than evaluative), empirically-driven baseline of practitioners' conceptions and employment of WAW, we conducted a triangulated, mixed-methods study using surveys, interviews, and instructional documents.

There are many ways to learn about WAW. One way is by examining textbooks. Initially, WAW textbook choices were limited for US practitioners to Elizabeth Wardle and Doug Downs' *Writing about Writing*, Wendy Bishop's *The Subject is Writing*, Eleanor Kutz's *Exploring Literacy*, or books on language (but not on writing specifically). More recently, books such as *Focus on Writing* (McMillan) and *Language Diversity* (Looker-Koenigs) appeared, and *Writing about Writing* was published in subsequent editions. Added to this small set are published lists (e.g., "Teaching Resources"). Across these texts are examples of assignments such as autoethnographies and activity-based genre studies. But it is not clear from such examination that WAW practitioners use only these textbooks; it is also not clear how or why WAW practitioners choose their materials, nor how they would enact WAW in the classroom.

Another way to learn about WAW is by examining individual classroom cases. Bird et al.'s *Next Steps* discusses mainly the implementation of specific WAW courses that, taken together, demonstrate a range of approaches in first year writing (FYW), English as a Second Language (ESL), writing across the curriculum (WAC) and professional writing (PW) courses. That said, the purpose of *Next Steps* was not to examine any patterns emerging from the individual cases. Whicker and Stinson examined published accounts of WAW, many from *Next Steps*, and developed a categorization scheme to plot approaches on various axes of attention to transfer, social aspects of writing (rather than social issues such as jobs and housing), and political issues involved in writing. They categorized the approaches as Process, Language/Literacy, Academic Discourse, and Context Analysis. Process focuses on the writer's own writing process, the process of famous authors, or process research. Language and Literacy pays more attention to political matters; these courses examine issues of diversity and social justice through topics such as literacy sponsors. Academic Discourse deals primarily with either similarity and difference in academic discourse generally or with differences among disciplines and genres. Context Analysis appears to focus on transfer, such as "teaching students to analyze communities, activity systems, and/or genres as a means of more efficiently learning to write in local contexts" (Whicker and Stinson). Whicker and Stinson conclude that further research is needed to determine the efficacy of a focus on student dispositions and transfer in writing studies courses.

While revelatory, these examinations of small sets of individual textbooks or a few individual cases are not enough to understand the fullness of WAW in practice. The next step is to consider many cases together in a cognitively flexible manner in order to attain a deeper layer of understanding. Cognitive flexibility is the ability to think in multiple, adaptive ways to acquire expertise in complex, ill-structured domains (Spiro et al.). This report argues that the goal of cognitive flexibility is to avoid oversimplifying or overregularizing by acknowledging that "knowledge is not as simple and orderly as it might first seem in introductory treatments" (16). Conceptually, WAW as a subject domain is both complex and ill-structured; many interwoven parts interact contextually, and "patterns of combination are inconsistent across case applications of the same nominal type" (2). Borrowing from Kristopher Lotier's metaphor for analyzing the history of postprocess–zooming in on individual cases and zooming out to consider a group of cases–we may come to similarly understand WAW at an advanced level: "At a lower resolution, fine-grained distinctions . . . become invisible. But, sometimes, invisibility is useful. In some cases, too much information produces conceptual static, unnecessary noise" (6). In other words, rather than relying on published texts inflected by the specific practices of individual experts or concentrating, as Lotier has done, on WAW's roots in previous composition pedagogy, we have borrowed Lotier's guiding metaphor to study a diverse range of contemporary practitioners. Our goal is to understand more about WAW as conceptualized and instantiated in widespread practice.

Besides offering an understanding of how practitioners define and instantiate WAW, this study also contributes to composition studies by providing a field-based look at how the theoretical principles of an approach transpire in teaching. This study is significant as the first survey of instructors since Downs and Wardle's small survey ("Reimagining") that asks about WAW teaching practices and beliefs, and it should be useful to practitioners (especially novices) and experienced scholars alike. In reporting descriptively and empirically, we aim to discuss our findings as impartially as possible, without evaluation. Although we are not evaluating WAW in any way, it is appropriate to mention that Cochran and Babcock were using approaches consistent with WAW at the outset of the study, and all three authors are members of the WAW Standing Group. Dean came to the pedagogy later but is an active practitioner.

## WAW in the Literature

As a teaching practice, WAW has multiple origins. One traces back to Aristotle and his dual emphasis on knowledge of and practice in rhetoric (Bird et al., "Writing" 13). Regarding more contemporary pedagogy, WAW may evolve from postprocess (Lotier). Another perspective is that contemporary WAW practice is traceable to Doug Downs, who, in his 2004 dissertation, outlined a course asking students to read, discuss, write about, learn to conduct library research on, and perform composition research, with attention to writing and discourse theory, research methods and questions, and students' own literacy experiences. In Downs' model, students created a research question, designed research methods, and reported/speculated on their findings; students also reflected on themselves as writers (83). Downs argues that FYW should lead students to interrogate their conceptions about writing in dialogue with the larger field. This kind of pedagogy, Downs argues, is difficult to enact given the training of FYW teachers, which he considered to be lacking in theory (at least circa 2004). Downs also attempted to counter the belief that anyone can teach writing, regardless of their specialized disciplinary knowledge. Downs and Wardle later explain that WAW teaches students "flexible and transferable declarative and procedural knowledge about writing" helping them understand writing as "situated, motivated, contingent, material or embodied, and epistemic" ("Reflecting" 279) and something that is collaboratively and dynamically used and produced within "communities of practice" to generate new knowledge, and a skill learned and developed over time (280).

In 2005, the WAW Special Interest Group (SIG) of the CCCC began, and Elizabeth Sargent and Cornelia Paraskevas published *Conversations about Writing*. For a 2007 *College Composition and Communication* (*CCC*) article, Downs and Wardle investigated the teaching of writing studies in an FYC class entitled "The Writing about Writing Course" (564). Many compositionists, including several of our study participants, credit this 2007 *CCC* article as kicking off interest in WAW. Its publication caused a stir (and more than a few misunderstandings), resulting in several published responses… and responses to responses. (Those unfamiliar with these exchanges can consult the pages of *CCC*; space prohibits lengthy discussion here.) The WAW approach gained exposure through Wardle and Downs' textbook, *Writing about Writing*, originally published in 2011. Wardle and Downs later reflected, "our field has knowledge and conceptions of writing that are valuable to students," specifically when we advocate a set of principles: "engage students with the research and ideas of the field, using any means necessary and productive, in order to shift students' conceptions of writing, building declarative and procedural knowledge of writing with an eye toward transfer" ("Reflecting"). Elsewhere, Downs and Wardle reported on a small survey of instructors who said that WAW empowers students by teaching them methods and content to "better understand themselves as writers and users of language" ("Reimagining" 136). During the rise of WAW, studies of the efficacy of WAW (Blaauw-Hara et al.; Moore) have taken on increasing importance, but their focus deviates from ours here, which is on course content.

We reasoned, however, that before becoming heavily invested in research on the effects or evaluation of WAW, scholars should establish a baseline of what WAW means to everyday practitioners and learn how they operationalize their definition by what they do. To find out more about instructors who use WAW, we performed a study investigating what WAW has come to mean to a diverse group of practitioners. The study population for our study includes graduate students, contingent faculty, and other everyday teachers using the pedagogy, in addition to some well-known WAW researchers.

## Methods

### *Research Questions*

Considering WAW's newness and the dearth of descriptive empirical research, we planned to study the range and boundaries of WAW, including how instructors define WAW and develop their classes. Thus, we developed these research questions to find how WAW is enacted and defined at a particular moment in the US and Canada:

1. How do participants define WAW conceptually?
2. How do participants define WAW operationally? That is, what themes, readings, and assignments do they include in WAW courses?

### *Data Gathering, Recruitment, and Dataset*

We reasoned that collecting multiple forms of data would help us discover how practitioners use and define WAW: instructor surveys, their course materials (e.g., syllabi, writing assignments, reading lists), and interviews of survey participants served as data for the study.

We gained permission to conduct the research from Cochran's IRB. In 2015, we posted an open invitation on the WAWN, WCenter, and WPA-L (now known as the Writing Studies listserv) listservs because they are active and highly populated; from these venues, we recruited 31 participants for the initial survey. These lists include primarily post-secondary instructors, so we expected—and found—all participants were at the post-secondary level. We did not purposefully sample for only US and Canadian practitioners, but all participants were located in those geographical areas.

We used survey, interview, and text analysis as primary data-gathering methods. We created the survey instrument (see Appendix) using Google Forms and distributed a link on the three aforementioned listservs. Based on survey responses, we sent a follow-up letter to those who agreed to be interviewed and to share course materials. Interviews were conducted from fall 2015 to spring 2016 via Skype; participants unable to complete a live interview responded to an emailed set of interview questions. During the recorded interviews, one researcher took notes and the other asked questions. The questioning interviewer also took backup notes. A research assistant listened to and transcribed the recordings, double-checking the notes.

For our sample, 31 US and Canadian instructors completed the survey; 8 sent course materials; 11 completed in-depth online interviews (4 live and 7 email interviews). One participant did not teach but was a writing center director. This sample was not selected randomly from all composition instructors in the US and Canada, so it does represent a self-selected group invested to some degree in WAW. Some participants are more experienced than others in teaching WAW, and, as a group, they work at a wide range of colleges and universities.

### *Method of Analysis*

This is a mixed-method study using grounded theory–an approach to data analysis that allows relevant information to emerge and discourages researcher's preconceptions from imposing upon the data–for analysis (Babcock 109-110; Corbin and Strauss). We examined surveys to determine categories of responses to each question. Both primary researchers individually counted answers to closed-ended questions and individually coded open-ended ones. We reviewed all Skype and email interviews and examined related course materials. We coded the interviews, syllabi, and other materials for readings, writing assignments, and course themes (topics). We worked through qualitative data recursively: after initial coding, we checked each other's work and discussed the codes until reaching a consensus. We completed the later analysis of our codes with modified grounded theory, using qualitative, interpretative methods. The back-and-forth, constant checking, re-checking, and consensus-making were quite rigorous but necessary because our survey contained open-ended questions, the answers for which had to be interpreted to be categorized. These rounds of coding gave us the structure to track comparison across our data sets.

Using the codes, we formulated holistic lists for each research question. We cross-referenced data points wherever participants mentioned relevant information (in survey responses, interviews, emails to the authors, or provided materials). Specifically, we created a full list of all course readings from the syllabi and then added any readings mentioned elsewhere in the data. We tallied the readings that more than one instructor mentioned. Similarly, using the syllabi and the other data, we created a full list of all writing assignments. Through grounded theory, we categorized and chunked the various assignments until we had a schema that encompassed what we saw in the data. Finally, using the lists and the original data, we developed a codebook to indicate which participants mentioned a given topic in order to create a list of course themes.

### *Limitations of the Study*

Certain limitations resulted from our desire to take a snapshot of WAW at a particular moment. We contacted no instructors outside of the aforementioned listservs, which meant excluding instructors outside of Canada and the US. We asked survey respondents neither their rank, years of experience with WAW, academic backgrounds, nor areas of expertise, although some participants volunteered this information. We did not ask survey respondents specifically about assignments, readings, goals, or objectives, although participants mentioned these in survey responses and some provided course materials. We later realized that the simplistic wording in some survey questions did not go far enough in asking why people assign what they assign—or even whether they view all their assignments as part and parcel of WAW (see Appendix for questions.) All participants self-identified as using WAW, but, unless participants provided a syllabus, we do not know whether their whole course or a portion of it fits into a WAW construct.

## Results

Below, we present the results of the research by topic. Some participants opted to use their real names, and we honor that choice in this article. We refer to anyone choosing anonymity by a participant number. Where pertinent, we report participants' views using their original language.

### *How Participants Came to WAW*

Participants came to WAW in various ways, including some survey respondents who were teaching in a program using WAW. All eleven interview subjects reported how they came to and why they preferred WAW. Three reasons emerged why interviewees chose WAW:

1. It fit with what they already knew about writing pedagogy or with their emerging philosophies (n=5).

   For instance, Barbara Bird said, "When I studied what [George Jardine 1742-1827] was doing, I thought, 'That's the way writing should be taught.'" Christina Grant found that WAW fit in with her "commitment to giving students the straight goods about rhetoric, writing, and the real communications world out there." Jeffrey Klausman wrote that WAW "made sense, especially in the context of the research I'd been reading."

2. It fit what they were already doing or wanted to do (n=3).

One participant was working with genre, one was developing a writing program, and one wondered why Donald Murray's writings could not be shared directly with students.

3. Their reason was inherent in the pedagogy itself (n=3).

   For example, Samuel Stinson wrote, "WAW approaches directly position students as writing researchers and provide students a critical apparatus for engaging not only the threshold concepts of our field but also educational transfer." Participant #17 indicated that they were "drawn to the pedagogy because of its emphasis on writing, and secondarily, research on writing." Barbara Lewis wrote, "It immerses college writers in theories about writing and composing; it allows and encourages self-reflection about writing practices; and raises their awareness about the choices they're making in communication, in general."

*Conceptual Definitions of WAW*

When asked to define WAW, survey participants called it an approach, a concept, a philosophy, a pedagogy, a curriculum, and a movement. Many indicated that the subject students write about in such a course is writing itself and mentioned academic writing and texts, professional writing, writing research, and "[w]hat other writers and researchers have said/discovered about the process of writing" (Barbara Lewis). Participants described WAW as the study of writing, genre, and adaptation. Jack Keningsburg declared it an approach in which writing is used "to inquire about writing itself"; Matthew Ortoleva called writing "the key learning tool" of a WAW approach. Several survey participants offered general definitions:

> "WAW offers opportunities for viewing writing through an ecological frame as well as intersecting with expressivist, cognitive, and social epistemic ways of understanding writing process. . . . WAW remains a flexible concept that subsumes theory, content, and curricular matters. The central theme of WAW pedagogy is writing and focusing on student understanding of writing." – Stinson

> "[Students] spend most or all of their time reading, writing, and talking about what experts and experienced writers have to say about their own struggles to write, their philosophies of what writing can do in the world, what learning to write with power and clarity has done–or not done—for them, and how they actually go about it." – Grant

As part of their definitions, some participants described their approach. Participant #6 wrote that their approach to WAW teaches students "about writing, rather than any one form of writing." Other course content included "the scholarship of our field" (Michaud), research methods, "what we know as writing professionals" (Stinson), theories and research from rhetoric/composition, the importance of metacognition, "how to learn to write" (Participant #6), and declarative and procedural knowledge about writing.

Taking what seems a proactive stance, Michael Michaud wrote:

> "someday the title 'Writing about Writing' needs to go away. [WAW] is what Writing Studies scholars SHOULD be and ARE, in many cases, teaching in their classes. We don't need an extra name for this kind of teaching, although perhaps we did initially. I see WAW as connected to a larger disciplinary movement to claim our knowledge and practices and to teach them to our students [and] . . . as connected to efforts towards writing majors/minors, etc. Someday it will seem silly that we needed a name for the thing that we should have been doing all along: teaching our students what we know (both the declarative and procedural aspects)."

### *Operational Definitions of WAW*

Beyond finding how participants explicitly defined WAW, we wanted to know how they enacted it in teaching; that is we wondered how their operational definitions of WAW were evidenced in their course goals, overall thematic focus/subject, topics, classroom activities, readings, and writing assignments. Although participants used a variety of terms to describe their courses, the categories grew out of our grounded theory analysis of data that allowed us to determine what WAW meant to the instructors, not just in theory but in practice.

#### Classroom Activities

Certain classroom activities help to define WAW as highly interactive and both cognitively and socially situated. Grant wrote, "Ideally, the approach also involves some research-supported pedagogical elements such as small class size, workshop format, student-versus teacher-led teaching, teacher-student conferencing, shared freewriting (i.e. inkshedding), lots of feedback on content (first) and lower order concerns (second), portfolio grading, and contract grading" and "thinking about others' ideas *in relation to themselves*" (emphasis in original). Other participants mentioned writing, metacognition, and practice with various genres, including "helping students practice writing" (Michaud).

### Course Goals

Part of the operational definition of WAW arose from the course goals and objectives participants listed in survey responses, interviews, or course materials. In our grounded theory analysis, we phrased these as objectives with infinitive verbs (some were already phrased that way). Students were to:

- understand how writing works
- learn different kinds of writing
- understand or theorize writing
- develop abstract knowledge about literacy, writing, and rhetoric
- "increase transfer through self-study, meta-cognition, and practice with various genres as examples of application of abstract concepts (such as rhetorical awareness and rhetorical situations, activity systems, discourse communities, etc.) rather than as ends unto themselves" (Participant #7).
- "acquire knowledge and experience that transfer to other writing situations" (Participant #16)
- "develop a flexible collection of writing process strategies" (Grant)

Although not all of these objectives are measurable, this list provides a start for designing WAW course objectives.

### Overall Focus of the Course

The definition of WAW also emerged from the focus of participants' courses. As expected, the most common subject and focus areas mentioned were writing and the study and practice of writing, though participants phrased it differently one to the next. Courses focused on "writing itself" (Kenigsberg); "understanding how writing works" (Pat Burnes); "writing—including the students' own texts" (Grant); "reflective awareness" (Burnes); and "writing (in a 'meta' way)" (Participant #22). People also mentioned as course foci writing as a "discipline," "writing studies disciplinary content" (TJ Geiger), and "research on composition, literacy studies, and rhetorical studies" (David Stock). Stock said writing appears as "both an activity and an object of study" with a "twin emphasis on writing and writing research." Finally, participants described the focus as "reading and writing about the activity of writing" (Lewis) and "students' reasons for writing and what they write and why" (Bradley Bleck).

### Specific Course Topics and Units

To further understand variations in the focus of the courses, we examined specific course content by asking participants what themes (meaning topics or units) they included. To probe the issue, we also examined their course materials. Following grounded theory techniques, we clustered data into categories that seemed to cohere, and then re-examined the data to further collapse and combine categories. In all, we counted eighty-seven different words or phrases regarding themes and topics, and each became a token. The top topics before combining like tokens were process, discourse communities, and genre. After combining like codes into categories, the top focus was Literacy, including visual, rhetorical, workplace, information, digital, alternative, and personal (all of these words collocated with Literacy). Specifically mentioned were literacy narratives and "critical literacy autobiographies," although in some cases it was difficult to determine if respondents meant these as topics students study (perhaps through assigned readings), as assignments they write, or both. Another prominent topic was Rhetoric, including visual and digital rhetoric, rhetorical situation, rhetorical awareness, rhetorical reading, and rhetorical analysis. The count for Rhetoric rises to twenty-seven if we include things like voice, style, exigence, audience, persuasion, and argument. After further combining and refining categories, Process gained the subcategories of invention, freewriting, revision, and "reading, writing, and thinking as processes." A final set of topics related to Social Considerations, which included discourse community, genre, and cultural studies (see Table 1.)

Table 1. Combined Course Topics

| Literacy | Rhetoric | Process | Social Considerations |
|---|---|---|---|
| Visual<br>Rhetorical<br>Workplace<br>Information<br>Digital<br>Alternative<br>Personal | Visual<br>Digital<br>Situational<br>Awareness<br>Analytical Reading<br>Voice<br>Style<br>Exigence<br>Audience<br>Persuasion<br>Argument | Invention<br>Free-writing<br>Revision<br>Reading<br>Writing<br>Thinking | Discourse community<br>Genre<br>Cultural studies |

Regarding themes and diversity, Grant said in an online interview,

> "One theme I might add is awareness of diverse rhetorical traditions. It's important for all students to acknowledge and value their home country's rhetorical traditions and not see them as deficits to their learning or development as writers and thinkers. We need to help all students move towards a truly global culturally and linguistically diverse future in order to embrace and mobilize all ways of seeing and being. . . . The power language and ideology of Euro-American English must be tempered with flavours and colours from across rhetorical worlds."

Reflecting that thematic approaches may change, Michaud wrote,

> "My WAW courses are always changing. I've done work with literacy narratives and with rhetoric. I've looked at writing process and auto-ethnography. But lately I've been branching out and making up my own WAW courses and assignments. It's like Doug and Liz's book was the inspiration, a model, and permission and now I have picked up the ball and run with it. I've turned a multi-major professional writing course into a WAW course in which we read work by . . . Deborah Brandt and Anne Beaufort. In my FYW courses I've designed units and courses entirely on revision and on the five-paragraph essay. I'm having fun with it and I see endless possibilities . . . once you make the switch from teaching other people's 'content' to teaching your own."

### Readings

As part of the definition of WAW, participants mentioned the types of readings used in their courses. These materials were used to help determine what people mean by WAW. Instructors included texts on writing, writing theory, writing research, and writing "introductory research articles" (Cat Mahaffey); instructional texts; "key disciplinary literature" (Ortoleva); scholarship/research on novice writers; scholarship from the discipline or field of writing studies; and "articles, chapters, and other texts by writing scholars" (Clay Walker). Walker also told us he assigns "readings on a variety of writing studies issues (e.g., genre studies, rhetorical reading, literacy studies)" and that "students read selected texts for class discussions in preparation for writing projects." Jennifer deWinter's students, on the other hand, choose a "keyword" from writing studies and then, in groups, research and write about it.

To find out more about course readings, we examined course material and actual references provided by eight instructors and eleven instructor interviews without duplicating information from six instructors who provided both. We found that several (not all) courses used *Writing about Writing* (1st or 2nd edition)[1]. The most popular reading (used by six instructors) was Wardle's "Identity, Authority, and Learning to Write in New Workplaces." When asked in an interview about readings, Lewis said she used "excerpts from . . . Peter Elbow, Annie Dillard, Stephen King, John Barth, Berthoff and others." Participant #10 specified "readings from Robert McRuer, Helene Cixous, Gloria Anzaldua, Geneva Smitherman, Lisa Delpit, etc." Readers may note that the list includes not only writing studies scholars but people in other areas, such as philosophers and both literary and popular writers. We found five readings used in common by four instructors; these include three about discourse communities, one about activity theory, and one about literacy sponsors. Of readings used in two or more courses, all but two readings (92%) appeared in the first and second editions of *Writing about Writing*. However, of the 105 readings mentioned by only one participant, eighty-two, or 78%, did not appear in the *Writing about Writing* textbook. This suggests that shared readings are often textbook based, but that, outside of that context, people tend to choose different and non-overlapping readings, even some apparently from outside of writing studies itself. We cannot assume causality, so perhaps the textbook is driving the pedagogy, or perhaps Wardle and Downs included readings that were already popular. The entire list of readings can be viewed in "Readings for WAW Courses" on the WAW Blog (https://writingaboutwriting.net/2023/05/17/readings-for-waw-courses/).

### Writing Assignments

When asked to define WAW, several participants mentioned types of assignments (n=30) as a defining program element; for example, three said assignments focused on the topic or nature of writing. Others mentioned rhetorical analysis, "'authentic' writing tasks" (Dan Bommarito), and assignments that "end with students reflecting on what they have done and often comparing that to what they have been reading about" (Burnes). Bommarito said that "writing is the centerpiece of all the assignments." In many courses, students do primary research; in some primary and library research assignments, students researched academic or professional writing, writing process, or writing pedagogy: "The major writing projects also concern writing issues, such as exploring the writing and genre conventions in a professional field" (Walker).

We examined all the data for mention of specific writing assignments. The following list includes both unique and common assignments, ordered by the most to least common assignment category:

- Research writing: annotated bibliographies, source evaluation, library research paper, synthesis paper, research or professional conference proposal or presentation, literature review, bibliographic essay
- Reflections: literacy narratives, portfolio reflections (including letters), writing logs, autoethnographies on writing, writing to discover self, think-aloud protocol analysis, reflections of writing process and product, letter arguing for grade
- Analysis of texts in context: rhetorical analysis, genre analysis, exploring writing in a particular field, profession, or discipline
- Analysis of writing as a contextualized act or sociocultural phenomenon (could include primary research): discourse community analysis, science accommodation writing activity, new media
- Summary and responses: writing about readings, writing to learn, extended definitions (could be argumentative)
- Exploratory: prewriting, writing to explore, journaling, freewriting
- Argument: a theory of writing, writing to prove your point, critique, critical summary, grading rubric
- Explanatory writing-to-learn and instructional writing: extended definition of writing studies terms, research on key writing studies concepts, "Five-part Guide" to explain reading, writing, and revising
- Peer review: of presentations and drafts (often written out as a memo or letter)

Despite perceiving an emphasis in WAW on genre study, few respondents reported assigning genres outside of personal narratives, analyses, arguments, research papers, and reader responses. Though these assignments mainly focused on writing studies content, the genres are common to many composition courses, with some exceptions: Several people assigned a letter (e.g., one attached to a portfolio), a genre often left for professional writing courses; several assigned research reports on students' first-hand research. A few assigned presentations, multimodal writing (e.g., online portfolios that could contain a variety of genres), or new media writing assignments. Overall, the preponderance of assignments called for academic and personal writing; though some were professional writing assignments, no civic writing appeared.

## Discussion

Despite going into the study with no preconceptions about how WAW would be defined or enacted by participants, we found diverse definitions. However, one common theme emerged: these college instructors consider "writing itself" to be the focus of WAW courses. But WAW emerged as more than a pedagogy. They also defined WAW as a movement, a philosophy, and a concept/subject matter. As a pedagogical and curricular approach, WAW asks students to read and write about disciplinary literature in writing studies and to use writing to inquire about their own writing processes and writing in communities.

WAW is becoming common in composition pedagogy, finding its way into writing-related courses and gaining proponents. However, not all of our study participants define themselves as WAW proponents. Answering whether they considered themselves a proponent or explorer of WAW, a clear majority, 65% (n=20) considered themselves proponents, and 20% (n=16) identified as explorers (five said both; one gave an off-topic answer). This result reflects the variety of stances toward WAW of the composition instructors who participated and may reflect distinctions in how much autonomy individual instructors have in a given teaching context.

Understandably, WAW course goals vary, but most courses include goals regarding learning about and understanding writing studies and writing itself; other goals are to learn for transfer, develop writing processes, and improve metacognition about writing. The course subject or focus is writing, and the disciplinary content is predominantly writing studies (including research) and students' reflective awareness. Instructors teach content and research methods of writing studies as well as common writing and rhetorical skills and genres, drawing from the humanities and social sciences in their approach to writing studies. This emphasis on writing studies content is the most predominant way that WAW pedagogy is distinguished from other composition pedagogies.

We found the main course topics and units of courses to be *Process, Rhetoric, Literacy,* and *Social Considerations*; we believe these categories are consistent with and confirm the conclusions of Whicker and Stinson, who found the four theoretical axes of WAW to be *Process, Language/Literacy, Academic Discourse,* and *Context Analysis* (i.e., teaching for transfer).

Interestingly, many WAW courses rely, in part, on rhetorical analysis as a key to introducing students to writing studies, likely reflecting the instructors' own background in rhetorical studies. Classroom activities, while drawing on forms common to other composition pedagogies, also commonly include practicing and reflecting on writing and writing research. Assignments focus on the topic of writing (including rhetorical analysis), academic writing, and professional writing. Reflection and metacognition are usually included. Early uses of WAW– like the one highlighted in Downs' dissertation–tended to be in FYW, typically a course requiring a research paper. In this study, however, some instructors reported using WAW with writing center tutors or graduate students, others in undergraduate courses before or beyond FYW, including ESL courses. This finding is consistent with the range reported in *Next Steps.* Just as FYW is not students' only opportunity to learn to write, WAW is not limited to FYW, a point Wardle highlights in an interview: "At the end of the day, first year composition is still just one class at one place at the beginning of a student's educational experience. And we already know that that will never be enough. . . . We need to work with faculty from across all the years and all the disciplines as well, so they can continue the work with student writers" (Olejnik 64).

Our analysis showed that many instructors explicitly identified WAW with the Wardle and Downs *Writing About Writing* textbook, while others were initially drawn to WAW by the 2007 Downs and Wardle article or discovered the approach on their own or with books like Wendy Bishop's *The Subject is Writing*. We found that the Wardle and Downs' text liberates some and confines others. We did not expect, but found, that some equate this textbook with the pedagogy. (That the textbook and the pedagogy share a name is perhaps a source of this conflation). Other individuals developed their own approaches, perhaps starting with readings that appear in the Wardle and Downs book and then adding their own. Our study was not about the textbook, nor did we ask about it, but eight survey respondents referred explicitly to it and some apparently expected us to know what they were talking about (e.g., "the text").

The identity relationship between WAW and the textbook *Writing About Writing* arose repeatedly. Several respondents shared Participant #20's view: "I take issues with some aspects of the textbook *Writing about Writing*, but the concept works." For some, such as Participant #26, the textbook enables sophisticated teaching: "What I appreciate most about the text is that I learn while teaching it, and it doesn't dumb things down for the students." Keningsburg's initial reaction to some of Wardle and Downs' work was "omg hell no would that ever work in a classroom. I thought then that it was important for teachers to know, but not necessarily for students to read. I am–slowly–coming around to having my students read more of the dense, abstract stuff as a way to frame the more concrete, practical stuff." This comment revealed an initial disinclination to use WAW based on the Wardle and Downs textbook, but he became more of a proponent "with each passing semester." One participant remarked that "the Downs and Wardle book just seemed much too bulky," though we don't know if this is meant literally–as in the book's physical properties–or conceptually. Yet other participants reported having a wider vision of WAW than captured by *WAW*. One wrote, "It's important to consider WAW's expanded definition and not just the Wardle and Downs approach." Participant #10 mentioned that new TAs used Wardle and Downs' book, but that the department had added readings for teaching multimodality, using "none from *WAW* 2nd ed. because we found the chapter to be pretty useless for our needs." That participant added, "WAW [the textbook] doesn't address the role identity plays in the creation and negotiation of texts."

The many instructors who selected alternative readings do not, apparently, identify WAW with only *Writing about Writing*, the textbook. Thus, using a WAW reader may be, for some, a way to teach their expertise and flexibly to forge new pathways; for others, the textbook felt unnecessary. In both cases, it seems that, as an approach to teaching writing, WAW allows practitioners to draw on their writing studies background and interests when selecting the course readings.

Given what practitioners in our study reported about their classes, the range of approaches is consistent with those reported in *Next Steps.* Moreover, instructors vary in their approach in ways that reinforce the categories derived by Whicker and Stinson. Some see WAW as a distinct pedagogy with unique features, including those for which Downs advocates. Some participants incorporated WAW with other approaches (one used cultural studies, and another mentioned its compatibility with critical pedagogy). Some were explorers who reported that they came to WAW because it fit in with what they already knew or what they had already been doing before WAW was named as such. The most vocal proponents in our study had come to use WAW as the basis for their entire course, incorporating the strands of writing scholarship they saw as important for their goals. For some participants, WAW appears to have altered their previous conception of what a writing course should be. The range of assignments, while predominantly academic writing, certainly suggests that WAW is adaptable to various types of writing courses (including levels from developmental to graduate); nothing in the data suggests it is necessarily limited to academic writing. Nor does using WAW limit instructors to any given approach: it "has never been a single monolithic curriculum" (Whicker and Stinson ). WAW also seems flexible for participants who reported changing topics and readings from semester to semester or course to course; recall Wardle's comment that even the same WAW instructor may take different approaches to the same end ("Reflecting" 281).

Most writing assignments in our study were academic, a finding similar to findings by Graves et al. and by Melzer in studying composition and WAC pedagogy. But the strong emphasis on self-reflective metacognition through self-study, auto-ethnographies, and literacy narratives in WAW enables expressivist writing in an academic setting, and many instructors included personal narratives of some sort. The assignments promoting reflection, coupled with data-gathering–especially of one's own writing and writing processes–helps WAW blend the expressivist and the academic insofar as the subject matter combines writing *itself* and writing *my self.* Perhaps this idea explains some participants' strong feelings about WAW (two participants used the word "love"). Some participants applauded WAW as a route to help students make transitions into college and into becoming researchers. WAW is indeed unique in its emphasis on studying writing per se—as an act, process, phenomenon, set of genres, and so on.

Finally, WAW is likely to change along with the discipline. WAW themes and readings follow scholarship in the field, so works like Linda Adler-Kassner and Elizabeth Wardle's textbook edition of *Naming What We Know* can encourage variation in the readings selected for a WAW course. In addition, philosophical changes in the discipline can also inflect WAW pedagogies and materials. One example would be WAW's relationship to postprocess. If the move from composition to writing studies is, in fact, a paradigm shift resulting from the end of postprocess (Lotier), we might expect other approaches and theories–like WAW–to ascend disciplinarily. Conversely, if this move is not a paradigm shift–if WAW is, rather, a phenomenon that is "inextricably bound-up with and connected to" postprocess (122)–we would have a way to understand how WAW draws from several composition pedagogies and movements, incorporating elements of process, genre, and reflective writing into assignments of largely academic and expressivist (i.e., reflective) writing.

Then again, perhaps our disciplinary context doesn't quite fit with Lotier's framework. A study like the one represented by this article is important at this time not only because WAW is becoming a standard in composition pedagogy, but because WAW draws from the whole of composition and rhetoric, the whole of writing studies and sister fields such as linguistics, literature, and education. WAW practitioners do assign mostly familiar academic genres for students to write in, but this study has demonstrated that WAW practitioneres also draw from a wide range of readings in writing studies. In this regard, WAW is perhaps not a living offshoot of postprocess, but a natural outgrowth of the entire writing studies field. Practitioners come to WAW from various traditions and approaches: historical, rhetorical, genre studies, social constructivism, Soviet psychology, even expressivism. All these have a place and a space in WAW.

With apologies to Walt Whitman: Does WAW contradict itself? Very well then it contradicts itself. (But it is large, it contains multitudes.)

In practice, then, WAW takes the logical step from writing in the disciplines, investigating discourse communities, and having teachers teach from genres that they know and use, to the idea of teaching writing studies content in the composition course (which is, presumably, the instructors' expertise). Because of the strong emphasis on writing studies as content emerging from the WAW movement, we propose that the term *writing studies pedagogy* better captures the diversity and richness of perspectives through which students can learn about and practice writing via WAW.

## Ideas for Future Research

The study results hint at pedagogical connections we did not investigate explicitly. First among those was expressed by one reviewer for this article, who was surprised that so many participants used rhetorical analysis in their coursework. But, considering the array of backgrounds of composition instructors—many who were schooled in rhetorical analysis—it seems logical that they would emphasize this humanities-based approach in their WAW courses. More to the point, the instructors chose to include the content of writing studies while retaining many of the types of writing assignments common to composition classes of all sorts. Second, the emphasis on learning about writing and writing studies, rather than simply learning how to write, appears to be one of WAW's most distinguishing features, which we might choose to explore more.

Much research work remains for studying WAW. We suggest a large-scale quantitative study of WAW course syllabi and a full-scale study of readings and writing assignments used in WAW courses that would expand the findings of this study. Starting with the reading and writing assignments we found in this study, we wonder: would one find a canon developing in the larger community of WAW instructors? Similarly, syllabus analysis could include a study of specified goals and objectives that would broaden and deepen the findings here.

Surveys of a larger group of instructors could reveal more about WAW reading and writing assignments, including how they may have changed since the inception of this study. An interview study could reveal more about how instructors' backgrounds relate to their choice of readings and writing assignments, going into more depth about what they consider central to writing studies and WAW. From such studies, we might learn more about why instructors make the choices they do. Such studies could research the effects of using WAW to teach graduate teaching assistants, writing center tutors, and/or WAC/WID instructors: Would perceptions of writing studies or composition instruction differ across time, curricular level, and program type? How might their teaching and perspectives compare to those who learned to teach writing in more traditional ways? It would also be useful to consider more broadly how WAW may be used with various student populations (e.g., in secondary, developmental, and ESL courses). Further research could then follow-up on studies of WAW efficacy, examining effects on transfer of WAW pedagogy compared to non-WAW approaches.

As with many qualitative studies, we end–happily–with more questions than when we began.

## Acknowledgments

Thanks to Julie Samaras, who assisted with transcribing. Thanks also to the participants for their time and generosity. Thanks to the anonymous reviewers for their thoughtful comments and to Dawn An for her careful reading of this article.

## Notes

1. *Writing about Writing*'s 3rd, 4th, and now 5th editions hadn't appeared when we collected our data, but because our research is not about the textbook, its readings–no matter the source–remain relevant. This snapshot is historical.

## Appendix: Survey Questions

1. Do you consider yourself to be a proponent of WAW or more of an explorer in WAW?
   To what extent and in what ways?
2. How do you define "writing about writing"?
3. What kinds of themes do you include in your course? (These themes may appear in readings, units, assignments, etc.)
4. For what level of students do you use WAW?
5. What delivery method do you use?
6. Who uses writing about writing at your institution?
7. Anything else you want to tell us:

I agree to participate in a follow-up interview (potentially by phone or email). I understand that my participation in this interview is completely voluntary, and also understand that I may withdraw my consent at any time before, during, or after the study.

I agree to submit materials to be used as data in the study. (If you agree you may be asked to submit your syllabus, WAW assignments, and any other relevant materials such as rubrics or WAW reading lists).

__ yes, use my real name __yes, use a pseudonym _ no

## Works Cited

Adler-Kassner, Linda, and Elizabeth Wardle. *Naming What We Know: Threshold Concepts of Writing Studies.* UP of Colorado, 2015.

Babcock, Rebecca, et al. "Grounded Theory." *Theories and Methods of Writing Center Studies: A Practical Guide*, edited by Jo Mackiewicz and Rebecca Day Babcock, Routledge, 2019, pp. 109-117.

Babcock, Rebecca, Cynthia Cochran, and Aliethia Dean. "Readings for WAW Courses." Blog. Writing About Writing Network. May 2023, https://writingaboutwriting.net/2023/05/17/readings-for-waw-courses/. Accessed 27 Oct. 2023.

Bird, Barbara, et al. *Next Steps: New Directions for/in Writing about Writing.* Utah State UP, 2019.

—. "Writing about Writing: A History." *Next Steps: New Directions for/in Writing about Writing.* Utah State UP, 2019, pp. 13-20.

Bishop, Wendy. *The Subject is Writing.* 4th ed., Heinemann, 2006.

Blaauw-Hara, Mark, et al. "Is a Writing-about-Writing Approach Appropriate for Community College Developmental Writers in a Corequisite Class?" *Composition Studies,* vol. 48, no. 2, 2020, pp. 55-73.

Corbin, Juliet, and Anselm Strauss. *Basics of Qualitative Research: Techniques and Procedures for Developing Grounded Theory.* SAGE, 2003.

Downs, Doug. *Teaching Our Own Prison: FYC Curricula and Public Conceptions of Writing.* 2004. University of Utah, PhD dissertation.

Downs, Doug, and Elizabeth Wardle. "Reimagining the Nature of FYC Trends in Writing-about- Writing Pedagogies." *Exploring Composition Studies,* edited by Kelly Ritter and Paul Kei Matsuda. U of Colorado P, 2012, pp. 123-44.

—. "Teaching about Writing, Righting Misconceptions: (Re)envisioning 'First-Year Composition' as 'Introduction to Writing Studies.'" *College Composition and Communication*, vol. 58, no. 4, 2007, pp. 552- 85.

Graves, Roger, et al. "Undergraduate Writing Assignments: An Analysis of Syllabi at One Canadian College." *Written Communication,* vol. 27, 2010, pp. 293-317.

Looker-Koenigs, Samantha. *Language Diversity and Academic Writing: A Bedford Spotlight Reader.* Bedford, 2018.

Kutz, Eleanor. *Exploring Literacy.* Pearson, 2003.

Lotier, Kristopher M. *Postprocess Postmortem.* WAC Clearinghouse and U of Colorado P, 2021.

McMillan, Laurie. *Focus on Writing: What College Students Want to Know.* Broadview, 2018.

Melzer, Dan. *Assignments across the Curriculum: A National Study of College Writing.* Utah State UP, 2014.

Moore, Miriam. "Using 'Writing about Writing' Pedagogy with L2 and Developmental Readers and Writers at the Community College." *Empowering the Community College First-Year Composition Teacher*, edited by Meryl Siegal and Betsy Gilliland. U of Michigan P, 2021, pp. 49-60.

Olejnik, Mandy. "Changing Conceptions of Writing: An interview with Elizabeth Wardle." *Writing Program Administration,* vol. 42, no. 3, 2019, pp. 59–64.

Read, Sarah, and Michael J. Michaud. "Negotiating WAW-PW Across Diverse Institutional Contexts." *Next Steps,* edited by Bird et al., Utah State UP, 2019, pp. 159-71.

Sargent, M. Elizabeth, and Cornelia C. Paraskevas. *Conversations about Writing.* Thompson/Nelson, 2005.

Spiro, Rand, et al. *Cognitive Flexibility Theory: Advanced Knowledge Acquisition in Ill-structured Domains.* Center for the Study of Reading, U. of Illinois at Urbana-Champaign, 1988. Technical Report no. 441.

"Teaching Resources." *Writing About Writing Network.* 2021, https://writingabout-writing.net/category/resources/teaching-resources/textbooks/. Accessed 27 Oct. 2023.

Wardle, Elizabeth. "Identity, Authority, and Learning to Write in New Workplaces." *enculturation* vol. 5 no. 2. (2004). http://enculturation.gmu.edu/5_2/wardle.html. Accessed 28 Oct. 2023.

Wardle, Elizabeth, and Doug Downs. "Reflecting Back and Looking Forward: Revisiting 'Teaching about Writing, Righting Misconceptions' Five Years On." *Composition Forum,* vol. 27, 2013, https://www.compositionforum.com/issue/27/reflecting-back.php. Accessed 27 Oct. 2023.

—. *Writing about Writing: A College Reader.* Bedford-St. Martin's, 2011.

—. *Writing about Writing: A College Reader.* 2nd ed, Bedford-St. Martin's, 2014.

Whicker, John, and Samuel Stinson. "Axiology and Transfer in Writing about Writing: Does It Matter Which Way We WAW?" *Composition Forum,* vol. 45, 2020. https://compositionforum.com/issue/45/axiology.php. Accessed 27 Oct. 2023.

# Building Our Ideals into Program Structures: Democratic Design in Program Administration

*Brad Jacobson and Rachael W. Shah*

This article argues for a Deweyan "democratic design" approach to program leadership that builds programmatic ideals into leadership practices. To illustrate democratic design in practice, we draw from case studies of two partnership programs based in writing studies—a writing partnership between the University of Arizona and area high schools and a collaboration between Salt Lake City Community College and the University of Utah—that utilize community advisory boards and democratic processes to work toward stakeholder-oriented approaches to leadership. Through these case studies, we emphasize three core principles of democratic design, including stakeholder leadership, political vision, and epistemic equity, that can be applicable across a range of programmatic opportunities. For leaders in composition studies who see collaboration as central to their mission, democratic design can serve as a linchpin for aligning processes with values.

---

The changing landscape of composition calls for new approaches to leadership. As Tom Miller and Joddy Murray argue, many of our field's challenges might also spark opportunities to rearticulate leadership approaches to align with a civic vision of writing studies: critiques about the value of the humanities invite us to design research partnerships that demonstrate the power of rhetoric for the public good; broad expansions of adjunct labor call for the fostering of less-hierarchical structures for decision-making that include non-tenure-track faculty and local stakeholders; pressures to prepare graduate students for a greater diversity of careers offer an impetus to launch internship programs that allow students to work with community organizations and community colleges; and the increasing emphasis on student recruitment and retention invite faculty and administrators to build initiatives that cultivate student engagement through community-based learning. Composition faculty working in public partnerships have explored the potential of such community-based collaborations to foster more rhetorically-aware student writing (Barrett; Young and Morgan) and spark rich teacher development (Leon, Pinkert, and Taylor).

Yet public partnerships must wrestle explicitly with the ethics of program leadership, given the stark power dynamics that tend to privilege university stakeholders (Kannan et al.). When faculty coordinate engagement initiatives and broker partnerships with nonprofits, K-12 institutions, and community colleges, effective and ethical administration requires conceptions of leadership that move beyond the simplistic view of one designated individual holding authority. Public engagement calls for coalitional approaches to collective action, methods for program decision-making that are responsive to power differentials, and mechanisms for creating accountability to constituencies inside and beyond the university—strategies that are important not only for community engagement and cross-institutional programs, but also for the many kinds leadership that composition faculty hold, such as administering writing programs, chairing departments, and coordinating WAC projects, among other possibilities.

While the subfields of writing program administration and writing center studies have hosted deep conversations about ethical leadership, we suggest that public partnerships offer another generative site for reflecting on leadership in composition and rhetoric. Leaders in community writing have called for moving beyond a rationalistic, transactional view of reciprocity, which has traditionally guided discussions of ethics in community engagement (Opel and Sackey). Scholars have proposed strategies for making community-based programs more attentive to less-powerful stakeholders, drawing on a range of frameworks including community organizing (Goldblatt), indigenous Filipino worldviews (Bernando and Monberg), Cherokee principles (Cushman), intercultural inquiry (Flower), and Scandinavian Participatory Design (Brizee and Wells). In this article, we extend this active conversation by drawing from John Dewey to introduce democratic design as a framework for conceptualizing a stakeholder-oriented approach to leadership. While many compositionists use terms like *democratic* to describe the aims of a class, a program, or the field at large, this term is notoriously hazy (Wan), and there is a need for more concrete discussions of what a democratic vision might mean in the context of writing studies leadership. Emerging from a study of two public partnerships grappling with stark power differentials, democratic design, as we describe it here, offers a deeply practical approach to ethical leadership that seeks to center the insights of those most impacted by a program or initiative. In this article, we offer a grounded approach to building these ideals into program structures.

John Dewey provides the theoretical inspiration for this model of democratic design. He posits that democracy is more than a governing system, but also a "social idea" that could permeate work, school, and everyday life (143). As he explains, democracy "consists in having a responsible share according to capacity in forming and directing the activities of the groups to which one belongs . . . [I]t demands liberation of the potentialities of members of a group in harmony with the interests and goods which are common" (147). In other words, democracy as a social ideal means that people have opportunities to shape the structures they participate in, which requires recognition of their capacities to contribute to the common good. Todd DeStigter reminds us that to Dewey, democracy is not a static goal, but rather an "end in view," an ongoing collaborative process. DeStigter writes, "Understanding an aim as an end in view means that people should think of going through the process of working toward a desirable end as part of the end itself" (15). He suggests that the end goals and the processes of a Deweyan approach should be seen as indistinguishable, as the activities of a group need to be characterized by the same values as the goals of the social project (16). The conception of democratic design for collaborative leadership we develop in this article emphasizes the need to build programmatic ideals into leadership practices.

In what follows, we illustrate democratic design through case studies of two partnership programs based in writing studies. Wildcat Writers, which we have each coordinated, is a high school-university writing exchange program in Arizona guided by an advisory board consisting of teachers from the participating high schools and university. The second case study examines a collaboration between Salt Lake Community College (SLCC) and the University of Utah ("the U") to coordinate a range of initiatives to better support students transferring from SLCC to the U in English studies. This partnership models collaborative leadership that includes undergraduate and graduate students, as well as faculty from both institutions.

We developed these case studies using transcripts of group interviews with stakeholders from the university and partnering organizations, co-authored documents by university and community representatives, and our own experience as coordinators of Wildcat Writers. For the first group interview, we reconvened five founding advisory board members from Wildcat Writers; in addition to the two of us, participants included high school teachers Taylor Johnson, Kate Street, and Maria Elena Wakamatsu. In a set of separate group interviews conducted via Zoom, we interviewed leaders of the SLCC-U partnership: one interview with Stephen Ruffus, the former English Department chair at SLCC, and Christie Toth, then Assistant Professor at the U, and one interview with Toth and Lisa Bickmore, a more recent English Department chair at SLCC. Conducting group interviews was important to allow for participants to build on each others' thoughts, illustrating the type of knowledge production we call for in the piece. With IRB approval,[1] the Wildcat Writers and SLCC-U collaborative interviews were recorded, transcribed, and coded by both authors using Eclectic Coding (Saldaña). We use participants' real names, with their permission, as a way to honor their intellectual contributions.

The Wildcat Writers program and SLCC-U collaborative are grounded in different contexts and hold different goals, but they share striking similarities in their visions of shared, cross-institutional leadership structures that reflect Dewey's view of democracy. After introducing the case studies, we identify and discuss key aspects of democratic design, including stakeholder leadership, political vision, and epistemic equity. Our goal is to consider these emerging themes as principles to consider not only for public partnerships, but also for collaborative leadership across a range of programmatic and institutional contexts. For those of us committed to Deweyan democracy, democratic design offers opportunities to integrate our ideals into leadership structures by actively engaging participants more deeply in the process.

### Case Study 1 Introduction: Wildcat Writers Advisory Board

Wildcat Writers has supported high school-university writing exchanges for more than 20 years. Developed to promote college access pathways for minoritized students and offer college students opportunities to engage with communities outside the university, the program recruits teachers from secondary schools predominantly serving students underrepresented in higher education. High school and college writing teachers are paired to plan a linked curriculum in which their students work together throughout a semester. University classes include first year composition, advanced rhetorical theory and composition, creative writing, and professional writing. Projects range from feedback exchanges on writing to extensive youth participatory action research projects. While the program started with just a few teachers, it grew to support the participation of up to 30 teachers and 600+ students in some years.

Wildcat Writers is guided by an advisory board consisting of Wildcat Writers teachers from the high schools and university. When it started in 2009, there were five of us who met once a month to make decisions about the program: Which teachers should be paired? What grants should we apply for? What should we do when a partnership falters? How should we talk about our work with broader publics? As Wildcat Writers has grown, the advisory board has taken on a more prominent role. Advisory board members mentor partnership teachers, attend program planning meetings, help gather materials for class visits, and troubleshoot issues. In recent years, board members have also attended weekend-long visioning retreats, developed a handbook of effective practices which is updated and distributed to teachers each year, and launched a monthly newsletter. The Wildcat Writers advisory board functions to illuminate many of the possibilities and challenges of democratic design.

### Case Study 2 Introduction: Cross-Institutional Leadership in the SLCC-U Writing Transfer Partnership

Writing faculty at Salt Lake Community College and the University of Utah have partnered to support students transferring from SLCC to the U in writing studies, which has also allowed them to strengthen both departments in areas like enrollment, retention, and faculty development. University faculty member Christie Toth built relationships with faculty at SLCC and collaborated with transfer students from SLCC to conduct a study about how students experience moving from one institution to the other. This research led to a set of recommendations to support students transferring from SLCC to the U, including a summer bridge program open to any SLCC student considering the U's writing and rhetoric studies major/minor or certificate program in professional and technical writing. The summer course was developed to introduce students to the field of writing studies by having them learn from writing studies scholars in the region, involving faculty from both institutions as co-teachers. This locally sourced curriculum means students meet the writers of the works they read, allowing students to build a network of support from both SLCC and the U. The class is also facilitated with the help of one or more transfer students who provide mentorship.

The SLCC-U partnership has continued to grow and now includes an associate degree in writing, 300-level U classes taught on the SLCC campus, a community college professional apprenticeship program that places graduate students in community college classrooms, and a student advisory board. The partnership has also fostered an informal inter-institutional disciplinary community in which faculty and graduate students attend speaking events and participate in reading groups hosted by the partner institution. The brief narrative illustration we offer here does not fully capture the rich work happening in the SLCC-U partnership, and we refer readers to publications emerging out of that partnership to learn more about this impressive work (Ruffus et al.; Toth; Toth and Ruffus; Toth, Sullivan, and Calhoon-Dillahunt). In our discussion that follows, we focus on aspects of this partnership, along with the Wildcat Writers advisory board, that illustrate democratic design.

## Democratic Design for Collaborative Leadership in Action

The Deweyan idea of democracy as a "social idea" reminds us of the rich capacity participants have to shape the programs, systems, and organizations that impact them. If the leaders of programs and initiatives in writing studies wish to seek democratic ends, we must build leadership models that incorporate these ideals. In this section, we explore the ways in which Wildcat Writers and the SLCC-U collaborative exhibit principles of what we call democratic design. As we explore the key themes of (1) stakeholder leadership, (2) political vision, and (3) epistemic equity, we can begin to see the ways in which these programs align their leadership processes with their stated values.

### *Stakeholder Leadership*

Too often, Carrie Leverenz argues, program administrators assume a Rawlsian ability to make ethical decisions from behind the "veil of ignorance," attempting to understand a problem without taking into account the social location from which they see. She cites feminist philosopher Seyla Benhabib, who argues for processes that enable differing voices to engage in discussion, as it is impossible to anticipate the concrete realities of others' experiences absent their voices. In her call for more ethical WPA decision-making, Leverenz argues for program administration that directly involves representatives of impacted constituencies, especially when those constituencies have been marginalized. The democratic design framework we saw emerge from the case studies emphasizes such stakeholder leadership as essential.

In our conversation with the Wildcat Writers participants, high school teacher Maria Elena Wakamatsu described the advisory board as "an accountability system," a way to allow community stakeholders to have input into decisions that determine whether the program is serving their interests. Here, Wakamatsu offers a vision of accountability rooted in responsiveness to marginalized stakeholders rather than to powerful granting agencies, university administrators, wealthy donors, or promotion and tenure review committees. It would be "easier," she suggested, to focus on the university's priorities and rely on assumptions about the interests of community participants, but the range of advisory board positionalities aims to allow community interests to emerge in decision-making processes. Involving those impacted by a program in leadership functions to rework accountability into an ethical concept instead of a neoliberal mandate, along the lines of Shari Stenberg's call for feminist repurposing of austerity discourses. Wildcat Writers' commitment to accountability has inspired programmatic and procedural changes over the years, from small alterations of which nights and where to hold meetings to more substantial shifts in the application process and the professional development program.

The development of the SLCC-U bridge course is also an example of stakeholder leadership, as transfer students and faculty from both institutions had a significant role in developing the program. The project began with a study to better understand local transfer experiences, involving transfer students as research assistants compensated through the U's Undergraduate Research Opportunity Program. As Toth explained, the positioning of undergraduate research assistants transitioned to "thinking of ourselves as co-researchers" who conducted surveys and interviews of transfer students and collaborated to make recommendations, including the idea for a summer bridge course. Toth described to us the day the University faculty went to a faculty meeting at SLCC to propose this bridge course, which was originally designed to be taught by faculty from the U. "The immediate response [at SLCC], I can remember the meeting really vividly, was, 'Wow! Why would you teach that course by yourself?'" The SLCC faculty rightly argued for leadership roles in the process for conceiving and implementing the bridge program. Since then, Toth has co-taught the course with different faculty members from SLCC along with student co-teachers who have transferred to the U from SLCC. An advisory board including students and alumni of the partnership has also been formed so "it's not just me [Toth] making those judgment calls or even us [SLCC and U faculty] making those judgment calls. That we have a body of students that we're responsible to and can vet those decisions with." This advisory board has offered important insights to improve student experience in the program, such as recommending a workshop on imposter phenomenon and a formal peer mentoring program for post-transfer students.

Writing about WPA work, Jeanne Gunner suggests that the increased communication that emerges through a collaborative leadership structure allows the team "to see and share perceptions about the program" from different perspectives, leading to triangulation and better responsiveness (257-258). Similarly, stakeholder leadership in Wildcat Writers and the SLCC-U collaborative creates space for a greater range of people impacted by a program to join in programmatic decision-making, allowing these programs to remain more responsive to participant interests. In fact, SLCC English department chair Lisa Bickmore warned against using the SLCC-U partnership as a model of what types of programs to adopt, rather than as an example of the importance of stakeholder leadership: "It would be easy to say, 'What we need is a *this*, a *this*, a *this*, a *this*, a *this*, we'll do it like *that*—like they did it at the U and maybe make some modifications.' But to me, one of the most powerful things about this model is that, by and large, we built it together." Creating opportunities for stakeholders to co-build, co-lead, and co-determine how programs are responding to the interests of marginalized stakeholders becomes an essential feature of democratic partnerships because of the opportunities for ethical accountability and responsive programming.

### *Political Vision*

By prioritizing accountability to marginalized communities, both Wildcat Writers and the SLCC-U partnership seek to disrupt the way education typically works. The political nature of this work is strongly articulated in the words of Wildcat Writers board member Wakamatsu, a former community organizer of undocumented farm workers. Her statement is worth quoting in full:

> Whoever you recruit to an advisory board, they have to understand that this is a highly political program, because what you're talking about is about educating and empowering people, kids in Title I schools, okay. Poor kids. Empowering them so that they know and feel they belong in college and that they can do just as well as anybody else. That is a very political statement, and you know what? There are a lot of people out there in high schools and district offices who are afraid of those of us trying to do this . . . . People who don't believe that this is any business of the university and certainly not any business of a high school, because they're trying to bring up test scores. If it doesn't advance what they're doing with the Common Core or with the canned curriculum or with our assessment scores, it's like, 'No.' It's like, 'What the hell are you doing working on a college curriculum? Why do you have your kids working on that when they can't even pass the damn [state test]?' A lot of times, administrators don't see the end game.

Here, Wakamatsu uses a political lens to identify with powerful clarity how the status quo in education, with its focus on test scores and its assumptions about the capabilities of minoritized youth, denies certain groups college access. She recognizes that advisory board members—and the organization itself—must embrace this political vision that calls attention to inequality and attempts to intervene in structures positioning some students as less-than.

Higher education scholar Gina Ann Garcia has similarly argued for attention to the political nature of organizational structures in postsecondary education in her work studying Hispanic-serving institutions (HSIs). Too often, she suggests, universities admit students from previously excluded populations yet continue to operate in the same way. Garcia argues that an educational organization must align its mission, governance, and community standards in order to serve minoritized students; for example, institutions should center those students' experiences in curriculum and include those from historically marginalized groups in pluralistic models of decision-making (137-139). This holistic approach recognizes the ways an entire organization needs to be aligned under a political vision in order to claim a justice-oriented mission.

For Wildcat Writers, changing the mission statement of the program was one such attempt at creating a justice-oriented political alignment. The program initially started as the "Service Learning Program," and the advisory board elected to remove references to service learning in program materials after discussion about the impact of this terminology. As high school teacher Taylor Johnson recalled, the service learning language reinforced a university-driven relationship in which the college students might think "we're providing a charitable thing" rather than engaging in a partnership. The status quo around community engagement often positions marginalized populations as recipients of service, sending messages to both community members and college students that reinforce hierarchies of worth and capability. The advisory board revised the mission statement to emphasize "reciprocal learning," codifying the program's aim of collaboration between secondary and college students (and their teachers). The political vision to see the inequalities perpetuated by normative educational dynamics and intervene through program design is a key role of the advisory board.

The SLCC-U partnership holds a similar political perspective. As Toth articulated, community colleges are often overlooked in state, disciplinary, and university priorities, and "if community colleges are invisible, ignored or denigrated, think about the students that are being ignored, rendered invisible, and denigrated in that process"—often first-generation and BIPOC students. Attention to hierarchies in the education system has become a cornerstone of the partnership, as expressed in its vision statement, which outlines seven principles guiding the initiative ("Articulating"). Two of these principles, "centering students" and "educate for social justice", exemplify the political vision of the SLCC-U partnership. The statement charges those involved in the partnership with a "moral obligation" to recognize "that the educational experiences and opportunities of students—particularly the often structurally disadvantaged students at SLCC—are more important than professional or disciplinary 'turf'" (6). This stance is important in the historical context of SLCC-U relations, as the institutions have often seen each other as competitors for credit hour production and teaching opportunities. In foregrounding marginalized students, the partnership seeks to take a clear-eyed look at inequities in the postsecondary system, which offers more status and more per-pupil funding to four-year universities: as the vision statement asserts,"ultimately, our work together is motivated by a shared commitment to challenging the social injustices reproduced by the educational system in which we labor and learn" (5). This explicitly political vision is also articulated in the value, "address material conditions," which will "require us to engage politically…to address the broader labor structures, *especially the labor conditions of contingent faculty,*" as well as factors that limit students' educational access (Toth, Sullivan, and Calhoon-Dillahunt 105, emphasis in original). The vision statement works to encourage political clarity in understanding the trajectories of inequality that shape the partnership context, from the marginalization of community college students to exploitative labor conditions for adjunct faculty.

We want to be careful to acknowledge that no education program can fully step outside problematic political dynamics. Moreover, marginalized communities have many reasons to distrust university intervention, as Indigenous scholar

Linda Tuhiwai Smith recognizes, and small changes like altering terminology or drafting a mission statement is only a start, given the work that must be done. Nevertheless, we see a political vision as central to developing leadership structures that seek to disrupt traditional power relations.

### *Epistemic Equity*

A key component of bringing a political vision to program leadership is addressing whose knowledge is considered valuable *in all the practices and administrative levels of a program.* As adrienne maree brown argues, "How we are at the small scale is how we are at the large scale," which means to us that a core principle must show up in specific practices and organizational structures from the highest level of an organization down to small interactions (52). In short, the work toward social justice must look like the world the work is trying to achieve. A core principle we argue is key to democratic design is challenging inequalities around knowledge production. In public partnerships, for example, knowledge is often conceptualized as flowing from the university to the community, a view that must be actively countered at every level of a program. Marginalized stakeholders are often not seen as credible knowledge-makers, a phenomenon philosopher Miranda Fricker calls "epistemic injustice." Fricker argues that institutions relying on a shared culture or an abstract commitment to epistemic justice may not succeed, and she suggests designating a subgroup responsible for upholding epistemic virtues. An advisory board can function as such a subgroup when it takes responsibility to shape power dynamics. Both Wildcat Writers and the SLCC-U partnership have created processes and protocols to foreground epistemic equity at all levels of programming.

In the Wildcat Writers program, the advisory board models the idea that all partners bring valuable knowledge to the program by distributing decision-making across the board, as discussed above. In addition, the board positions experienced high school teachers as "mentors" to both secondary and college instructors in the partnership. This attention to epistemic equity flows out from the advisory board to impact other programmatic levels. Board member Maria Elena Wakamatsu explained that when she mentors pairs of secondary and college teachers, she seeks to shape the knowledge power dynamics between the two. She stresses to the secondary teachers that they often have more expertise in areas such as classroom management and backward design than their college partners, frequently graduate students new to teaching. She shared, "When I tell high school teachers that they are more experienced than their [GTA] partner, they're always shocked. . .I say, 'You've gotta help them out . . .'" Here, Wakamatsu helps the secondary teachers resist hierarchies that position university knowledge as more valuable. The advisory board mentor's role is not only to navigate practical matters but to set a tone of reciprocal learning between university and secondary teachers. A reflection protocol following a meeting further prompts teachers to discuss what they learned from the other.

High school teacher Taylor Johnson agreed that the teacher relationship sets the tone for the entire partnership, especially when the teachers help students to see that the "high school students also have something different to offer." Secondary students in Wildcat Writers are often intimidated at the idea of collaborating with a college student (Shah) and college students sometimes join the program with a hierarchical lens of "mentorship," views that have to be aggressively countered. As the board members argued, encouraging epistemic equity works best when that balance is modeled at multiple levels of a program, from administration, to teachers, to students.

Explicitly recognizing experiential knowledge is another way to promote epistemic justice in university-community partnerships and other programs. Rigoberto Reyes, a community organizer, notes that university representatives frequently exude "a certain know-it-all arrogance, not stopping to recognize that who better to know what the problems, issues, and priorities are than the people who are being directly affected by the problem" (2). In democratic design, credibility comes from hands-on experience in the program rather than the number of articles published, a high-status title, or political connections. The Wildcat Writers advisory board, for example, is different from executive boards in non-profits, which are often composed of people with connections to powerful spheres who may not have experience in the day-to-day work. When discussing what made the board effective, our interviewees stressed that board members must have participated in the program, "probably more than once," according to secondary teacher Kate Street, because this experiential knowledge is invaluable. Similarly, in the SLCC-U collaboration, Toth sought to involve transfer students as co-researchers in her exploration of how to smooth the transition from community college to the university. The experiential expertise of transfer students is also highlighted through their role as co-facilitators in the summer bridge course, as the SLCC-U partnership recognizes that successfully transferring to the university serves as a valuable qualification for teaching students about to undergo this experience.[2]

Honoring experiential knowledge also opens up pathways for wider ranges of stakeholders to participate as co-authors of program documents. When we asked Stephen Ruffus, formerly of SLCC, for suggestions for how to promote democratic knowledge exchange in the face of hierarchies between universities and community colleges, he suggested "writing those connections" through the co-creation of texts. For example, in addition to co-authoring the vision statement discussed in the previous section, SLCC and U faculty and students have collaborated on a variety of texts and publications, including a recently published book (Toth). In our conversation, Toth referred to this book not as a monograph, but as a "polygraph" that includes co-authored and solicited mini-essays that feature a range of stakeholders in the SLCC-U partnership. SLCC English department chair Bickmore emphatically argued that this collaborative and relational model of scholarship shaped the dynamics of the SLCC-U collaboration, as it involved a university professor "ceding that territory" to the voices of others and co-developing the argument rather than "employ[ing] your labor to get to my idea" in a tenure-earning book. The writing process was built on an awareness of the rich knowledges held by community college students and faculty. The co-written texts in the SLCC-U partnership are therefore important not just for their content but for the process by which they were constructed, intentionally involving a variety of stakeholders in the drafting.

Similar to how high school teachers Wakamatsu and Johnson described epistemic equity as trickling down from the advisory board to teachers to students in Wildcat Writers, Bickmore outlined how honoring traditionally-marginalized knowledges through faculty co-writing has implications at multiple levels of the SLCC-U partnership. She explained that epistemic equity in her context often required challenging the limiting discourses that framed universities as where knowledge is made and community colleges where teaching occurs. These discourses have to be "decoded," with political vision, for the ways that they frame community colleges as "lesser institutions, there for students who can't 'make it' in better institutions"—which is really "another way of talking about race, class, and all the divides that our students live in and among." Demonstrating epistemic equity at the level of co-designing a bridge class or co-authoring a book, then, positions the community college as a place of knowledge production, which has the potential to impact students, "because it allows students to frame the work that they're doing when they come to community college as real intellectual work themselves." In short, pursuing epistemic equity at the highest levels of program administration and representation can impact a variety of stakeholders. As Bickmore argued, "Doing the work of decoding [those discourses], recognizing in each other the capacity for, the potential for, and the already-have-done-it-ness of knowledge-making is a way of harnessing something really new" in the state education system.

This stance echoes Dewey's commitment to democratic social organization by honoring the epistemic capacities of individuals to shape conjoint activity. As DeStigter suggests, a Deweyan approach to democracy as a way of life is as much about process as product. He explains that when individuals are engaged with each other in activity, "[they] begin to think of the activity in terms of the outcome, thereby defining and deepening the view of what they do and why they are doing it" (16). From this perspective, it is critical that the activities in which a group participates are characterized by the same ideals that describe the intended aim. In other words, when a program claims to pursue greater social equality as an end goal, then it should also strive toward equity in whose knowledges are valued in everyday program interactions. As both case study partnerships aim to address hierarchies between universities and their partner institutions, that stance should be present in how different knowledges are valued in program practices, such as the drafting processes for Toth's book or reflection protocols that ask secondary and university teachers to share what they learned from one another. Many programs in writing studies that espouse justice-oriented goals or values related to democracy may have opportunities to integrate the related value of epistemic equity into programmatic processes.

## Possibilities and Limitations: Toward Democratic Design in the Field of Composition

The Deweyan idea of democracy as a "social idea" reminds us of the rich capacity participants have to shape the programs, systems, and organizations that impact them. In this article, we have offered democratic design as one way to move toward a form of leadership that values and reflects the knowledges and interests of participants. Epistemic equity—a conscious effort to honor stakeholder knowledges throughout the organizational structure—serves as the defining characteristic of our model, acting as a mechanism for stakeholder leadership and creating space for voices that can sharpen a political vision. As Bickmore of SLCC argued, "At every level where we talk about systems of higher education, it's important to recognize knowledge-making where it occurs, and that it occurs everywhere. Recognizing it means, then, that you can actually use it." This recognition of marginalized knowledge is especially critical in public partnerships to better understand the impacts of partnerships and resist the ways universities often fail to engage communities ethically, even in partnerships that seem to emerge from progressive ideals (Kannan et al; Mathieu). The model of democratic design, emerging from public partnerships, may also speak to broader conceptions of leadership in writing studies, as many of our programs are similarly impacted by sharp power imbalances and epistemological hierarchies. Democratic design, an "end in view" approach to building programmatic ideals into collaborative leadership structures, can be a partial answer to these imbalances, serving as an accountability system to less-powerful stakeholders, as Wildcat Writers board member Maria Elena Wakamatsu asserted.

Yet democratic design comes with its own thorny questions and limitations. In particular, participants in our study asked whether it is ethical to ask marginalized stakeholders to dedicate labor toward program leadership, and, if so, how much is too much to ask? Toth shared, "As one student told me, and I think about this everyday, 'It's not my job to fix you people. It's your job to fix you people.'" If stakeholders are going to be invited to take on program improvement, how can administrators act in light of the potential costs and risks to marginalized participants? These questions point to long-standing tensions in community engagement scholarship. Collaborating with university classes can be a burden on community partners (Stoecker and Tryon), and that burden is heightened when taking on a leadership role. The ethics around asking marginalized stakeholders to serve on an advisory board are especially complex given that participants can face barriers to board participation, such as transportation and accessibility (Grabill), and an element of risk when advocating for stakeholder interests in ways that may be unpopular with those who hold more power. High school teacher Street noted that serving on the advisory board requires a willingness to "put your neck out," and Wakamatsu added that several advisory board members had "paid dearly, quite frankly, to be part of this program" in terms of opportunities for advancement at the district office, because advocating for students to have access to college-level curriculum sometimes required being at odds with administrators. The inherent risks of centering stakeholder interests were discussed in the SLCC-U partnership, as well. Toth's initial involvement came during her pre-tenure years at the U, and from this unstable positionality she had to advocate for institutional change to create more authentic transfer pathways.

The Wildcat Writers advisory board members also noted that participation on the board led to work-life balance compromises. Due to the differing schedules of high school and university faculty, meetings often overlapped with time that would otherwise be reserved for family. Board member Johnson and co-author Brad Jacobson remembered bringing their young children to meetings. In an illustration of the human costs of advisory board work, Johnson added that in a recent conversation about patience, her daughter said simply, "Mom, I've learned how to wait."

Given the burden of democratic design for participants, compensation becomes an important way to honor the labor of stakeholders. In the SLCC-U partnership, students able to participate as co-researchers, co-developers, or co-teachers, are paid for their labor, and, if it's useful to them, get tuition-free credit that counts toward a writing and rhetoric studies minor or major. All forms of compensation, including stipends for advisory board service, are available to students of any documentation status. In our roles coordinating advisory boards, we have pursued opportunities such as grant-funded stipends, research assistantships, and credit-bearing internships in an effort to recognize the labor burden involved, yet these options have not always been available. For stakeholders who are not rewarded for service in a tenure portfolio, "the sudden invitation to serve on a committee or collaborate on a project may be perceived as simply more work without more compensation" (Leverenz 16).

Leverenz suggests inviting forms of participation that benefit stakeholders in ways they value, such as inviting contingent faculty to co-lead a workshop when professional development counts for merit evaluation. We sought creative ways of providing professional value, such as mailing letters to high school principals on university letterhead that celebrated teachers' contributions and hosting a Wildcat Writers teaching award, but it is also worth noting that advisory board members' motivations were more complex than monetary or professional advancement. For example, Johnson found deep satisfaction in opportunities to "tell the story" of Wildcat Writers through scholarship, potentially leaving a professional legacy by impacting other programs.

The participants in the Wildcat Writers advisory board conversation were also quick to note that the costs of participation were counterbalanced by meaningful social connections forged through the board. Following up on a comment about the impact of board commitments on family time, Johnson remarked that "the offset to that [labor and time burden] is that the board can feel like a family." Other interviewees agreed, sharing memories of dancing together at a board member's wedding and making pizza before meetings. Street emphasized, "It can't just be another meeting that you have to go to," and Wakamatsu described how sharing food and wine helped give a relational feel to gatherings. This kind of relationality was also evident in our interviews about the SLCC-U partnership. For example, Toth shared that SLCC-U faculty and current and former students had attended her "non-baby shower/baby party." This theme reminded us of Steven Alvarez's argument for *confianza*, or the ongoing, intentional process of establishing mutual trust through listening, valuing home knowledges, and building relationships. As he illustrates, such relationality is foundational to community literacy work. When Johnson says the board "can feel like a family," she suggests that opportunities for social interactions are not fillers to be included only if there's time; rather, in some contexts, they make the work possible, helping participants–administrators included, we would emphasize–weather the risks and costs of democratic design.

In addition to considering time for individual participants, it is also important to acknowledge another aspect of time: democratic design may not meet the expectations of efficiency and traditional metrics many institutional leaders desire. Democratic design takes time to build relationships of trust, to share perspectives, to make decisions and, if necessary, change course. brown describes making the case for collaborative decision-making "to people who use the words 'efficient; and 'ASAP' to describe everything good," arguing that the real "heart of efficiency" occurs when people who will be involved in the work have trust and alignment (230). Without collaborative commitment, participants may not give their full energy toward the project, slowing it down. For brown, taking the time to involve impacted communities in decision-making not only allows organizations to identify more ethical goals–what is efficiency for if it doesn't lead us to the desired result?–but it also allows organizations to move toward those goals more effectively. Leaders in writing studies fields will need to make a creative and rhetorical case for a democratic design approach when advocating for institutional support or justifying democratic structures to skeptical colleagues or administrators. For example, to fund stipends at her current institution, co-author Rachael Shah accessed an external grant focused on improving teacher quality by arguing that secondary teachers participating on an advisory board would build teacher capacity. The SLCC-U partnership utilized undergraduate research funds to develop their co-researcher approach. Leaders might also look to others doing participatory research or program design at their institutions for inspiration on how to justify this work. Rachael recently connected with minority health disparities researchers who utilize community advisory boards (CABs) because they recognize that the validity, reach, and impact of inquiry can be augmented by democratic approaches.

Measuring impact and what counts as success raises other questions for leaders utilizing democratic design within accountability-focused models. While some partnerships, like Wildcat Writers and SLCC-U, lend themselves to data collection on student impacts that tend to be valued by administrators, democratic design reminds us that measuring results must also align with the means. Echoing Garcia's call for HSIs to seek legitimacy by meeting traditional measures of success (e.g., graduation rates) while valuing transformational practices like developing critical consciousness and ethnic identity, we see promise in combining traditional metrics and processes with a broader range of data and participatory approaches. In addition to identifying metrics valuable to administrators or external funders, democratic designed partnerships could work to develop their own metrics aligned with programmatic values. For example, a partnership that values reciprocal learning could analyze written reflections for the depth of response in describing what students learned from their partners. In this way, the program evaluation process itself can become an opportunity for democratic design, as a range of stakeholders can be involved in determining which outcomes to track (for external and internal purposes), how to go about gathering data and participant input, and/or how to interpret results (Sabo Flores; Shah). Using more expansive data markers and evaluation processes alongside established research on student success (like high-impact practices) could help to present a holistic picture that sustains democratic design. At the same time, we acknowledge that a democratically designed evaluation comes with its own ethics and labor tensions, so this is far from a simple answer.

As we continue to pursue this work, we have encountered other questions: How can programs grapple with the slippery nature of representation—who can speak for a community or group? For example, does an advisory board that only includes teachers sufficiently represent the communities involved in Wildcat Writers?[3] How should factors like race and class be considered when thinking about representation? How might programs navigate the tension in the importance of having people of color in leadership of an initiative that primarily serves minoritized communities without overburdening teachers or students of color? Are programs that draw on democratic design in danger of falling under an "inclusion delusion" (Kannan et al.), in which the appearance of community participation provides a smokescreen or false sense of security that allows for problematic practices? And how might the contexts of particular programs bring additional ethical questions to the fore? Democratic design has limitations, to be sure. We want to be clear that we are continually negotiating institutional dynamics in our own leadership capacities, and what works in one situation may not work in another. We look forward to learning from others enacting strategies to justify and build democratic design in their unique programmatic and institutional contexts.

Qualified as our call is, we believe democratic design–through stakeholder leadership, political vision, and epistemic equity–can provide a hopeful approach to change. While we have focused our discussion on public partnerships that link composition studies in the university with broader constituencies, we also see these principles as applicable within departments and programs themselves. Readers in a variety of leadership positions might consider strategies from these case studies, including advisory boards, stakeholder co-authorship, collaborative research across institutional positionalities, mission statements that center marginalized stakeholders or epistemic equity, and discussion protocols that disrupt knowledge hierarchies. Could writing programs draw upon democratic design as they establish a student advisory board, invite NTT faculty to help drive curricular decision-making, or work with neurodivergent students to create a teacher workshop on neurodiversity? Many English departments have mission statements that claim to center marginalized knowledges and a range of potential outcomes, but how might they build in stakeholder accountability beyond tracking readings on syllabi or student graduation rates and job placements? How could program leaders incorporate insights from students who feel excluded or marginalized from writing classroom practices?

Democratic design as a metaphor reminds us that all leadership structures are built, and processes that may be taken as given are actually choices that carry significant consequences for stakeholders. A program's end goals cannot be divorced from its leadership structure, as decisions about structure define whose knowledges are valued within a program. We argue here that the epistemic equity central to the Wildcat Writers advisory board and the SLCC-U writing studies partnership is a necessary condition for such a collaborative leadership structure. For leaders in composition who see collaboration as central to their mission, democratic design can serve as a linchpin for aligning processes with values.

## Acknowledgments

We thank the participants in this research for sharing their time and expertise with us, and we thank the Wildcat Writers community for supporting us across many years of collaboration and friendship. We also want to thank Shelley Rodrigo and an anonymous reviewer for their thoughtful feedback that helped strengthen this piece.

## Notes

1. IRB # 16186, University of Nebraska-Lincoln.

2. New processes may be needed when epistemic equity is a goal. Toth shared that while it can be difficult for undergraduate students to "get a word in" during a faculty-dominated discussion, they were able to contribute more in small group settings. Toth reminds us that maintaining epistemic equity does not always mean everyone in the same room hashing things out; there are "massive power asymmetries" that will never be equal.

3. The Wildcat Writers advisory board has since included undergraduate students. Husker Writers, which Rachael went on to coordinate at a different institution, has also included undergraduate and high school students on the board.

## Works Cited

Alvarez, Steven. *Community Literacies en Confianza.* NCTE, 2017.

"Articulating SLCC-U Partnerships in Writing Studies: Reimagining Relations, Making Change." SLCC-U Partnership, 2018, us.utah.edu/faculty-resources/transfer-pathways/mou-folder/humanities/SLCC-U%20Writing%20Studies%20Vision%20Statement%202018.pdf.

Barrett, Kenna. "Where Professional Writing Meets Social Change: The Grant Proposal as Hospitality." *Composition Studies,* vol. 41, no. 1, 2013, pp. 70-83.

Bernando, Shane and Terese Guinsatao Monberg. "Resituating Reciprocity within Longer Legacies of Colonization: A Conversation." *Community Literacy Journal,* vol. 14, no. 1, 2019, pp. 83-93. https://doi.org/10.1353/clj.2019.0020.

Brizee, Allen, and Jaclyn Wells. *Partners in Literacy: A Writing Center Model for Civic Engagement.* Lexington, 2016.

brown, adrienne maree. *Emergent Strategy: Shaping Change, Changing Worlds.* AK Press, 2017.

Cushman, Ellen. "Gadugi: Where the Fire Burns." *Activism and Rhetoric,* edited by Seth Kahn and Jonghwa Lee, Routledge, 2011, pp 80-85.

DeStigter, Todd. "The Tesoros Literacy Project: An Experiment in Democratic Communities." *Research in the Teaching of English*, vol. 32, no. 1, 1998, pp. 10–42.

Dewey, John. *The Public and Its Problems.* Swallow, 1927.

Flower, Linda. *Community Literacy and the Rhetoric of Public Engagement.* Southern Illinois UP, 2008.

Fricker, Miranda. "Epistemic Justice as a Condition of Political Freedom." *Synthese,* vol. 7, no. 190, 2013,pp. 1317-1332.

Garcia, Gina Ann. "Decolonizing Hispanic-Serving Institutions: A Framework for Organizing." *Journal of Hispanic Higher Education,* vol. 17, no. 2, 2018, pp. 132–147. https://doi.org/10.1177/1538192717734289.

Goldblatt, Eli. *Because We Live Here: Sponsoring Literacy Beyond the College Curriculum.* Hampton Press, 2007.

Grabill, Jeffrey T. "Shaping Local HIV/AIDS Services Policy through Activist Research: The Problem of Client Involvement." *Technical Communication Quarterly,* vol. 9, no. 1, 2000, pp. 29-50.

Gunner, Jeanne. "Collaborative Administration." *The Writing Program Administrator's Resource: A Guide to Reflective Institutional Practice*, edited by Stuart C. Brown and Theresa Jarnagin Enos, Routledge, 2002, pp. 253–262.

Kannan, Vani, et al. "Unmasking Corporate-Military Infrastructure: Four Theses." *Community Literacy Journal,* vol. 11, no. 1, 2016, pp. 76-93. https://dx.doi.org/10.25148/CLJ.11.1.009251.

Leon, Kendall, Laurie A. Pinkert, and Kathryn Trauth Taylor. "Developing Accounts of Instructor Learning: Recognizing the Impacts of Service-Learning Pedagogies on Writing Teachers." *Composition Studies,* vol. 45, no. 1, 2017, pp. 39-58.

Leverenz, Carrie. "What's Ethics Got to Do With It? Feminist Ethics and Administrative Work in Rhetoric and Composition." *Performing Feminism and Administration in Rhetoric and Composition Studies,* edited by Krista Ratcliffe and Rebecca Rickly, Hampton, 2010, pp. 3-18.

Mathieu, Paula. *Tactics of Hope: The Public Turn in Composition.* Boynton Cook, 2005.

Miller, Thomas P., and Joddy Murray. "Reimagining Leadership after the Public Turn." *College English,* vol. 79, no. 5, 2017, pp 435-450.

Opel, Dawn, and Donnie Sackey. "Reciprocity in Community-Engaged Food and Environmental Justice Scholarship." *Community Literacy Journal,* vol. 14, no. 1, 2019, pp 1-6. https://dx.doi.org/10.25148/CLJ.14.1.009052.

Reyes, Rigoberto. "Engaged Pedagogy: Reflections from a Barriologist." *Engaging Pedagogies in Catholic Higher Education,* vol. 2, no. 1, 2016, pp. 1-3. https://doi.org/10.18263/2379-920X.1012.

Ruffus, Stephen, et al. "It's Not Just the English Department: Reimagining Two-Year/Four-Year Relations Across English, Linguistics, and Writing Studies." *ADE Bulletin,* vol. 158, 2020, pp. 23-42.

Sabo Flores, Kim. *Youth Participatory Evaluation: Strategies for Engaging Young People.* Jossey-Bass, 2007.

Saldaña, Johnny. *The Coding Manual for Qualitative Researchers*. 3rd ed., SAGE, 2016.

Shah, Rachael W. *Rewriting Partnerships: Community Perspectives on Community-Based Learning.* Utah State UP, 2020.

Stenberg, Shari. *Repurposing Composition: Feminist Interventions in a Neoliberal Age.* UP of Colorado, 2015.

Smith, Linda Tuhiwai.. *Decolonizing Methodologies: Research and Indigenous Peoples.* Zed Books, 1999.

Stoecker, Randy, and Elizabeth Tryon. *The Unheard Voices: Community Organizations and Service Learning.* Temple UP, 2009.

Toth, Christie. *Transfer in an Urban Writing Ecology: Reimagining Community College-University Relations in Composition Studies.* NCTE, 2023.

Toth, Christie, Patrick Sullivan, and Carolyn Calhoon-Dillahunt. "Reconstructing the Disciplinary Matrix of Writing Studies. *College Composition and Communication,* vol. 71, no. 1, 2019, pp. 86-116.

Toth, Christie, and Stephen Ruffus. "Inter-Institutional Partnerships for Academic Freedom: Reversing 'The Great Credit Grab.'" Symposium: Academic Freedom, Labor, and Teaching Two-Year College English. *Teaching English in the Two Year College,* vol. 45, no. 4, 2018, pp. 338-342.

Wan, Amy. *Producing Good Citizens: Literacy Training in Anxious Times.* U of Pittsburgh P, 2014.

Young, Debra Dimond, and Rachel Morgan. "The Impact of Critical Community-Engaged Writing on Student Understanding of Audience." *Composition Studies,* vol. 48 no. 3, 2020, pp. 35-52.

# Course Designs

## BTW 250: Principles of Business Communication

*A. Kay Emmert, Andrew Moss, David Morris, and Andrew Bowman*

### Course Description

At the University of Illinois at Urbana-Champaign (UIUC), as with many research-oriented institutions, an increasingly popular option for writing courses includes a technical and professional communication (TPC) curriculum. Recent developments in TPC pedagogy have turned toward course designs and teaching practices oriented around social justice. At the same time, new developments in TPC administration recognize the role of non-tenure-track (NTT) faculty in teaching TPC courses and staffing TPC programs.[1] The course we describe here, BTW 250: Principles of Business Communication, uniquely brings together these two branches of TPC research: we applied an ecological, social justice-based frame to our course and our course revision process, producing a course that serves contemporary students while stimulating a communal professional culture among formerly isolated instructors.

BTW 250 is a multi-major professional writing course offered by the Department of English in service to students in other disciplines at UIUC. The course teaches students to apply the principles of successful professional communication to workplace writing. Because the course meets UIUC's general education requirement for advanced composition, students complete complex writing tasks in a multidisciplinary setting that requires analysis and synthesis, application of writing as a process through drafting and revision, and creation of 20-30 pages of original composition. As a service course and a general education advanced composition course, BTW 250 features instruction in specific business communication through the broader lens of writing pedagogy.

The course's major assignments and scaffolded instruction are built around five student learning objectives (SLOs):

1. Compose effective business communication in written and/or multimodal forms.
2. Adapt content and delivery to specific professional conventions, audiences, and situations.
3. Take part in collaborative work to create effective professional communication.
4. Identify and make use of resources to make informed, responsible, goal-oriented writing decisions.

*Composition Studies 51.2 (2023): 106–116*

5. Develop and follow a recursive process of investigation, task definition, drafting, feedback, revision, and editing.

Over the past few decades, TPC courses have most commonly taught communication genres (emails, memos, letters) or professional development genres (resumes, cover letters) (Read and Michaud; Waltman et al). This approach often has the unintended consequence of instilling in students the belief that genre is static at the expense of developing adaptable skills, and just as importantly, fails to engage student emotions such as curiosity, which is a propellant of learning (Cavanagh). For our institution, previous designs of BTW 250 centered on textbooks, role-playing, and genres and configured an economy of work populated by homogenous identities and stereotyped versions of work and writing.

As a corrective to this static and potentially discriminatory configuration, the redesigned BTW 250 grounds students' learning and writing in their own experiences and their own research about their work and fields. For example, the first two major assignments ask students to write a professional literacy narrative, research the literacies of the profession they are pursuing, and write a procedure manual for a position they would like to hold when they graduate. We encourage students to look beyond a published job description or examples of procedure manuals they might themselves have read; instead, students bring forward the unique insights of their research and reflections about professional literacy to write their procedure manuals. Typical of all the assignments in the new BTW 250, this sequence prompts students to learn, know about, and make changes to the business writing and working conditions of their profession.

Through this curriculum, we argue that the success of TPC courses depends on students connecting personally with the material, and that connection is strongest when provided by the students' own contexts. When students engage personally, the exigence of writing situations becomes less theoretical and more emotionally charged, thus providing a stronger motivation to learn and grow. The curriculum focuses on students' diversity (especially in their majors and concentrations), what students report as immediately useful, and what we are not ashamed to call "fun." To teach students from agriculture, accounting, computer engineering, and Spanish (to name but a few of our students' majors), our course grounds each of its assignments in students' expertise or their research about their majors and professions. For example, what was previously a "complaint letter," featuring a fictional customer service complaint and resolution, is now a request for time off to a supervisor they work under (or hope to work under in the future). In this problem-solving message, students make a case for managing their workload using arguments about values and priorities that have grounding in a real world that is visible and valuable to students.

## Institutional Context

Revising our BTW 250 course required us to work within dramatically changed labor conditions at UIUC and elsewhere, and this affected both our method and our pedagogies. Enrollment in our BTW courses steadily dropped over the 2010s as students found other ways to satisfy their general education requirements. No financial resources were available to revise our courses. No professors specializing in professional communication were hired; indeed, the Center for Writing Studies suffered a contraction in funding and discontinuation of tenure lines. In this respect, our program in Professional Writing (PPW) fit into a clear national trend: as of 2009, a majority of TPC service courses in the U.S. were being taught by contingent faculty (Melonçon and England 405), a pattern that has grown more prevalent ("Curricular Challenges"). The PPW was staffed administratively and instructionally by NTT faculty and graduate students ranging in specializations and years of experience. In part because of this defunding, the program over the 2010s became increasingly isolated from the campus, the Center for Writing Studies, and the English department more broadly.

In part as a result of this isolation, BTW 250's course designs grew difficult to navigate and somewhat distant from current practices in writing pedagogy. From 2010-2019, the PPW's courses were built on a wiki, written by one program director and adopted as the foundational text and source of knowledge for instructors and students. Because of its single authorship, this wiki and the program that depended on it did not always cohere or facilitate meaningful collaboration among instructors. The course designs housed in the wiki were remarkably recursive (a recursiveness facilitated by the interlinked, web-based pages and resources). However, the assignment sequences felt maze-like for new instructors and many students, who proportioned much time and energy to navigating course materials rather than teaching and learning with them. The complexity of course resources and assignments focalized in one grand scenario meant to give them unity: students were asked to play the role of a new hire at a generically named corporate business. This attempt at grounding the class in students' experiences, in the eyes of many instructors, normalized one particular and outmoded definition of professionalism; further, it asked students to adopt a persona that erased a student's identity, experiences, and point of view. Administratively, although accounting for a significant portion of the English department's students, the PPW sank very low on the department's list of priorities. It was tasked with keeping administrative costs down and managing other processes, such as the English department's social media, newsletter, and the redesign of its webpage.

Dedicated but largely isolated NTT and graduate instructors did their best in individual sections to adapt this curriculum, slowly shifting over the 2010s from textbook- and genre-based instruction to instruction built with online materials and focused on writing as a reflective process. Their innovations provided some excellent material on which to revise BTW 250 when, in Spring 2020, a new team of NTT faculty were appointed to lead the PPW and tasked with attracting more students from a wider range of majors. Working toward this goal required an examination of all the program's courses, and most significantly, its core course, BTW 250. In the two years that followed, a program that had once been spearheaded by one academic professional became a collaborative team bringing extensive classroom experience, passion for effective, up-to-date course design, and keen awareness of the working conditions of graduate students and NTT faculty to an overhaul of one writing class.

## Theoretical Rationale

Throughout our curriculum revision process, we strove to balance the skills and experiences of our instructors with the writing needs of our heterogenous group of students. Historic enrollment data showed that BTW 250 drew students from across our campus, so the class would need to prepare students to write professionally in many different workplaces. Often TPC curricula and textbooks rely heavily on narrow conceptions of genre to solve this problem, providing models that can be adapted to fit most professions. While we believe generic knowledge is an important part of TPC education, our curriculum emphasizes how genres (and the writers who compose them) must adapt to fit their context and goals. In doing so, we move away from an emphasis on generic form and instead focus on function through a phronesis-based genre ecology approach (Doan 295). This approach emphasizes the relationship between the documents students create and the desired consequence the documents are created to achieve. The ecology approach also provides students with a model for understanding the professional writing process and its many occluded, or unofficial, genres.

Making the course revision through this ecological approach makes sense; after all, our work is embedded in a university and professional economy whose pressures and problems are diverse. Our new curriculum is part of another widening of the TPC field: the curricular and scholarly emphasis on identity and history. TPC scholarship's social justice turn seeks to redress many historical and pedagogical failures in TPC education (Agboka and Dorpenyo; Walton et. al). In general, an outmoded (in every sense of the term) approach to business writing often asks students to assume a normative identity and persona and assume readers with a similar identity and persona: a white cis man in a pinstriped suit working in an investment bank on the east coast of the US.[2]

We were confident in this theoretical basis for our new curriculum, but to turn it into a course that would serve our students, we needed to enfranchise our NTT and graduate instructors in the process. Seth Kahn argues, "A carefully developed ecological frame can help show us what we miss when we think too big," but also "it's important to remember that what often seem to be quintessentially local problems aren't—or aren't just" (116). It's common to overlook the essential role of NTT faculty and graduate employees when administrative visions focus on the broader mission of a program, department, or campus. To create a more just work environment for contingent faculty in TPC programs, Lisa Melonçon and Peter England recommend that "TPC administrators, with support of their departments, need to make every effort to enfranchise contingent faculty in all decisions that directly impact their teaching lives" (406). It was important to the program's ethos and commitment to justice to consult instructors of the program, integrating their feedback into the final versions of the program's values, student learning objectives, and course design.

## Critical Reflection

### *Course Design Process*

In redesigning BTW 250 we prioritized making a pedagogically sound and adaptable class that would serve our students' needs, but we knew that was not a sustainable goal without generating a more collegial culture in the PPW. Improving the health of the program as a complex system meant taking a social justice approach with all involved: students, instructors, administrators, staff. As Kahn argues, "Not only are the people who work with us in our programs and on our campuses part of complex systems (and understand I mean that very inclusively: students, administrators, staff, all of us), but they're people (and so are we) whose lives and livelihoods often depend on the health of the environment" (115). The health of the program impacts the lives of people in very real ways, and we wanted that impact to be positive for all involved. Moreover, a healthy program would provide the basis for assessing, revising, and improving our course so that we could meet student needs as it evolved over time. Such improvability would further help programs who send their majors to BTW 250; a strong, evolving course would remove the need for faculty in the served programs to look for other courses (or create their own) to fulfill their students' educational needs around writing. Moreover, a healthier, continuously improving course provides greater stability for nontenure faculty, as their employment security would be less susceptible to dramatic changes in staffing needs.

Our instructors provided the insight and work needed to revise the course, as they have a diversity of valuable expertise and experience related to pedagogy, student well-being, and various writing disciplines. Some also brought experience in professional fields outside academia. Due in part to the trend of TPC programs being more likely to employ stable, long-term, full-time contingent faculty ("A Portrait" 231), all had years of experience as successful writing instructors at UIUC. However, we faced an obstacle in capitalizing on our instructors' knowledges: years of decentralization. We worried that imposed curricular changes would be met with hostility or apathy. Because so many instructors had been teaching the course with little oversight or support, we needed to assess current approaches across sections. Assignments, student learning outcomes, policies, and methodologies varied depending on the instructor. Instructors came from a range of academic specialties (writing studies, literary studies, and creative writing) and often split their time teaching classes across multiple programs. Non-tenure-track faculty were employed on a year-to-year basis, and graduate employees were often juggling multiple part-time appointments to support themselves. Moreover, many of our instructors had independent research and publishing projects of their own, served on departmental or campus committees, and were otherwise contributing unpaid labor to various functions of the university. In short, our instructors were invested but overworked, and they were unlikely to welcome a new curriculum unless they had input in developing it. Our method of revision, therefore, needed to involve BTW instructors and benefited from their participation.

With our cultural goals in sight, we began the process of revising BTW 250 in summer 2020 by gathering many of our instructors and asking a simple question: What do we think is important for students to learn in a business writing course at UIUC? We wanted to understand what people had been teaching, but we didn't want simply to collect assignments. Using Dynamic Criteria Mapping (Broad), we collected diverse student writing from past BTW 250 courses, removed all identifying information, and redistributed the samples to our instructors, asking two questions: First, in a given writing piece, what did the student writer do well that the participating instructors valued? Second, what did the student writers try to do (perhaps less successfully) that the participating instructors valued? We collected answers to these questions using a Moodle discussion board designed for the purpose, and we followed this with a two-hour discussion with participating instructors on Zoom. From the instructors' answers on Moodle and in the Zoom discussion, PPW staff made a list of professional writing values that our instructors generally agreed were important to teach. Through several drafts, feedback from BTW instructors, and Zoom meetings, PPW staff produced a visual representation of our program's values. We used this representation as the basis of our new BTW 250 student learning objectives and course curriculum, and to help orient new BTW instructors to teaching BTW 250.

Because this preliminary work required little of individual instructors and provided professional development, we asked them to do it on a volunteer basis. Converting these discussions into a curriculum required more complicated work, and while we wanted to incorporate instructor input, we were also keenly aware of systemic reliance on unpaid contingent labor. Nationwide, nontenure faculty already carry a substantial teaching load for which they are not satisfied with the corresponding compensation ("A Portrait" 231). Because we had no independent budget, we diverted research funds into a limited number of $500 stipends to pay five NTT faculty to collaborate on the next phase of the BTW 250 curriculum revision project. This team met regularly with program staff to assess survey data, program resources, and syllabi from comparable courses on campus and at other universities. Building on this research, the team created an outline of the assignment sequence, which was then distributed to all program instructors for feedback and questions. We used this feedback to refine the new major assignment sequence further. Once the assignment sequence was set, the program staff took over the scaffolding of low-stakes tasks and the creation of a Moodle template. Finally, we spent a year piloting the new curriculum with two different sets of instructors, collecting feedback and further refining the course and orientation materials. These efforts proved not only helpful in enfranchising contingent instructors, but also in providing professional development opportunities for NTT faculty, which, according to Melonçon et al., is largely lacking in TPC programs ("A Portrait" 231).

From this process, we learned three potentially helpful lessons about course revision. First, a productive process begins with taking stock of everyone and everything in the ecological frame, including students, instructors, program administrators, advisors, and other departments. When we began by considering how we could leverage everyone's perspectives, priorities, and expertise in the design process, differences in discipline and pedagogy became useful tools in course design. We relied on and tried to reward differences in expertise, building in academic freedom so that instructors (graduate and NTT faculty) could shape the curriculum to their pedagogy and be responsive to the needs of their particular students.

Second, productive course revision on this scale must continue beyond a single revision. As opposed to a jarring replacement of one curriculum for another based on the interests of a small group, we built relationships and methods that would allow the curriculum to evolve and keep the course relevant to the needs of its stakeholders. This ongoing revision can make use of advancements in writing pedagogy applied within local conditions and through the abilities and passions of instructors.

Third, we learned that curriculum revision provides a professional development opportunity, but that we had to balance that opportunity with a sense of what labor we could consider part of instructional duties, and what labor we would need to compensate fairly. For example, we could ask instructors to provide feedback, answer brief surveys, volunteer material they already had, and do anything that might reasonably be accomplished in a single professional development meeting. These sorts of participation helped with sharing pedagogical ideas, creating community, and encouraging instructors toward instructional innovation. On the other hand, we fairly compensated instructors who created new content, conducted research, or did anything else requiring a significant time and labor commitment. This mix of monetary compensation and communal professional recognition lent value to instructors and encouraged them to participate in further professional and curricular development.

### *Piloting the Course*

After a year of piloting our new curriculum, preliminary feedback from students and instructors suggests that students find the course material easy to engage. A majority report that the course effectively teaches adaptable, transferable professional writing skills. Instructors have experimented with and adjusted to new writing assignments and methods. Moreover, individual instructors have made thoughtful adjustments in scaffolding instruction. We're encouraged by the initial results, and we've identified some areas for adjustment and support for instructors.

The new curriculum's recommitment to and reconception of process has produced some promising results. While process assignments are certainly not new for BTW 250, we included more reflective writing and ways for students to draw on their own experiences and interests to access writing assignments and grow knowledge. An emphasis on reflective writing is new for many of our instructors, and instructors and students continue to experiment with productive prompts. Originally, the new curriculum called for students to reflect often on their professional experiences, but many students didn't have much professional experience, so instructors have adjusted, prompting students to access their academic and life experiences and translate them into professional situations. We're planning to hold professional development sessions and collect resources for instructors on teaching with reflective writing next year, and we hope this will generate new ways to incorporate reflective writing into the course.

The commitment to process has fostered greater growth and experimentation for instructors and students. Students and instructors across our program report similar experiences with one early major assignment in particular, the Procedure Manual. This assignment asks students to define and describe processes in their workplace after an initial "Onboarding" assignment. Initially put off by the unfamiliar genre, instructors quickly apprehended its forms and affordances and built scaffolded assignments that made the assignment accessible. Students completed manuals that were as quotidian as making dinner and as weighty as managing clients at KPMG with the same kinds of successes and failures. A wide variety of possible approaches allowed students to build their own competencies. Moreover, students and instructors had enough room to experiment and learn together about work, genre, and writing in this assignment. In a one-semester course, it can be difficult to create room for pedagogical experimentation, but we see great results from instructors and students learning together. We're committed to creating more opportunities for this cooperative discovery.

## Conclusions

There is no single method to make every individual feel valued, but conversations with instructors uncovered a common feeling: instructors tended to feel valued through ongoing yet relatively unstructured teaching conversations with program staff and other instructors. Ongoing interactions gave instructors assistance they needed to solve problems and rethink pedagogies, and the unstructured quality helped make pedagogical discussions collegial rather than hierarchical. Some instructors see an administrative hands-off approach as a sign of respect and trust. For others, this can be isolating, providing few opportunities for colleagues and program administrators to provide immediate and responsive positive feedback. Approaching curriculum revision the way we did provided "home-grown professional development opportunities" (Melonçon and England 406) for creating a sense of worth through monetary compensation, the sharing of ideas that result in observable change, and timely acknowledgement of the value of those contributions.

While continuous improvement of a program through a carefully developed ecological frame may sound like extra administrative labor, looking purposefully at how students, administrators, and faculty all depend on the health of the environment creates less chaos and strain than a reactionary approach that deals with problems as they arise and never resolves root causes. The course design affects student engagement; instructor knowledge affects course design and delivery; the course design determines possible directions for instructor professional development. Support, financial and otherwise, impacts the ability of instructors and staff to commit time to these efforts, and that time translates directly to the level of development and buy-in for the course. All these forces, working together, create the health of the program. If we were to take any one problem—curriculum design, student engagement, instructor buy-in, instructor support, program support, programmatic infrastructure, the role of the service course in relation to other programs—other problems slip by and any attempts at continuous improvement would be crippled by the need to respond to isolated problems as they arise.

We find the initial results of our BTW 250 revisions quite promising in and of themselves, but our improvements to the ecological frame of the program excite us the most. Our redesigned course will only work if we make the process ongoing and recursive. In assessments and reviews of this curriculum going forward, we plan to draw again on our instructors, conduct new research, assess student learning, and make adjustments on an annual or biannual basis. With invested, communicative instructors engaged with our students, relevant research, and our institutional environment, we're confident that we can now update our curricula in this and other courses on an ongoing basis. We further hope that this will keep our pedagogy effective without sudden, dramatic curricular changes that temporarily lower pedagogical quality and impose ruinous labor burdens on our already overworked instructors.

## Acknowledgment

We would like to thank the instructors in the BTW program, all of whom contributed in some way to our revised BTW 250 course design. In particular, John Dudek, Joe Grohens, and Zack McVicker did much of the work to design the high-stakes assignment sequence and supporting materials. We appreciate their expertise and effort.

## Notes

1. For a discussion of the status and promise of the field in which our course is situated, see Melançon, et al. "A Field Wide Metasynthesis;" Melançon "Current Overview;" Rude; Bridgeford and St Amant; and Schreiber et al.

2. For two interventions in the state of the TPC classroom we describe using this somewhat provocative example, see Cox's approach to queer rhetorics in professional communication and Agboka's discussion of the need to decolonize the field of TPC.

## Works Cited

Agboka, Godwin Y., and Isidore K. Dorpenyo. "Curricular Efforts in Technical Communication After the Social Justice Turn." *Journal of Business & Technical Communication*, vol. 36, no. 1, 2022, pp. 38–70.

Agboka, Godwin Y. "'Subjects' in and of Research: Decolonizing Oppressive Rhetorical Practices in Technical Communication Research." *Journal of Technical Writing & Communication*, vol. 51, no. 2, Apr. 2021, pp. 159–74.

Bridgeford, Tracy, and Kirk St Amant. *Academy-industry Relationships and Partnerships*. Taylor & Francis, 2017.

Broad, Bob. *What We Really Value: Beyond Rubrics in Teaching and Assessing Writing*. Utah State UP, 2003.

Cavanagh, Sarah Rose. *The Park of Learning: Energizing the College Classroom with the Science of Emotion*. West Virginia UP, 2016.

Cox, Matthew B. "Working Closets: Mapping Queer Professional Discourses and Why Professional Communication Studies Need Queer Rhetorics." *Journal of Business & Technical Communication*, vol. 33, no. 1, 2019, pp. 1–25.

Doan, Sara. "Teaching Workplace Genre Ecologies and Pedagogical Goals Through Résumés and Cover Letters." *Business and Professional Communication Quarterly*, vol. 84, no. 4, 2021, pp. 294–317.

Kahn, Seth. "Towards an Ecology of Sustainable Labor in Writing Programs (and Other Places)." *Writing Program Administration*, vol. 39, no. 1, 2015, pp. 109-121.

Melonçon, Lisa. "Curricular Challenges of Emphasis Degrees in Technical and Professional Communication." *Sharing Our Intellectual Traces: Narrative Reflections from Administrators of Professional, Technical, and Scientific Communication Programs*, edited by Tracy Bridgeford, Karla Saari Kitalong, and Bill Williamson, Baywood Publishing Co, 2014, pp. 179-200.

Meloncon, Lisa. "Current Overview of Academic Certificates in Technical and Professional Communication in the United States." *Technical Communication,* vol. 59, no. 3, 2012, pp. 207-222.

Melonçon, Lisa, and Peter England. "The Current Status of Contingent Faculty in Technical and Professional Communication." *College English*, vol. 73, no. 4, 2011, pp. 396-408.

Melonçon, Lisa, et al. "A Field-Wide Metasynthesis of Pedagogical Research in Technical and Professional Communication." *Journal of Technical Writing & Communication*, vol. 50, no. 1, 2020, pp. 91–118.

Melonçon, Lisa, et al. "A Portrait of Non-Tenure-Track Faculty in Technical and Professional Communication: Results of a Pilot Study." *Journal of Technical Writing and Communication*, vol. 46, no. 2, 2016, pp. 206-235.

Read, Sarah, and Michael J. Michaud. "Hidden in Plain Sight: Findings from a Survey on the Multi-Major Professional Writing Course." *Technical Communication Quarterly*, vol. 27, no. 3, 2018, pp. 227-248.

Rude, Carolyn D. "Mapping the Research Questions in Technical Communication." *Journal of Business and Technical Communication,* vol. 23, no. 2, 2009, pp. 174-215.

Schreiber, Joanna et al.. "Guest Editors' Introduction: Revisiting the Service Course to Map Out the Future of the Field." *Programmatic Perspectives*, vol. 10, no. 1, 2018, pp. 1-11.

Waltman, Jean, et al. "Contingent faculty in a tenure track world." Center for the Education of Women, University of Michigan, May 2010, www.cew.umich.edu/PDFs/SloanFinalReport5-10.pdf. Accessed 28 July 2022.

Walton, Rebecca W., et al. *Technical Communication after the Social Justice Turn: Building Coalitions for Action*. Routledge, 2019.

# English 5519 & 700: Introduction to the Theories and Practices of Composition Teaching

*Antonio Byrd and Virginia M. Schwarz*

## Course Description

The University of Missouri-Kansas City (UMKC) and San Francisco State University (SFSU) both offer English graduate programs with teaching assistantships; those students awarded an assistantship are required to take an introductory course in composition theory in practice. At UMKC, this course is English 5519: Teaching Writing: Theories, Histories, Contexts, Practices. At SFSU, this course is English 700: Introduction to Composition Theory: Issues of Composition Theory, Research, and Classroom Practice. Most MA and PhD institutions have a version of this course where the goal reads something like this: introduce issues related to the theories and practices of teaching college-level writing. As early-career, tenure-track faculty who graduated from the same doctoral program in composition and rhetoric, we view introductory composition pedagogy courses as an important space to welcome students into the larger discipline. However, in teaching this course for the first time, accomplishing this wasn't always straightforward, and we struggled with two primary concerns: one, how do we avoid repeating our own introduction to the field that reified its whiteness; and, two, how do we engage graduate students from across English disciplines–including creative writing, Teaching English to Students of Other Languages (TESOL), linguistics, literature, and composition–with course materials, instruction, and assignments?

Grappling with these questions, we formalized a cross-institutional partnership to support each other in creating and teaching anti-oppressive, inclusive versions of our graduate introductory composition courses. We met weekly before the semester began, and, in Fall 2021, we piloted parallel courses that consciously decentered canonical white scholarship in the field and revealed historical silences to highlight that writing is a political and cultural action with resounding consequences for students. In these courses, we also designed class discussions and major assignments that encouraged graduate students to engage composition studies critically and decide for themselves how they might leverage the course for their own academic and professional goals. We believe that this approach helped us and our students intervene in the tendency to replicate whiteness as the default perspective in the field. In this course design, we describe our overlapping course descriptions and rationale, followed by separate reflections in which we give an overview of our syllabi and think through our instructional innovation and the benefits of a cross-institutional collaboration.

## Institutional Context

Our experiences teaching introductory graduate courses occurred at two different Research II institutions. Antonio Byrd teaches at UMKC, one of four campuses in the University of Missouri System, and the only urban public research university in the system on the western side of Missouri. At the graduate level, the UMKC English department offers a master of arts, a master of fine arts, and an interdisciplinary doctorate (iPhD). Students in the iPhD program split coursework between English (as their primary discipline) and a co-discipline, the most popular of which are art history, curriculum and instruction, history, and the Humanities Consortium. Most graduate students across all programs identify as white. First year doctoral and masters graduate students may apply for a teaching assistantship. Funding for the upcoming year determines the number of available positions doctoral faculty may offer these newly admitted students but they are guaranteed teaching assistantships for up to three years or more in some cases. Graduates of the program typically remain in the region and establish careers in public schools or higher education. Others leverage their research skills into working as industry professionals in publishing, marketing, healthcare, technical writing, or they seek further doctoral study out of state.

Most graduate students study creative writing or literary studies; rarely do graduate students intend to study composition and rhetoric. Thus, intellectual investment in ENG 5519 is not a given, and students may express reservations about how well they understand composition and rhetoric. On occasion, students realize they want to learn more about the field, so they switch their research interests at the beginning or in the middle of their coursework. Graduate teaching assistants teach either ENG 110, an introductory course to college writing, or ENG 225, an introductory course to research methods. Graduate teaching assistants receive professional support through monthly practicum meetings with the Director of Composition. However, ENG 5519 is unique in that it provides formal engagement in the scholarship and practice of composition studies in a credit-based course taught by tenure-track composition and rhetoric faculty.

Virginia Schwarz teaches first year writing and graduate-level composition courses at San Francisco State University (SFSU), one of 23 universities in the California State University public system. SFSU is a Hispanic-Serving Institution and Asian American and Native American Pacific Islander-Serving Institution. At the graduate level, the English department offers MA degrees in composition, linguistics, literature, and TESOL with certificates in computational linguistics, immigrant literacies, teaching of composition, and teaching of post-secondary reading. Students in the composition MA must take English 700 as part of the curriculum, but graduate students across English studies or from other disciplines—like creative writing, education, or ethnic studies—may opt into the course as an elective or for the teaching of composition certificate. Additionally, any graduate student who applies to teach first year writing as a teaching assistant must take English 700. The curricular location of the course means that the class hosts a range of student interests, goals, prior experiences, and demographic backgrounds. For example, in a typical English 700 section, students of color are the majority, and many students identify as first-generation, returning students, and working students. Student ages range from 24-64. Graduates of the MA or certificate programs typically find careers in community colleges as teachers, writing tutors, and administrators. However, some also find work as industry professionals or go on to PhD programs. Like Antonio, Virginia serves a variety of graduate students and attempts to balance a range of student needs.

## Theoretical Rationale

In conceptualizing our respective introductory courses, neither of us felt like we had an example of the course we wanted to build, so we began by thinking about what critical graduate education might look like. Kevin Kumashiro's work in teacher education and theorization of "harmful repetitions" gave us a useful framework for understanding how we might approach education at the graduate level and helped us reflect on our pedagogical and curricular interventions (67). This theoretical rationale explores how we hoped to practice anti-oppressive teaching strategies, resist replicating our own prior graduate education, and enact ethical citation practices.

Drawing on Judith Butler's *Excitable Speech: A Politics of the Performative*, Kumashiro argues that an instructor may deploy anti-oppressive pedagogy in their classroom but still teach in a way that upholds traditional values of what education looks like. Kumshiro writes, "people often consider some practices and relations to be part of what schools and society are *supposed to be*, and fail to recognize how the repetition of such practices and relations — how having to experience them again and again — can help to maintain the oppressive status quo of schools and society" (68). In other words, educators enacting anti-oppressive practices in their classrooms may still remain loyal, intentionally or unintentionally, to routines that function in oppressive ways. For example, in a graduate context, students may read about feminist and queer theories, yet an instructor may demand that students analyze those works only through a rational lens, denying the use of bodily and emotional experience as sources of knowledge-making. Because the majority of our students are or will become educators, we wanted to surface and examine these tensions with each other and also foreground them in class discussions.

We found harmful repetitions can also persist through curricula, passed along through generations of select graduate students who become professors themselves. Specifically, early career faculty can be in the daunting position of teaching a graduate seminar for the first time; this is daunting because they are unlikely to have prior experience designing and leading graduate classes for an entire semester. This was the case for us. While we had both worked as peer mentors for graduate students as PhD candidates–Antonio as a writing center assistant director and Virginia as a writing program assistant director–neither of us had formal training in teaching graduate students or designing graduate-level courses. We felt nervous and were tempted to reuse the material from our own graduate education–revisit mentors' syllabi and assignments and rely on comprehensive examination lists to assign readings and complete course preparation. After all, there could be social and professional risks in adopting our own critical teaching stances. It also takes time to get to know an institution and develop meaningful, context-specific course materials.

For us, however, looking back would mean replicating the historical focus on white scholarship in the field and harming our students. When we were PhD students, most of our professors had excluded or minimized contributions by scholars and teachers of color. This shaped the way Virginia understood her current responsibilities as an educator and the way Antonio perceived his future white colleagues. For example, the curricula and reading lists did not include any community college scholars. So Virginia rarely felt connected to these readings because they never reflected her own realities as a community college instructor working with first-generation, transfer, returning, and non-traditional age students. In fact, Virginia ended up taking courses from the School of Education to learn more about college student experiences and the exclusionary and oppressive processes embedded in higher education. Meanwhile, Antonio worried that centering majority white scholarship in coursework and in the comprehensive exam would leave his colleagues underprepared for teaching and mentoring students of color in other contexts, let alone for being allies to colleagues of color. We felt there was a danger in drawing on only the materials we were given as students to teach future scholars, teachers, and practitioners of writing.

Thinking about graduate courses as citational acts—acts that respond to what came before and set up what comes after—helped us further shape our reading lists. In the academic cycle, the scholarship most often cited and published shapes the default curriculum of graduate seminars. In turn, graduate seminars—in master's and doctoral programs—show students a representation of contemporary discourses, knowledge, and movements that matter. In their work, Cana Uluak Itchuaqiyaq and Jordan Frith argue that "citational practices do infrastructural work and are a discursive base upon which entire disciplines . . . are built" (11). They posit that writing operates as infrastructure and suggest that we can analyze the infrastructure of our citation practices for how they benefit some groups over others for how citations shape the architecture of research. Itchuaqiyaq and Frith point out that technical communication, and by extension composition and rhetoric, are facing a moment of infrastructural breakdown because multiply-marginalized scholars have critiqued exclusionary citation practices.

Thus, early in our course design, we recognized the imperative to adopt inclusive and even anti-oppressive teaching practices in graduate student spaces, but we also wanted to keep open minds about how our courses might unintentionally still echo white voices. For example, as Clare Russell argues in her study of writing pedagogy education, addressing critiques about representation in superficial ways can also lead to instances of "curricular tokenism," that is, "utilizing scholars or theories in a manner that appears inclusive, but ultimately does not facilitate translation from theory to practice" (56). Specifically, in a survey of graduate curricula, Russell found the time devoted to language diversity and race to be "limited in both coverage and presence," and when instructors did assign readings on these topics, the same scholars stand in for issues and are repeated rather than engaged with (55). In other words, the challenge we faced in these course designs was to go far enough, consciously, in decentering whiteness.

A central question emerged for us: How can we prioritize equity, inclusion and diversity in curricular coverage without enacting harmful repetitions that limit us and our students? In exploring the answer to this question, our own course designs presented in this article not only center marginalized voices; the designs also change the conversation about how we understand and address racial and social justice within the profession and the world writ large. Ethical citation practices also contain important lessons for writing education pedagogy: In order to teach or work with students embodying a range of backgrounds and experiences, graduate students will need to critically engage issues of racial and social justice as future teachers, managers, entrepreneurs, writers, and other positions where they may exert power over civic and professional communities or others may exert power over them.

## Critical Reflection

In the following critical reflections, we consider our subject positions, readings to set up the cultures for our courses, and the interactions and discussions we had with students over the Fall 2021 semester. We also note our perceptions of the strengths and missed opportunities of these course designs and the changes we might make in the future. Our critical reflections include some of the texts we assigned to introduce students to competing debates about the political, cultural, and social purposes of first year classrooms. We found that framing composition studies as a place of tension invited students to discover where they stood and then identify the consequences of their positions for the first year composition students they taught.

### *Suddenly, an All-In-One Course: Antonio Reflects*

As a teacher, I design courses that balance students' needs with the expectations of the field according to contemporary scholarship and professional standards under social justice frameworks, such as critical race theory. Thus, I encountered the following primary challenge: preparing majority white graduate teaching assistants from different strands of English Studies to teach first year composition courses that enrolled mostly BIPOC and international students. Virginia and I had similar goals to adopt a "social justice theme and humanizing course content" (Schwarz, this article). Because she had taught a version of the course in a previous semester and our teaching interests aligned, I drew on her course design as a template and began to reshape it according to my own context and knowledge.

Throughout summer 2021, Virginia and I had weekly discussions on the choices we made about our course designs, sometimes borrowing each other's readings and assignments. These conversations became instrumental for my implementing a justice- and anti-racist-informed introduction to composition pedagogy. Looking back on our conversations, I notice that I avoid assuming that students knew nothing about oppression (Kumashiro); I did, however, assume that they may have trouble identifying linguistic injustice in writing classrooms given that the coursework in my department often centered white literature and creative writing. However, I had neither considered the lived experiences of my students nor that they were already oriented toward learning about social justice in an English program that did not always discuss these topics.

My final design highlighted tensions and debates across four different units. The first unit explored histories of the discipline while in Unit Two students and I discussed potential allyship with other subdisciplines in English Studies, such as creative writing, literature, and professional and technical communication. In Unit 3, I had students reflect on the relationship between teachers and diverse student populations in higher education. Finally, Unit 4 concluded the course with debates about the role and consequences of writing assessment for marginalized students. Throughout the course, students researched, wrote, and workshopped conference presentations in response to Staci Perryman-Clark's call for proposals for the 2022 CCCC Annual Convention. Using texts like

Iris Ruiz's *Reclaiming Composition for Chicano/as and Other Ethnic Minorities*, I wanted students to learn that the writing classroom doesn't just teach academic writing; it has always been, and continues to be, "uniquely beholden to social convention" and "unusually susceptible to social influence" (Fleming 14). Thus, I designed my course for students to ask questions about the politics of teaching writing; to reflect on how they themselves take up harmful or affirming ideologies about writing from their schooling, professional life, and lived experience; and to consider what ideologies they may pass onto their students in both productive and harmful ways.

I kept online discussion and in-person class activities open-ended for their response to steer graduate students away from accepting ideas in scholarship as is. Between classes, students read assigned articles in mixed-disciplinary reading groups. Using the Hypothesis tool on Canvas, students annotated articles and responded to one another's comments throughout the week. During class, the reading groups had time to read through their annotations and discuss key takeaways from their conversation. By mixing up different degree programs in the reading groups, I had hoped to show that peers' knowledge was just as valuable as the instructor's and that they had more in common across English Studies, pushing against the silos of academic disciplines.

Students brought themselves to the texts and to the in-class activities, sometimes at my prompting and other times on their own, so they could create meaningful connections to the debates the scholarship presented. However, I understood here an opportunity to have them think beyond "affirm[ing] their own sense of self" (Kumashiro 86). For example, the unit on social identities of students and teachers inevitably inspired students to speak from their own identity about how higher education changed their relationship with their families. Literary graduate students and creative writing graduate students especially enjoyed reading the tensions among composition, creative writing, and literature and felt affinity for the scholarship written about their discipline. Of course, our academic and social identities can be affirmed and our practices in individual categories may be oppressive themselves. As Kumashiro writes, "the solution is for all of us to rethink our practices constantly. Anti-oppressive research involves responding to other researchers and their research in ways that interrupt our complicity with multiple forms of oppression" (Kumashiro 88).

Thus, in-class activities challenged graduate students to create strategies for how they could best support multiply-marginalized students different from them in their classrooms, given the precarity of their well-being amidst the COVID-19 pandemic. Meanwhile, students themselves offered candid yet careful critiques on the lack of diversity among graduate teaching assistants in the department and inadequate stipends each semester. Debates on the relationship between literary studies and composition and the potential allyship with creative writing led me to invite students to strategize what first year composition could draw from their sibling disciplines in English Studies and vice versa. Our attempts to show relationships among identities and disciplines were meant to complicate disciplinary and social identity silos, discover new points of inquiry from their subject positions, and welcome careful reflections on social justice pedagogy. These rhetorical design choices culminated in conference presentations at the end of the semester that reflected a wide range of interests, with some focusing on areas of bigotry I had not addressed, such as a presentation on using labor-based contract grades for neurodivergent students.

While students did see the value of my framing of composition under a critical race studies lens, the course also presented unintended challenges in terms of disciplinary knowledge and social justice pedagogy. First, the debates left my students yearning for answers to the issues I presented to them. For example, affirming students' right to their own language through alternative assessment practices like labor-based contract grades was attractive to GTAs; some wanted to implement contract grades the following spring semester. However, they also felt the specter of Standard Written English dominating academic writing. Teaching assistants felt the need to balance supporting linguistic differences with stakeholder expectations (employers, for example) that college graduates hone their standard English. As one student told me, "I understand the problem, but I don't have any solutions from this course." Students desired to be researchers of teaching that made institutional change rather than repeating the expectations of the curriculum because they had invested themselves in some of the problems I had presented, especially with respect to supporting marginalized students. Secretly, that was my goal—to show students how unsettled teaching writing is and how it shifts according to the social and cultural moment of society and higher education. I left debates open and uncertain, which meant that students were responsible for developing practical solutions. While this seemed beneficial, next time, I may emphasize the importance of uncertainty in teaching and learning and explicitly address ways to think about solutions at the end of each class.

Second, graduate students in literary studies and in creative writing often felt unsure of whether they understood composition and rhetoric as a discipline. Even with a foundational history of the field and why first year composition came to exist, they wanted to grasp more theory; when they commented on articles or wrote their conference presentations, these students were unsure if they were "on the right track." What may be a point of frustration for them was a good sign that I was achieving my goal: rather than dismiss or resist the field, they discovered composition studies' relevance to them. My encouragement focused on situating their learning within a "regime of competence," an understanding that course content "operates within, but at the outer edge of, the learner's resources, so that at many points the game [or in my case the class] is felt as challenging but not 'undoable'" (Gee 70). Therefore, as an instructor, I was able to affirm that their thinking was grounded in the field of composition and rhetoric. I also explained that the field was at a point where it welcomed interdisciplinary concepts and research methods (Bazerman) even as those increase the "reading problem" (keeping up with new scholarship) in composition and rhetoric (Mueller 121).

Finally, while my assigned readings highlighted social issues related to race, with some nods toward class and first-generation status, the second unit stepped out of a social justice framework. The unit's topic—What counts as writing?—asked important questions about curriculum design in first year composition and negotiating power with college administrators, yet the unit failed to frame the question within social justice. Next time, I would redesign the unit to highlight how each discipline grapples with anti-racism considering the 2020 racial protests. All of academia had a reckoning, and English Studies was no different. As such, a redesign would first present debates on how literary students and creative writing can become allies as a discipline, followed by readings on how each discipline must contend with its own flavor of anti-racism and oppression in their scholarship and curriculum. For the remainder of the unit, students would design a first year composition curriculum that honors linguistic difference, features BIPOC scholarship in different media, and presents different kinds of genres under the rubric of social-justice pedagogy. Discussion about students' and teachers' social identities and the impact on their relationships in the classroom, followed by assessment design, would be foundational to return to the question of unit two: What counts as writing and who counts in a writing classroom? Assigned readings in future iterations of the course would consistently circle back to the social justice theme.

### *What Is A Writing Class For?: Virginia Reflects*

As a MA student in 2006, the first moment I felt that I belonged in composition was when I encountered the heated debates scholars were having about what a college writing class was for and what it should do (e.g., Tate; Lindemann; Elbow; Bartholomae; Hairston; Berlin). I found it fascinating that one course—first year writing—could cause so much disagreement and, at the same time, materialize so differently depending on the context and people in the room. Now, after teaching undergraduate writing courses at community colleges for 12 years, I understand how important those early conversations about teaching can be for graduate students who are developing their pedagogical values. This means my primary role as an instructor is to support students' exploration of their own beliefs about language and writing and locate those beliefs within historical and present-day writing pedagogy conversations.

This course design reflects my second iteration of this particular course. Drawing from conversations with Antonio, I divided this version of English 700 into three sections: composition's histories and tensions, composition pedagogy and assessment, and then, for the final three weeks, professional careers inside and outside academia. The course was structured around weekly readings and an online "pre-discussion post" due the day before the class met. Additionally, at the end of each unit, students wrote reflections in order to further process the ideas from class, especially in light of class discussions. To make this course more meaningful for students across disciplines, I designed reflection and discussion prompts that invited students to apply the curricular arc of our course to their own field of study by exploring similar historical silences, emergent best practices, and potential career paths. For students going into teaching, I also introduced scholarly and instructional resources so that each person developed the capacity to research the issues most salient to their future classrooms. For example, during the week foregrounding assessment, I assigned academic articles but also included many different examples of syllabi, rubrics, and grading contracts so that students could make connections between theories and practices and feel capable of exploring on their own. The culminating, end-of-term project was modeled from Antonio's conference presentation where each person investigated a topic of their choice.

Part of anti-oppressive teaching, for me, is asking questions about what knowledge has been minimized or discounted, and by extension, about what knowledge has been privileged or overrepresented. For example, while bringing this course to life, I felt a significant pedagogical tension: I wanted to skip past the race-evasive scholarship of the '90s and '00s that formed the foundation of my own introduction to composition, but I also did not want to elide the field's historical omissions. Further, I did not want to ignore the ways in which curricular tokenism (Russell) has typically played out in graduate programs. Instead, I felt compelled to respond to my own education in some way—not by forgetting it or dismissing it as unimportant, but by "repeating [it] with difference" (Kumashiro). To do this, I included several canonical debates in the third week of the course, while I also centered racism and white supremacy as key frames for understanding writing studies' historical turns and silences. Like Antonio, I assigned chapters from Ruiz's book *Reclaiming Composition for Chicano/as and Other Ethnic Minorities* alongside additional articles, like Royster and Williams' "Histories in the Spaces Left: African American Presence and Narratives in Composition Studies" and Lyons' "Rhetorical Sovereignty: What Do Native Americans Want From Writing?" I also included readings about diverse teacher identities to open opportunities to talk through our own embodied realities and what commonalities and differences we may have with the people in our classrooms (e.g. Cedillo and Bratta; Alexander and Rhodes). For practical classroom strategies, we primarily discussed works by scholars, teachers, and students of color that were published within the last five years. When writing instruction is humanized and situated within personal and social contexts, the role of early canonical texts can shift: graduate students can still find value in the exchanges, but they can also reflect on their inherent incompleteness.

In this way, English 700 ended up functioning as a meta-course, where students processed all of my pedagogical choices through the lens of both students and teachers. Consequently, I often shared stories about my early teaching moments to model growth, humility, and the need to continuously revisit our own practices. For example, as a white instructor with racial privilege, I acknowledged my own experiences and limitations and kept an open mind about how students across identities, marginalized and privileged, might react to a text. This means that in different moments of the course, readings that were significant for me or for one group of students might be common sense for others. Like in the undergraduate classroom, topics always play out differently depending on who is in the class, what community knowledge they bring, and how they interact with peers. Graduate students are often under the impression that they need to demonstrate knowledge or aim for correctness, an approach that can be in direct conflict with productive conversations about identities. In these moments, students experience the choices I make that mediate our interactions—questions, interjections, silences—and, hopefully, they develop their own repertoire for facilitating critical conversations. In sum, whether posting to an online discussion forum, using collaborative annotation tools, or going over readings during class, English 700 was a space where people–as teachers and learners–came together to voice and workshop their ideas.

While my goal of creating a classroom culture that could sustain conflict and learning has remained the same in moving from undergraduate to graduate courses, teaching graduate students has been different in terms of negotiating deeply entrenched values. At SFSU, many graduate students in English 700 have first-hand experience with racism and linguistic oppression and come into the class determined to learn tools that will better serve undergraduate writers. However, because this graduate course is so much about holding a mirror to our own values as teachers and people, several older adults have been uncomfortable with and resistant to talking about social issues that did not confirm their worldviews. When I teach this course, I email students two weeks ahead of time letting them know the theme of the class and giving them a copy of the course description. On the first day, I opened with Asao B. Inoue's CCCC speech (printed in *CCC*) and the concept of white language supremacy. While the majority of students were excited about the class and on board with the content, one white woman left the class crying. Throughout the course, she centered her experience as an ESL instructor working with students who had recently immigrated to the United States. It would be a disservice to them, she argued, to not correct their grammar. Every semester, I have had a version of this student—usually white—who refuses to acknowledge that racism is a factor in educational outcomes. I have also had two older males confront me during class about what they called politically correct course content. For me, these graduate students present a challenge: how can I better support folks at this stage—emotionally and cognitively—while not giving them too much class time or too much of my behind-the-scenes energy, thus making them and their views the focus of the class and missing opportunities to mentor and support other students? In a future iteration of this course, I would like to rearrange the order of Inoue's CCC's speech and think of a way to scaffold some of the key concepts. I would also like to collaborate with other professors more so that I might have a rough idea about how to understand students coming from outside composition.

As Kumashiro argues, "students come to school not as blank slates, but as individuals who are already invested in their thoughts, beliefs, and desires" (72). Although we explored differing views through readings, in future classes, I would like to engage these perspectives more deeply by calling attention, in discussions and in personal reflections, to our own beliefs and values about education and how our own identities and experiences shape our decision making processes. For example, many of the conflicts that emerged in this class were a result of disagreements around what an undergraduate writing class is for, a question that continuously surfaced throughout the semester in one form or another. In thinking about assessment, several students passionately argued that composition courses are for demystifying academic and linguistic standards and how those standards came to be. Many felt that talking about grades and grading was an important conversation to have with their own students. Other students felt first year writing courses were for teaching specific language skills or research processes and there would not be enough time to address much else. So while I could still present practical ways teachers and scholars are reconciling these tensions, next time, I would like to slow down and ask graduate students more difficult questions about what success can look like, what "transferable knowledge" is, and, like Antonio, what counts as writing in different contexts and why. In sum, I would like to rethink class discussions in ways that more fully include not only composition's silenced histories but also the educational histories of the people in the room. This means, in future semesters, I plan to create several opportunities for graduate students to share what about my approach or text selection feels incomplete in light of their own disciplinary, academic, professional, and personal experiences.

### Collective Takeaways: Graduate Classrooms as Citational Interventions

In both of our graduate courses, we wanted to resist the temptation to repeat curriculum and control students' responses to and application of the disciplinary conversations. These goals were tricky to navigate as new graduate faculty, where both of us, at times, felt compelled to provide easy answers, lean into practical topics, and manage day-to-day expectations about graduate student labor (like reasonable reading and workloads). This cross-institutional partnership allowed us to see graduate education as a site to amplify and actualize the social justice commitments of the field. English 5519 and 700 can function as citational interventions that challenge and change which texts get circulated in our disciplines, institutions, and communities. In making this so, we contextualized dominant contributions to the field alongside critical, anti-oppressive frames.

While these were the conversations we had as new graduate faculty, we suspect that many others can relate to copying and pasting a course from another person or, over time, from semester to semester. We also feel it is very typical to want to redesign or update a course but not know how to start. Despite these shared challenges, in designing an introductory graduate course, we realized that, as professors, we have the (sometimes unacknowledged) privilege of circulating a cycle of citation practices and that either reinscribe or interrupt racism and other forms of oppression (Delgado). We invite others into this discussion of designing introductory graduate-level courses that intervene in curricular tokenism and center various approaches to social justice.

### Works Cited

Alexander, Jonathan, and Jacqueline Rhodes. "Flattening Effects: Composition's Multicultural Imperative and the Problem of Narrative Coherence." *College Composition and Communication*, vol. 65, no. 3, 2014, pp. 430-454.

Bartholomae, David. "Inventing the University." *Writing on the Margins*. Palgrave Macmillan, 2005, pp. 60-85.

Bazerman, Charles. "Standpoints: The Disciplined Interdisciplinarity of Writing Studies." *Research in the Teaching of English*, vol. 46, no. 1, 2022, pp. 8–21.

Berlin, James. "Rhetoric and Ideology in the writing class." *College English*, vol. 50, no. 5, 1988, 477-494.

Cedillo, Christina V., and Phil Bratta. "Relating our Experiences: The Practice of Positionality Stories in Student-Centered Pedagogy." *College Composition and Communication* vol. 71, no. 2, 2019, pp. 215-240.

Delgado, Richard. "Imperial Scholar: Reflections on a Review of Civil Rights Literature Commentary." *University of Pennsylvania Law Review*, vol. 132, 1983, p. 19.

Elbow, Peter. "Being a Writer vs. Being an Academic: A Conflict in Goals." *College Composition and Communication,* vol. 46, no.1, 1995, pp.72-83.

Fleming, David. *From Form to Meaning: Freshman Composition and the Long Sixties, 1957-1974.* University of Pittsburgh Press, 2011.

Gee, James Paul. *What Video Games Have to Teach Us about Learning and Literacy.* Palgrave Macmillan, 2004.

Hairston, Maxine. "Diversity, Ideology, and Teaching Writing." *College Composition and Communication,* vol. 43, no.2, 1992, pp. 179-193.

Inoue, Asao B. *Labor-Based Grading Contracts: Building Equity and Inclusion in the Compassionate Writing Classroom.* The WAC Clearinghouse; University Press of Colorado, 2019.

Inoue, Asao. B. "How Do We Language So People Stop Killing Each Other, or What Do We Do about White Language Supremacy?" *College Composition and Communication* vol.71, vol. 2, 2019, pp. 352 - 369.

Itchuaqiyaq, Cana Uluak, and Jordan Frith. "Citational Practices as a Site of Resistance and Radical Pedagogy: Positioning the Multiply Marginalized and Underrepresented (MMU) Scholar Database as an Infrastructural Intervention." *Communication Design Quarterly,* vol. 10, no. 3, 2022, pp. 10–19.

Kumashiro, Kevin. "Against Repetition: Addressing Resistance to Anti-Oppressive Change in the Practices of Learning, Teaching, Supervising, and Researching." *Harvard Educational Review,* vol. 72, no. 1, 2002, pp. 67–93.

Lindemann, Erika. "Freshman Composition: No Place for Literature." *College English,*vol. 55, no. 3, 1993, pp. 311-316.

Lyons, Scott Richard. "Rhetorical Sovereignty: What Do American Indians Want from Writing?" *College Composition and Communication,* 2000, pp. 447-468.

Mueller, Derek N. *Network Sense: Methods for Visualizing a Discipline.* The WAC Clearinghouse, 2017.

Royster, Jacqueline Jones, and Jean C. Williams. "History in the Spaces Left: African American Presence and Narratives of Composition Studies." *College Composition and Communication,* vol. 50, no. 4, 1999, pp. 563-584.

Ruiz, Iris D. *Reclaiming Composition for Chicano/as and Other Ethnic Minorities.* Palgrave Macmillan, 2016.

Russell, Clare Jennifer. *Curricular Inquiry: A Survey Of Writing Pedagogy Practicum Instructors.* 2020. Wayne State University, Doctoral Dissertaton. https://digitalcommons.wayne.edu/oa_dissertations/2425

Tate, Gary. "A Place for Literature in Freshman Composition." *College English,* vol. 55, no. 3, 1993, pp. 317-321.

## Where We Are

### Ungrading: Where We Are and Where We Might Go

*Ellen C. Carillo*

I couldn't be more excited to have the opportunity to contribute to this Where We Are section focused on ungrading. I don't know that I heard the term "ungrading" prior to the COVID-19 pandemic. Over the past twenty years, I have certainly employed what I have come to understand as forms of ungrading, such as portfolio grading, peer assessment, self-assessment, and process letters, but the term "ungrading" was not one I had come across. Anecdotally, the same seems to be true of many of my colleagues. And so I am going to take this opportunity to reflect on ungrading by addressing the role the COVID-19 pandemic continues to play in current discussions of ungrading. I will also describe what I believe to be a newly emerging impetus for ungrading, namely students' mental health, and, finally, I'll address where we might go from where we are.

The pandemic brought new urgency to ungrading, a form of assessment with a long history. The pandemic exposed and exacerbated the disparities and injustices in the education system and posed a range of challenges for students— and disproportionately so for students of color. The murder of George Floyd in the early months of the pandemic further magnified these injustices. Because the pandemic affected students of color disproportionately, racial equity became a significant impetus for employing ungrading practices during and since the pandemic. Instructors, including many in writing studies, sought out and continue to seek out alternative grading practices that are not beholden to "white language supremacy. . .the structural condition that determines the standards by which literacy practices are judged in most if not all writing classrooms" (Inoue 27). Many postsecondary instructors and entire writing programs across the country continue to employ ungrading practices to signal their commitment to racial (and often linguistic) equity.

Current discussions surrounding the need for more equitable assessment practices have built upon this foundation and are beginning to include attention to students' intersectional identities in ways that go beyond race and language. In my short-form book, *The Hidden Inequities in Labor-Based Contract Grading,* for example, I argue for adopting assessment practices, like engagement-based grading, that acknowledge students' disabilities, including anxiety and depression, and don't neglect students who are multiply marginalized.

Others in writing studies are currently expanding the scope of scholarship on ungrading even further. As I write this piece, I am also putting together a special issue on ungrading for the journal *Pedagogy: Critical Approaches to Teaching Literature, Language, Composition, and Culture.* As such, I have the privilege of drawing on those articles as examples of where we are now (even though the special issue itself won't be published for another year or so). Some contributors to the special issue are interested in how instructors' racial identities and their positions in the academic hierarchy (i.e., whether they are contingent, tenured, and so on) affect the extent to which they can successfully ungrade—or even have an interest in ungrading. Other contributors are studying different populations of students, including community college students, international students, and multilingual students to determine whether ungrading and, specifically, which forms of ungrading might suit these populations. Others, still, are exploring why some students are motivated and others demotivated by ungrading practices. Through quantitative studies, these researchers promise to help us better understand the potential of ungrading, but also its problems and limits.

One pattern I have noticed in recent research, including in the anonymous feedback I have collected from my own students, is the relationship between some ungrading practices and reduced levels of stress. Since I have started using engagement-based grading, for example, the most common feedback students share about this form of assessment is that it reduces their stress levels. Notably, this feedback is consistent across curricular levels and across courses in the English major and the general education curriculum at my institution. One student explained: "This approach in grading helped me a lot. I currently work 40-60 hours a week. I take care of my siblings as well as help my mother who is on disability. I have to work to help maintain the mortgage. Having this flexibility and grading scale made me less stressed. I did not feel pressured at all." Another student noted, "It makes me motivated to do the work because I know I'm gonna get half credit for even trying. The flexibility in this class has helped me a lot with my learning disability. It reduces stress knowing that I don't have to rush to get an assignment done." A third student described how ungrading was especially useful later in the semester: "As the semester progressed, I was getting very burnout and exhausted. Therefore, the system of grading helped me to still contribute by having flexibility of deadlines." This feedback is indicative, I would argue, of a newly emerging impetus for ungrading: students' mental health.

Students are struggling. Anything we can do as instructors to mitigate—or at least refrain from adding to students' stress—positions students to learn more and may even have the potential to help them reach graduation, suggests "The Lumina Foundation-Gallup State of Higher Education 2023" study. The 6,008 students currently enrolled in a postsecondary education program who participated in the study include 763 students pursuing a certification; 1,296 students seeking a certificate; 1,571 students pursuing an associate degree; and 2,378 students seeking a bachelor's degree. The report explains that these students "are finding it just as difficult to remain enrolled in their programs as they did the year before. But now, more students—Black, Hispanic and male students in particular—are considering stopping out of their coursework. Emotional stress and mental health are the top reasons they are considering pausing their studies" (3). Overall, 41% of percent of enrolled students "say they have considered stopping out in the past six months, up from 37% in 2021." Additionally, the study explains, "more than half (55%) of students who have considered stopping out cite emotional stress as a reason they considered leaving, and almost half (47%) considered it due to mental health reasons." Notably, the Lumina Foundation and Gallup published a related report that drew on the same data but highlighted the specific findings related to students' mental health. As its title suggests, the report, "Stressed Out and Stopping Out: The Mental Health Crisis in Higher Education," underscores the relationship between students' declining mental health and decreased retention rates. Several other recent studies (Colarossi; Lipson et al.; Elharake et al.) corroborate students' mental health struggles.

## Where We Might Go

While some early studies suggested an increase in students' stress levels as a result of particular ungrading practices (Spidell and Thelin; Inman and Powell), recent writing studies scholarship since the pandemic has consistently reported more favorable responses from students, particularly in terms of reduced levels of stress (Gabor; Larson; O'Meara; Ubbesen, et al.; Nastal). Thus, the time seems ripe to conduct targeted research on the relationship between ungrading practices and stress levels across populations of postsecondary students. This research would help instructors, writing program administrators, and other stakeholders learn more about students' stress, an increasingly significant barrier to student success and degree completion, and one that might be mitigated by ungrading practices.

As well as potentially supporting retention efforts, the drop in postsecondary enrollments might also be addressed by using ungrading as a recruitment tool. In addition to surveying currently enrolled students, as discussed above, the Lumina Foundation-Gallup study surveyed unenrolled adults: 3,004 adults who were previously enrolled in a postsecondary program but never earned their bachelor or associate degree and 3,003 "never-enrolled adults" (2). The study reports that "about 3 in 10 unenrolled adults [including previously enrolled and never-enrolled adults] say emotional stress (30%) or personal mental health (28%) are very important reasons why they are not currently enrolled" (14). Working alongside recruitment offices and advisors, the field of writing studies can help prospective students understand how ungrading practices, like those used in many first year writing programs, might help ease the transition into postsecondary institutions and potentially lower levels of stress for new students.

In addition to exploring collaborations between the field of writing studies and offices of recruitment and retention, I hope our work with ungrading will expand in other ways in the coming years. For example, expanding the scope of our discussions to address the importance of creating inclusive pedagogies, as opposed to just inclusive assessments, seems crucial. These discussions might more consistently address how to develop assignments informed by Universal Design for Learning guidelines, as well as the importance of inclusive notions of time, including flexible deadlines. In disability studies, this concept is called crip time, a more flexible approach to time than is usually present in the education system in which "students are expected to arrive on time, absorb information at a particular speed, and perform spontaneously in restricted time frames" (Price 63). In her study of thirty-five students with both documented and undocumented disabilities, Tara Wood found that "students' anxiety might be alleviated through cripping time, increasing flexibility, avoiding rigidity, and lowering the stakes of writing (particularly in the beginning stages of a course)" (270). Unlike normative time frames, crip time recognizes that people move, engage, and process information at different rates and speeds. In order to better meet the needs of our students who are experiencing anxiety and other mental health issues, we would be wise to explore more deeply these inclusive pedagogical practices that emerge from disability studies.

I would also encourage instructors to explore how ungrading practices can complement the ubiquitous ChatGPT (and similar AI programs) to support students' learning and mental health simultaneously. ChatGPT is a powerful, generative tool that can help mitigate writer's block and the anxiety students have surrounding writing. Instead of having to stare at a blank screen, ChatGPT generates for students something from which they can work, some ideas they can think alongside. Like ungrading, in other words, ChatGPT has the potential to reduce students' stress surrounding writing. As we look toward the future of ungrading, we would be wise to think about how the tools we have within writing studies can be harnessed simultaneously to reduce our students' stress levels.

I would be remiss if I didn't also address the mental health of postsecondary instructors, including the increasing levels of stress that instructors are experiencing. Experimenting with, refining, and justifying ungrading approaches to students and skeptical administrators can be time-consuming and stressful. Often these approaches are not supported by learning management systems and take some amount of manual input. Creating more flexible policies, such as removing deadlines might increase one's workload (and make it less predictable), particularly if one teaches several classes across multiple institutions. Moreover, because writing classes tend to be smaller than other classes, students will sometimes seek emotional support from their writing instructors, confiding in them as they would in counselors or therapists, thereby increasing the emotional labor expended by writing instructors. Just as we need to consider how the tools we have in Writing Studies can help us reduce our students' stress levels, we also need to explore (or develop) the tools that might do the same for us.

Ungrading is not a simple fix, whether one is looking to mitigate the inequities within the education system or address students' mental health issues. Still, ungrading has the potential to be a transformative tool that not only encourages us, as educators, to be flexible but seems flexible enough itself to meet our needs as a discipline.

The value of ungrading may also lie well beyond our discipline in its use as an enrollment and retention tool. Writing studies, a field at the forefront of research and scholarship on ungrading, has the opportunity not just to contribute to discussions of ungrading but also help shape them, and by extension, help shape the enrollment and retention programs at postsecondary institutions. The research already being conducted on ungrading and that which I have called for in this short piece have the potential to highlight the measurable contributions of writing studies not just to the curricular and assessment goals of postsecondary institutions, but to the enrollment and retention goals of these very same institutions.

## Works Cited


Carillo, Ellen C. *The Hidden Inequities in Labor-Based Contract Grading.* Utah State UP, 2021.

Colarossi, Jessica. "Mental Health of College Students Is Getting Worse." *The Brink*, 2022. https://www.bu.edu/articles/2022/mental-health-of-collegestudents-is-getting-worse/

Elharake, Jad A., et al. "Mental Health Impact of COVID-19 Among Children and College Students: A Systematic Review." *Child Psychiatry & Human Development*, vol. 54, 2022, pp. 913-925.

Gabor, Cathy. "Just One More Thing?: International Students' Perceptions of Contract Grading." *Pedagogy*, special issue on ungrading, edited by Ellen C. Carillo. Forthcoming.

Inman, Joyce Olewski and Rebecca A. Powell. "In the Absence of Grades: Dissonance and Desire in Course-Contract Classrooms." *College Composition and Communication* vol. 70, no. 1, 2018, pp. 30-56

Inoue, Asao B. *Labor-Based Grading Contracts: Building Equity and Inclusion in the Compassionate Writing Classroom*, 2nd ed. The WAC Clearinghouse; University Press of Colorado, 2022.

Larson, Kara Kristina. *Labor-Based Grading Contracts in the Multilingual FYC Classroom: Unpacking the Variables.* 2021. University of South Florida, Doctoral dissertation.

Lipson, Sarah Ketchen, et al. "Trends in College Student Mental Health and Help-Seeking by Race/Ethnicity: Findings From the National Healthy Minds Study, 2013-2021." *Journal of Affective Disorders*, vol. 306, 2022, pp. 138-147.

Lumina Foundation and Gallup. "The State of Higher Education 2023." 2023, https://www.gallup.com/analytics/468986/state-of-higher-education.aspx

—. "Stressed Out and Stopping Out." 2023, https://www.luminafoundation.org/resource/stressed-out-and-stopping-out/

Nastal, Jessica. "A Sociocognitive Grading Model for First-Year Writing Classes." *Pedagogy*, special issue on ungrading, edited by Ellen C. Carillo. Forthcoming.

O'Meara, Katherine Daily. "'In absolute control of my own grading destiny': Student Reflections on Engagement-Based Grading Contracts." *Pedagogy*, special issue on ungrading, edited by Ellen C. Carillo. Forthcoming.

Price, Margaret. *Mad at School: Rhetorics of Mental Disability and Academic Life*. University of Michigan Press, 2011.

Spidell, Cathy and William H. Thelin. "Not Ready to Let Go: A Study of Resistance to Grading Contracts." *Composition Studies* vol. 34, no 1., 2006, pp. 35-69.

Ubbesen, Molly, et al. "Accessible Ungrading." *Pedagogy*, special issue on ungrading, edited by Ellen C. Carillo. Forthcoming.

Wood, Tara. "Cripping Time in the Composition Classroom." *College Composition and Communication* vol. 69, no. 2, 2017, pp. 260-286.

# Defining Ungrading: Alternative Writing Assessment as Jeremiad

*Megan Von Bergen*

Around the time I was asked to write this essay in summer 2023, West Virginia University announced massive budget cuts (Quinn). As I drafted the essay, the university completed them, laying off hundreds of faculty across departments from English to forestry. The whole World Languages, Literatures, and Linguistics department vanished (Slade). Faced with such crises and when asked where we are in ungrading, I was tempted to respond that our choices about classroom writing assessment are insignificant. Ungrading will not prevent administrators, university boards, or state-level educators from disinvesting in higher education, nor will it address the social conditions that led to this moment. Yet ungrading, oriented towards a keen awareness of social justice, may work as a sort of jeremiad in assessment—making it possible for us to speak boldly about the challenges that face us and rise to meet them.

Though this Where We Are section is titled "Ungrading," use of the term *ungrading* is more common outside the discipline of rhetoric and composition than inside it. Outside the discipline, it largely refers to a fluid set of assessment practices, and some scholars deploy the term to refer to a particular version of alternative assessment: students assigning their own grades in consultation with their teachers (Eyler). Others deploy *ungrading* as an umbrella term, capturing alternative versions of assessment from fields as diverse as postsecondary computer science and high school English, as for instance in Susan Blum's collection *Ungrading.*

The discipline of rhetoric and composition refers rarely to ungrading broadly—but rarely enough that its use as the title for this Where We Are is a notable exception. Rhetoric and composition refers more commonly to contract grading, or labor-based contract grading, engaging one of a small handful of key scholarly texts, among them Danielewicz and Elbow, Shor, or Inoue. These writers propose assigning students' grades on the accumulation not (only) of teachers' subjective, qualitative judgments of student work but on students' quantitative efforts across the term.

Yet even within (labor-based) contract grading discourses, the practices educators use vary widely. As I write this, I am also working on an annotated bibliography of research on (labor-based) contract grading in rhetoric and composition. Among the practices I have documented as associated with contract grading are the following:

- Self-assessments and collaborative work to invite students to establish their own criteria for a project (Litterio)
- A menu of participation options, to invite students to engage the course in ways that suit their skill set (Gomes et al.)

- Embedded tutors to connect students to on-campus resources (Klotz and Reardon)

Contracts may be partially labor-based (Danielwicz and Elbow) or entirely labor-based (Inoue); they may be used for an entire course (Inoue) or for a single, big project (Medina and Walker), and they may be negotiated (Shor) or unilateral (Danielwicz and Elbow). Virginia Schwarz has argued that this variation justifies defining labor-based grading less as a singular practice than a genre of assessment—a view that makes visible the variation and creativity that educators use in (re)fashioning alternative writing assessment for their classrooms. These variations show that the concept we often call contract grading is not any one concept at all but an ever-changing set of practices that teachers remix and adapt based on students' needs, institutional support, and their own labor conditions.

This is where the term *ungrading* becomes useful. In contrast to contract grading, which despite the increasing variation associated with the practice too often implies a singular model, ungrading pushes us past the details of any one model to consider the values or goals underpinning how we develop that arrangement and where we are trying to get with it. Conversations about the particularities of assessment practices—whether to use a negotiated or unilateral model and what role self-assessments play—have their place, of course. But in using the word *ungrading*, we de-emphasize these particularities so often determined by our locatedness and professional contexts. Instead, we shed light onto our choices and goals—our refusal to carry out a stereotypical duty of (writing) educators and our attention to new ways of being and teaching, defined by the distinctive commitments we hold to ourselves, our labor, our students, and our institutions.

Changes within the literature on ungrading appear in three major waves: the first, in the 1960s and 1970s; the second, in the mid-2000s; and the third, which is ongoing, in the late 2010s and early 2020s. Notably, each wave coincides with a period of social injustice and change. During the first wave, faculty—including graduate students at UW-Madison—employed "degrading" to keep students' GPA high enough to avoid the Vietnam draft (Fleming 117). Years later, Ira Shor explicitly situated his negotiated contract in contrast with the "neoliberal capture of school and society," aiming to give students a measure of power in a social context that denies them that (17). And, in the ongoing third wave, ungrading, especially when used to address linguistic bias and affirm students' own language, addresses pervasive anti-Black violence in the United States (Inoue). In the years since Inoue's scholarship, more than twenty articles on the use of ungrading have appeared in print. At the Conference of College Composition and Communication in 2023, at least eleven separate sessions engaged with questions about alternative writing assessment, suggesting sustained interest in taking up assessment practices that may help us meet ongoing injustices. Yet across all three waves, for educators and scholars facing the challenges of their present moment—perhaps feeling helpless amidst the oppressive structural forces of war, neoliberalism, or racism—ungrading functions as a tool of (possible) response to injustice and social change.

Indeed, much of the research on alternative writing assessment opens with a mini-jeremiad on grades and grading, complaining that grades interfere with and diminish learning (Bauman; Birdsall; Reichert) and/or that grades disincentivize and penalize students who are not enculturated into the linguistic norms of academic language (Inoue; Santos; Tinoco). Regardless of whether a given model is a robustly labor-based approach or a tiny step away from conventional grading practices, a core part of what makes any given assessment model ungrading is its sense of resistance or pushback against established and often discriminatory norms in writing assessment across our communities more broadly.

I want to be clear here. I am not arguing that ungrading is defined as an innately socially just model of grading, as though a method of writing assessment — inextricably hierarchical — can solve the world's ills. The fallings-short of ungrading are well-documented. Scholars demonstrate the hardship it may create for neurodivergent/disabled students (Carillo; Kryger and Zimmerman) and for BIPOC students and faculty, especially pre-tenure faculty (Craig). Attention to ungrading as presumptively antiracist assessment can also, as Sherri Craig points out (Barrios et al.), distract from other, equally (or more) urgent efforts supporting Black students, such as curricular changes. Even BIPOC scholars enthusiastic about ungrading, such as Laila McCloud, observe that it demands more labor of them, "keeping receipts," so their authority and role in the classroom is not challenged (103). Like any other method of assessment, ungrading can perpetuate injustice—perhaps more so if we as scholars and teachers assume the method is equitable and employ it without careful attention to student and institutional needs.

My argument is more narrow. Ungrading can, a little and in complicated ways, work for social justice. But ungrading consistently responds to perceived social injustice, with research and practice spiking in response to widespread social evils. Ungrading is a kind of canary in the coal mine, a way to signal that educators and their students are uncomfortable with the status quo and eager for change, willing to change up commonplaces in their classroom as deeply rooted as grades in an attempt to address those inequities.

This brings me back to the question of where we are.

We are—as I demonstrated above—currently seeing a flourishing of research and writing on ungrading, with attention to ungrading spiking across both conferences and journals in rhetoric and composition.

We are also amid a period of heightened social inequities, including in higher education. In addition to the closures at West Virginia University, UNC-Chapel Hill has experienced two active shooter threats, and the Supreme Court has ruled race-conscious admissions illegal (Totenberg). We cannot ungrade our way out of such crises. These are crises of values, of deprioritizing the cultivation of opportunities for public education and the civic sphere. Disoriented values will not be fixed by adopting, say, a labor-based assessment model over a qualitative one. Ungrading does not have that much power.

But ungrading is also not impotent in the face of these crises. As a canary in the coal mine, a flashing warning indicator for ongoing injustice, ungrading pushes us to acknowledge that yes, the way our society is organized does harm to people; that yes, the way we teach and assess writing perpetuates that harm. Ungrading invites us to the work of reimagining writing education and assessment around the human needs of the students we teach, their own locatedness in society and the identities they bring to our classrooms. Ungrading will not always do justice in the writing classroom, but it does urge us as educators to recognize and respond to injustice in the ways that are open to us within our classrooms, institutions, and communities.

One way to frame ungrading —staked on its frank acknowledgement of ongoing injustices and its desire (if not its capacity)—is as a jeremiad. A rhetorical genre that highlights "present fail[ings]," the jeremiad urges, in response, that audiences rekindle their "shared values" and restore the larger "communities [in] which they" live and work (Ringer 632). Indeed, I feel as though my own writing in this piece participates in the genre of jeremiad, at least a little — I do not produce a standard definition of ungrading but open by acknowledging the social ills we face and urge us as educators and researchers to reconsider how our assessment work may speak beyond our classroom walls to the needs of this present moment. There are, of course, limits to the jeremiad analogy, notably the genre's typically conservative bent (633). Yet I find the comparison apt, a way to draw out what seem core underlying functions of ungrading, particularly poignant at this social moment: its clear, extended engagement with existing social and pedagogical ills, its assumption of certain core values shared among educators, and its urging educators to return, in a new way, to those values.

This is ultimately where I believe the definition of ungrading lies—not in a tallying up of particular moves (though that work has its place) but in challenging conventional notions of writing assessment oriented around merit with more accessible, equitable alternatives. The work of teasing out the advantages and disadvantages of this model or that one and its function is necessary; it is also necessary to get beyond the particularities of any given model. Broadly, ungrading is imaginative work that requires us to think critically about the ways our current practice falls short of both good pedagogy and of fairness or justice for our students. It also requires us to adopt new assessment models. This work is not done once, forever; it is done and redone at the beginning of each new academic semester. Jeremiads, despite their conservative reputation, can in fact move us forward (Ringer 633). In drawing attention to the imaginative role of ungrading, I hope that I can frame it as a tool—which, to be clear, does not always work the way we hope it will—that enables us as educators to acknowledge and rise to meet the challenges facing us.

### Works Cited


"2023 CCCC Convention Program - Conference on College Composition and Communication." *Conference on College Composition and Communication*, 17 Mar. 2023, cccc.ncte.org/cccc/2023-cccc-convention-program.

Barrios, Barclay, et al. *Labor-Based Hope: Three Counternarratives on Complicating Antiracist Grading Practices*. Conference for College Composition and Communication, 2023.

Bauman, Marcy. "What Grades Do with Us, and How to Do Without Them." *Alternatives to Grading Student Writing*, edited by Stephen Tchudi, WAC Clearinghouse, 1997, pp. 162-78, https://wac.colostate.edu/books/ncte/tchudi/.

Birdsall, Eric R."Avoiding Whadjaget with No-Grade, Graded Papers." *College Composition and Communication*, vol. 30, no. 2, May 1979, p. 220-22, https://doi.org/10.2307/356334.

Blum, Susan Debra, editor. *Ungrading: Why Rating Students Undermines Learning (and What to Do Instead)*. First edition, West Virginia University Press, 2020.

Carillo, Ellen C. *The Hidden Inequities in Labor-Based Contract Grading*. Utah State UP, 2021.

Craig, Sherri. "Your Contract Grading Ain't It." *WPA Journal*, vol. 44, no. 3, Summer 2021, pp. 145-46.

Danielewicz, Jane, and Peter Elbow. "A Unilateral Grading Contract to Improve Learning and Teaching." *College Composition and Communication*, vol. 61, no. 2, 2009, pp. 244-68.

Eyler, Josh. "The Call is Coming from Inside the House: How Grades can Undermine Learning and Jeopardize Our Students' Wellbeing." Teaching, Learning, and Innovation Institute, 22 May 2023, Zoom. Plenary Session.

Fleming, David, et al. "TA Experimentation, 1966-1969." *From Form to Meaning: Freshman Composition and the Long Sixties, 1957-1974*, U Pittsburgh P, 2011, pp. 93-132.

Gomes, Matthew, et al. "Enabling Meaningful Labor: Narratives of Participation in a Grading Contract." *The Journal of Writing Assessment*, edited by Asao Inoue et al., vol. 13, no. 2, 2020, http://journalofwritingassessment.org/article.php?article=152.

Inoue, Asao. *Labor-Based Grading Contracts: Building Equity and Inclusion in the Compassionate Writing Classroom*. WAC Clearinghouse, 2019, https://wac.colostate.edu/books/perspectives/labor/.

Klotz, Sarah, and Kristina Reardon. "Crafting a Writing Response Community Through Contract Grading." *Journal of Response to Writing*, vol. 8, no. 2, 2022, pp. 106-26.

Kryger, Kathleen, and Griffin X. Zimmerman. "Neurodivergence and Intersectionality in Labor-Based Grading Contracts." *The Journal of Writing Assessment*, vol. 13, no. 2, 2020, http://journalofwritingassessment.org/article.php?article=156.

Litterio, Lisa M. "Contract Grading in the Technical Writing Classroom: Blending Community-Based Assessment and Self-Assessment." *Assessing Writing*, vol. 38, 2018, pp. 1-9, https://doi.org/10.1016/j.asw.2018.06.002.

Medina, Cruz, and Kenneth Walker. "Validating the Consequences of a Social Justice Pedagogy." *Key Theoretical Frameworks*, edited by Angela M. Haas and Michelle F. Eble, Utah State UP, 2018, pp. 46-67, https://doi.org/10.7330/9781607327585.c002.

McCloud, Laila. "View of Keeping Receipts: Thoughts on Ungrading from a Black Woman Professor." *Zeal: A Journal for the Liberal Arts*, vol. 1, no. 2, 2023, pp. 101-05.

Quinn, Ryan. "West Virginia University's Unprecedented Proposed Cuts Become Clear." *Inside Higher Ed*, 11 Aug. 2023, www.insidehighered.com/news/faculty-issues/tenure/2023/08/11/west-virginia-universitys-unprecedented-proposed-cuts-become.

Reichert, Nancy. "Practice Makes Perfect: Contracting Quantity and Quality." *Teaching English in The Two Year College*, vol. 31, no. 1, 2003, pp. 60-68.

Ringer, Jeffrey M. "Working With(in) the Logic of the Jeremiad: Responding to the Writing of Evangelical Christian Students." *College Composition and Communication*, vol. 68, no. 4, 2017, pp. 629-54.

Santos, Marc C. "How I Implemented Asao B. Inoue's Labor-Based Grading and Other Antiracist Assessment Strategies." *CEA Critic*, vol. 84, no. 2, 2022, pp. 160-79, https://doi.org/10.1353/cea.2022.0019.

Schwarz, Virginia M. "Patterns, Negotiations, and Ideologies: Contract Grading as Genre." *Writing the Classroom: Pedagogical Documents as Rhetorical Genres*, edited by Stephen Neaderhiser, Utah State UP, 2022, pp. 60-76.

Shor, Ira. "Critical Pedagogy is Too Big to Fail." *Journal of Basic Writing*, vol. 28, no. 2, 2009, pp. 6-27.

Slade, Duncan. "West Virginia University Faces Budget Cuts and Layoffs. Here's What to Know." *Mountain State Spotlight*, 11 Aug. 2023, mountainstatespotlight.org/2023/08/08/wvu-budget-cuts-deficit-faculty-layoffs.

Tinoco, Lizbett, et al. "Openings, Risks, and Antiracist Futures at a Hispanic-Serving Institution." *The Journal of Writing Assessment*, vol. 13, no. 2, 2020, http://journalofwritingassessment.org/article.php?article=151.

Totenberg, Nina. "Supreme Court Guts Affirmative Action, Effectively Ending Race-Conscious Admissions." *NPR*, 29 June 2023, www.npr.org/2023/06/29/1181138066/affirmative-action-supreme-court-decision.

# Ungrading: Self-Assessment, Effort, and Motivation

*Hannah T. Davis*

> A single grade hardly sums up the complicated mixture of strengths and weaknesses present in students' work, and if an instructor's goal is to teach invention, feedback, revision, and other process-oriented skills, grading one final product misses the point entirely.
>
> —Michelle Cowan

After spending several weeks guiding first year writing (FYW) students through an iterative process of invention, research, drafting, and revision, taking the time to meet with students and provide feedback on drafts, I dread the moment at which I have to mark student writing with a grade. Writing products are important, and I want students to learn to meet audience and genre expectations and communicate effectively; however, as Michelle Cowan expresses, a "single grade" on a single draft does not tell the full story of what I teach or what I hope students will learn. Perhaps most importantly, the grade often signals to students the end of learning, and, in many cases, carries an emotionally charged message about good writing or writers.

Inspired by the positive outcomes detailed in Susan Blum's edited collection *UNgrading: Why Rating Students Undermines Learning (and What to Do Instead)* and in an effort to better align my process pedagogy with my assessment practices, I decided to try ungrading. Because the current conversation is largely theoretical, I wondered how student learning would compare across traditionally-graded, portfolio-graded, and ungraded sections of the same course. In a recent IRB-approved study, I taught three sections of FYW that were identical in terms of content, assignments, and pedagogy but implemented a different approach to grading. Based on other instructors' anecdotal results and the theoretical frameworks of ungrading, I thought that the evidence from my study would be clear: the ungraded students would demonstrate learning and engage more authentically with writing as a process. Though my ungraded students did write recursively and reveal insights about their learning through reflection, so, too, did my graded students. As I reflect on my data and my experience teaching the course, I find myself with new questions about ungrading:

1. Are we using self-assessment as effectively as we could?
2. What should we make of students' effort-based self-assessments?
3. Does being grade-motivated mean students won't learn?

In a submitted manuscript about this study, titled "From Performative to Productive: A Proposal for Formative Self-Assessment," I explore the value of self-assessment as student-generated feedback on their writing. Current approaches to ungrading suggest that self-assessment is used reflectively and holistically, offering students a space to reflect on their writing and learning (Stommel, "Ungrading"; Blum; Chiaravalli) but not used as a source of feedback on their writing products. While these summative self-assessments can provide opportunities for students to reflect, I am not convinced that they are the best approach to helping students engage in metacognition, develop skills for writing transfer, or implement their learning. I initially followed that path, though, asking students–regardless of how they were graded–to self-assess their writing products upon submission of the assignment. My goal was for students to analyze their writing (and to acknowledge room for additional revision or to revise) prior to receiving my feedback and, in the graded sections, a grade. However, my data reveals that, even in the ungraded section of my course, students' summative self-assessments were more likely to be performative, used to prove or justify a desired grade. As I reflect on this finding, it seems obvious that my students–who drafted, received feedback, and revised multiple times before the deadline–would view their final drafts as the best writing they can produce. At the end of a recursive process, students are proud of the work that went into their writing and, understandably, want to demonstrate the ways in which their writing succeeds in meeting the assignment or genre expectations. In my study, then, summative self-assessment did not prompt students to think critically about or analyze their writing. Instead, self-assessment may be more valuable when implemented as formative assessment (Andrade) and, as with reflection (Taczak), used throughout the process to teach students to analyze their writing, make choices during revision, and implement what they learn from this self-generated feedback. Used solely as summative assessment, self-assessment can serve as a replacement for traditional grades (Kohn) but may inadvertently inhibit students' ability to assess or improve their writing. Formative self-assessment, on the other hand, allows students to provide feedback on their writing in process and use that feedback during revision, thus demonstrating their writing knowledge and their learning.

The performative nature of students' summative self-assessments arises, in part, from their emphasis on effort. Effort as grade justification aligns with Heidi Andrade's claim that "Students are not stupid: if they know that they can influence their final grade, and that their judgment is summative rather than intended to inform revision and improvement, they will be motivated to inflate their self-evaluation" (6). Perhaps more generously, and as noted above, students want to acknowledge and be rewarded for their hard work. In my course, students tended to view the quality of their writing favorably as a result of the work that went into the assignment. While graded students were more likely to use effort to fill any perceived gaps between writing quality and desired grade, ungraded students also rounded up to an A for effort. For example, multiple ungraded students self-assessed two or more of their major assignments as an A- or below yet awarded themselves As for their course grades.

Scaffolding and providing feedback on self-assessments may equip students with the metacognitive skills necessary for accurate self-assessments (Yan and Brown). However, I question whether effort-based assessments are entirely inaccurate. In the case of my ungraded students, they did accurately assess their writing yet also placed value on their effort. As proponents of labor-based grading argue, assessing students' effort, or work in the course, not only prioritizes writing as a process over writing products but is also an anti-racist approach to writing assessment that offers a means of fairly assessing students of diverse racial, linguistic, and socioeconomic backgrounds (Inoue). Though I am not convinced that effort is entirely equitable (Carillo), students' effort-based assessments raise an interesting perspective worth further consideration: Is effort another word for process? Considering Cowan's statement in the epigraph and my own struggle with process pedagogy in a system that has traditionally graded products, I do see value in assessing, or asking students to assess, effort. However, I am not sure that effort-based assessment teaches students to analyze their writing or fully prepares students for writing transfer. Is it possible, then, to assess both process and product in writing courses? Notably, my students did not assess effort in their formative self-assessments, focusing instead on the effectiveness of their writing and how to improve their drafts. Perhaps the question is less about whether to and more about when or for what purpose to assess writing processes and products.

Lastly, arguments for ungrading often emphasize intrinsic motivation: "Grades do motivate, but they don't motivate the kinds of peak experiences that can happen in a learning environment" (Stommel, "Why"). Alfie Kohn similarly argues that any form of extrinsic motivation is antithetical to learning. These sentiments suggest that all extrinsic motivation is bad and that students are more likely to become intrinsically motivated once grades are removed. It seems to me that we may be putting unnecessary expectations on students when we suggest that ungrading is a path to intrinsic motivation, especially in the context of a required course such as FYW. According to Gretchen Rubin, people respond differently to internal and external expectations, and some learners need extrinsic accountability to meet their goals. What if, for example, students improve as writers, engage in authentic reflection, and demonstrate learning but need the course requirements or the prospect of a good grade to motivate them to invest in the coursework? Is their learning any less real or valuable than that of a student who was intrinsically motivated? If Rubin is correct, it seems unrealistic to expect that removing grades or other extrinsic motivators will inherently increase intrinsic motivation.

In fact, extrinsic motivation might be the very reason some students find the accountability necessary to learn. When surveyed about their motivations to write, about half (six out of fourteen) of my ungraded students chose an extrinsic motivator—course requirement or getting a good grade—as their primary motivation. Interestingly, eight out of nine students in the portfolio-graded section chose getting a good grade as their primary motivation (as compared to three students per class in the ungraded and graded sections). It seems, then, that the presence or lack of grades did not determine students' motivations. This finding leads me to wonder whether motivating learning and motivating students to learn might be two separate challenges that require different approaches. Certainly, intrinsic motivation may be more desirable or more sustainable for lifelong learning (Kohn), but does that make intrinsic motivation a prerequisite for getting students to learn? Considering the discussion of effort above and approaches such as contract grading, it seems we have agreed that some extrinsic motivators—assignment deadlines, amount of work to complete, etc.—are acceptable. Though I have my own questions about grades, I am not sure that positioning grades as antithetical to learning is productive, and I worry that the messaging around intrinsic motivation and learning may inadvertently put off students who do not have interest in or feel motivated by our courses. This is especially true if Rubin is right that individual needs for accountability differ. If encouraging learning is the goal, we might first consider what motivates our specific students.

Ungrading challenges us to shift our thinking about our goals for students, what it means to learn, and what role assessment serves in our courses. In return, we should challenge ungrading by continuing to ask questions and test our theories. I am currently asking what it means to motivate learning and what students need in order to learn. My study and the resulting data clarified something for me: I care most about teaching students to engage with writing as a recursive process, to analyze and assess their writing, and to use reflection as a tool for writing, learning, and transfer. Ungrading may allow me to accomplish these objectives, but I'm not yet convinced that grading will not.

## Works Cited


Andrade, Heidi L. "A Critical Review of Research on Student Self-Assessment." *Frontiers in Education*, vol. 4, 2019, pp. 1-13. DOI: 10.3389/feduc.2019.00087.

Bloom, Lynn Z. "Why I (Used to) Hate to Give Grades." *College Composition and Communication*, vol. 48, no. 3, 1997, pp. 360-71. https://doi.org/10.2307/358403.

Blum, Susan D., editor. *UNgrading: Why Rating Students Undermines Learning (and What to Do Instead)*. West Virginia UP, 2020.

Blum, Susan D. "Just One Change (Just Kidding): Ungrading and Its Necessary Accompaniments." Blum, pp. 53-73.

Carillo, Ellen C. *The Hidden Inequities in Labor-Based Contract Grading.* Utah State UP, 2021.

Chiaravalli, Arthur. "Grades Stifle Student Learning. Can We Learn to Teach Without Grades?" Blum, pp. 82-88.

Cowan, Michelle. "A Legacy of Grading Contracts for Composition." *Journal of Writing Assessment,* vol. 13, no. 2, 2020. https://escholarship.org/uc/item/0j28w67h.

Inoue, Asao B. *Antiracist Writing Assessment Ecologies: Teaching and Assessing Writing for a Socially Just Future.* The WAC Clearinghouse, 2015.

Kohn, Alfie. Foreword. Blum, pp. xiii-xx.

Rubin, Gretchen. *The Four Tendencies.* Harmony, 2017.

Stommel, Jesse. "Ungrading: an FAQ." *Jesse Stommel,* 06 Feb. 2020, www.jessestommel.com/ungrading-an-faq/.

—. "Why I Don't Grade." *Jesse Stommel,* 26 Oct. 2017, www.jessestommel.com/why-i-dont-grade/.

Taczak, Kara. "Reflection is Critical for Writers' Development." *Naming What We Know: Threshold Concepts of Writing Studies,* edited by Linda Adler-Kassner and Elizabeth Wardle, Utah State UP, 2015, pp. 78-81.

Yan, Zi, and Gavin T. L. Brown. "A Cyclical Self-Assessment Process: Towards a Model of How Students Engage in Self-Assessment." *Assessment and Evaluation in Higher Education,* vol. 42, no. 8, 2017, pp. 1247-62. DOI:10.1080/02602938.2016.1260091.

# We're All Still Grading: A Call for Honesty in Writing Assessment Discourse

*Maggie Fernandes, Emily Brier, and Megan McIntyre*

In recent years, a series of crises have hit academic workplaces with implications for how many instructors think about grading and its ties to the systemic oppression of our most vulnerable students. Such ongoing crises include the 2020 COVID-19 lockdown and its continued impacts on students, the systemic attack on Critical Race Theory, the effects of inflation on precariously employed faculty and graduate students, and the continued dismantling and corporatization of public education. Within these tumultuous times, ungrading became a beacon in higher education for pedagogical change. But here's the truth: We're all still grading.

Amidst all this tumult and transformation, we still teach in places that assign grades. We give letter grades at the end of each semester; some of us also give multiple, mandatory mid-term letter grades to indicate a student's progress in our course. Our students deserve to understand how grades—grades that often significantly impact their future—work in our classes. Saying we don't care about grades or we don't believe in grades doesn't seem sincere when we are still giving grades at the end of the semester. Acknowledging these facts is a vital foundation for having an honest conversation about writing assessment practices and their impacts on our students.

And that's why we argue against the language of ungrading and for more detailed, specific, contextual discussions of alternative writing assessments, assessments built on a disciplinary foundation and the work of writing studies scholars like April Baker-Bell, Asao Inoue, Carmen Kynard, Geneva Smitherman, and others who have spoken and written about writing studies, writing assessment, and their relationships to linguistic justice.

Specifically, we have two related concerns:

1. The language of ungrading misrepresents how students experience our courses, as well as the responsibilities that most writing instructors have. We should be honest with our students and ourselves about the fact that our classes are graded, and we need to confront how standards are intentionally and unintentionally communicated not just via letter and numerical grades but also through how we frame writing assignments, tasks, and feedback to individual students.
2. Relatedly, the popular and non-disciplinary discourse about ungrading, while effective in sparking conversations about problematic assessment practices, flattens the critiques of normative and oppres-

*Composition Studies 51.2 (2023): 148–154*

sive writing assessment that our field has challenged for decades. We must turn to specific conversations in writing studies related to linguistic diversity and disability justice to develop practical assessment approaches that reduce harm done to our most vulnerable students.

## Against Ungrading and for Alternative Assessment Practices

We object to the language of ungrading because it doesn't allow us to be honest about assessment with our students and, perhaps more importantly, with ourselves. To a certain extent, the ambiguity around what we mean by ungrading feels intentional. It's difficult to pin down ungrading as a framework. For Susan Blum, one of the foremost voices on ungrading in higher education, ungrading is a "growing movement" of teachers who believe that grading should be critically interrogated and removed (2). For Jesse Stommel, ungrading is an ethic, a philosophy, a politic, and a lens by which we deconstruct grades in our classrooms (84). In other words, ungrading is not a set of practices; in fact, part of the work of ungrading is for instructors to deconstruct their need and adherence to grading practices that rely on normative standards and distract from actual learning.

And, as three people who use variations of contract-grading approaches in our classes, we get it: grading and grading systems are bad. Institutions wield those systems against their most vulnerable members in ways that should make us all deeply uncomfortable. But ungrading as both a term and a movement does not necessarily allow us to undo or disrupt those harms.

The field of writing studies pedagogy needs specificity about alternative assessment practices that help us engage in honest and transparent assessment as a form of harm reduction. We can't escape the institutional reliance on course grades without activist efforts, but we can—through honest alternative assessment practices—reduce the harm that grades do to students. To do that, though, we need practices that work in specific ways, in specific contexts, for specific people. We need discussions of those practices that acknowledge the specific and inherent messiness of grading and feedback in writing classes. And we can't accomplish these disciplinary goals if we lean so heavily on the disembodied, non-disciplinary conversations that dominate popular discourse about ungrading.

We're not saying that any writing teacher who takes up ungrading in their classrooms is being willfully dishonest. We're sure that we share many of the same values around alternative assessment, which is to say that we believe that there are many approaches that serve our students better than traditional grading. But we do wonder if ungrading—as a movement, as a framework, and especially as language we share with our students—mostly makes instructors feel good, to echo Sherri Craig's poignant critique of antiracist assessment approaches in writing classrooms. Does our attachment to ungrading reveal more about our own desire to brand ourselves as innovative, radical, and equitable teachers than it does about the actual practices of assessment that occur in our classrooms (Craig 145)?

Moreover, the use of ungrading within writing assessment conversations is limited by the myriad approaches that fall under the umbrella of ungrading, including specifications grading, student self-assessment, labor-based contract grading, digital badges, or any number of other alternative assessment practices that come with their own sets of allegiances, histories, and baked-in problems. Ungrading allows us to seem unbothered about specific issues with our alternative assessment practice of choice. However, writing teachers and members of a discipline invested in linguistic variety, equitable assessment, and process-based literacy instruction need more specific frameworks for thinking about assessment, and those frameworks must be rooted in disciplinary knowledge and praxis, something that much of the popular ungrading discourse eschews. Is ungrading only an oppositional position meant to indicate that one is aware of issues in the neoliberal university, a cloak of progressivism that shows you know enough about teaching writing to know that things should be fixed? The harms of grades do not begin and end with the placement of a number or letter beside a text in a learning management system; rather, works such as Baker-Bell's *Linguistic Justice* and Inoue's *Antiracist Writing Assessment Ecologies* challenge us to take on racist modes of responding to student writing in all forms, including how we discuss writing with students in our lessons. How do these important challenges intersect with ungrading as a pedagogical approach in writing classes?

## Disciplinary Specificity in Assessment Conversations

While ungrading has been taken up in meaningful ways by practitioners in writing studies, especially in the years following the initial emergence of COVID-19, we take issue with how ungrading flattens critiques of normative and oppressive writing instruction and assessment that our field has challenged for decades. Specifically, scholars across writing studies have named issues of white language supremacy and linguistic injustice (Baker-Bell, 2020; Inoue, 2021), as well as how inaccessible pedagogies do harm to neurodivergent and disabled students (Carillo, 2021; Dolmage, 2017; Kryger and Zimmerman, 2020).

Too often, our conversations about assessment fail to consider wider conversations about writing pedagogy, literacy development, educational and linguistic equity, and linguistic variation. However, scholarship on the historical development of the discipline, for example, tells us much about what the goals and values of writing courses should be, and those goals and values impact assignments and assessments. We're thinking here of the ways that Carmen Kynard's historiographical work in *Vernacular Insurrections* gives us important insight into how writing instruction has historically excluded and harmed Black students and other students of color. These two things–a history of harm and the possible methods for redressing that harm–should fundamentally inform how we understand the relationships between writing courses (and their assessments) and the students they serve.

What then, precisely, would it look like to have a disciplinary conversation about alternative assessment practices that centers what we know about the writing process and writing instruction? First, it would involve uncomfortable honesty about how messy the writing process is and how writing standards and assessments perpetuate harm when relying upon single-standard, white mainstream English. Our students deserve as much clarity and honesty about grades and grading as we can give them, even if that means revealing the complexity within which we work.

Luckily, we have the work of Baker-Bell, Inoue, Kynard, and Smitherman to guide us in contending with the complex relationships among feedback, grading, assessment, and linguistic justice. And using the work of these scholars matters both because it is discipline-specific work and because building from the work of these scholars reflects our field's attention to citation justice. Our field has a long, ongoing tradition of grappling with citation justice and ethical attribution practices, both for our students and for ourselves. In other words, citation justice is not just about what ultimately ends up on our reference pages—it's about meaningfully and substantially engaging the work of marginalized scholars from within writing studies throughout our work on assessment. Work on disciplinary histories, language variation, and equitable writing pedagogy should fundamentally inform our decisions about writing assessment. We have a very specific set of discipline-specific concerns, values, and practices around assessment and feedback. Those discipline-specific concerns, values, and practice are reflected in the scholarship of the discipline.

## Toward Uncomfortably Transparent Futures

So yes, we are grading. We are carving out space in hostile departments, universities, and states to do less harm through grading. We are working with other composition practitioners to subvert oppressive systems which harm not only our students but us, which strip us of our humanity and ability to engage with others as whole humans, which makes us rank students against one another, to move toward a system that feels more humane. We are trying new things that are actually very old things, moving away from 100-point scales and ranked letter grades to engage with education itself, the gathering and co-creation of knowledge as a group of people moving toward educational and personal goals.

And we know: Asking for honesty about assessment makes us more vulnerable in spaces that may already be hostile to us, to our students, and to our practices. But honesty and specificity are the only ways forward if what we most want is a suite of approaches that allow us to reduce the harm that traditional writing assessments do to our students.

However, this disciplinary playing field is not equal to all in our discipline, nor should we, in our call to disciplinarity, pretend as much. Precariously employed and early-career writing studies practitioners of alternative assessment practices may have few if any incentives to be honest in their pedagogical disclosures to colleagues and peers. The messy reflections that we need are silenced and stifled by the inherent tensions between what we know and believe to be true about the unfairness of grading systems; the limitations of self-assessment; the top-down biases of creating requirements of length, genre, or topic for given assignments; and the desire to prove so-called rigor and necessity of composition courses to uninvested outsiders looking to cut faculty and liberal education hours by any means necessary. In a system not only of grades but precarity, soft and hard power over our jobs means that the systems in which we work are not always the systems in which we would most believe. But we have to at least be honest about what we're actually doing in our classes. Declaring ourselves beyond grades does not actually make it so, even if it makes us feel better.

Beyond our classrooms, we believe in the urgency of questions that advocates of ungrading raise. Ungrading, or alternative assessment practices more generally, largely represent the changes that individual instructors (and in some cases programs) can make. Individual instructors implementing classroom harm reduction practices does not redress the greater problems of grades in higher education; at most, we are postponing, obscuring, and unveiling the moment of grading in nontraditional ways.

The changes necessary will take real activism, working in cross-disciplinary solidarity with faculty, staff, and students for change at the institutional level. Such coalitional, cross-disciplinary activism is necessary and possible, as we've seen demonstrated by the oceanic swell in graduate student and faculty unionizing across the U.S. (Quinn, 2023a) and the resistance efforts of faculty at West Virginia University (Quinn, 2023b).

It is not as easy (or frankly marketable) to do risky, often-boring, rarely-lauded activist work. No one is going to change grades in a university system based on the actions of a few instructors; we must admit as much, to ourselves and others, as we use these guiding principles to talk back toward these grading systems writ large. No one is coming to do this work for us: The university certainly has no investment in throwing out grades in favor of a system that promotes non-compliance in its student body, or a perceived lack of certainty in the ranking of one's student population.

Until we get organized, we can be honest with ourselves and our students about the role of grades in our classrooms and use that honesty to deliberately employ alternative assessment practices to address racism and ableism in assessment. We can develop alternative assessment practices that are built upon disciplinary work and values. And we can tap into local university organizing efforts that would help make the ideals of ungrading more possible and more material for our students.

## Works Cited


Baker-Bell, April. *Linguistic Justice: Black Language, Literacy, Identity, and Pedagogy.* Routledge, 2020.

Blum, Susan. *Ungrading: Why Rating Students Undermines Learning (And What To Do Instead).* West Virginia UP, 2020.

Carillo, Ellen C. *The Hidden Inequities in Labor-Based Contract Grading.* UP of Colorado, 2021.

Craig, Sherri. "Your Contract Grading Ain't It." *WPA: Writing Program Administration,* vol. 44, no. 3, 2021, pp. 145-147. https://wpacouncil.org/aws/CWPA/asset_manager/get_file/604397?ver=1.

Dolmage, Jay T. *Academic Ableism: Disability and Higher Education.* U of Michigan P, 2017.

Inman, Joyce Olewski, and Rebecca A. Powell. "In the Absence of Grades." *College, Composition, and Communication,* vol. 70, no. 1, 2018, pp. 30-56.

Inoue, Asao B. *Antiracist Writing Assessment Ecologies: Teaching and Assessing Writing for a Socially Just Future.* WAC Clearinghouse and Parlor Press, 2015, https://doi.org/10.37514/per-b.2015.0698.

—. "Blogbook: Habits of White Language (HOWL)." *Asao B. Inoue's Infrequent Words.* https://asaobinoue.blogspot.com/2021/07/blogbook-habits-of-white-language-howl.html. Accessed 20 July 2023.

Kryger, Kathleen, and Griffin X. Zimmerman. "Neurodivergence and Intersectionality in Labor-Based Grading Contracts." *Journal of Writing Assessment,* vol. 13, no. 2, 2020, https://escholarship.org/uc/item/0934x4rm.

Kynard, Carmen. *Vernacular insurrections: Race, Black Protest, and the New Century in Composition-Literacies Studies.* SUNY UP, 2013.

Quinn, Ryan. "Grad Worker Unionization Is Booming, Even Down South." *Inside Higher Ed,* September 6, 2023. https://www.insidehighered.com/news/faculty-issues/labor-unionization/2023/09/06/grad-worker-unionization-booming-even-down-south

—. "Despite National Pushback, West Virginia Will Cut Faculty, Programs." *Inside Higher Ed,* September 15, 2023. https://www.insidehighered.com/news/faculty-issues/shared-governance/2023/09/15/desp ite-national-pushback-wvu-will-cut-faculty.

Smitherman, Geneva. *Word from the Mother: Language and African Americans*. Routledge, 2006.

Stommel, Jesse. "Do We Need the Word 'Ungrading?'" *Zeal: A Journal for the Liberal Arts*, Vol. 1, No. 2, 2023, https://zeal.kings.edu/zeal/article/view/22.

# Book Reviews

***Approaches to Lifespan Writing Research: Generating an Actionable Coherence,*** edited by Ryan J. Dippre and Talinn Phillips, University Press of Colorado, 2020. 265 pp.

*Reviewed by Nasih Alam, North Dakota State University*

During the closing speech of 2016 Dartmouth Summer Seminar for Composition Research and Conference, Charles Bazerman spoke about the Lifespan Writing Development Group that he had formed with his colleagues from various disciplines to investigate "how people find their separate paths to grow into writing creatures" (Preface xiii, 5). After attending Bazerman's workshop and plenary speech in that conference, a group of rhetoric and writing scholars shared an interest in doing research on literacy narratives from an eclectic range of sources. In keeping with that perspective, forty composition scholars from multiple disciplines met online and face-to-face between 2017 and 2018 to draft academic papers on lifespan writing; the result is this edited collection, *Approaches to Lifespan Writing Research: Generating an Actionable Coherence* (*LWR*).

Lifespan writing researchers generally cover the entire lifespan writing of one generation or "multiple generations" (6) in order to sketch a report on the rhetorical situation and the rhetorical tradition from different strata of society. Through diverse and inclusive perspectives, contributors of *LWR* focus on varied individuals' multi-genre writing and new media literacies to "support more people becoming more versatile and capable writers" (7). To study the composition process of lifespan research writing, contributors of *LWR* used qualitative, quantitative, and mixed methods of research to develop "more coherent understanding of lifespan writing" (8). Lifespan writing research acknowledges writing scholars' general view that writing is a rigorous and complex process; therefore, an individual's writing keeps evolving throughout their lifespan. In addition, lifespan writing research does not ignore the fact that individuals' writing development might also be affected by relationship struggles, financial difficulties, unemployment situations, diasporic tensions, legal convictions, jail terms, career choices, childcare issues, and deteriorating mental or physical health. *LWR* contributors have also interviewed people from various backgrounds and shown that it this evolving research field requires constant investigation of individuals' writing processes–not only from countries of the global south but also from other parts of the world. This inclusive approach promises the field of rhetoric and composition studies a nuanced understanding of lifespan writing from the global world.

*LWR* consists of two parts. The first part, "Embracing the Radical," contains six chapters, and the second part, "Leveraging our Traditions," comprises eight chapters. In addition to the two parts, *LWR* has introductory and concluding chapters jointly written by editors Ryan J. Dippre and Talinn Philips; the volume ends with Deborah Brandt's epilogue. All contributions share three characteristics: first, they agree that lifespan writing research needs continued exploration; second, they emphasize that every phase of writing contributes to an individual's literacy development over their life period; third, they collectively encourage readers to continue writing throughout the lifespan, for themselves and for others and in any platform of their choice.

Impressively, Yvonne Lee selected four generations of her family as her research participants. Following the interviews with her participants, Lee argues that multilingual writers from past and present generations get inspired by "multidirectional" and "multigenerational" sponsors of literacy to assimilate themselves with different surroundings over the period (139). Focusing on a single research subject rather than a family, Lauren Marshall Bowen studies an elderly man, Don, whose literacy practices alter substantially later in life. Citing Don's renewed conceptions of literacy even when he is sixty, Bowen shows how anyone can develop their literacy in writing in a new genre at any age. Similarly, James T. Zebrosky demonstrates how an academic scholar can gain literacy in multiple genres at any career stage. For example, Zebrosky himself becomes literate about retirement plans after his formal resignation from a tenure-track position at a university where he used to teach. This chapter illustrates that individuals can take stock of their growth of literacy on any given subject/topic at any time with affordances and sponsors of literacy (156). In addition to age and growth, lifespan writing research draws attention towards people with learning difficulties and health challenges. Apryl L. Poch and colleagues posit that researchers might want to share a space with people with learning disabilities, especially people on the autism spectrum, to study how writers of various capacities approach writing in the longitudinally.

Some of the contributions of this collection broach the idea of revisiting research participants even after a manuscript on lifespan writing is published. The idea is to continuously monitor how the participants of the earlier manuscript are navigating through their writing process and share their perspective on writing as it develops. To demonstrate this idea, Lauren Rosenberg narrates her interaction with Chief, her research participant in a previously-published monograph. Revisiting Chief after the publication of that monograph gives Rosenberg new ideas to explore lifespan writing in her future research; she postulates that lifespan writing researchers could benefit from examining how life-events and life-experiences inform, encourage, and discourage everyday writers throughout their lives. Like Rosenberg and Bowen, Jeff Naftzinger uses "a writer-informed approach" (82) to understand how everyday writers' definition of writing diverges from scholarly assumptions about their pattern of writing. If writing scholars learn from everyday writers' experiences, they can find new research gaps to address in lifespan writing research (81) and "may help other writers see the value of their writing and/or the value of studying that writing" (93).

Lifespan writing research includes addressing how writing participants methodize their writing processes in different contexts and situations. In order to understand how participants' writing approaches change over time and with the influence of new ideas, Kevin Roozen examines the everyday writing of participants and observes how that writing is shaped by the past and informs the "unpredictable futures" of writers, too (245).

In the conclusion of *LWR,* the editors write, "We ask readers, then, to treat this concluding chapter as a starter pistol in what will no doubt be a long and sometimes grueling (but also incredibly rewarding) task of researching writing through the lifespan" (254). Although *LWR* has done a brilliant job of delving into lifespan writing from a diverse range, future rhetoric and writing researchers might want to address how second-language writers in English approach writing in English after they begin settling in the U.S. It will be invigorating to interview more people to understand more in-depth how immigrant and the BIPOC (Black, Indigenous, and People of Color) communities approach everyday writing. Rhetoric and composition scholars will also want to continue including more participants from around the world.

Certainly, *LWR* has inspired budding researchers like me to emulate the book's research process to reconceptualize a theory of my own on lifespan writing research. To build "stronger political will for writing research" (259), I would like to extend the conversation around lifespan writing by focusing on my own community's approach to multilingual writing. Inspired by *LWR,* I plan to study how international students from the STEM fields approach writing during their lifespan and what methods and techniques they follow to translate their thoughts into words. By getting an overall picture of their literacy narratives, I aim to write about their rhetorical challenges, rhetorical tensions, and literacy progressions amidst their disparate personal challenges.

I would recommend that everyone new and experienced in the field of rhetoric and composition studies to read *LWR* and include it in undergraduate and graduate curricula. After poring over this book, undergraduate students might know why their individual everyday writing through their lifespan is as important as writings of their family members from different generations. Additionally, *LWR* might inspire undergraduate and graduate students to interview everyday writers, generate data from them, visit digital and physical archives to look at past artifacts to decipher the pattern of everyday writing during major geopolitical changes, and thereby to understand how that past informs the present in lifespan research writing. We might also include *LWR* in writing, rhetoric, and culture courses and have students to interview their family members or friends and to think about writing across the curriculum in different eras and various stages of people's lives through their lifespans. To carry on the lifespan research writing project, rhetoric and composition studies scholars need to continue sharing their research findings, informing more people about the importance of writing through our lifespans, and archiving documents as important artifacts for continual explorative and diverse research projects as a part of longitudinal study from across the world.

*Fargo, North Dakota*

***Multilingual Contributions to Writing Research: Toward an Equal Academic Exchange***, edited by Natalia Ávila Reyes. The WAC Clearinghouse and the University Press of Colorado, 2021, 357 pp.

*Reviewed by Gregg Fields, Chandler-Gilbert Community College*

The discipline of writing studies continues to explore ways to weave together various streams of scholarly engagement between second-language, multilingual, translingual, and a plethora of other third or fourth term approaches, each with their own unique, circumscribed ideologies. The edited collection *Multilingual Contributions to Writing Research: Toward an Equal Academic Exchange,* edited by Ávila Reyes, speaks to this complex context by equipping scholars from a variety of language backgrounds and engaging normatively monolingual scholars in the work of writing studies with cross-national and cross-linguistic implications. The collection pushes the discipline to examine more deeply its potential linguistic bias beyond the first year papers of students (where bias is more likely to be hidden by an emphasis on sentence-level clarity). Ávila Reyes accomplishes this shift by embodying translingual and crosslinguistic approaches into the mainstream scholarly context of U.S. composition scholarship directly. In this collection, we are led to experience scholarship beyond the particular language norm of Standard Written English, which I have described as sedimented white/western English (Fields 125). In engaging with this work, English-speaking monolingual composition scholars are moved into the position of linguistic limitation or—framed more positively, linguistic liminality—and perhaps like a therapeutic ice bath or sauna, it can be both healing and perhaps a bit uncomfortable for those unprepared.

As one of five manuscripts published in 2021 within the International Exchanges on the Study of Writing: Latin American Section Book Series, Ávila Reyes' edited collection (with assistant editors Lina Calle-Arango and Ana Cortés Lagos), *Multilingual Contributions to Writing Research* continues the series' mission to promote visibility and access to meaningful scholarship beyond the English monolingual institutions and locations within the U.S. This edited collection is a substantive transcontinental and translingual work, shuttling resources powerfully across the academic literacy cultures of Spanish, English, and Portuguese. For example, Reyes opens the collection by providing a strong theoretical underpinning and an introduction duplicated in three different languages to "to generate a more egalitarian dialogue across national spaces" (37). Further, all the chapters have abstracts present in Spanish, English, and Portuguese. This textual feature is something U.S.-based scholars should work to emulate in the future if we are to fully embrace our attempts to decolonize the scholarship of composition. US-based scholars could follow the collection's example by adding abstracts in Spanish (or perhaps in Chinese) to honor the second and third most commonly spoken languages in the United States and better produce "educated speakers who have deep translingual and transcultural competence" as set by the Modern Language Association in 2007.

In addition, by providing linguistic accessibility to geopolitical regions often unreachable or neglected by many U.S.-based, English-speaking scholars, Avila Reyes' collection embodies Latin American language practices in academia on par with Gloria Anzaldúa or Celia Ana Zentella. The collection is a credit to the discipline of writing studies because it expands the view of composition beyond the perceived borders of the U.S. context, a most needed exercise to decolonize and more accurately represent the discipline in all its fullness.

After the introduction, the collection is divided into four sections: 1) theoretical contributions, 2) multilingualism and university writing, 3) literacy practices and the teaching of writing, and 4) contributions from applied linguistics. The collection consists of 14 chapters with 35 contributors, and compositionists and language scholars will benefit substantially from each chapter as well as the multilingual experience as a whole. In this review, I strive to represent chapters based on the work's linguistic variety as equitably as possible. The chapters featured here are representative of such variety.

In Chapter 1, "¿Academic Literacies: Intereses Locales, Preocupaciones Globales? Academic Literacies: Local Interests, Global Concerns?," Theresa Lillis provides a strategically code-switched chapter, and she eases readers into this linguistic decolonization by providing metadiscursive logic for when and why she chose to include a section in English or Spanish. At one point, she writes in Spanish for the literature review on academic literacies noting, "various summaries of this review already exist in English" (39). She also provides a summary of Spanish, English, Portuguese, and French scholarly terminology and translations surrounding academic literacies and the richness that can be drawn by code-switching across these various semiotic resources.

In Chapter 2, Bob Broad takes a macro lens to look at large scale writing assessment and its impact and benefits when applied to local contexts. He emphasizes the agency of local faculty and students and provides a meaningful series of steps for engaging in effective localized Large-Scale Writing Assessment (LSWA). He aligns with the volume's purpose to affirm locally-oriented agency while also highlighting meaningful work in Chile published in 2019 in this area by Navarro, Ávila Reyes, and Gómez Vera.

In Chapter 5, Jaci Brasil Tonelli e Eliane G. Lousada discuss the disciplinary tension between French language and literature in "A Produção Textual no Curso de Letras-Francês: Uma Comparação das Capacidades de Linguagem Requeridas em Disciplinas de Língua Francesa e Literatura Francófona." The engagement with disciplinary tensions around textual production in a second language will give scholars a Freudian sense of *heimlich/umheimlich* where we are familiar with the general tension but intrigued by its situatedness in the Portuguese context of Brazil's Universidade de São Paulo. The authors suggest that a misalignment of genres across the language/literature divide contributes to students' struggles to produce effective and clear writing.

In Chapter 7, "'Ensayar una Voz': Un Análisis Interaccional de Prácticas en Torno a lo Escrito en Eventos de Escritura Colaborativa," Laura Eisner orients readers to students (ages 21-60) in an adult secondary school located in the city of San Carlos de Bariloche who attempt to develop an academic voice based on a privileged academic language. Using ethnographic analysis of approximately 300 hours of audio data and other weekly documentation throughout the school year, Eisner highlights ten examples of group interactions where students' differentiated roles produce co-constructed writing with una "voz autorizada" (192). Eisner concludes her work by highlighting the dialectic tension of acceptance and rejection of the authorized voice by these students, and she notes that this study, while centered on a particular set of student groups, could provide a meaningful lens for understanding more mainstream students in other secondary schools and universities.

In Chapter 12, Estela Inés Moyano draws on Systemic Functional Linguistics (SFL) as *el marco teórico* to establish a methodological approach for studying genre qualitatively in economic science. Inés Moyano analyzes students' synthesis of partial genres into a macro-genre, even providing lexical mapping of a selected sample of a larger corpus. Ultimately, through the application of theory, the chapter explains teachers' efforts to provide discursive disciplinary knowledge to student writers. This chapter is meaningful for those of us working with writing across disciplines. The collection offers further scholarship that engages with Chilean writing in Health Sciences and Engineering in Chapter 11, "Transformados por la Escritura: Concepciones de Estudiantes Universitarios a través del Currículum y de las Etapas Formativas."

As a whole, the depth and variety of scholarship present in this edited collection covers the gamut from theoretical to longitudinal to ethnographic, and across countries both north and south of the equator. Most importantly, the collection brings fully forward composition's translocal presence, particularly beyond American English academic contexts. The act of engaging with this work will challenge many in our discipline, particularly the large number of us who spend most of our time thinking of ourselves as English professors. The edited collection seems itself to be a critical artifact of movements in composition to engage in more equitable linguistic and cultural practices. The collection embraces the multifaceted and multilingual identity of writing studies by presenting scholarship on writing from English, Spanish, Portuguese,

Swedish, and French language contexts. To accomplish this, Reyes provides framing early on for the mindset shift necessary to engage with scholarship presented in multiple languages, and she suggests a surprisingly effective translation technology (Deepl.com/translator) for scholars who may not be fluent in academic forms of Spanish, English, or Portuguese. This allows a fairly easy process for translating the digital form of the text available from The WAC Clearinghouse. However, even monolingual scholars will find the paperback filled with fully English, fully Spanish, fully Portuguese, and code-switching chapters: We might all gain a little cognitive plasticity by attempting to translate the gems of research in those languages with which we are less familiar.

To add another lens for engaging with the text: I tend to consume texts using a variety of technologies beyond traditional reading. I often will use a text to speech app–@VoiceAloud Reader–on my phone when driving or Apple's accessibility reader on my laptop when doing other mundane household chores. It was encouraging to see the capabilities of accessibility technology as my laptop switched smoothly from different voices to match the code-switching within different parts of the text. Unfortunately, the free version of my phone app was not nearly as effective, requiring that I actively shift the voice from one language voicing to another, slowing the reading process. Nonetheless, between DeepL and my own resources, these technological affordances made the consumption of the collection's multilingual, code-switched research nearly as easy to digest as monolingual texts in our discipline. While living in Arizona does allow me the privilege of engaging with speakers and writers of multiple languages, reading academic research in this way is not as common in my life as I would like. Engaging with the multilingual research in this collection was one of the most intellectually refreshing experiences of my academic work this year.

The totality of the work and the tools provided for engaging this scholarship could be used to affirm multilingual students, expose first year writers to empathy practices, prime undergraduates for capstone projects in multilingual composition, equip new college writing teachers beyond traditional TESOL methods, and inspire masters and doctoral students toward new and meaningful culminating projects.

*Chandler, AZ*

## Works Cited

Fields, Gregg. "An Integrative Translingual Pedagogy of Affirmation and Resources Sharing." *Translingual Pedagogical Perspectives: Engaging Domestic and International Students in the Composition Classroom.* Edited by Julia Kiernan, Alana Frost, and Suzanne Blum Malley, Utah State UP, 2021, pp. 125-148. DOI:10.733/9781646421121.c006

MLA Ad Hoc Committee on Foreign Languages. "Foreign Languages and Higher Education: New Structures for a Changed World." *MLA.org,* 2007. http://www.mla.org/flreport. Accessed 15 Dec. 2022.

***Teaching through the Archives: Text, Collaboration, and Activism***, edited by Tarez Samra Graban and Wendy Hayden. Southern Illinois University Press, 2022. 333 pp.

*Reviewed by C.C. Hendricks, University of New Hampshire*

As scholars across the disciplines recognize, working in the archives can be daunting. An emerging scholar with archival experience, I have never felt confident enough to teach archival research. Yet, after reading *Teaching Through the Archives: Text, Collaboration, and Activism*, edited by Tarez Samra Graban and Wendy Hayden, I am excited to integrate archives into my courses. Hayden and Graban bring together a wide range of interdisciplinary voices to examine "what values have emerged from [Rhetoric and Composition scholars'] work with archives, what pedagogical uses of archives have made those values more visible, and how those values might transfer to other disciplines…" (17). Contributors build upon existing examinations of the archive as a teaching tool in the writing classroom (e.g., Buehl, et al.; Enoch and Jack; Hayden). This collection also contributes to archival methodologies that address the complex power dynamics between researcher, subject, and archive (e.g., Kirsch, et al.; Kirsch and Rohan; Ramsey, et al.). In constructing an archival pedagogy that both reflects the values of the field and is transferable to other disciplines, the essays in *Teaching through the Archives* come together to "narrate a theory and pedagogy that illuminate the larger issues endemic to the field's newest archival turn" (Hayden and Graban 14). In each of the essays, the archive serves as a site of learning for students, instructors, and archivists and provides opportunities to reflect on and enact change within the disciplinary, institutional, and local histories represented–and not represented–in the archives.

*Teaching through the Archives* includes sixteen essays, organized in three sections: "Archive as Text," "Archive as Collaboration," and "Archive as Activism." This "archive as. . ." approach reflects the emphasis on praxis present in every essay. Hayden and Graban organize the essays in this way to represent "the increasingly complex definitions of archive that drive each contributor's work in order to locate the rhetoricity of the archive about which they write" (6). These broad categories are effective in organizing the vast range of course models and theoretical frameworks included in each section.

The first section includes five essays, all of which coalesce around demystifying the research processes of archival work. For example, Lisa Mastrangelo integrates the archives into her first year writing course to teach students "slow research" skills and help them connect with their new campus community. Lisa Shaver prompts students to engage in gendered analysis of institutional archives to help them "cultivate a heightened feminist consciousness" (47). In "Arranging Our Emotions: Archival Affects and Emotional Responses," Jane Greer analyzes the contrasting emotional experiences of two students in her junior-level writing intensive class on women and rhetoric. Greer demonstrates the impact of indexing and archival organization on students' emotional responses to the archive. Like Mastrangelo and Shaver, Greer uses archival work to encourage students' critical reflection on their positionality and interpretive power as researchers. Katherine E. Tirabassi also emphasizes reflection in her undergraduate creative non-fiction course, in which students analyze and craft researcher narratives from the archives. Tirabassi's students employ creative writing to engage in "archival exploration," making room for expression of the unpredictable nature of working in the archives (80). In the final essay of this section, James P. Beasley has students interrogate a random assemblage of artifacts from the A.S. Hill papers in the Harvard archives, a highly-cited archive in histories of rhetoric and composition. Beasley's students practice rhetorical assemblage of these artifacts and pair them with new archival documents to build an alternative rhetorical theory that also expands traditional histories of the field. In all the essays in this section, students are active agents in the archive, gaining localized information literacies grounded in their lived experiences.

In the second section, instructor, archivist, and student contributors reflect on the archive as a site of interdisciplinary collaboration in five case studies. While the range of pedagogical contexts represented across the essays is broad, they all share a focus on reciprocity through collaboration. In their essay, Jennifer Enoch, et al. adopt *techne* to theorize how an undergraduate intern draws upon their knowledge of rhetorical theory to navigate unfamiliar writing contexts as an archivist for Florida State University's Museum of Everyday Writing. Also positioning the archive as a site for praxis, Shirley K. Rose, Glenn C. W. Newman, and Robert P. Spindler present the interdisciplinary workshop as a model for making institutional archives more accessible. They take up Krista Ratcliffe's method of rhetorical listening to invite stakeholders from across the curriculum to participate in the processes by which institutional archives are formed, collated, and shared with the community.

This invitation for feedback on the accessibility of archives resonates with the first essay in the collection to be co-authored by a student, "Recursion and Responsiveness: Archival Pedagogy and Archival Infrastructures in the Same Conversation," by Jenna Morton-Aiker and Robert Schwegler. A doctoral student in Schwegler's special topics course on archival research, Morton-Aiker reflects on her experiences working in the National Archives of Composition and Rhetoric, which were co-created by Schwegler. Morton-Aiker and Schwegler ultimately propose a "collaboratively authored infrastructure" approach to archival creation, in which regular user feedback is implemented to increase an archive's accessibility and impact (151). In the following essay, Erin Brock Carlson, Michelle McMullin, and Patricia Sullivan call for a collaboration between archival methodology and technical communication. The authors theorize the archive as a means of digital content management in an upper-level undergraduate technical communication course, where students assemble and index archives for client-based projects. Jonathan Buehl, Tamar Chute, and Laura Kissel collaborate on an undergraduate service-learning course on proposal writing, where, throughout the semester, students craft proposals for funded projects of increasing size while in consultation with institutional and local archivists. In all the essays in this section, collaboration through archival work results in both students' increased engagement with course material and the expansion of the archives in which they are working. Instructors looking for models of how to integrate archival work into their courses will particularly appreciate the practical examples offered in this section.

The final section includes six essays that approach the archive as "a site for locating epistemic omissions and gaps–gendered, raced, disciplinary, institutional, or material" (Hayden and Graban 11). Laura Proszak and Ellen Cushman employ archival work in a first year writing and upper-level undergraduate seminar for English majors to establish sustainable decolonial relationships between the institution and local communities. Proszak and Cushman recognize that while the final student projects fall short of the original intent of decolonization, archival work is effective in helping students gain new knowledge about themselves and their positions within local communities. Similarly, Michael-John DePalma explores how archival work in community-based writing courses can facilitate ethical relationships between student researchers and community members. Representing the instructors, archivists, and students involved in building the Jewish Heritage Fund of Excellence's Jewish Kentucky Oral History Project, Janice W. Fernheimer, Beth L. Goldstein, Sarah Dorpinghaus, and Douglas A. Boyd offer a "method for ethically encountering, creating, and preserving knowledge about the other using Jewish rhetorical practices" (244). Jeanne Law-Bohannon and Shiloh Gill Garcia's essay traces the development of an upper-level undergraduate archival project that chronicles untold stories of the Atlanta Student Movement into a nationally funded, multi-platform, public-facing research project. In "'Loving Blackness' as a First-Year Composition Student Learning Outcome in the Archives," Michelle S. Hite, et al. adopt bell hooks' theory of loving blackness as a methodology for promoting students' celebration of Black life in the archives when engaging with violent and disturbing artifacts, such as those surrounding the Atlanta child murders.

Courtney Rivard's essay, "'Flagged for Deletion': Wikipedia, the Federal Writers' Project, and First-Year Composition" offers one of the most interesting examples of student engagement with archive building in the collection. Rivard shares the experiences of an archival assignment gone awry. For the assignment, students created an original Wikipedia entry for one person from an institutional archive on the Federal Writers Project, but Wikipedia blocked the student entries, citing the subjects' lack of notability. This unexpected impediment provides Rivard and her students with a unique opportunity to interrogate the power dynamics and ethics imbricated in which histories are included and excluded from public archives.

*Teaching through the Archives* is a valuable read for anyone working in—or considering working in—the archives, including scholars, instructors, archivists, and students. Contributors offer course models and methodologies for teaching the archives that are adaptable to a variety of pedagogical, institutional, and local contexts. I especially appreciate contributors' recognition of the unpredictability of archival work, particularly when it does not go to plan, as in the essays by Beasley, Proszak and Cushman, and Rivard. This move models the reflexivity central to an ethical archival pedagogy grounded in praxis that is at the core of this collection. In addition, the multivocal and interdisciplinary authorship, especially in the integration of archivists and students as co-authors throughout the collection, models its overarching view of the archive as a site of reciprocal exchange of ideas and meaning-making. Collectively, the contributors not only demonstrate the vast pedagogical applications of archival work, but also contribute to theorizations of the archive as a site of active learning and agency.

*Manchester, NH*

## Works Cited

Buehl, Jonathan, et al. "Training in the Archives: Archival Research as Professional Development." *College Composition and Communication*, vol. 64, no. 2, 2012, pp. 274–305.

Enoch, Jessica, and Jordynn Jack. "Remembering Sappho: New Perspectives on Teaching (and Writing) Women's Rhetorical History." *College English*, vol. 73, no. 5, 2011, pp. 518-37.

Hayden, Wendy. "And Gladly Teach: The Archival Turn's Pedagogical Turn." *College English*, vol. 80, no. 2, 2017, pp. 133–58.

Kirsch, Gesa, and Liz Rohan, eds. *Beyond the Archives: Research as a Lived Process*. Southern Illinois UP, 2008.

Kirsch, Gesa, et al., eds. "Unsettling Archival Research across the Disciplines: Engaging Critical, Communal, and Digital Archives," special issue of *Across the Disciplines* vol. 18, no. 1/2, 2021. https://wac.colostate.edu/atd/special/archives/.

Ramsey, Alexis, et al., eds. *Working in the Archives: Practical Research Methods for Rhetoric and Composition*, Southern Illinois UP, 2010.

Ratcliffe, Krista. *Rhetorical Listening: Identification, Gender, Whiteness.* Southern Illinois UP, 2005.

***Creating a Transnational Space in the First Year Writing Classroom***, edited by William. Ordeman. Vernon Press, 2021. 187 pp.

*Reviewed by Donald Joseph, University of Pittsburgh*

In the past decade, broad conversations on transnational rhetoric in the classroom have allowed educators to interrogate transnational approaches to rhetoric and composition studies. During this time, there have been significant studies, such as Suresh Canagarajah's *Literacy as Translingual Practice: Between Communities and Classrooms* (2013), Christopher Minnix's *Rhetoric and the Global Turn in Higher Education* (2018), and Heather Robinson et al.'s., *Translingual Identities and Transnational Realities in the U.S. College Classroom* (2020). All of these studies have questioned the hybridity of language and the varied experiences that students have with language inside and outside of the classroom. Furthermore, these meaningful works have opened several avenues of thought to assemble scholarship that productively probes the world's increased interconnectedness due to globalization.

William Ordeman's edited volume intelligently assembles works from several researchers that pushes rhetoric and composition scholars to think through translingualism as a method of merging languages in the classroom as a productive means of instruction. This is done principally to highlight the linguistic skills and capabilities that students already possess and encourage students to use them. In the introduction, Ordeman situates the reader theoretically to expand upon what transnationalism means specifically for this edited volume, an understanding of the term that differs from traditional usages of transnationalism. Drawing upon Carrie Kilfoil's work, Ordeman nuances terms such as translingual and transnational, which are often conflated with one another such that the former typically refers the interplay of language as a site of diversity in higher education and the latter term refers to the crossing of national borders. According to Ordeman, "using transnational and translingual interchangeably reinforces a limited definition of rhetoric—that it is a strictly linguistic act" (ix). Furthermore, Ordeman details the various ways this edited volume intervenes in composition and rhetoric studies through ethnographic studies, pedagogy, and experiential learning. Ordeman, like all the authors in the text, sees rhetoric as highly contextual and based on individual experiences.

The volume contains eight chapters, divided into three major sections. The sections are logically assembled to craft a pedagogical roadmap for readers as we consider how to introduce transnational approaches in first year writing classrooms. As asserted by Oderman, work on transnational pedagogy has largely been entrenched in theoretical models. Where this project seeks to depart from pure theoretical scopes of thought is to think of and provide examples of praxis in the classroom with real-world accounts from instructors in higher education as they approach translingualism and transnationalism. For instance, some of these instructors engage with students living in border cities who experience transnational movement regularly, sometimes daily.

The first section, "Creating Transnational Spaces through Ethnographic Reflections," uses an ethnographic approach to innovative pedagogical models as instructors conduct qualitative research on their students. In their chapter on "Translanguaging and Academic Writing: Possibilities and Challenges in English-Only Classrooms," Abu Saleh Mohammad Rafi and Anne-Marie Morgan work with students in an English course to develop writing skills for students at a public university in Bangladesh. Their study challenges monolingual approaches to language, which can be found in many universities, that ultimately limit students as they attempt to express themselves in their second language. As a means of support, Rafi and Morgan allowed students to write bilingually in their local language (Bengali) and English to aid in their efforts to improve their written expression of English. Their findings showed that using two languages or translanguaging made the curriculum more accessible for all students. This further encouraged the authors to hypothesize that this experience of communicating simultaneously in English and Bengali permitted students to engage in cross-linguistic analysis that made it feasible for students to have a greater understanding of rhetoric across cultures and languages.

Section two, "Creating Transnational Space through Pedagogical Designs Focused on Genre," takes a different approach to classroom discourse, classroom activities, and writing prompts. This section includes chapters that craft wonderful activities to be easily implemented into transnational classrooms; the activities are designed to facilitate assignments and discussions for first year students. Asmita Ghimire and Elizabethada A. Wright's chapter "All Writers Have More Englishes to Learn: Translingual First-Year Composition Classes' Promotion of Composition's Threshold Concepts" seeks to reconstitute the omission of transnational and translingual peoples in composition and rhetoric. For Ghimire and Wright, first year classes have the potential to expose monolingual students to the value of a translingual education and to translingual faculty and students that work in and among several languages. A key component of their study is to show how having a classroom of native and non-native English-speaking students, imbues students in negotiations that, according to them, promotes five threshold metaconcepts. These metaconcepts include: "1) writing is an activity and a subject of study, 2) writing speaks to situations through recognizable forms, 3) writing enacts and creates identities and ideologies, 4) all writers have more to learn, and 5) writing is a cognitive ability" (86). The assemblage of these five metaconcepts proves useful when thinking about the diversity of one language (English, in this case) and as one thinks about the lack of homogeneity in language, which Ghimire and Wright do as they provide sample assignments that were used in the classroom as well as measurements of success (e.g. rubrics).

The third section, "Creating Temporary Transnational Space through Assignment Design," focuses on the construction of assignments and course modules to promote student success. Maria Houston and Ekaterina Gradaleva's chapter on "Learning by Writing: Possibilities of Tele-Collaborative Transnational Education in and Beyond a First-Year Writing Classroom" invites us to look at not only first year writing students in the United States, but also second-year engineering students enrolled in an English class in Russia. Furthermore, Houston and Gradaleva make a plea for the professionalization of faculty who are open to teaching in a "transnational composition classroom" and in doing so, offer a guide to how to approach such a method. In order to accomplish their study (with Houston residing in the U.S. and Gradaleva in Russia), the two used a virtual, tele-collaborative approach to writing with specific goals for their students. For example, their International Conference Project (ICP) engaged with second-year sophomore students at a technical college in Russia and first year freshman students at a private Catholic college in Ohio with specific goals and stages in mind. Clearly stated, "the ICP was to allow students to analyze and evaluate their current composing practices in new media spaces and develop skills and competencies to 'write in the world' for global audiences" (128). Some media platforms used include Facebook Chat, Facebook Group, and Skype.

Ordeman's assemblage of such diverse chapters allows readers to engage with and think through the act of writing in transnational classrooms as a form of praxis. Despite the differences in approaches among chapters and especially among the three parts that divide the manuscript, one can consider all the chapters to better engage with transnational writing pedagogy in first year rhetoric and composition classrooms and beyond. Such a project, as Ordeman states in the introduction to the book, is necessary due to the lack of work on transnational writing practices in classrooms. The chapters about teaching students from diverse socio-linguistic and cultural backgrounds are useful because they allows instructors from varying backgrounds to take salient examples and make use of such approaches in their classrooms. This text opens several avenues for research that encourage transnational dialogue in the classroom. Future projects aligned with Ordeman's edited volume could work with multilingual communities that use more than two working languages; this would open yet newer avenues related to rhetoric and composition. Furthermore, and as suggested by Ordeman, future research could consider the impact of cosmopolitanism on pedagogical research as the world becomes more globalized.

*Pittsburgh, PA*

## Works Cited

Canagarajah, Suresh, editor. *Literacy as Translingual Practice: Between Communities and Classrooms*. Routledge, 2013.

Kilfoil, Carrie. "What's the Difference Between 'Translingual' and 'Transnational' Composition?: Clarifying the Relationship Between Two Terms" Transnational Writing: A Blog for the Conference on College Composition and Communication Transnational Composition Group at the Conference on College Composition and Communication, 9 September 2016.

Minnix, Christopher. *Rhetoric and the Global Turn in Higher Education*. 1st ed., Springer, 2018.

Robinson, Heather M., et al. *Translingual Identities and Transnational Realities in the U.S. College Classroom*. Routledge, 2020.

***Desegregation State: College Writing Programs after the Civil Rights Movement***, by Annie S. Mendenhall, Utah State University Press, 2022. 208 pp.

*Reviewed by Jessica Edens McCrary, Georgia State University and Emory University*

From her vantage point at Georgia Southern University's Savannah Campus, which until 2018 was Armstrong Atlantic State University, Annie S. Mendenhall has written an important text advancing how we understand composition studies alongside complex desegregation policy, practice, and outcomes in colleges and universities across the U.S. South. She draws on historical sources of policies established by the University System of Georgia (USG) from the late 1960s through the 1980s as well as interviews and archival material from Savannah's two public colleges, Savannah State (historically Black) and Armstrong (historically white). Pairing this material with a detailed overview of court cases related to desegregation, *Desegregation State* overwhelmingly shows that desegregation established "a set of policies and norms for literary remediation that affected writing instruction for decades afterward" (35). The rest of the book provides a historical account of eras in writing programs—remediation, testing, and assessment—as spaces of direct and indirect desegregation policy for two public schools in Savannah from the early 1970s through the 1980s.

*Desegregation State* is an essential read for composition scholars interested in the systemic ways writing programs were informed by desegregation policies. While this might appear most applicable to colleges and universities in the U.S. South, I suggest that there are valuable historical contextual lessons for any U.S. postsecondary institution. Though I provide here a brief overview of the themes and her thesis, a full read is necessary to really understand the complexities of institutional policies today and the legacies of racism pervading everything from admissions to retention programs. With proper historical context and recognition of the systemic challenges Black students have faced, we can begin to uncouple our contemporary writing programs, retention and progression efforts, and admissions and testing policies from twentieth-century established practice. Scholars working in writing program administration roles in testing, basic writing programs, first year composition, writing centers, and writing across the curriculum (WAC) will find this a helpful reference for understanding the problematic theories and ideas driving the establishment of many of those programs.

In the late 1990s, my family moved from Michigan to Savannah, where the complicated educational landscape of the South was apparent and confusing to a white, Northern, adolescent transplant. I have since earned nearly three degrees from Georgia's public institutions; I have worked in the USG for nine years. Mendenhall's book provides meaningful explanation of legacies of desegregation I observed in everything from "pre-college English" to the widely disputed Regents Test, a USG graduation requirement for decades.

*Desegregation State* evaluates writing programs for the systemic limits built into them by educational policy, which we often understand as rooted in anti-Black racism, and provides specific institutional history to help us articulate our understandings. Mendenhall's work proves—sometimes to a point of exhaustion—how organizations like Georgia's Board of Regents' (which oversees the USG) paltry effort at desegregation post *Brown v. Board of Education* created policies that established "desegregation as remediation." In other words, colleges and universities established remedial writing programs as their response to "addressing" what they observed as the linguistic insufficiencies of Black students. Colleges and universities also latched onto cultural deprivation theory, a concept borrowed from psychology, "to explain how culture and environment influenced learning" (33). Cultural deprivation theory would become the foundation for remedial programs. thereby becoming the basis for most states' desegregation plans (41). Through a cultural deprivation theory lens, the "insufficient" linguistic practices of Black students would be explained away for decades; meanwhile, policies continued based on a faulty premise. In its early years of disciplinary leadership, the Conference on College Composition and Communication's (CCCC) stance on pedagogy influenced the era of desegregation-as-remediation: "By emphasizing cultural integration and writing remediation, the discipline normalized remedial pedagogies focused on vocabulary, speech, and logic" (47). To scale remediation and address "the problem of increasing minority student enrollment," Special Studies departments were established at all USG institutions by 1974 (Mendenhall citing Georgia Board of Regents).

Mendenhall traces how the USG's desegregation plan evolved, under continued scrutiny by federal offices and watchdog organizations like the NAACP Legal Defense Fund, which kept pushing southern states via lawsuits and policy revisions. Mendenhall's research shows how much of the language the US Department of Health, Education, and Welfare (HEW) used, with the intention of prompting states to broaden enrollment goals by focusing on admission and retention, backfired. In response to HEW, institutions used thinly-coded language of "academic standards"—crucial for "defining institutional quality"—to encourage "white colleges to limit remedial writing instruction" (84). In other words, HEW's language was used to support USG institutions' plans for further restricting admissions rather than drive wider access.

As the USG revised its plan based on legal pressure, language surrounding affirmative action also plagued the intentions-versus-results of large-scale policy.

Popular definitions for the so-called disadvantages facing college students in the 1970s downplayed vestiges of slavery and legalized racial exclusion impacting realities for Black Americans. As Mendenhall shows, such language was manipulated by anti-affirmative action leaders to suggest race was one in a list of "disadvantaged" identity groups to address. Such subtle manipulations of language are constant in *Desegregation State* amd demonstrate the longstanding discrimination Black students face(d) in USG institutions.

Mendenhall also shows how those interpreting the court cases and federal policies guiding desegregation in the 1970s were continually caught up in equality, rather than equity, as the means for successful integration. HEW required states to revise institutional missions to eliminate references to race to encourage students to apply to secondary education institutions based on program rather than on the racial identity of the college. This meant public Black colleges, already neglected by states and disparaged by white communities, "now had to abandon their mission to serve Black students and focus on recruiting white students who considered them inferior" (86). This approach neglected ideas we recognize today as key to retaining students across marginalized groups, namely that students need more than strong academic programs to be successful: They need teachers whose expectations assume their success, support programs and staff, and psychological safety. None of these were part of the USG's plan, at least through the 1980s.

Mendenhall illustrates the legacy of standardized testing for college admissions and placement testing for determining writing level–and the problematic nature of this practice since inception–even as retention and assessment policies evolved. Only after the COVID-19 pandemic have policies on testing finally begun to budge, despite ample early evidence that minority students were negatively impacted by white racial bias in standardized tests of writing and reading (68-70). Mendenhall's well-built arguments show how "indicators of prestige and effectiveness" like standardized test scores, retention rates, and institutional selectivity, were based on norms that benefited historically white colleges and universities (65). By the 1980s, remediation programs were seen as ineffectual, which posed a delicate problem for the USG because so many of its remediation programs were tied to federally-approved plans for desegregation. This period exacerbated a tension composition scholars felt, namely of writing program growth set against racially-biased suggestions of their necessity. Meanwhile, the debate to define and measure academic standards continued, and institutions shifted investment to growing programs like writing centers and WAC.

Mendenhall adds essential historical context to composition studies as a discipline. She illustrates how even those with the best of intentions were perhaps basing their approach to basic writing on white-biased assumptions of success and linguistic practices—the problematic theories grounding desegregation plans in the first place notwithstanding. While many educators were not carrying out those policies intentionally to advance racist agendas, that is what often occurred in the USG in practice. Compositionists' involvement in the standards established in testing is one strong example of how this played out in practice, and is discussed in detail in chapter three of the book. Mendenhall shows that composition was singled out in the 1970s for its "racial bias in the hiring process," evidencing composition as a "white-oriented discipline" (97).

Mendenhall's work advances foundational scholarship in our field, including Janet Emig's and Mina Shaughnessy's work on composing practices and basic writing. Importantly, Mendenhall suggests their foundational work has roots in white cultural assumptions on Black linguistic practices. Rather than reject outright the important work done as composition studies theorized alongside a legacy of desegregation, Mendenhall's work suggests that by understanding the roots of racism built into college writing programs, we can continue the work of disassembling practices that devalue historically excluded students and pursue the longer-term objective of finally providing higher education that serves students equitably. The book builds toward important questions related to the legacy of composition studies that demand action; I leave you with one: Can historically white institutions avoid succumbing to political pressures that plagued desegregation progress for decades, or will they acknowledge "the reality of racism" and our role in redressing it (32)? This question is relevant not only to administrators across postsecondary education. The insights Mendenhall exposes call those of us working in composition departments and running writing programs to actively consider the ways our programs have fallen short based on legacies of discrimination built on white-coded and white-serving policies.

*Atlanta, Georgia*

## Works Cited

Emig, Janet. *The Composing Process of Twelfth Graders.* NCTE, 1971.

Shaughnessy, Mina P. *Errors and Expectations: A Guide for the Teacher of Basic Writing.* Oxford UP, 1977.

***Languaging Myths and Realities: Journeys of Chinese International Students***, by Qianqian Zhang-Wu, Multilingual Matters, 2021, 280 pp.

*Reviewed by Shreya Sangai, York University*

With advancements in globalization, acquiring Western education is no longer a mirage-like aspiration for non-Western students; it is more attainable than ever before. Many students travel from their home countries to foreign lands, especially North America and the UK, to pursue a college education. However, these students may struggle linguistically in classes that are delivered in languages that aren't their primary language. To support the diverse language needs of the increasingly heterogeneous student community, universities offer resources like writing, tutoring, and language learning centers. These resources are sometimes limited by certain assumptions about students' linguistic practices. Qianqian Zhang-Wu's *Languaging Myths and Realities* critically examines these resources to present their shortcomings and offers interventions to build better systems for multilingual international students' needs. For Zhang-Wu, the existing scholarship focuses on tertiary-level Chinese international students who are at the graduate level. As a result, undergraduate students' experiences often get overlooked (8).

*Languaging Myths and Realities* is organized into three parts, subdivided into fourteen chapters. Part 1 introduces Zhang-Wu's research problem and questions: Who are the international students, and how are they conflated with immigrant students? Part 1 urges educators and policymakers to urgently de-homogenize international students' needs and create customizable linguistic support models. In Part 2 (Chapters 4 through 7), she shares her research data, which iterates the variabilities among the twelve Chinese students (of both international and immigrant status) who make up her sample. In order to create customizable models of support, Zhang-Wu demonstrates that the participants' previous language training and educational experiences signal their preparedness for American classrooms. Part 3 of the book debunks the following myths:

- Myth 1: TOEFL results accurately predict international students' abilities to function linguistically on college entry
- Myth 2: An English-only policy is necessary for college classrooms to help international students improve their linguistic functioning in English
- Myth 3: *First Year Writing* guarantees international students' successful writing performances in content-area courses
- Myth 4: English is responsible for all the challenges facing Chinese international students

- Myth 5: Chinese international students are well supported in American higher education, linguistically and academically. (xv)

Zhang-Wu posits that the first step to identifying the needs of international students is to accurately define them so that the particularity of their identity and circumstances is better understood. She unpacks inaccurate descriptors like "crossing state borders for education" that collapse the distinction between international students and their immigrant counterparts, and uses the Institute of International Education's characterization—"[a]nyone who is enrolled at an institution of higher education in the United States who is not a US citizen, an immigrant (permanent resident) or a refugee" (qtd. in Zhang-Wu 4). This definition underscores the salience of international students' purpose and presence: education and temporariness.

Zhang-Wu's research shows that compared to immigrant students, international students come from relatively secure socio-economic backgrounds with less dependence on loans. They have different experiences with native languages and English, which makes their classroom experience vastly distinct from the immigrants who may already be acclimated to the Western educational systems. For instance, international students must undertake the TOEFL exam to affirm that they are linguistically proficient to be in an American classroom; however, such a qualification is not imposed on immigrant students. Moreover, scoring well on TOEFL does not guarantee any success; international students are still considered linguistically under-prepared to tackle "acculturation stressors," which further impedes their adjustment within and outside the classroom (7).

When discussing languaging struggles, Zhang-Wu draws attention to international students' coping methods within and outside the classroom. She combines two data collection methods—digital ethnography and a traditional qualitative approach—to compare their classroom and personal interactions. To access the information first-hand, she joins the WeChat group, where students shared their difficulties with classroom engagement, assignment instructions, and other stressors in college life. Unlike the monolingual classroom, where students think and speak in one language, Chinese students, like other multilingual speakers, shuttle between their mother tongue and the classroom language. WeChat is their familiar, safe space because they share and clarify their confusion about lectures, assignment instructions, and social dynamics. Using traditional qualitative analyses, Zhang-Wu finds that Chinese students have different pedagogical exposures, which further impact their classroom and outside participation. For instance, the students trained in traditional schools that focus more on the national entrance examination and less on English struggled more than those from a foreign language regular high school, where the attention was given to both. However, Zhang-Wu quickly points out that her research did not verify this claim for each case. For her, despite the training, an individual's motivation to blend into the culture significantly determined their success in languaging and acculturation journeys.

After identifying the backgrounds of the twelve participants, Zhang-Wu unpacks theoretical frameworks that demarcate academic and social English to emphasize the layers of linguistic challenges. She engages primarily with Jim Cummins, "one of the pioneering scholars in examining academic English," to define key terms of the study, including basic interpersonal communication skills (BICS) and cognitive academic language proficiency (CALP) (16). BICS, or the social language, "focuses on the conversational fluency of the target language" (16). CALP "relates to students' ability to understand and express, in both oral and written modes, concepts and ideas that are relevant to success in school" (16). Zhang-Wu acknowledges that while Cummins' definitions offer critical foundational concepts to understand different kinds of languages within English that international students have to incorporate quickly, his dichotomous division is misleading. While CALP does not consider the shifts in language use as it moves between disciplines, BICS facilitates classroom and community participation. Each category's utility extends beyond the purposes that Cummins identifies. Furthermore, Zhang-Wu points out that this classificatory approach "may lead to deficit views on the rich cultural and linguistic resources that [international] students bring to the classroom" (16).

Alison Bailey broadens Cummins' grouping of language by classifying academic English into school navigational language (SNL)—language to communicate with teachers and peers in the school setting—and curriculum content language (CCL)—the language used in the process of teaching and learning content material" (Bailey and Heritage 15). For Zhang-Wu, while Bailey recognizes that multiple registers of English work concurrently in the classroom, she overlooks the fact that the students are constantly moving across and between classroom and socializing spaces. Often, the two spaces and their language function overlap. For example, the classroom discussions or an instructor's office hours are neither exclusively in SNL nor CCL. Instead, they rely on students' capability to intuitively adapt their language as the situation demands. Such rapid adjustment is almost undoable for Chinese international students who may not be conversant in English, let alone distinguish between CCL and SNL.

To tackle the challenges mentioned above, Zhang-Wu suggests that their language proficiency and languaging skills must be contextualized to create adequate support structures for Chinese and other international students to function better in formal and less formal settings. She proposes an ecological approach which enables the readers to unpack the relationships between home and target language, their relationships with each other, and their relationship with the speaker. Zhang-Wu presents her take on Bronfenbrenner and Morris's bioecological model, which situates the international students' linguistic, cultural, and educational transitions "in different layers of environments and developmental processes" (24). She adds that Canagarajah's and Garcia's conceptualization of "languaging" as "dynamic communicative practices in action" to show that Chinese international students draw on all their resources to function linguistically in their cross-cultural experience (24).

Towards the conclusion of her research, Zhang-Wu looks back at her participants' university experiences to add more agents to her earlier proposed model, like tutors, teaching assistants, and offices for international students that aim to smoothen out students' acclimation. She is mindful that altering external factors is a challenging bargain; however, the "active change agents" can carefully consider their practices to support international students better. For instance, instead of thrusting a monolingual, English-only approach in the classroom, Zhang-Wu writes, instructors should "cultivate a welcoming attitude toward cultural and linguistic diversity across the institution" (229). International students must be seen as dynamic individuals with ambitions to learn and grow in global contexts and not simply as English language learners.

As an international student in North America, I found Zhang-Wu's bioecological model akin to a radical vision that the teachers, departments, and administrators must aspire for; however, I am concerned about its applicability on two levels. First, when Zhang-Wu discusses socio-cultural and political factors such as race, citizenship, and English proficiency, she depersonalizes and abstracts them. The assumption that these factors are out there and not embodied by faculty, TAs and tutors, who are expected to create customizable support models, is an obvious fallacy. Second, the readers may need more information about some actionable ways of using Zhang-Wu's model. For instance, how do we develop non-monolingual classrooms? What skills do faculty, TAs, tutors, and other agents need to acquire to make this leap? The readers are left with a lot to consider about our ways of teaching and learning, but we don't yet know what more we need to do to create equitable classrooms. Despite these limitations, Zhang-Wu's insights help us consider how international students are defined and why the current scaffolds are inadequate. Her analyses can be extended to international students of other nationalities with varying particularities. Finally, Zhang-Wu's call for action that the university, its faculty, teaching assistants, and tutors must see international students as already whole unto themselves, not merely deficient English practitioners, is irrefutable.

*Toronto, Canada*

## Works Cited


Bailey, Alison L. and Heritage, Margaret, eds. *Formative Assessment for Literacy, Grades K-6: Building Reading and Academic Language Skills across the Curriculum.* Corwin Press, 2008.

Bronfenbrenner, Urie, and Morris, Pamela A. "The Bioecological Model of Human Development." *Handbook of Child Psychology*, edited by Richard Lerner and William Damon, John Wiley & Sons, Inc., 2006, pp. 793-828.

Canagarajah, Suresh. "Codemeshing in Academic Writing: Identifying Teachable Strategies of Translanguaging." *The Modern Language Journal*, vol. 95, no. 3, 2011, pp. 401-417. jstor.org/stable/41262375.

Cummins, Jim. "BICS and CALP: Empirical and Theoretical Status of the Distinction." *Encyclopedia of Language and Education: Vol. 2. Literacy*, 2nd ed., edited by Brian V.. Street and Nancy H. Hornberger, Springer, 2008, pp. 71-83.

García, Ofelia. "Education, Multilingualism, and Translanguaging in the 21st Century." *Social Justice through Multilingual Education*, edited by Tove Skutnabb-Kangas, Robert Phillipson, Ajit K. Mohanty, and Minati Panda, Multilingual Matters, 2009, pp. 140-158.

***Grounded Literacies in a Transnational WAC/WID Ecology: A Korean-U.S. Study***, by Jay Jordan. University Press of Colorado, 2022. 118 pp.

*Reviewed by Eunhee Seo, George Mason University Korea*

Transnational WAC/WID movements in U.S. higher education advocate for more inclusive writing policies and pedagogies that incorporate linguistic and cultural diversity and localized knowledge and practices into global perspectives (Hall and Horner). This growing awareness toward plurality in transnational WAC/WID methods is exemplified by Zawacki and Cox's dictum: "Think globally. Research locally. Teach consciously" (12). Jay Jordan's *Grounded Literacies in a Transnational WAC/WID Ecology: A Korean-U.S. Study* adds a more nuanced discussion to this conversation through analysis of the WAC/WID movement in Korean higher education, which is still in its beginning and lacks institutional and programmatic support. Jordan's lived experience as a participant in this transnational WAC/WID movement serves as an insightful guide for writing teachers, scholars, administrators, and/or those taking on intersecting roles in a similar context.

The seven chapters in Jordan's three-year, cross-campus longitudinal study delve into the situatedness of Second Language (L2) academic literacy practices. The first three chapters provide a background understanding to the study context and design. Chapter 1 traces the history of English education in Korea by juxtaposing conflicting perceptions and ambivalent attitudes toward English language ideologies in Korean society—manifested by the labels *guknaepa* (those who learn English domestically) versus *haewaepa* (those who learn overseas) (19). The next chapter takes the reader to a vivid scene at the University of Utah Asia Campus—from the start-up campus' inception to the daily operation of programs and curricula, all of which are entangled with their local culture and major stakeholders. Chapter 3 evinces Jordan's thoughtfully crafted qualitative method that yields rich and thick descriptions of the "transnational experiments" (20). The most notable are students' anxieties and struggles relating to the varying demands of academic literacy practices, their coping strategies and resistance toward certain practices (e.g., extemporaneous speech) to promote a self-image of perfection, and their evolving L2 literacy identities in the transnational space over time.

Chapter 4 frames embeddedness as the "sensitizing concept" of the study and thereby gives readers a glimpse of "transnational complexities" from participants' viewpoints (59). Jordan argues that, despite the challenge of a "double shift" in FYW and WAC/WID, students tap their prior educational experiences and cultural repertoires to orient themselves to new academic and professional discourses and conventions in two different disciplines (42).

Readers will see that sensitivity to the local context and student population helps faculty members revise and innovate their curriculum and pedagogy to deal with a complex interplay of student needs and disciplinary goals.

Chapter 5 concentrates on "instances of coping" observed in students' academic language and literacy practice and on faculty members' adaptive teaching that reflects the complex interconnection of ecology, network, and negotiation in this cross-border education site (62). Jordan's narrative depicts how students construct and negotiate their subject positions to resist certain academic demands of faculty members as well as to create interactional opportunities to access authentic linguistic resources in the transnational space (Norton-Pierce; Pavlenko, "Access"). On one hand, the students' actions (e.g., frequenting professors' office hours or finding employment in the psychology lab) are understood as an attempt to establish "intersubjectivity with the speakers of target language" (Pavlenko, *The Bilingual Mind* 303), a gesture to gain legitimacy in the target language community (Wenger). On the other hand, Alice's transformation from an L2 learner to an L2 user–or "star English teacher"(78)–upon graduation indicates that the social meaning of the English language in Korean society is viewed as symbolic capital promising educational opportunities and economic viability (Bourdieu). Similar to the previous chapter, the great takeaway from the practitioners' perspective is the faculty's sensitivity and responsiveness toward students' emergent academic needs in the new ecological context. Faculty members constantly negotiate their expectations by crafting a space for scaffolding students' learning and socialization into a new educational culture and discourse community.

The following chapter highlights the ramifications of transnational education in reference to Korea's linguistic internationalization effort through a case study of one student (David) with a hybrid identity (half-Korean and half-American). The narrative illustrates how David's English language proficiency and his home- and school-based literacy practice enhance both his language tutor role among students in the Asia Campus and also his relatively smooth socialization into the academic discourse community. By contrast, the study also illuminates that David's identity—one living in a bilingual and bicultural world—is often in conflict with the dominant perceptions of him by people in the target society. They see him as a model minority in the transnational space—a seemingly American student (*haewaepa*) with highly proficient English skills at the Asia Campus but a high-performing Korean student at the U.S.-based campus. The strength of this chapter is in vivid observations and careful reflections of the transnational education scene and the depiction of students' multiple identities in flux. It offers valuable pedagogical implications to practitioners involved in cross-border education: how to weigh expectations of the home campus and host country with the realities of local conditions and particularities of student backgrounds.

The final chapter draws inspiration from pedagogical and administrative perspectives and centers on the "ways of transfer" (101) observed in both students and faculty members in earlier chapters. Jordan maintains that, in the transnational educational context, students and faculty alike should be able to repurpose and reapply their prior knowledge and practices from previous contexts into a new disciplinary and social context by navigating both linguistic and cultural differences and the constraints and affordances of the available resources on site (100-01). Readers will also appreciate Jordan's advocacy for a "transnational administrative effort to recruit and develop writing-focused faculty" locally and internationally, even though there are various (un)predictable administrative challenges surrounding transnational campus operation at an early stage (103). Based on the claim that literacy development and teaching involve the "whole world" (106), the book concludes with an invitation to scholars, teachers, and administrators who interact with international and multilingual students to consider the idea of "[cultivating] sensitivities to writing and to writing's surrounds" (105) to achieve higher education's internationalization goals.

One of the greatest values of this book is that it situates writing research in a transnational site and presents fresh, rich, and vibrant insights about L2 literacy practices. It examines linguistic, educational, cultural, ideological, material, disciplinary, and administrative complexities involving various stakeholders within the cross-border educational context. Further work on broadening the ownership of English to L2 users who possess multicompetence—the knowledge of more than one language in the same mind—will eventually benefit the entire institutional community and the host country (Cook). Understanding the "foundational awareness of literacy's particular complexity" (102), as shown in instances of participants' struggles, requires a much deeper understanding of language and disciplinary socialization processes from the perspective of L2 users who both belong to more than one discrete or conflicting discourse community and also need to internalize the values, norms, and interests of the target community by becoming an insider (Canagarajah 151).

Continued work is also needed to examine ways to facilitate students' disciplinary socialization processes by empowering them to take advantage of discursive situations as a resource for their original voice (Canagarajah 169). Anyone who has been working in a similar context to Jordan's description would support his advocacy for cross-institutional efforts to align curriculum and course goals and coordinate courses across programs, departments, and campuses (102). As higher education's transnational partnership under internationalization continues, this book will continue to invite diverse audiences who work in a similar context to generate discursive practices about teaching and researching writing, planning and administration of writing intensive (WI) courses and programs, as well as ongoing faculty training, mentoring, and exchange in cross-border educational sites.

*Incheon, South Korea*

**Works Cited**


Bourdieu, Pierre. *Language and Symbolic Power.* Edited by John Thompson, Translated by Raymond, Gino and Matthew Adamson. Polity P, 1991.

Canagarajah, A. Suresh. *Resisting Linguistic Imperialism in English Teaching.* Oxford UP, 1999.

Cook, Vivian. *Portraits of the L2 User.* Multilingual Matters, 2002.

Hall, Jonathan, and Bruce Horner, eds. *Toward a Transnational University: WAC/WIC across Borders of Language, Nation, and Discipline.* UP of Colorado, 2023.

Norton-Pierce, Bonny. "Social Identity, Investment, and Language Learning." *TESOL Quarterly,* vol. 29, no. 1, 1995, pp. 9-31. https://doi.org/10.2307/3587803.

Pavlenko, Aneta. "Access to Linguistic Resources: Key Variable in Second Language Learning." *Estudios de Sociolinguistica,* vol. 1, no. 2, 2000, pp. 85-105. https://doi.org/10.1558/sols.v1i2.85.

Pavlenko, Aneta. *The Bilingual Minds and What It Tells Us about Language and Thought.* Cambridge UP, 2014.

Wenger, Etienne. *Communities of Practice: Learning, Meaning, and Identity.* Cambridge UP, 1998.

Zawacki, Terry M., and Michelle Cox, eds. *WAC and Second Language Writers: Research towards Linguistically and Culturally Inclusive Programs and Practices.* Parlor P, 2014.

***Stories of Becoming: Demystifying the Professoriate for Graduate Students in Composition and Rhetoric***, by Claire Lutkewitte, Juliette C. Kitchens, and Molly J. Scanlon. University Press of Colorado, 2022. 202 pp.

*Reviewed by Gabriella Wilson, Syracuse University*

Engaging recent scholarship regarding graduate education and the professionalization of rhetoric and composition graduate students, *Stories of Becoming: Demystifying the Professoriate for Graduate Students in Composition and Rhetoric* provides reflective questions and insight into the discipline while arguing for a different approach to graduate education (Badenhorst et al.; Brooks-Gillies et al.; Macauley). Addressing the current state of higher education generally and rhetoric and composition specifically, the authors examine trends across U.S. higher education to consider how reductions in student retention in English courses, subsequent decreases in funding, and the elimination of many tenure-track positions impacts graduate education. Based on a study spanning four years, the authors conducted a nationwide survey of two hundred new assistant professors in the field of composition and rhetoric and engaged in follow-up interviews with ten survey participants. The authors collected and analyzed professional documents from the interview participants, including CVs, cover letters, and teaching philosophies, using the professional documents to interrogate the professional academic identity construction of their participants.

Exposing the intricacies of navigating transitions from graduate student to full-time faculty and balancing the many demands and roles each position encompasses, including teaching, research, service, and administration, the book is informative for graduate students and those developing graduate education curricula alike. The book provides context and strategies for its rhetoric and composition graduate student audience as it reviews the current academic job market and demonstrates why discussions about the job market must expand beyond R1 tenure-track positions. In this way, the book not only tells a story about academic professionalization through its study of early-career faculty but also engages in the academic professionalization of graduate students as it contextualizes the discipline.

The first chapter emphasizes the importance of stories in the discipline, arguing that stories allow humans to relate to each other and allow for reflection on "who we are and who we are becoming" as scholars of rhetoric and composition (22). Embracing narrative inquiry as a method, the authors interrogate constructions of academic and professional identities by examining the identity construction of their research participants. They also explore disciplinary commonplaces circulating in rhetoric and composition to uncover micronarratives about the discipline that resist "disciplinary lore about the job market, hiring processes, and new-faculty transition" (28). Chapter one's exploration of academic identity construction becomes a connecting thread continued in chapters two and three, wherein the authors discuss how professional documents constructed for the job market provide insight into the professional identity construction of academics.

In chapter two, the authors explore graduate students' job market preparedness, arguing that graduate students feel their doctoral programs "helped students develop an effective strategy for the job search" (40). However, despite this phenomenon, the authors stipulate that participants were still overwhelmingly worried about their chances in the job market; participants argue that their graduate education left them feeling unprepared for jobs outside of R1 tenure-track positions. As a result, the authors claim that how we talk about the job market matters and that framing the job market as something to be survived by graduate students reinforces "the institutional practices that make it daunting and worrisome" (41). Instead, the book argues that graduate education should address the changing landscape of the academic job market and encourage graduate students to use their time on the job market "as a personal learning experience in crafting a professional identity" (43). The chapter concludes with strategies for graduate students to use when approaching the job market, including monitoring job ads and looking at professional organizations' position statements to think critically about how to craft their professional identity through professional documents.

Chapters three and four zoom in on the ways that faculty members are expected to split their labor between teaching, research, service, and administration (TRSA), which they define as a "tetrad." Highlighting a central tension throughout the book, the authors stipulate that how the tetrad is interpreted changes as graduate students transition into faculty positions; for instance, some institutions may value teaching or administration over research. As the text makes clear, this is markedly different from how graduate students are taught to value research. Thus, the authors advocate for doctoral programs to better prepare graduate students for their transition into new faculty by providing resources on how to manage their time and responsibilities according to the tetrad. It's important to note that the authors contrast their construction of the tetrad with the traditional triad known as teaching, research, and service. This is because they argue that administration is often overlooked by graduate education and needs to be more clearly addressed by doctoral programs to prepare graduate students to transition into their role as faculty.

Chapter five discusses how to transition from the time management expectations required during graduate school to the ones necessary as a faculty member. Reflecting on how institutional identity and requirements regarding faculty time management heavily influence the construction of faculty members' professional identities, the authors are careful to examine how a "lack of explicit communication regarding expectations of the position" leaves faculty members feeling confused and hesitant (105). The book argues that, as early as possible, graduate students should learn about the institutional demands and time constraints that will be placed on them as they transition into full-time faculty roles.

Chapter six focuses on the importance of collaboration and learning to collaborate with diverse people. The authors claim that doctoral programs should encourage more collaboration between doctoral students and faculty and amongst doctoral students, especially within administrative positions. The authors contend that doctoral programs should grant graduate students in those positions more power, autonomy, and exposure to the intricacies and hard work necessary to embody an administrative role. Through analysis of professional documents, the authors provide insight into how "collaboration is a part of and affects our graduate experiences. . . our professional time, and the elements of TRSA" (126). The authors argue that fostering collaborative relationships across various contexts, such as with other graduate students or WPAs, prepares graduate students for administrative work where they will be expected to work within and across departments and diverse faculty while producing writing visible to others (140).

The authors conclude by offering three suggestions for redeveloping graduate education. These revisions include developing even more support resources, which would include more research into the experiences and needs of new faculty and creating creative funding opportunities for graduate students and new faculty alike. The second revision is formalizing professional development across the discipline; importantly, the authors stipulate that professional development is an ongoing process, so professional development opportunities should come from a variety of sources, including invested, horizontal mentoring relationships (Keller; VanHaitsma and Ceraso). Finally, the authors argue that graduate education needs to do a better job of capturing the day-to-day activities of new faculty to better prepare graduate students to meet the various demands placed on them in terms of research, service, teaching, and administration, within the institutional contexts they navigate post-graduation.

As a graduate student, reading this book was informative for considering how I position myself in the discipline and the goals I have for my academic career. Ever since deciding to pursue a doctoral degree, I've been told about how awful and dismal the job market is. But while the text is careful not to paint a cheery picture of current conditions, it makes clear there are a variety of jobs and experiences available to graduate students after graduation. This text is helpful for other graduate students as they begin to consider how they wish to locate themselves in the discipline and contend with the creation of their professional identity on the job market. It is also helpful for administrators and professors in charge of developing graduate curricula and on job hiring committees, who can attend to the various suggestions included in each chapter detailing ways for graduate education to be more responsive to current market conditions. The text is clear about the influence of graduate education on the overall direction of the discipline, making transparent what is at stake in the current neoliberal landscape.

*Syracuse, NY*

**Works Cited**

Badenhorst, Cecile, et al. *Re-imagining Doctoral Writing*. The WAC Clearinghouse, 2021. doi.org/10.37514/INT-B.2021.1343.

Brooks-Gillies, Marilee, et al. *Graduate Writing across the Disciplines: Identifying, Teaching, and Supporting*. The WAC Clearinghouse, 2020. doi.org/10.37514/ATD-B.2020.0407.

Keller, Elizabeth J. *Rhetorical Strategies for Professional Development: Investment Mentoring in Classrooms and Workplaces*. Routledge, 2018. doi.org/10.4324/9781351246187.

McCauley, William. *Standing at the Threshold: Working through Liminality in the Composition and Rhetoric TAship*. UP of Colorado, 2021.

VanHaitsma, Pamela, and Steph Ceraso. "'Making It' in the Academy through Horizontal Mentoring." *Peitho*, vol. 19, no. 2, 2017. https://cfshrc.org/article/making-it-in-the-academy-through-horizontal-mentoring/.

Williams, Andrea, and Tanya Rodrigue. *Standing at the Threshold: Working through Liminality in the Composition and Rhetoric TAship*. UP of Colorado, 2021.

## Contributors

**Nasih Ul Wadud Alam** is completing his master's degree in rhetoric, writing, and culture in the department of English at North Dakota State University. Hailing from Bangladesh, he has nine scholarly articles published in peer-reviewed university journals from Bangladesh. Moreover, he is a regular contributor to *The Daily Sun*, a daily newspaper published in English from Dhaka, Bangladesh.

**Rebecca Day Babcock** is the William and Ordelle Watts Professor at the University of Texas Permian Basin. She teaches courses in writing and linguistics and serves as Freshman English Coordinator and Director of Undergraduate Research. While widely published in writing centers, her latest book focuses on humanities content related to the oil industry.

**Andrew J. Bowman** is a PhD Candidate in the Center for Writing Studies and a former Assistant Director of the Program in Professional Writing at the University of Illinois. He's co-author of "This is What Solidarity Looks Like: A Model of Thick Solidarity" in *The Invisible Professor* (WAC Clearinghouse, 2022).

**Emily Brier** is Instructor of English Studies at Western Carolina University. A poet, community writing facilitator, and writing teacher, her recent research focuses on alternative assessment practices, LGBTQ+ writing spaces, and Appalachian literature and culture. More information about her can be found at her website, emilybrier.com.

**Antonio Byrd** is Assistant Professor of English at the University of Missouri Kansas City where he teaches courses in professional and technical communication, multimodal composition, composition studies, and qualitative research methods. His work has appeared in *College Composition and Communication*, *Composition Studies*, *Literacy in Composition Studies*, and *Technical Communication Quarterly*.

**Ellen C. Carillo** is Professor of English at the University of Connecticut and the Writing Coordinator at its Waterbury campus. She is the author of *Securing a Place for Reading in Composition*, A *Writer's Guide to Mindful Reading*, *Teaching Readers in Post-Truth America*, *The Hidden Inequities in Labor-Based Contract Grading*, and the *MLA Guide to Digital Literacy*.

**Cynthia Cochran**, a former writing center director, teaches creative and expository writing at Illinois College. She researches developmental and first-year writing pedagogy, including AI in composition. Since 2017, she has worked closely with colleagues at the University of Pinar del Rio in Cuba on English language teaching/assessment. She enjoys gardening with her husband, Bob.

**Maria Conti Maravillas** is Assistant Professor of English and a Composition Program Coordinator at Youngstown State University. She specializes in writing program and writing center administration, diverse student populations, and instructor professional development. Her work appears in *Composition Forum* and *Community Literacy Journal.* She enjoys helping students who have had negative writing experiences find a way forward.

**Hannah T. Davis** is a Writing Studies Lecturer in the Thompson Writing Program at Duke University. She studies writing pedagogy with a particular interest in first year writing. Her current research brings together creativity theory and learning theory to consider the roles of metacognition, motivation, and confidence in students' writing processes.

**Aliethia Dean** is a PhD student and graduate instructor at Texas Tech University. Aliethia's research interests include technical and global communication, composition, usability, and UX studies.

**Gregg Fields** is residential faculty and FYC program co-lead at Chandler-Gilbert Community College in Arizona. He has book chapters on affirmational translingual approaches, metacognition, and advanced language acquisition. With 10 years experience teaching writing in a variety of modalities, he also explores WAC/WID in fully-integrated learning communities.

**Kay Emmert** is Co-Director of the Program in Professional Writing at the University of Illinois. She has presented on how emotion affects the teaching of business writing and the role of contingent instructors in curriculum development, and she has co-authored a chapter on thick-solidarity among labor unions in academia.

**Maggie Fernandes** is Assistant Professor of Rhetoric and Composition at the University of Arkansas. Her research interests focus on digital cultural rhetorics, digital content moderation on social media platforms, and writing assessment across classroom contexts and online environments. Her work has appeared in *Kairos*, *Enculturation*, and *Reflections: A Journal of Community-Engaged Writing and Rhetoric.*

**Kristie S. Fleckenstein** is Professor of English at Florida State University, where she teaches graduate and undergraduate courses in rhetoric and composition. Her research interests include feminism and race, especially at the intersection of material and visual rhetorics in the writing classroom and in civic life.

**Scott Gage** is Associate Professor of English and Director of First-Year Composition at Texas A&M University-San Antonio. His research addresses the intersection of rhetoric, violence, and composition studies.

**C.C. Hendricks** is Assistant Professor and Director of First-Year Writing in Communication Arts & Sciences and core faculty member of Women's and Gender Studies at the University of New Hampshire. She is a mom and feminist rhetorician. She has held many Writing Program Administrative positions and teaches undergraduate and graduate courses in composition and English education. C.C. has also served as a consultant in writing centers and a Writing Across the Curriculum program. Her work has appeared in *Peitho*, *The WAC Journal,* and *Across the Disciplines.*

**Brad Jacobson** is Assistant Professor of English at The University of Texas at El Paso where he teaches English education and writing studies courses. His research on teacher development and school-based writing opportunities has appeared or is forthcoming in several journals and edited collections, including *Written Communication*, the *Journal of Literacy Research*, and *Writing Program Administration.*

**Donald Joseph** is a Ph.D. candidate at the University of Pittsburgh in French and Francophone Studies. He works on 20th and 21st-century Middle Eastern and Maghrebi literature and cultural production in French, Arabic, Catalan, and Spanish to engage with migration studies, masculinity studies, queer theory, and critical race studies.

**Neal Lerner**, Professor of English at Northeastern University, teaches undergraduate and graduate courses in writing and the teaching of writing. Lerner is the author or co-author of eight books and over 40 peer-reviewed articles and book chapters on the history, theory, and practice of learning and teaching writing.

**Talitha May** is an artist and adjunct assistant professor at Portland State University where she teaches writing and rhetoric courses.

**Jessica Edens McCrary** is a PhD candidate in rhetoric and composition at Georgia State University. With a disciplinary background in history, her work is focused in archival research, feminist rhetorics, and writing program administration. Her scholarship has appeared in *College English* and the *Journal of the Georgia Association of Historians.*

**Megan McIntyre** is Assistant Professor of Rhetoric and Composition and Director of the Program in Rhetoric and Composition at the University of Arkansas. She was formerly Writing Program Director at Sonoma State University and the Assistant Director of Dartmouth College's Institute for Writing and Rhetoric. She received her PhD from the University of South Florida in 2015, and her research interests include digital rhetoric and writing, antiracist pedagogy and writing program administration, and archival research methods.

**David Morris** is Teaching Assistant Professor of English and Co-Director of the Program in Professional Writing at the University of Illinois. He's author of P*ublic Religions in the Future World: Postsecularism and Utopia* (University of Georgia Press, 2021).

**Andrew Moss** is Senior Lecturer in English and the Program in Professional Writing at the University of Illinois. He teaches courses in international business communication and grant writing.

**Shreya Sangai** is a PhD student in the Department of Humanities at York University. Her areas of interest are multilingualism, anti-racism pedagogies, raciolinguism, and graphic representations of conflict, trauma, and survival.

**Virginia M. Schwarz** is Assistant Professor at San Francisco State University where she teaches first-year writing and MA and certificate courses in the graduate composition program. Virginia researches graduate education, faculty development, and anti-oppressive approaches to teaching, learning, and assessment. She would like to thank her former English 700 students for making this course design possible.

**Eunhee Seo** is Assistant Professor of English for Academic Purposes (EAP) at George Mason University Korea and concurrently serves as the EAP Program Coordinator. In this role, she communicates with programs across the curriculum and engages with program faculty across campuses. Her research focuses on exploring issues in Second Language (L2) writing, English for Academic Purposes, language and identity/ideology, and teacher education (including student teachers). Her previous publications appear in *Korean Journal of Applied Linguistics* and *Studies in English Education.*

**Rachael W. Shah** is Associate Professor of English at University of Nebraska-Lincoln. She is the director of the Nebraska Writing Project, and she teaches classes in pedagogy, community literacy, and teacher education. Her book *Rewriting Partnerships: Community Perspectives on Community-Engaged Learning* was published in 2020.

**Alison Y. L. Stephens** is Lecturer in the Writing Program at Northeastern University specializing in sections of Advanced Writing in the Disciplines for multilingual writers. She was formerly a Multilingual Writing Support Specialist at Northeastern University and at the University of Oregon.

**Megan Von Bergen** is a scholar of (alternative) writing assessment with a focus on the history of grades/grading in first year composition courses and the emergence of labor-based grading.

**Gabriella Wilson** is a PhD student in the Composition and Cultural Rhetoric program at Syracuse University. Her research interests include rhetorics of care, transnational feminism, disability studies, craft and materiality, and feminist and antiracist pedagogies.

**Qianqian Zhang-Wu** is Assistant Professor of English and Director of Multilingual Writing at Northeastern University. Her research focuses on multilingual writing and issues on language, race, and power. Zhang-Wu is author of the award-winning book *Languaging Myths and Realities: Journeys of Chinese International Students.* Her work appears in *TESOL Quarterly* and *Research in the Teaching of English* among many others.

## 2022 Reviewers

Linda Adler-Kassner
Wendy Anderson
Cecile Badenhorst
Hadi Banat
Christopher Ryan Basgier
Logan Bearden
Beth Boquet
Tyler Branson
Beth Brunk-Chavez
Elizabeth Buck
Antonio Byrd
Amy Cicchino
Richard Colby
Crystal Colombini
José Cortez
Dominic DelliCarpini
Doug Downs
Dana Lynn Driscoll
Katherine Fargo Ahern
Romeo Garcia
Roger Gilles
Kristi Girdharry
Matthew Gomes
Morgan Gresham
Leigh Gruwell
Carrie Hall
Joe Harris
Ashley Holmes
Davena Jackson
Radhika Jaidev
Florianne Jimenez
Seth Kahn
Michelle LaFrance
Christina LaVecchia
Rebecca Lorimer Leonard
Corey McCullough
Teaira McMurtry
Ligia Mihut
Lillian Mina
Jessie Moore
Michael Neal
Jim Nugent
Katherine O'Meara
Timothy Oleksiak
Laurie Pinkert
Mya Poe
Shakil Rabbi
Gwendolynne Reid
Kevin Roozen
Shirley Rose
Tony Scott
Ryan Shepherd
Amanda Marie Sladek
Trixie Smith
Shelley Staples
Darci Thoune
Katherine Tirabassi
Christie Toth
Phuong Minh Tran
Lisa Tremain
Crystal VanKooten
Alexis Walston
Elizabeth Wardle
Scott Warnock
John Whicker
Courtney Adams Wooten
Lacey Wootton
Pavel Zemliansky

## Now with Parlor Press!

*Studies in Rhetorics and Feminism*
**Series Editors: Jessica Enoch and Sharon Yam**

*Emerging Conversations in the Global Humanities*
**Series Editor: Victor E. Taylor**

*The X-Series*
**Series Editor: Jordan Frith**

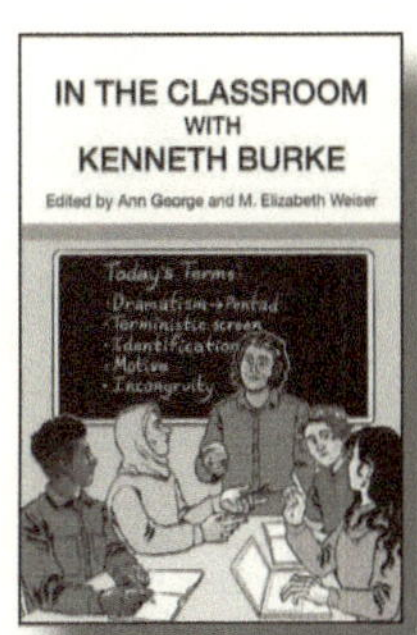


## New Releases

*In the Classroom with Kenneth Burke* by Ann George and M. Elizabeth Weiser

*Design for Composition: Inspiration for Creative Visual and Multimodal Projects* by Sohui Lee and Russell Carpenter

*Writing to Learn in Teams: A Collaborative Writing Playbook for Students Across the Curriculum* by Joe Moses and Jason Tham

*Rhetorical Listening in Action: A Concept-Tacticc Approach* by Krista Ratcliffe and Kyle Jensen

*Reimagining the Humanities* edited by Edited by Barry Mauer and Anastasia Salter

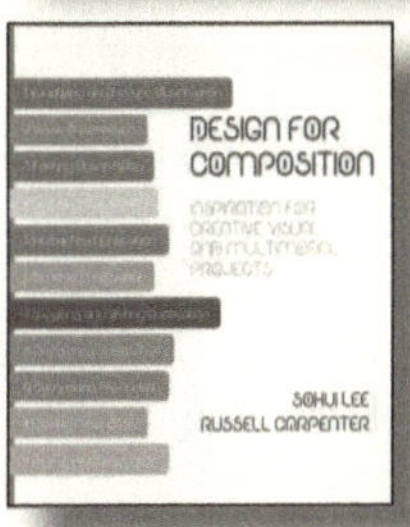


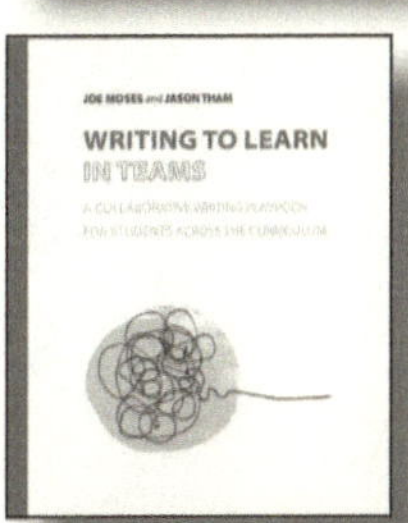


## MLA Mina Shaughnessy Prize and CCCC Best Book Award 2021!

*Creole Composition: Academic Writing and Rhetoric in the Anglophone Caribbean,* edited by Vivette Milson-Whyte, Raymond Oenbring, and Brianne Jaquette

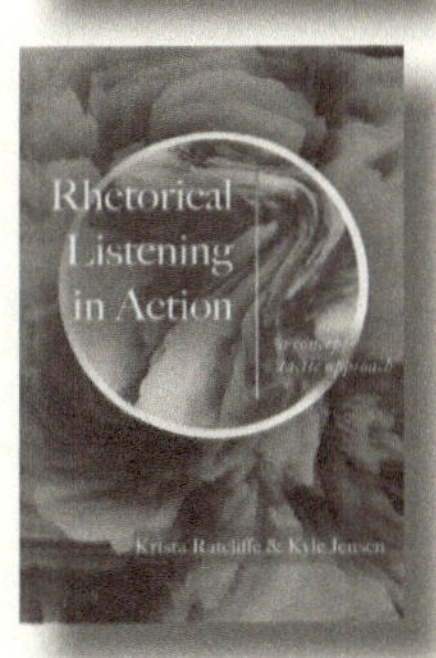


## Check Out Our Website!

*Discounts, blog, open access titles, instant downloads, and more.*

www.parlorpress.com

*Composition Studies* **Discount:** Use CS20 at checkout to receive a 20% discount on all titles not on sale through February 1, 2024.

www.ingramcontent.com/pod-product-compliance
Lightning Source LLC
Chambersburg PA
CBHW032023050726
47590CB00006B/2282

* 9 7 8 1 6 4 3 1 7 4 4 2 6 *